THE STRUCTURE
OF PROTECTION
IN DEVELOPING
COUNTRIES

BELA BALASSA AND ASSOCIATES

THE STRUCTURE OF PROTECTION IN DEVELOPING COUNTRIES

Published for
The International Bank for Reconstruction and Development
and the Inter-American Development Bank
by The Johns Hopkins Press, Baltimore and London

CONTENTS

v

APPENDICES

LIST OF TABLES

vii

APPENDIX TABLES

PREFACE

This volume reports on the findings of a research project on the structure of protection in developing countries, sponsored by the World Bank and the Inter-American Development Bank. The choice of this topic reflects a preoccupation on the part of the two institutions with the economic policies followed by developing countries, among which the policies of protection have particular importance.

Research on the volume was directed by Bela Balassa, Professor of Political Economy at The Johns Hopkins University, in his capacity as consultant to the Economics Department of the World Bank. He was aided by several collaborators who carried out the country studies on the basis of a common methodology. The countries studied include Brazil, Chile, Mexico, West Malaysia, Pakistan, the Philippines, and for comparison, a developed country, Norway.

The volume presents a comparative evaluation of the results of the country studies and explores the effects of protection on resource allocation, exports, and economic growth. The experience of the seven countries studied is also utilized to derive some general conclusions on protection in developing countries and to provide guidelines for an "ideal" policy of protection.

It is hoped that, apart from their interest to the economics profession, the methods and the results presented in this volume will be useful in the practical work of international and national organizations. In various respects, the findings of the research project have already been utilized at the World Bank; the dissemination of the results should contribute to their increased use by the two sponsoring institutions as well as by the developing countries themselves.

ANDREW M. KAMARCK
Director, Economics Department
World Bank

INTRODUCTION

The policy of import substitution followed by most developing countries since World War II has had the twin objectives of improving the balance-of-payments position of these countries and providing for the development of their manufacturing industries. The principal argument for this policy has been that, because of the slow increase of demand from the industrial nations, the expansion of traditional exports cannot ensure high rates of economic growth and balance-of-payments equilibrium in the developing countries.

Whatever the intrinsic merits of this policy, its application has rarely been based on a consistent program of action. Rather, the existing system of protection in many developing countries can be described as the historical result of actions taken at different times and for different reasons. These actions have been in response to the particular circumstances of the situation, and have often been conditioned by the demands of special interest groups. The authorities have generally assumed a permissive attitude toward requests for protection and failed to inquire into the impact of the measures applied on other industries and on the allocation of resources in the national economy. The interaction of tariffs and exchange rates and their effects on exports have been generally disregarded; nor have the implications of duties on raw materials and intermediate products for the protection of finished manufactures been taken into account.

In general, we find a tendency to restrict the consideration of the effects of a policy instrument to the objective actually pursued, with little attention given to the multiplicity of instruments and objectives and their interrelationships. Thus, devaluation has been considered in its effects on the balance of payments, and tariffs in their impact on the development of manufacturing industries. At the same time, the tariff levied on a particular commodity has been assumed to influence the imports of only that commodity.

From the point of view of resource allocation, however, the joint effects of the various policy instruments are relevant. Tariffs on inputs and the overvaluation of the currency associated with protection penalize export industries and partly or wholly offset the apparent protection of import-substituting activities. The structure of protection also influences resource allocation within the import-competing sector, and affects the firm's choice between selling in domestic and in foreign markets.

These considerations point to the need for appraising the effects of the existing system of protection in developing countries. This is the purpose of the present volume which provides criteria for the evaluation of the system of protection and applies these criteria in the study of seven countries carried out on the basis of a common methodology. It further endeavors to offer guidelines for policy formulation.

In the evaluation of the system of protection, use has been made of the effective protection measure that has been developed in recent years.[1] Effective rates of protection indicate the extent of protection of processing activities by taking account of tariffs on the product itself and on the inputs used in its manufacturing. Since the protection of a particular processing activity is also affected by the extent of overvaluation of the currency as compared to the hypothetical free trade situation, we have further calculated net effective rates by adjusting for the difference between the actual exchange rate and the rate that would apply in a free trade situation. Finally, we have devised a measure to express the extent of the bias against exporting and in favor of import substitution in individual industries.

The calculation of these measures requires information on the input structure of individual industries that are provided in input-output tables. The lack of such data has not permitted us to include any African countries in the investigation. Furthermore, considerations of data availability and regional balance have led us to select three countries from Latin America (Brazil, Chile,

---

[1] Cf. H. G. Johnson, "The Theory of Tariff Structure, with Special Reference to World Trade and Development," in *Trade and Development* (Geneva: Librairie Droz, 1965); Bela Balassa, "Tariff Protection in Industrial Countries: An Evaluation," *Journal of Political Economy*, December 1965, pp. 573–94; and W. M. Corden, "The Structure of a Tariff System and the Effective Protective Rate," *ibid.*, June 1966, pp. 221–37. Also, W. M. Corden, *The Theory of Protection* (Oxford: Clarendon Press, 1971).

and Mexico) and three from Asia (West Malaysia, Pakistan, and the Philippines). For comparison, we have also studied a European country (Norway).

The volume consists of two parts. The first chapter, supplemented by Appendix A, provides the conceptual framework and the methodology for the country studies. The following four chapters of Part I supply some general information on the national economies of the countries under study; present the results of the estimates for the individual countries; offer an appraisal of the results; and suggest guidelines for protection policies. The country studies themselves are presented in Part II, comprising seven chapters.

Chapter 1 introduces the concepts designed to evaluate the structure of protection. It further describes the instruments of protection used in the individual countries and considers various problems involved in measuring effective protection. These relate to calculations made from price and tariff observations; the choice of input coefficients and the definition of value added; the treatment of nontraded goods; and the problems of classification and averaging. Several of these questions are discussed in a more rigorous fashion, together with some theoretical considerations, in Appendix A.

As background material to the country studies, Chapter 2 provides some salient economic statistics for the countries in question. Market size and the orientation of manufacturing industries, economic growth and structural change, factors affecting economic growth, export performance, and changes in the composition of exports and imports are examined in the chapter. The data pertain to the period 1950–67.

Chapter 3 presents the estimates of nominal and effective rates of protection for the seven countries under study. A comparison is made between the results obtained in calculations based on domestic input-output coefficients and those utilizing input-output coefficients that are assumed to reflect free trade conditions. Under both alternatives, estimates are provided for primary activities and for manufacturing, for import-substituting and export industries, as well as for major commodity groups. In the presentation of the results, separate consideration is given to the interindustry structure of protection, the extent of import protection, and the bias against exports.

The findings reported in the previous chapter are evaluated in Chapter 4. After a discussion of the "static" or allocative cost of protection, the "dynamic" costs, including the absence of opportunities for utilizing large-scale production methods and the lack of incentives for technological change, are discussed. The chapter also provides some tentative calculations on the economic loss due to protection, and an appraisal of the effects of protection on export performance and economic growth.

The results of the country studies are utilized in formulating guidelines for a policy of protection in developing countries. While emphasis is given to the need for tailoring policies to the particular circumstances of the individual countries, it is suggested that some general conclusions apply to all of them. These relate to the choice between tariffs and quantitative restrictions; the incentives to traditional and nontraditional primary activities; the preferential treatment of manufacturing industries; and the choice between import substitution and exports of manufactured goods. Finally, some consideration is given to an "ideal" system of protection.

The country studies of Part II were undertaken by my collaborators Joel Bergsman and Pedro S. Malan (Brazil), Teresa Jeanneret (Chile), Gerardo Bueno (Mexico), John H. Power (West Malaysia and the Philippines), Stephen R. Lewis, Jr., and Stephen E. Guisinger (Pakistan), and Preben Munthe (Norway). I am indebted to them for having valiantly and patiently participated in the difficult task of carrying out a collective research effort.

The research project has been financed by the World Bank, with contributions made to the cost of the Latin American studies by the Inter-American Development Bank. Members of a Study Group, jointly organized by the two institutions, have provided helpful suggestions on the draft manuscript. Its members were Andrew M. Kamarck (chairman), John Adler, Louis Goreux, Ravi Gulhati, George Kalmanoff, Benjamin King, Enrique Lerdau, Moeen Qureshi, Herman van der Tak (World Bank), and John deBeers and Joaquin Gonzalez (IDB). Tibor Scitovsky participated in the deliberations of the Study Group and served as an outside reader. His incisive comments were of much help in improving the manuscript.

I have also had the cooperation of the participants of the research project of the Development Centre of the Organisation for Economic Co-operation and Development (OECD); this was undertaken parallel with our project and dealt with the more general issues of industrialization. Joel Bergsman, Stephen Lewis, and John Power took part in both research projects. Lewis and Guisinger also published certain of their results in the *American Economic Review* and the *Journal of Political Economy*. Some of my own work connected with the project appeared in the *American Economic Review*, the *Journal of Political Economy*, *Oxford Economic Papers*, and *Quarterly Journal of Economics*. These journals have given permission for the use of published material.

For suggestions made on parts of the study I am indebted to Jagdish Bhagwati, Max Corden, Maurice Scott, and Daniel Schydlowsky. I am also grateful to Deborah Sullivan who performed her task as research assistant with intelligence and competence and to Thomas Silcock who did an excellent job as editor. But my greatest debt is to my secretary, Anne Jeffery, who has borne the burden of drafting and redrafting the individual chapters.

BELA BALASSA
Project Director

THE STRUCTURE
OF PROTECTION
IN DEVELOPING
COUNTRIES

PART I

CHAPTER 1

CONCEPTS AND MEASUREMENT OF PROTECTION

Bela Balassa

Nominal and Effective Protection

In contributions to the theory of international trade, economists have traditionally limited their attention to trade in final commodities, as if all stages of fabrication were undertaken domestically. In so doing, they have followed in the footsteps of David Ricardo, whose famous example concerns trade in cloth and wine between England and Portugal. Accordingly, comparative advantage has been defined in terms of the costs of production incurred at all stages of fabrication taken together.

Such a simplification might have been appropriate in Ricardo's time, but its usefulness has greatly diminished with the increasing complexity of the structure of world trade. In an analysis of trade flows under present-day conditions, one needs to take account of the international division of the production process through trade in raw materials and intermediate products. Instead of considering the comparative advantage of a country in, for example, clothing, we have to separately indicate its advantages and disadvantages in cotton growing, spinning, weaving, and clothing manufacturing. Comparative advantage will then be defined with reference to the costs of processing at a *given* stage of fabrication rather than in terms of the sum of processing costs at all stages; thus, a country may import cotton cloth but export raw cotton and clothing.

These considerations have profound implications for the study of protection. Traditionally, it has been assumed that domestic producers and consumers respond to the price-raising effects of tariffs by expanding the production and reducing the consumption of the commodity that has come to be protected. Introducing trade in raw materials and intermediate inputs does not affect the decisions taken by consumers—they will continue to react to changes in product prices brought about by the imposition of tariffs. For the producer, however, not only tariffs on the product will be relevant but also tariffs levied on material inputs, such as industrial materials, fuels, and parts and components used in the production process. Although tariffs on the product itself provide protection to the firm or industry by allowing domestic prices to rise above import prices, tariffs on material inputs reduce the extent of protection by raising the cost of material inputs and can be regarded as a tax on the processing of such inputs.

Accordingly, distinction needs to be made between nominal or product protection and effective protection or the protection of value added. The nominal rate of protection of a particular commodity is defined as the percentage excess of the domestic price over the world market price, resulting from the application of protective measures. If tariffs are the only protective measures used and they are not prohibitive in the sense that they would exclude all imports, the domestic price of competing domestic commodities of identical quality will equal the sum of the c.i.f. import price and the tariff, and the nominal rate of protection will equal the ad valorem rate of tariff (tariffs expressed as a percentage of import value). For exports, domestic prices may be raised through export subsidies and the nominal rate of protection will equal the rate of subsidy on f.o.b. value. (Export taxes can be regarded as negative subsidies, since they reduce domestic prices and give rise to negative nominal protection.)

The effective rate of protection expresses the margin of protection on value added in the production process rather than on the product price. It is defined as the percentage excess of domestic value added, obtainable by reason of the imposition of tariffs and other protective measures on the product and its inputs, over foreign or world market value added. Thus, while the nominal rate of protection pertains to the product and affects decisions taken by consumers, the effective rate of protection indicates the joint effects on the processing activity of tariffs on the product itself and on its inputs, and it influences the producer's choice.

The effective protection measure is a relatively new concept in economic discussions but has long been known to businessmen whose main concern is how tariffs on the product and its inputs affect the protection of their processing activity. It has special importance in developing countries where tariffs are high and differences between tariffs on inputs and outputs are often substantial. The concept will be used in this volume to evaluate the structure of protection in the seven countries under study. These are Brazil, Chile, and Mexico in Latin America; West Malaysia (hereafter called Malaya), Pakistan, and the Philippines in Asia; and Norway in Western Europe.

While comparisons will be made between nominal and effective rates, our discussion will center on effective protection that affects decisions by producers and thus the allocation of resources among industries. Furthermore, we will exclude from our purview the fiscal implications of the system of protection, although tariffs and export taxes often partly serve revenue purposes. This is so especially for export taxes which are sometimes used as substitutes for taxes on the incomes of exporters.

Calculating Effective Protection

As an illustration of the concept of effective protection, consider a product (clothing), whose c.i.f. import price is $1.00 and the cost of its material inputs (textile fabrics) on the world market $0.60, corresponding to a value added in clothing manufacturing of $0.40. Converted at the going exchange rate of 100 pesos to the dollar, the price of the product will be 100 pesos, of which the world market cost of material inputs is 60 pesos, and the foreign (world market) value added in clothing manufacturing 40 pesos. A 20 percent tariff on clothing will raise the domestic price of the product to 120 pesos, while a 10 percent duty on textile fabrics increases material costs to the domestic producer to 66 pesos. Protection will thus enable firms to operate with a value added of 54 pesos—the difference between the domestic price of clothing of 120 pesos and the material cost of 66 pesos—compared with a value added of 40 pesos abroad. The margin of 14 pesos means that the effective rate of protection of the domestic processing activity—the percentage excess of domestic over world market value added—will be 35 percent.[1]

Apart from tariffs on inputs and outputs, the effective rate of protection also depends on the share of value added in the product price. Consider, for example, pharmaceutical products imported in bulk into Central America duty-free that bear a 15 percent duty in packaged form. If bulk pharmaceuticals cost 90 percent of the packaged product on the world market—i.e., foreign value added is 10 percent of the product price—and the import price is 100 pesos, domestic value added will be 25 pesos (the difference between the domestic price of 115 pesos and the 90 pesos paid for bulk pharmaceuticals).

---

[1] For the relevant formulas and a discussion of the assumptions underlying the analysis, see Appendix A.

In raising the price of the product by 15 percent, protection thus enables domestic producers to operate with a domestic value added 2.5 times higher than value added in the world market—i.e., the effective rate of protection is 150 percent. It follows that relatively low nominal protection may entail high effective protection if value added is a small proportion of the product price. In the examples, the effective rate of protection is greater on packaged pharmaceuticals than on the manufacture of clothing, although the latter had higher nominal protection.

Let us now consider an export industry, for example, meat, which has to sell at world market prices but pays for material inputs, such as fodder, at domestic prices augmented by a tariff. If fodder and other material inputs account for 60 percent of the price of meat on the world market and are subject to a 10 percent duty, the effective protection of meat will be negative; i.e., the system of protection applied penalizes meat processing. If the world market price of meat is taken to be 100 pesos, the tariff-induced increase in the domestic cost of material inputs from 60 to 66 pesos will entail a decline in value added from 40 to 34 pesos, so that domestic beef producers could compete in world markets only if they operated with a value added 15 percent lower than abroad. Thus, the effective rate of protection is -15 percent.

To fully compensate the meat producer for the increase in costs due to tariffs on material inputs, an export subsidy of 6 percent would be needed. This subsidy would raise the price of meat, along with domestic value added in meat processing, by 6 pesos which equals the excess cost of material inputs due to tariffs. By comparison, a 10 percent export subsidy would more than offset the increase in material costs, and provide an effective protection of 10 percent (the difference between domestic value added of 44 pesos and world market value added of 40 pesos, as a percentage of the latter) to the meat industry.

These results indicate that tariffs, as well as export subsidies, provide protection to domestic processing activities by raising the value added obtainable by the firm or industry. It is also apparent from the last example that if the rates of tariffs (subsidies) were the same on the product itself and on its material inputs, they would equal the rate of effective protection of the processing activity.

More generally, the effective rate of protection will be higher than, equal to, or lower than the rate of tariff (export subsidy) on the product, depending on whether this tariff (export subsidy) exceeds, equals, or falls short of the average rate of tariffs on material inputs. Effective rates of protection will be negative if tariffs raise the cost of material inputs by a larger absolute amount than they raise the price of the product. In our first example, if the tariff on clothing were 4 percent (i.e., 4 pesos) instead of 20 percent, and the tariff on textile fabrics remained 10 percent (i.e., 6 pesos), domestic value added would be 38 pesos and the effective rate of protection -5 percent.

"Net" Effective Protection

Protection permits domestic industries to operate with a value added higher than that under free trade, thereby providing incentives for the movement of domestic resources (land, labor, and capital) into protected industries. Other things being equal, the higher the effective rate of protection, the greater will be this inducement, and a ranking of protective activities by effective rates of protection will indicate the relative incentives provided by protection. Such a ranking focuses attention on the interdependence of economic activities and highlights the fact that the protection of any one industry will have to be at the expense of others.

We can visualize this interdependence by considering the effects of protection on the exchange rate. The imposition of tariffs makes it possible to maintain balance-of-payments equilibrium at a lower exchange rate (i.e., fewer units of domestic currency per dollar) than that existing under free trade. But the lower the exchange rate, the lower will be the price of imports, and hence the protection provided by a given tariff. The exchange rate that maintains balance-of-payments equilibrium will decline further as the number of protected industries increases, thereby reducing the extent of protection accorded to any one of them.

As an illustration, let us return to the case of the clothing industry. If the tariff on clothing is 20 percent and no other industries are protected, the domestic price of clothing will be 20 percent higher under protection than under free trade since tariffs on a single product can hardly affect the exchange rate. But if all manufactured goods are protected, the exchange rate will be lower than it would be in a free trade situation. Assume, for example, that the free trade exchange rate is 110 pesos to the dollar as compared with a rate of 100 pesos in the case of the all-round protection of the manufacturing sector. A world market price of $1.00 will then correspond to a domestic price of 110 pesos under free trade when the higher exchange rate applies, as compared with a price of 120 pesos under protection. The overall protection of manufacturing industries has thus raised the domestic price of clothing by 9 percent— from 110 to 120 pesos—rather than by 20 percent as a simple observation of the tariff would indicate.

In adjusting for the difference between the actual and the free trade exchange rate, we can estimate the *net* effective protection of individual industries. In the previous clothing example, we will now compare the domestic value added of 54 pesos to a world market value added of 44 pesos, calculated at the free trade exchange rate of 110 pesos to the dollar, rather than to a value added of 40 pesos, calculated at the going exchange rate of 100 pesos to the dollar. Correspondingly, the net (adjusted) effective rate of protection will be 23 percent instead of 35 percent.

It appears, then, that the exchange rate observed under protection tends to overvalue the domestic currency as compared to the free trade situation, and effective rates calculated at this rate will overstate the extent of protection of individual industries. In turn, the degree of discrimination against export activities is understated since exports are penalized by the low (overvalued) exchange rate: producers receive fewer pesos per dollar than they would get under free trade. In the meat example with a 6 percent subsidy, the domestic equivalent of world market value added will be 44 pesos at the free trade exchange rate as against 40 pesos domestic value added. Thus, while the effective rate of protection calculated at the exchange rate prevailing under protection was nil, the net effective rate will be approximately −9 percent.

More generally, the measures of protection applied and the exchange rate are interdependent, and they can be combined in various ways to ensure balance-of-payments equilibrium. Yet the effective rate of protection is measured at the going exchange rate, and hence depends on the particular combination chosen. To estimate net effective protection it is therefore necessary to adjust for the overvaluation of the exchange rate as compared to the hypothetical free trade situation.

The extent of overvaluation as compared to the free trade situation in turn depends on the ability of the country's industries to expand exports at constant costs and to sell abroad at the going world market price. The more responsive is the foreign demand for, and the home supply of, exports to price changes, the greater is the ease of reallocation and the lower the degree of overvaluation. This may be illustrated by taking the extreme case of exports being produced at constant costs and sold at the going world market price. The elimination of tariffs would then lead to a reallocation of resources from import-competing to export industries with no change in export prices, and balance-of-payments equilibrium could be maintained without a devaluation. Effective rates of protection calculated at existing exchange rates would not require an adjustment in such an event, since the extent of overvaluation of the exchange rate as compared to the free trade situation is nil.

In most developing countries, however, the shift of resources from import-competing to export industries would entail increasing costs in producing exports and/or a lowering of their dollar prices in foreign markets. Such a resource shift, then, necessitates raising the exchange rate; i.e., balance-of-payments equilibrium can be maintained only if the elimination of protection is accompanied by a devaluation of the currency. It also follows that averages of effective rates, calculated at the going exchange rate, will not appropriately indicate the extent of protection in individual countries, and international comparisons need to be made by adjusting for the extent of overvaluation of their currencies as compared to the hypothetical free trade situation. Apart from the foreign elasticities of demand for, and supply of, the country's exports, the magnitude of this adjustment is also affected by the domestic elasticities of demand for imports and supply of exports. The relevant formulas are shown in Appendix A (pp. 326–28).

The expression "overvaluation" has been used here to compare two situations of balance-of-payments equilibrium: one under protection and another under free trade. A further adjustment would need to be made if there was an unintended loss of foreign exchange reserves or temporary short-term capital movements under the existing system of protection, because in such a situation imported goods as well as exports would be undervalued, thereby providing an incentive to import and a disincentive to export.

Domestic vs. Export Markets

We have considered so far some conceptual problems relating to the measurement of protection in particular industries. It is of further interest to analyze the incentives that protection provides to firms in a given industry in favor of producing for the domestic market (import substitution) and against exporting. In home markets, the firm can obtain the tariff-inclusive domestic price while—in the absence of export subsidies—it gets the world market price on export sales. Yet, unless the firm is reimbursed for tariffs paid on imported materials, it has to pay the the same price on material inputs whether these are used in domestic production or in exports.

In the clothing industry example, protection raises the domestic price to 120 pesos while the export price is 100 pesos. With inputs costing 66 pesos domestically, value added in import substitution is 54 pesos; by contrast, to compete successfully in export markets, the firm would have to operate with a value added of 34 pesos. There are cases when exporting would even require negative value added; i.e., the domestic value of material inputs exceeds the price at which exportation could take place.

For a given industry, the extent of the bias against exporting can be expressed by calculating the percentage excess of domestic value added in import substitution over that obtainable in exporting. With value added in import substitution of 54 pesos and that in exports of 34 pesos, the extent of the bias against exporting will be 59 percent. As we contrast domestic value added obtainable in import substitution and in exporting, no adjustment is made for overvaluation as compared to the hypothetical free trade situation.

The bias against exporting could be reduced if the firm were reimbursed for tariffs levied on imported inputs utilized in exported commodities, although producers using domestic materials would still be penalized by the higher prices of materials due to protection. In the absence of drawbacks on imported inputs, the same incentives could be provided to exports and import substitution if the rate of export subsidy equaled the tariff rate on the same product. In this eventuality, the domestic producer would get the same price irrespective of whether he exports or produces for the protected domestic market.

Instruments of Protection

We have considered so far the case when protection takes the form of tariffs or export subsidies. Developing countries, however, also apply other policy instruments to protect their domestic industries. Among measures that directly affect the protection of particular activities, we can distinguish "price" and "nonprice" measures. The former include ad valorem and specific tariffs, import surcharges, advance deposits for imports, and multiple exchange rates; the latter comprise quotas, licensing, and exchange controls. In an indirect way, the extent of protection is also affected by other types of policy measures, such as profit taxes, credit policy, and social security arrangements. These, however, fall outside the scope of the present inquiry which is concerned with the protective measures proper. An exception has been made for indirect taxes which often serve a function similar to tariffs.

All price measures can be expressed more or less easily in terms of ad valorem tariffs that are levied as a percentage of import value. Several of the countries included in the investigation, however, apply specific duties instead of, or in addition to, ad valorem tariffs. The ad valorem equivalent of specific duties has been estimated by relating the amount of duties paid to the unit value of imports. The various types of import surcharges applied in Brazil and Chile have also been expressed in terms of import value. Finally, in Mexico where tariffs are calculated as a percentage of the "official price" of imports, often different from the price actually paid, tariffs have been expressed as a proportion of the latter.

The tariff equivalent of advance deposits (prepayment requirements) on imports applied in Brazil and Chile has been calculated on the basis of information on the length of the period for which advance deposits had to be made, the size of the deposit, and the interest rate on loans designed to make such deposits. For example, if the importer had to make a deposit in U.S. dollars six months in advance for 50 percent of the import value and the going rate for dollar loans was 18 percent a year, we have added 4.5 percent to the rate of tariff.

Export subsidies applied in Mexico have been treated in the same way as tariffs; the export taxes levied in Brazil, Malaya, and the Philippines have been regarded as negative tariffs. Finally, for the multiple exchange rates used in Pakistan, the percentage difference between the exchange rate actually applied and the basic rate has been regarded as a tariff (export subsidy) or import subsidy (export tax), depending on whether the former is greater or smaller than the latter.

Mention should also be made of the existence of trade preferences and special regimes. In the case of Norway, we have avoided this problem by making estimates for the year 1954, i.e., for the period prior to the establishment of the European Free Trade Association (EFTA). In Malaya, Commonwealth preferences became rather unimportant in 1963 and 1965, the years for which calculations have been made, and we have assumed that the remaining preferences simply enabled higher-priced Commonwealth products to compete with, say, Japanese goods and have made no adjustment on this count. Similar considerations apply to U.S. preferences in the Philippines.

The situation is more complicated in Chile where tariff preferences and special regimes abound. There are substantial differences in tariffs on some imports according to whether these came from countries that are or are not members of the General Agreement on Tariffs and Trade (GATT), and there is a variety of special regimes that benefit particular regions, industries, and institutions. These cases have been handled on their individual merits as described in Chapter 7 and Appendix D.

The described price measures of protection influence foreign trade and resource allocation through their effects on domestic prices. In turn, nonprice measures set permissible levels of imports directly in quantitative terms. By limiting the amount imported, they lead to a rise in the domestic prices of commodities subject to such restrictions. The excess of domestic over foreign prices can be regarded as an "implicit tariff," since under competition imports will be the same whether this price differential has been due to the imposition of tariffs or quotas. Comparisons of domestic and foreign prices are generally not necessary for exports where the rate of subsidy or export tax provides an appropriate indication of the nominal rate of protection. Thus, the following remarks pertain to comparisons of domestic prices and the prices of actual or potential imports.

Making Price Comparisons

Among the countries included in the investigation, quantitative restrictions in the form of licensing apply to imports in Pakistan and Mexico, thereby necessitating comparisons of domestic and import prices. Accordingly, a distinction has been made between "nominal tariff protection" and "nominal implicit protection"; the former refers to the tariff equivalent of all price measures of protection while the latter denotes the percentage difference between domestic and import prices. Depending on the measure of nominal protection used in the calculations, we have further distinguished between "effective tariff protection" and "effective implicit protection."

Whenever domestic prices exceed the sum of import prices and the tariff, imports are effectively limited by quotas, and tariffs serve only a revenue function. Quota recipients will then enjoy a profit equal to the difference between the scarcity margin due to the restriction of imports and the tariff which accrues to the government. In both Pakistan and Mexico, we have also found cases where tariffs exceed the difference between the domestic and import prices of identical commodities. In such instances, tariffs are prohibitive (there are no imports) and domestic competition or profit maximization by a monopolist has resulted in a price lower than the sum of the import price and the tariff.

Prohibitive tariffs exist in other countries also, thus making price comparisons necessary. Since the industrial breakdown used in the country studies generally includes a variety of commodities, some of which may be subject to prohibitive tariffs, we have made price comparisons whenever imports were less than 10 percent of domestic consumption. There are several such instances in Brazil, Chile, and the Philippines, a few in Malaya and, apart from agriculture, none in Norway.

When tariffs are prohibitive, the effective rate of protection estimated from tariff observations indicates the extent of "potential" protection and that estimated from price comparisons shows "realized" protection. While potential protection indicates the "cushion" available to domestic producers, the extent of protection actually utilized will be relevant for the allocation of domestic resources.

In making price comparisons, we have taken the ex-factory price to be the relevant domestic price; whenever domestic prices were available on a different level (for example, wholesale), adjustments have been made for transportation costs and trade margins. Factory prices have next been compared to the c.i.f. import price. For commodities which are not imported because of either prohibitive tariffs or quantitative restrictions, we have estimated the c.i.f. price that would obtain if imports were to take place. For this purpose, we have used the prices of potential suppliers and added transportation costs to the country of destination. In the case of Mexico, comparisons have been made with U.S. prices; in the other studies, U.S. and Japanese prices have chiefly been used.

For standardized goods, comparisons of domestic and foreign prices are relatively straightforward. But quality differences between the domestic and the foreign variety of a particular commodity create problems in price comparisons for differentiated products. It is often alleged that the quality of products is lower in developing countries than in the developed nations whose products predominate in world trade. If this were so and if quality differentials pertained only to the product and not to its inputs, the extent of protection of domestic manufacturing calculated from price comparisons would be understated, since the observed price difference does not reflect the lower quality of the domestic product. By contrast, the effective rate of protection would be overstated if in developing countries the quality of inputs was inferior but this was overcome through the more careful processing of the product.

It should be emphasized that such problems do not arise when tariffs are the relevant measures of protection, since any price differential can then be ascribed to differences in quality. Thus, if the rate of tariff is 20 percent but the foreign variety of a commodity sells for 10 percent more than the competing domestic product, we may assume that there is a 10 percent quality differential which would persist with or without tariffs. But whenever tariffs are prohibitive or imports are effectively limited by quotas, the difference between domestic and foreign prices may reflect the effects of protection as well as quality differences. For example, a 10 percent price differential may express the extent of implicit protection or, alternatively, may correspond to a 20 percent nominal protection combined with a 10 percent quality differential.

The magnitude of the problem due to quality differences, and the methods applied in dealing with them, necessarily vary from country to country. The problem does not arise in Norway where price comparisons had to be made only for some foodstuffs that are not subject to quality differences. In Pakistan most of the commodities under consideration are standardized products so that we could avoid making adjustments for quality differences. In Mexico, it has been possible to compare separately the prices of low quality and high quality consumer goods; however, a downward adjustment has been made for the prices of domestically produced machinery. In the Philippines, we have adjusted downward the prices of most domestically produced goods that do not compete with imports. In other cases, adjustments have been made depending on the particular circumstances of the situation.

Although we have tried to take account of differences in product quality, no attempt has been made to consider what has been called "irrational preference" for foreign goods. It is difficult to define, let alone measure, such a phenomenon, and it would take us far into problems of welfare economics to pursue the matter. We have therefore restricted ourselves to stating that if consumers' preferences for foreign goods could be regarded as irrational, our calculations would overstate the extent of protection in developing countries, because part of the tariff or price differential would simply offset the irrational preferences.

It has further been necessary to take account of indirect taxes. The imposition of indirect taxes on the product itself does not affect its protection as long as such taxes are applied at the same rate to domestically produced and to imported varieties. However, higher rates of indirect taxes on imports, as in the Philippines, raise the level of protection; higher rates on domestic goods, as in Brazil, lower it.

In turn, the imposition of indirect taxes on material inputs reduces the effective rate of protection, since these taxes raise the cost of inputs to the domestic producer while leaving his receipts unchanged. In the earlier clothing example, a 10 percent indirect tax on the tariff-inclusive values of both outputs and inputs will not change net receipts but will increase the cost of material inputs from 66 to 72.6 pesos, thereby reducing domestic value added from 54 to 47.4 pesos and the effective rate of protection from 35 to 18.5 percent. We have made such adjustments in estimating the effective rate of protection in all the country studies.

Input Coefficients and the Definition of Value Added

In all previous examples we have assumed that input-output relations in the world market are known; moreover, we have disregarded the possibility that the imposition of tariffs might induce producers to increase—or to reduce —the amount of material inputs used per unit of output. However, for individual countries, information is available only on the relative proportions of material inputs and value added under protection, and the imposition of tariffs might have affected these proportions. This raises certain problems in measurement which are considered here and, in a more rigorous fashion, in Appendix A.

Information on the value of output, the value of material inputs, and value added in individual industries under protection is available in the input-output tables of the countries included in the investigation. In all cases, we have used the most recent input-output table and for two countries, Brazil and Malaya, calculations have been made for two separate years. The use of domestic input-output tables means that world market values had to be derived indirectly from the domestic values observed under protection. The adjustment can be indicated by an example.

Let us return to the case of the clothing industry where the domestic price of the product is 120 pesos and the domestic value of material inputs per unit of output is 66 pesos. To derive world market values we divide domestic output and input values by the corresponding ratio of domestic to import (or export) prices. With a 20 percent tariff on the output and a 10 percent duty on the material inputs, these price ratios will be 1.2 for the former and 1.1 for the latter. The corresponding world market values are 100 pesos and 60 pesos, and the effective rate of protection 35 percent, just as when we started out from the free trade situation.

It follows that if protection does not induce a change in input coefficients, it is immaterial if we measure effective protection from domestic values or from world market values. However, if the imposition of tariffs induces substitution among material inputs or between material inputs and the primary factors (labor, land, and capital) whose remuneration is included in value added, the assumption of constant input coefficients will involve an error irrespective of whether effective rates are calculated from domestic or from world market values. The problem of input substitution is discussed in Appendix A; some results on the possible extent of errors due to substitution are reported in Chapter 3.

Note further that the estimation of effective rates of protection from domestic input-output tables is sensitive to errors of observation since world market value added is obtained as a residual—the difference between the derived world market value of output and that of material inputs. The application of this method will thus magnify errors in the output and input values of domestic input-output tables as well as in the ratio of domestic and foreign prices of inputs and outputs. Yet input-output tables are subject to considerable errors in the developing countries, since these countries encounter many difficulties in the collection of statistical data.

The errors of observation in the input-output tables of developing countries as well as the errors of measurement in estimating effective rates on the basis of these tables suggest the need for making estimates from world market (free trade) values. Such estimates also permit us to derive comparable results for countries with input-output tables of differing composition. Furthermore, as noted in Chapter 3, a comparison of the results obtained by the use of domestic and free trade coefficients can be used to evaluate the importance of substitution among inputs.

But how can we derive the input-output coefficients that would apply under free trade conditions? For various reasons, the input-output tables of developing countries could not be used for this purpose. First, the classification schemes employed differ among countries and hence the industry breakdowns are not comparable. Second, as we have noted, the input-output tables of the developing countries are often subject to considerable error. Third, to the extent that there is substitution among inputs, the high levels of protection prevalent in developing countries might have distorted the input-output coefficients.

For lack of free trade input-output coefficients pertaining to developing countries, we have decided to make use of an input-output table based on the data of the industrial nations. The table has been constructed by utilizing the input-output tables of the Common Market countries that employ the same classification system. We have relied primarily on the tables of Belgium and the Netherlands where tariff levels are low; hence, input-output relationships are not likely to have been much distorted by substitution among inputs due to the effects of tariffs on domestic prices.

This solution may be objected to on the grounds that the use of an input-output table based on data for the industrial nations is not appropriate for evaluating the structure of protection in countries at an earlier stage of industrialization. However, as argued in Appendix A, the error possibilities in the results due to differences in the structure of production in developed and in developing countries may not be large. At any rate, the results are useful in providing a "sensitivity analysis" of the estimates of effective protection derived from different sets of input-output coefficients.

Irrespective of the choice of the input-output coefficients, the measurement of protection involves a comparison of domestic and world market value added in the processing activity. Value added can in turn be defined in gross or in net terms, depending on whether we include or exclude the depreciation of buildings, machinery, and equipment. To measure the extent of protection, the latter formulation is more appropriate since it takes account of the fact that investment goods are inputs and, in large part, internationally traded inputs. Even in the short run, firms make allowance for depreciation to ensure their continuing operation through the reinvestment of the proceeds.

The free trade input-output table provides information on depreciation; hence estimates based on this table refer to the effective rate of protection on net value added. Data on depreciation are also available in the domestic input-output tables of Chile, Malaya, Mexico, Norway, and the Philippines but not for Brazil and Pakistan. Accordingly, a net concept of value added has been applied to the first group of countries and a gross concept to the second.

The application of the net concept of value added involves deducting the domestic value of depreciation from domestic value added and the world market value of depreciation from world market value added. For this purpose, we need information on the average tariff on the particular items included in depreciation. Information in the appropriate detail is available for Chile and Mexico but not for the other countries. For the latter, we have rather arbitrarily assumed that electrical machinery, nonelectrical machinery, and construction individually account for one-third of the total, and have derived an average tariff on depreciation accordingly.

The error committed thereby is rather small, as is the difference between effective rates of protection calculated on a net and a gross basis. The reason lies in the small share of depreciation in the product price. If this share is 5 percent of the world market price, and depreciation is not subject to duty, the effective rate of protection in the previous clothing example will be 40 percent on net value added as compared with 35 percent on gross value added. More generally, the effective rate of protection on net value added will be greater than, equal to, or less than the effective rate of protection on gross value added, depending on whether the tariff on depreciation is less than, equal to, or greater than the effective rate on gross value added. In the case of Chile, where both concepts have been applied, the difference in the two sets of results rarely exceeded one-tenth of the effective rate of protection and the rank correlation between the two is .96.

The Treatment of Nontraded Goods

In estimating the effective rate of protection from price observations, we have compared domestic factory prices to the c.i.f. import price for actual or potential imports; for exports, the price differential has been assumed to equal the rate of export tax or subsidy. As exports are measured in f.o.b. prices, the different valuation base gives rise to problems in the case of commodities that are presently imported but would be exported under free trade conditions with a more favorable exchange rate. There may also be commodities that would not be traded even in the absence of tariffs because transportation costs to or from foreign countries outweigh the cost differential.

These possibilities could not be taken into account in the present study. In comparing the factory price with the c.i.f. import price, we have also neglected the difference in the cost of transportation to the place of consumption from the two sources of supply. Yet if the cost of transporting the commodity to the main consuming centers is greater from the port or other points of entry than from domestic factories, the effective rate of protection will be underestimated since we do not take account of the "natural protection" provided by transport costs. The opposite conclusion holds if transport costs are higher from domestic factories than from the ports.

Under the assumptions made, we could proceed in a straightforward fashion whenever the domestic input-output table was expressed in producer (ex-factory) prices, but adjustments have been necessary if inputs and outputs were valued in user prices. In the latter eventuality, we have expressed the value of output in producer prices by deducting from output value the cost of transporting the final product and the wholesale and retail margins. We have made no such adjustment in regard to individual material inputs, which were also valued at user prices, since the relatively small error possibility did not warrant making the necessary calculations.

Transportation and domestic trade are nontraded goods (services) that do not enter international trade. Other nontraded inputs include construction, electricity, gas, water, communications, banking, and insurance. In assuming that the value of production is made up of material inputs and value added, we have so far disregarded these inputs. They will now be discussed.

The treatment of nontraded inputs in the calculations depends on the assumptions made in regard to the responsiveness of their supply to changes in domestic prices. In this study, two alternative assumptions have been made. First, it has been assumed that the same primary factors are used in producing nontraded inputs as in producing traded goods, so that the available amounts of these factors limit both kinds of activities. This method, first proposed by W. M. Corden, entails including value added in the production of nontraded inputs with value added in processing in the industry in question.

The procedure suggested by Corden presupposes a method of price determination which may not be realistic in developing countries, and it also raises questions concerning the division of the gain among the producers of traded and nontraded goods. An alternative procedure, called the "Balassa method," assumes that nontraded goods are supplied at constant costs and that their prices vary by the amount by which protection raises or reduces the cost of material inputs used in their production. As noted in Appendix A, this method assumes that the effective rate of protection of nontraded goods is zero.

A comparison of the results obtained by the use of the two methods indicates the degree of sensitivity of the estimates to alternative ways of treating nontraded goods. In Mexico, Malaya, the Philippines, and Norway, the overall averages of effective rates derived by the use of the Balassa and Corden formulas are identical if domestic input-output coefficients are used; they differ by about one-fifth if free trade coefficients are applied. Nor do the differences for individual commodity categories exceed 10 percent in any of these countries.

In Brazil and Chile, the discrepancies in the overall averages calculated under the two alternative results amount to about 15 or 25 percent, depending on whether we use domestic or free trade coefficients. Except for a few cases where effective rates are very high, differences of similar magnitudes are also shown for individual commodity categories. Finally, in Pakistan, averages of effective rates obtained by the use of the Corden method are about one-half of those calculated by the Balassa method, irrespective of the choice of the input-output coefficients. Pakistan, however, is a special case since the category of nontraded goods includes unreported material inputs.

Although the assumptions about nontraded inputs affect the level of effective rates, with the exception of Pakistan the ranking of industries by their effective rates is practically the same under the two alternatives. Correspondingly, while effective rates of protection have been calculated under both alternatives at existing exchange rates, net effective rates have been calculated only by the use of a single formula. Because of its computational advantage in adjusting for overvaluation as compared to the hypothetical free trade situation, we have used the Corden method for this purpose.

Problems of Classification and Averaging

For calculating the effective rate of protection in the industrial breakdown of the domestic and the free trade input-output tables, it was necessary to establish a correspondence between the classification scheme of these tables and the tariff classification schemes used in the individual countries. Subsequently, tariffs, as well as ratios of domestic to foreign prices, had to be averaged for each industry of the relevant input-output table.

Ideally, one should calculate averages of tariffs (or price ratios) for each cell of the input-output table (i.e., for the output and for each use of the products of a given industry) by using sales weights that express the product composition of output and of its particular uses. In practice, apart from a few cases, such distinctions could not be made in the country studies due to lack of information on the product-by-product breakdown of sales to individual industries.

In some countries, not even data on the product composition of output were available, so that we had to introduce alternative weighting procedures. Among possible alternatives, weighting by the country's own imports is subject to a downward bias: low tariffs associated with high levels of imports are given large weights, high tariffs that restrict imports have small weights, and prohibitive duties zero weights. The use of unweighted averages, too, entails considerable error possibilities. This method involves assigning equal weights to all products within a particular industry under the assumption that the "law of large numbers" will lend meaning to the results. But in the countries under consideration, the assumption underlying this procedure is rarely fulfilled since the relative importance of individual commodities differs within each industry.

In view of the deficiencies of weighting tariffs by the country's own imports or calculating unweighted averages, we have decided to use world trade weights in averaging tariffs whenever domestic sales data were not available. The composition of world trade can be taken as an approximation for the structure of world consumption (production) under the assumption that the effects of the "idiosyncrasies" of national tariff levels are compensated on the world level. Distortions in the composition of imports due to protection will be especially small in the industrial countries whose tariffs are relatively low. Therefore, we have taken the combined imports of the major industrial countries to represent world market weights. Although the use of these weights may give rise to error because of differences in the industrial structure of the developed and the developing countries, within a given product category the margin of error is likely to be relatively small.

A combination of sales weights and world market weights has been utilized in cases when the latter provides a more detailed commodity breakdown than the former. Sales weights could not be employed, however, in calculations based on free trade input-output coefficients. In all such calculations we have used the combined imports of the major industrial countries as weights.

Data on the imports of the industrial countries are available according to the four-digit U.N. Standard International Trade Classification comprising about 110 commodity categories. Whenever the national tariff classification was more detailed than the four-digit SITC, tariff averages were calculated to get to the four-digit level by using the country's own imports as weights. This procedure has been considered superior to calculating unweighted averages, since at this level of disaggregation the bias that results from weighting by the country's own imports is likely to be relatively small while unweighted averages are hardly useful for a group containing only a few items.

We have noted that for export products, the nominal rate of protection has been assumed to equal the rate of subsidy while export taxes have been considered negative tariffs. For export products that are not subject to either a subsidy or a tax, tariffs have been assumed to be nil even in cases when the tariff classification includes a duty on their imports. Finally, in cases when an industry produces imports as well as export products, tariffs (price ratios) on the former and subsidies (taxes) on the latter have been averaged by the use of sales weights.

Thus far we have dealt with the problem of averaging nominal rates of protection (tariffs, subsidies, and price ratios) according to the breakdown of the input-output table. The resulting averages of nominal protection as well as the effective rates calculated for individual industries have further been averaged for major industry groups. This has been done both to indicate differences in the extent of protection among these groups and to compare the structure of protection in the individual countries.

Averages of effective rates of protection have been calculated for the commodity groups listed in Table 1.1, which shows the breakdown of the free

TABLE 1.1: Composition of Product Groups

I	Agriculture, forestry, and fishing:	01 Agriculture and forestry, 02 Fishing
II	Processed food:	10 Meat products, 11 Prepared food products, 12 Sugar, 13 Confectionary, 14 Dairy products, 15 Cereal products, 16 Other food products, 18 Oils and fats
III	Tobacco and beverages:	17 Beverages, 19 Tobacco
IV	Mining and energy:	03 Solid fuels, 04 Gas, 05 Iron ore mining, 06 Nonferrous metal ores, 07 Petroleum and natural gas, 09 Other minerals
V	Construction materials:	08 Basic construction materials, 45 Nonmetallic mineral products
VI-A	Intermediate products I:	21 Thread and yarn, 28 Lumber, 31 Wood pulp, 35 Leather, 39 Synthetic materials, 40 Other chemical materials, 44 Petroleum products, 46 Glass and glass products, 48 Pig iron and ferromanganese, 49 Steel ingots, 54 Nonferrous metals
VI-B	Intermediate products II:	22 Textile fabrics, 29 Wood products and furniture, 32 Paper and paper products, 37 Rubber products, 38 Plastic goods, 41 Chemical products, 50 Rolled steel products, 51 Other steel products, 55 Metal castings, 56 Metal manufactures
VII	Nondurable consumer goods:	23 Hosiery, 24 Clothing, 25 Other textile articles, 26 Shoes, 33 Printing and publishing, 36 Leather goods other than shoes, 66 Precision instruments, 67 Toys, sport goods, jewelry
VIII	Consumer durables:	62 Automobiles, 64 Bicycles and motorcycles
IX	Machinery:	57 Agricultural machinery, 58 Nonelectrical machinery, 59 Electrical machinery
X	Transport equipment:	60 Shipbuilding, 61 Railroad vehicles, 65 Airplanes

Source: Office Statistique des Communautés Européennes, *Tableaux 'Entrées-Sorties' pour les pays de la Communauté Européenne Economique*, October 1964.

Note: Arabic numerals refer to the industry classification of the free trade input-output table.

trade input-output table. In the country studies, we have also classified the industries of the domestic input-output table according to this scheme.

Nominal rates of protection pertaining to the individual industries of the domestic input-output tables have been averaged by supply weights. In averaging effective rates of protection, we have used "derived" world market value added as weights because this weighting scheme ensures that the average effective rate equals the effective rate calculated directly from data on domestic and world market value added for the group as a whole (see Appendix A).

Data on value added are not available in the industry breakdown of the free trade input-output table which contains only coefficients but not absolute numbers. To express the relative importance of individual industries, we have averaged the effective rates of protection calculated from these coefficients by using the combined imports of the industrial countries as weights. The weighting scheme applied has thus been the same as that used in averaging nominal rates of protection for individual industries.

The described procedures have also been applied in averaging nominal and effective rates of protection for primary activities and for manufacturing, as well as for exports, import-competing goods and non-import-competing goods. With some exceptions, the first group has been defined to include industries which exported more than one-tenth of their output; industries importing more than one-tenth of domestic consumption have been considered import-competing; all other industries have been included in the non-import-competing category. For reasons mentioned in Chapter 3, this categorization could not have applied to Brazil and Pakistan.

Uses of the Effective Protection Measure

Among the possible applications of the effective protection measure, we will consider its uses to indicate the incentive effects of protection, to measure the cost of protection, and to evaluate alternative investment projects. Under certain assumptions, ranking by effective rates of protection calculated at existing exchange rates will indicate the relative incentives provided to particular activities. In adjusting for overvaluation as compared to the hypothetical free trade situation, we can also estimate the net incentives that protective measures provide. For example, an industry with positive effective protection calculated at existing exchange rates may have negative *net* effective protection after adjustment for overvaluation, and thus suffer discrimination as a result of the imposition of protective measures.

These conclusions follow if production takes place under constant costs and there is no substitution among inputs in response to changes in relative prices resulting from protection. If these conditions are met and if monopolistic market structures do not result in "above-normal" profits and wages, value added in particular activities will also equal the cost of processing, so that the effective rate of protection will indicate the excess of domestic over foreign processing costs and can then be used to measure the cost of protection to the national economy.

Another use of the effective protection measure is in project appraisal. It has been suggested that projects should be ranked according to the domestic cost of foreign exchange saved in import substitution or earned in exporting. Domestic costs may be defined in terms of the cost of processing of the product in question (direct costs) or as the combined cost of processing at the last and at earlier stages of production (direct plus indirect costs). If the former definition is adopted, the effective rate of protection can be reinterpreted in terms of the domestic cost of saving or earning foreign exchange. A 50 percent net effective rate of protection on a commodity produced under protection will then mean that in the particular case the domestic cost of saving a dollar through import substitution is 50 percent greater than the exchange rate; in turn, a −20 percent net effective rate for an export commodity will indicate that its domestic cost is 20 percent less than the exchange rate. By contrast, including indirect costs in the calculations would involve averaging effective costs of protection at various stages of fabrication. The relative merits of the two alternatives are discussed in Appendix A.

The domestic costs of processing may be higher than costs on the world market for various reasons. The country's resource endowment may not be suitable for the production of the commodity in question; there may be waste of materials or inefficient organization of the production process; or the smallness of domestic markets may not permit the use of large-scale production methods in manufacturing industries. We will return to the discussion of these sources of excess costs in Chapter 4.

In the event of imperfect competition, however, the excess of domestic over world market value added may partly be absorbed by "above-normal" profits. Although indications are that such cases exist, especially in Pakistan, the amount of excess profits could not be estimated because of lack of information on the capital stock and because of the difficulties encountered in determining the "normal" profit rate. Nor have we attempted to estimate the excess value added absorbed in the form of higher wages due to the monopolistic power of labor unions, although there is evidence that such is the case in some Chilean industries.

The conclusions will also be affected if production does not take place under constant costs. It is apparent that, in an industry which has expanded under protection, the use of domestic input-output coefficients in the calculations will tend to overstate the effective rates of protection in increasing-cost industries and understate it in decreasing-cost industries. The reason is that effective protection is measured at existing output levels where costs per unit exceed costs at lower output levels in increasing-cost industries but are smaller in decreasing-cost industries. The opposite conclusion follows if we use free trade coefficients; we will now overstate effective protection in decreasing-cost industries and understate it in increasing-cost industries.

In agriculture, costs tend to rise with increases in output since expansion would involve the use of poorer land and/or the more intensive cultivation of the existing land. In manufacturing, increasing costs may be due to interfirm differences in costs. In developing countries, however, there is often only one firm, or very few firms, in a particular industry, so that the error committed in assuming constant costs may not be large.

Still, the constant cost assumption will not be fulfilled if protection affects the prices of the primary factors of production (on this point, see Appendix A, pp. 336–37). Furthermore, input substitution in response to changes in relative prices resulting from protection may affect the estimates of effective protection, as well as the ranking of industries by effective rates, depending on whether domestic or free trade coefficients are used in the calculations. This problem will be considered in Chapter 3.

A further qualification should also be made. While effective rates of protection are calculated with respect to value added, in a country with underemployment the expansion of protected activities would not necessitate drawing away labor from other industries. In such an eventuality, the resource-pull and resource-push effects of protection would be better indicated by the effective rate of protection on profits rather than on value added, while, from the point of view of the national economy, account would have to be taken on the employment effects of protection. These considerations have relevance for, for example, Pakistan, but data limitations did not permit estimating the effective rate of protection of profits. At any rate, owing to the year-to-year variability of profits, little confidence can be placed in estimates for particular years.

We have seen that substitution among inputs and nonconstant costs of production introduce error possibilities in calculations of effective rates of protection and influence the ranking of industries by effective rates. Nevertheless, effective rates of protection are superior to nominal rates that are subject to the same sources of error and have additional shortcomings inasmuch as they take no account either of the protection of inputs or the relative importance of value added in the product price. At the same time, the uncertainties due to the described sources of error can be reduced if we estimate effective rates by using both domestic and free trade input-output coefficients. Estimation by the use of the two sets of coefficients also provides a "sensitivity analysis" of the results, which is especially useful in the face of error possibilities in output and input values.

In this volume, our conclusions regarding the structure of protection in the individual countries will be based on results derived under both sets of coefficients. Moreover, in the analysis of the results, emphasis will be given to averages for groups of industries where the error possibilities are further reduced. Industries will be classified according to the character of their final products (for example, agriculture and manufacturing), the stage of fabrication (for example, intermediate products and final goods), and their major market outlets (import substitution and exports).

Effective rates of protection will also be used to indicate the cost to the national economy due to protection, and an attempt will be made to provide an estimate of this cost. While the error possibilities that influence the ranking of industries by effective rates will affect such estimates to a lesser degree, the numerical results will necessarily include above-normal profits and wages just as in the case when the estimates are made from nominal rates of protection.

Conclusions

In this chapter, we have presented some concepts that are useful in evaluating the structure of protection in developing countries. We have first compared the nominal rate of protection (product protection) and the effective rate of protection (protection of value added). The former is defined as the tariff equivalent of the protective measures applied and it equals the percentage excess of domestic over foreign prices due to the imposition of such measures. Apart from tariffs (and other protective measures) on the product itself, the effective rate of protection is also affected by tariffs on material inputs and by the share of value added in the product price. It is defined as the percentage excess of domestic value added, obtainable under protection, over foreign or world market value added.

Rates of nominal and effective protection are calculated at the existing exchange rate and need to be adjusted for the difference between this rate and the exchange rate that would obtain in a free trade situation. Such an adjustment is necessary since the imposition of protective measures permits balance-of-payments equilibrium to be maintained at an exchange rate lower than the rate that would prevail under free trade. The lower exchange rate, in turn, reduces the price of imports and thus lessens the protection provided by a given tariff. Further adjustments are required if the existing exchange rate did not ensure equilibrium in the balance of payments during the period under consideration.

If production takes place under constant costs and there is no substitution among inputs in response to changes in relative prices due to protection, ranking of domestic industries by effective rates will show the incentives provided by the imposition of protective measures in relative terms while effective rates adjusted for overvaluation as compared to the hypothetical free trade situation indicate the net protection of processing activities in absolute terms. In the absence of above-normal profits and wages in protected industries, estimates of net effective protection can also be used in project selection and in estimating the cost of protection.

One may further analyze the incentives provided in favor of import substitution and against exporting in protected industries. Bias against exporting arises because firms can obtain the tariff-inclusive price in home markets whereas—in the absence of export subsidies—they get the world market price on export sales. The results are further affected by drawbacks on imported inputs used in export industries.

Estimates of effective rates of protection, calculated at the actual and the hypothetical free trade exchange rate, and those on the bias against exporting will be used in appraising the structure of protection in the seven countries under consideration. Before presenting the results, however, in Chapter 2 we provide some information on the economic structure, growth performance, and trade pattern of these countries.

PATTERNS OF ECONOMIC STRUCTURE, GROWTH, AND TRADE

Bela Balassa

Market Size and the Orientation of Manufacturing Industries

The size of domestic markets influences the choice of economic policies and the effects of these policies, both because of large-scale economies obtainable in the manufacturing sector and because of the impact of market size on domestic competition. The existence of economies of scale limits the ability of small countries to develop manufacturing industries that cater exclusively to domestic markets and raises the cost of production in these industries. Moreover, the size of the home market limits the possibilities for domestic competition.[1]

These considerations indicate the need to compare the size of domestic markets in evaluating the system of protection applied in the seven countries under study. But how is market size to be measured? If we used population as a criterion, Pakistan would appear to be the largest country in the group with a population of 107.3 million in 1967, followed by Brazil (85.7 million), Mexico (45.7 million), the Philippines (34.7 million), Chile (9.2 million), Malaya (8.5 million), and Norway (3.8 million).[2] Population figures will

---

[1] For a detailed discussion of the advantages of large markets, see Chapter 4, pp. 76–80.

[2] Since 1968 data for several of the economic indicators used in this chapter were not available at the time the book went to press, for the sake of comparability, we have used data for 1967 throughout.

hardly be appropriate for the purpose at hand, however, since the purchasing power of the population also depends on per capita incomes. Thus, for indicating the opportunities for large-scale production and domestic competition, national income data are superior to population figures.

A comparison of gross domestic products shows less variation among the countries in question than does population, and it also gives a different ranking. Brazil and Mexico are now in first place with a gross domestic product of about $24 billion in 1967, followed by Pakistan, $13.2 billion; the Philippines, $9.0 billion; Norway, $7.5 billion; Chile, $4.9 billion; and Malaya, $2.4 billion (Table 2.1). Changes in the ranking reflect disparities in incomes per head that in 1967 ranged from nearly $2,000 in Norway to $123 in Pakistan. Among the other countries of the group, per capita incomes were about $500–550 in Chile and Mexico, and $260–80 in Malaya, Brazil, and the Philippines.

Comparisons of gross domestic products are affected to a considerable extent by the choice of the exchange rate used to convert data expressed in national currencies into dollars. Apart from the fact that the exchange rates employed by the United Nations and adopted here do not take account of the variety of rates used in some of the countries, the use of exchange rates as conversion ratio gives rise to bias in the comparisons.

First, conversion of national income data at exchange rates will overstate national incomes in countries with high levels of protection, since high protection will be associated with low exchange rates.[3] Second, as the relative prices of services (nontraded goods) tend to rise with per capita incomes, conversion at exchange rates will understate value added in the service sector—and hence the gross domestic product—in low-income countries and overstate them in high-income countries.[4]

The second source of bias can be avoided if we restrict the definition of market size to industries where large-scale economies can be obtained. Then, in addition to excluding service industries where economies of scale are practically nonexistent, we will exclude agriculture from our purview since the establishment of farms of efficient size does not require large national markets. Thus, if market size is to indicate the possibilities open to producers for exploiting economies of scale and the extent of potential competition, the domestic consumption of manufactured goods appears to be an appropriate indicator.[5]

The domestic consumption of manufactured goods has been estimated by adjusting the value of the domestic output of manufacturing for the imports and exports of manufactured goods. Table 2.1 provides alternative definitions

---

[3] For differences between actual and free trade exchange rates, see Chapter 1, pp. 7–9.

[4] For a detailed discussion, see Bela Balassa, "The Purchasing-Power Parity Doctrine: A Reappraisal," *Journal of Political Economy*, December 1964, pp. 584–96.

[5] Needless to say, such data indicate the actual size, and not the potential future size, of national markets.

TABLE 2.1: Market Size and Trade Shares of Manufacturing, 1967[a]

		Brazil	Chile	Mexico	Malaya	Pakistan	Philippines	Norway
1. Population (thousands)		85,655	9,137	45,671	8,540	107,258	34,656	3,784
2. Gross domestic product ($ million)		23,379[c]	4,928	23,736	2,400[c]	13,194	8,979	7,524
3. GDP per capita ($)		273	539	520	281	123	259	1,988
4. Manufacturing output ($ million)	A	15,672	2,239	11,153	1,062	3,755	3,787	5,299
	B	12,708	1,673	8,078	779	3,236	2,401	4,506
5. Exports of manufactures ($ million)	A	347	58	372	163	269	310	1,135
	B	164	43	243	75	263	86	967
6. Imports of manufactures ($ million)	A	1,036	519	1,524	553	826	786	2,267
	B	949	477	1,463	481	755	739	2,045
7. Domestic consumption of manufactured goods[b] ($ million)	A	16,361	2,700	12,305	1,452	4,312	4,263	6,431
	B	13,493	2,107	9,298	1,185	3,728	3,054	5,584
8. Exports as a proportion of manufacturing output (percent)	A	2.2	2.6	3.3	15.3	7.2	8.2	21.4
	B	1.3	2.6	3.0	9.6	8.1	3.6	21.5
9. Imports as a proportion of the consumption of manufactured goods (percent)	A	6.3	19.2	12.4	38.1	19.2	18.4	35.3
	B	7.0	22.6	15.7	40.6	20.3	24.2	36.6

Sources: U.N., Statistical Yearbook; U.N., Yearbook of International Trade Statistics; U.N., Commodity Trade Statistics; U.N., Yearbook of National Accounts Statistics.
[a] A includes food processing, beverages and tobacco, while B excludes them. Both A and B exclude unwrought metals.
[b] The consumption of manufactured goods has been derived by adding imports to, and deducting exports from, the value of manufacturing output.
[c] Our estimate.

of the manufacturing sector. Definition A, employed in industrial statistics, includes processed food, beverages, and tobacco under manufactured goods but generally excludes unwrought metals. Definition B conforms to the classification used in trade statistics where manufactured goods are defined to include all commodities in classes 5 to 8 of the U.N. Standard International Trade Classification except for unwrought metals. Thus the difference between the two definitions is that the former includes, and the latter excludes, processed foods, beverages, and tobacco.[6]

Differences in the values of the consumption of manufactured goods under the two definitions range from 13 percent in Pakistan to 29 percent in the Philippines; for the remaining countries, the corresponding figures are Brazil and Malaya, 18 percent; Chile, 21 percent; Norway, 23 percent; and Mexico, 26 percent. However, apart from the relative positions of Pakistan and the Philippines, the ranking of countries by the size of the domestic market for manufactured goods is the same irrespective of the definition used.

Given the relatively small importance of economies of scale in food processing, beverages, and tobacco,[7] we will employ the narrower concept in defining market size. This measure will give a different ranking of the countries in question than GDP, partly because the pattern of consumption varies with per capita incomes, and partly because there are intercountry differences in the degree of vertical integration and in the share of imported intermediate products in manufacturing output.

In the ranking of countries by the domestic consumption of manufactured goods (Table 2.1), Brazil occupies first place ($13.5 billion) and is followed by Mexico ($9.3 billion). Norway ($5.6 billion), however, now ranks ahead of Pakistan ($3.7 billion) and the Philippines ($3.1 billion) which in turn are followed by Chile ($2.1 billion) and Malaya ($1.2 billion). By comparison, the domestic market for manufactured goods exceeds $17 billion even in smaller industrial nations, such as the Netherlands and Sweden.

These data are expressed in domestic prices which are themselves affected by the system of protection. For comparability, we have therefore revalued the figures in terms of world market prices. The world market value of manufacturing output has been estimated by "deflating" domestic values by the average net nominal rate of protection of manufactured goods, which expresses the percentage difference between domestic and world market prices of manu-

---

[6] A third concept of the manufacturing sector has also been used in the country studies. This excludes construction materials, in addition to processed food, beverages, and tobacco. The rationale for this definition is that construction materials enjoy a considerable degree of natural protection due to transportation costs.

[7] For example, in grain milling, sugar manufacturing, and wine production, efficient scale operations are possible in plants that are relatively small compared with the domestic markets of the countries under consideration. On the other hand, economies of scale assume importance in the processing of fruits and vegetables.

factured goods after adjustment for the difference between the actual and the hypothetical free trade exchange rate.[8] Since the countries in question can hardly affect the world market prices of manufactured goods, there is no need, however, to adjust the dollar values of exports and imports which are expressed in f.o.b. and c.i.f. prices, respectively.

The adjusted data show a further reduction in intercountry disparities and an improvement in the relative positions of Norway and Malaya. The domestic consumption of manufactured goods in world market prices has been estimated as $10.3 billion in Brazil, $8.1 billion in Mexico, $5.5 billion in Norway, $3.4 billion in Pakistan, $2.9 billion in the Philippines, $1.7 billion in Chile, and $1.2 billion in Malaya. Such an adjustment would hardly affect the value of manufacturing output in the Netherlands and Sweden.

It should be added that the openness of national economies increases the effective size of home markets, since trade in manufactured goods permits the exploiting of scale economies through greater specialization in domestic industries. The extent of openness, measured by import-consumption and export-production ratios in manufacturing, is affected by the size of the domestic market itself as well as by the country's trade policies and its level of economic development.[9]

Norway's liberal trade policy largely explains that, in terms of both the share of imports in the domestic consumption of manufactured goods (37 percent) and that of exports in manufacturing output (22 percent), it ranks ahead of several of the countries of the group with a smaller domestic market. Imports account for 41 percent of the consumption and exports for 10 percent of the production of manufactured goods in Malaya, which also follows liberal trade policies but is at a lower level of industrial development than Norway (Table 2.1).

By contrast, due to high levels of protection, the share of imports in the consumption of manufactured goods in Brazil has declined to 7 percent, while exports hardly surpass 1 percent of the value of manufacturing output. Import substitution has proceeded less far in Mexico where the share of imports in the domestic consumption of manufactured goods approaches 16 percent, and exports account for 3 percent of output. In Chile the narrow domestic market limits the possibilities of developing industries that produce intermediate goods, machinery, and transport equipment. This explains that the import share exceeds one-fourth; the share of exports in Chile's manufacturing out-

---

[8] Data on the net nominal protection of manufacturing defined in a narrower sense are provided in the country chapters; they relate to the estimates for the entire manufacturing sector derived by the use of domestic input-output coefficients.

[9] Various studies have shown that per capita imports and exports of manufactured goods are inversely related to market size. Cf., for example, H. B. Chenery, "Patterns of Industrial Growth," *American Economic Review*, September 1960, pp. 624–54.

put is, however, less than 3 percent and about half of these exports are sold to LAFTA (Latin-American Free Trade Association) countries under preferential arrangements. Finally, in Pakistan, imports provide about 20 percent, and in the Philippines 24 percent, of the consumption of manufactured products, while exports—bolstered by subsidies—account for 8 percent of manufacturing output in Pakistan but less than 4 percent in the Philippines.

The Rate of Economic Growth

Among the countries under study, the Philippines had first place in the growth league in the first half of the 1950s but occupied third place (behind Mexico and Brazil) in 1955–60 and fourth place (behind Mexico, Malaya, and Pakistan) in 1967. A decline in the growth rate of GDP is also shown in Brazil, while economic growth accelerated in the other countries of the group. For the period as a whole, Mexico had the highest growth rate (6.4 percent) while the rate of growth of GDP averaged about 6 percent in the Philippines, 5 percent in Brazil and Malaya, and 4 percent in Chile and Norway (Table 2.2).[10]

But, with population rising at an annual rate of less than one percent, Norway had the second highest rate of growth of per capita incomes (3.0 percent) over the entire seventeen-year period and attained first place in 1960–67. The average annual rate of increase of population exceeded 3 percent in the Philippines and Mexico; it was 3 percent in Brazil and Malaya; and slightly over 2 percent in Chile and Pakistan. Among these countries, the ranking in terms of the rate of growth of per capita incomes is Mexico, 3.2 percent; the Philippines, 2.7 percent; Brazil, 2.0 percent; Chile, 1.7 percent; and Malaya and Pakistan, 1.6 percent.

In the calculation of growth rates of GDP, sectoral growth rates are weighted by the share of each sector in the base year, expressed in domestic prices. However, domestic prices are influenced by the system of protection applied, and the contribution of the individual sectors to the gross domestic product is more appropriately indicated if it is expressed in world market prices. This is so because world market prices rather than the domestic prices distorted by protection indicate the alternatives available for the country.

It follows that in developing countries that protect their manufacturing industries at the expense of primary activities, calculations made at domestic prices will overstate the contribution of the former, and understate that of the latter, to national income. The rate of growth of GDP will then be overstated or understated, depending on whether value added in manufacturing industries was rising at a faster or at a slower rate than in primary activities.

---

[10] In the case of Malaya, data relate to the period 1955–67.

TABLE 2.2:   Growth Rates of Population, GDP and Its Main Components[a]

(*Percent*)

	Brazil	Chile	Mexico	Malaya[c]	Pakis-tan	Philip-pines	Norway
Gross domestic product[b]							
1950–55	5.5	3.1	6.2	na	1.5	8.6	2.9
1955–60	5.9	4.1	5.8	3.6	3.5	5.0	3.5
1960–67	3.9	5.0	7.2	5.8	5.6	5.1	5.0
1950–67	5.0	4.2	6.5	4.8	3.8	6.1	3.9
Population							
1950–55	3.0	2.3	3.1	2.7	2.2	3.1	1.0
1955–60	3.0	2.5	3.3	3.1	2.1	3.1	0.9
1960–67	3.0	2.5	3.4	3.1	2.1	3.4	0.8
1950–67	3.0	2.4	3.3	3.0	2.1	3.3	0.9
Per capita incomes							
1950–55	2.6	0.8	3.0	na	−0.6	5.3	1.9
1955–60	2.8	1.6	2.5	0.4	1.4	1.8	2.6
1960–67	0.9	2.4	3.7	2.6	3.4	1.6	4.2
1950–67	2.0	1.7	3.1	1.6	1.6	2.7	3.0
Manufacturing (value added)[d]							
1950–55	7.9	4.3	6.1	na	9.6	12.0	3.8
1955–60	10.0	2.4	6.2	3.2	6.0	7.7	4.2
1960–67	4.7	7.0	8.3	12.2	8.3	4.5	5.8
1950–67	7.1	4.8	8.1	8.0	8.0	7.8	4.5
Agriculture (value added)							
1950–55	5.4	1.4	5.5	na	0.1	7.3	−0.4
1955–60	3.8	0.8	3.5	2.9	2.7	2.9	0.4
1960–67	4.5	2.0	4.0	4.2	3.3	4.6	−0.1
1950–67	4.6	1.5	4.8	3.6	2.2	4.9	0.0

Sources: U.N., *Yearbook of National Accounts Statistics;* U.N., *Demographic Yearbook;* Banco de Mexico, *Cuentas Nacionales y Aceros de Capital Consolidadas y por Tipo de Actividad.*
  [a] Data in market prices for Brazil and Mexico and in factor costs for the other countries.
  [b] Net domestic product for Chile and the Philippines.
  [c] The latest benchmark year is 1966 rather than 1967; apart from population, data for the entire period relates to 1955–66.
  [d] For Brazil, this includes mining and quarrying, construction, electricity, gas and water.

While we may assume that the countries included in the study cannot affect the world market prices of manufactured goods, this assumption does not hold for some of their agricultural and mining export products. Such products should therefore be valued at the world market prices that would obtain in the event that protective measures were eliminated in the country in question. This adjustment has been made in revaluing the contribution of individual sectors to the gross domestic product by deflating value added measured at domestic prices by the net effective rate of protection for each sector.[11]

To recalculate the rate of growth of GDP at world market prices, we need

---

  [11] Effective rates of protection for agriculture, mining, and manufacturing are shown in the country chapters; they have been calculated by the use of domestic input-output coefficients. Effective protection in the service sectors has been assumed to be nil.

to revalue value added in the individual sectors in world market prices for the base year of the national income calculations. While estimates of effective protection are generally available for years other than the base year, we have assumed that these also pertained to the base year.[12] Although this assumption undoubtedly introduces errors in the calculations, the results will indicate approximate magnitudes.

The adjusted growth rates, with unadjusted figures in parentheses, for the 1950–67 period are Brazil, 4.9 (5.0) percent; Chile, 4.2 (4.2) percent; Mexico, 6.3 (6.4) percent; Malaya, 4.8 (4.8) percent; Pakistan, 3.3 (3.8) percent; the Philippines, 6.0 (6.1) percent; and Norway, 4.0 (3.9) percent. It appears then that growth rates calculated from data expressed in domestic prices overstate the rate of growth of GDP in world market prices especially in Pakistan, with smaller differences shown for Brazil, Mexico, and the Philippines. In all these cases, the relatively high growth rates shown in the highly protected manufacturing sector explain the results. In turn, the unadjusted and adjusted estimates are identical in Chile where manufacturing grew at a rate not exceeding the average and in Malaya where effective rates of protection in primary production and in manufacturing are practically the same. Finally, the opposite result is obtained in Norway because of the low growth rate exhibited in the relatively highly protected agricultural sector.

Changes in Economic Structure

Increases in agricultural output were not commensurate with the rise of the gross domestic product in any of the countries under consideration, and only in Mexico, Brazil, Malaya, and the Philippines did food production grow faster than population. From the period 1952–54 to 1965–67, per capita food production increased by 34 percent in Mexico, 22 percent in Brazil, 18 percent in Malaya, and 6 percent in the Philippines. By contrast, Chile experienced a decline of 4 percent, Pakistan 7 percent, and Norway 8 percent.[13]

Measured in 1967 prices and exchange rates, per capita value added in manufacturing in 1950 was about $300 in Norway, $70 in Chile and Mexico, $30 in Brazil, $20 in the Philippines, $15 in Malaya, and $5 in Pakistan. In the following seventeen years, the rate of expansion of manufacturing value added was about 8 percent in Mexico, Malaya, Pakistan, and the Philippines; 7 percent in Brazil; 5 percent in Chile; and somewhat less in Norway.[14]

---

[12] In Brazil and Malaya where effective protection has been estimated for two different years, we have used the results for the years 1966 and 1965, respectively.

[13] Food and Agriculture Organization, *Production Yearbook, 1968.* Data prior to 1952 are not available.

[14] Tables 2.1, 2.2, and 2.3. Growth rates for Malaya refer to the 1955–67 period, and the 1950 figure has been obtained by extrapolating backwards.

Apart from Mexico surpassing Chile by a substantial margin, the ranking of these countries by per capita value added in manufacturing has not changed during this period, and despite relatively rapid increases in countries at lower levels of industrialization, absolute differences have become greater. The data for 1967 are Norway, $540; Mexico, $155; Chile, $100; Brazil, $60; the Philippines, $45; Malaya, $30; and Pakistan, $15. For several of these countries, the figures change again if value added in manufacturing is expressed in world market prices. The adjusted figures for 1967 are Mexico, $130; Chile, $60; Brazil, $45; the Philippines, $35; and Pakistan, $6.[15] No adjustment has been necessary for Norway and Malaya.

Intercountry differences in value added per head in manufacturing reflect differences in the productivity of the primary factors of production and their allocation among sectors. As an approximation, we may use per capita income data to indicate relative levels of productivity while the share of manufacturing in the gross domestic product, measured at factor cost, provides an indication of the proportion of the factors of production employed in this sector.[16] In 1967, this share was 27 percent in Norway, 24 percent in Mexico 19 percent in Chile, 17 percent in the Philippines, and 11–12 percent in Malaya and Pakistan (Table 2.3).[17] Comparable estimates are not available for Brazil but the relevant figure for this country may approach 25 percent.

The share of manufacturing in GDP is influenced by the share of the service sectors which tends to rise with the growth of per capita incomes, owing to increases in both the prices and the volume of services at higher income levels. To adjust for the effects of these differences, we have calculated the share of manufacturing in value added in commodity production, defined to include agriculture, forestry, and fishing; mining and quarrying; manufacturing; construction; as well as electricity, gas, and water.

In line with the observed differences in the rate of growth of agriculture and manufacturing, the relative share of the former declined and that of the latter increased in all the countries under consideration. Although the largest changes in relative shares took place in Pakistan, Malaya, and the Philippines, these countries still have the lowest share of manufacturing and the highest share of agriculture in commodity production. Thus, in 1967 the pro-

---

[15] For the method of adjustment, see p. 33 above.

[16] Per capita value added in manufacturing by definition equals the share of manufacturing in the gross domestic product multiplied by GDP per head. In symbols, $MVA/P = MVA/Y \cdot Y/P$. In using per capita income data to represent productivity levels, we put emphasis on intercountry differences in overall efficiency and neglect differences in capital and natural resources per head.

[17] The data slightly underestimate the share of manufacturing in Chile and the Philippines, because in these countries the calculations refer to the net, rather than the gross, domestic product and the depreciation of machinery and equipment excluded from the former is of greater importance in manufacturing than in the other sectors.

TABLE 2.3: Industrial Origin of the Gross Domestic Product, 1950 and 1967[a]

(Percent)

Sector	Brazil[b] 1950	Brazil[b] 1965	Chile[b] 1950	Chile[b] 1967	Mexico 1950	Mexico 1967	Malaya 1955	Malaya 1966	Pakistan 1950	Pakistan 1967	Philippines[b] 1950	Philippines[b] 1967	Norway 1950	Norway 1967
1. Agriculture, forestry, and fishing	28.7	29.6	14.0	9.1	18.2	12.8	40.2	29.2	59.9	46.1	39.8	31.0	15.0	7.4
2. Mining and quarrying	{ 23.8	{ 26.8	5.3	8.1	2.5	1.0	6.3	7.7	0.0	0.3	1.3	1.8	1.1	1.1
3. Manufacturing			17.3	19.0	20.8	23.9	{ 11.2	11.2	5.9	11.8	10.2	17.2	25.6	27.2
4. Construction			2.7	3.0	3.5	4.4		4.7	0.8	4.6	4.0	3.7	8.8	7.5
5. Electricity, gas, and water			0.6	1.3	0.5	1.5	1.3	2.0	0.0	0.8	(1.2)	(1.5)	2.0	3.0
Commodity production (1 to 5)	52.5	56.4	39.9	40.5	45.5	43.6	59.0	54.8	66.6	63.6	56.5	55.2	52.5	46.2
6. Transport, storage, and communication	7.4	{ 43.6	6.5	8.7	3.4	3.0	3.0	3.6	5.2	6.6	(2.3)	(3.2)	14.9	19.4
7. Public administration and defense	7.6		9.7	12.1	5.3	5.6	7.1	6.8	4.4	5.7	6.6	} 41.6	3.7	4.5
8. Private services[c]	32.5		43.9	38.7	45.8	47.8	30.9	34.8	23.8	24.1	34.6		28.9	29.9
Services (6 to 8)	47.5	43.6	60.1	59.5	54.5	56.4	41.0	45.2	33.4	36.4	43.5	44.8	47.5	53.8
9. Gross domestic product	100.0	100.0	100.0	100.0	100.0	100.0	100.0	100.0	100.0	100.0	100.0	100.0	100.0	100.0
Share of manufacturing in commodity production	na	na	43.4	46.9	45.7	54.8	na	20.4	8.9	18.6	18.1	31.2	48.8	58.9
Share of agriculture in commodity production	54.7	52.5	35.1	22.5	40.0	29.1	68.1	53.3	89.9	72.5	70.4	56.2	28.6	16.0

Sources: U.N., Yearbook of National Accounts Statistics; Banco de Mexico, Cuentas Nacionales y Aceros de Capital Consolidadas y por Tipo de Actividad.

[a] Data in current factor costs for Brazil, in constant market prices for Mexico, and in constant factor costs for the other countries.

[b] Net domestic product.

[c] Includes wholesale and retail trade; banking, insurance, and real estate; ownership of dwellings and miscellaneous services.

portion of value added generated in manufacturing was nearly 60 percent in Norway, 55 percent in Mexico, about 45 percent in Chile, 35 percent in Brazil, 30 percent in the Philippines, and approximately 18–20 percent in Malaya and Pakistan. In the same year, the share of agriculture in commodity production was about 70 percent in Pakistan, 55 percent in Malaya and the Philippines, slightly over 50 percent in Brazil, 30 percent in Mexico, 23 percent in Chile, and 16 percent in Norway.

The relative shares of the individual sectors having been calculated at domestic prices, the estimates are again affected by the system of protection employed. Adjusting for differences between domestic and world market values[18] entails a substantial downward revision in the share of manufacturing and a corresponding upward revision in that of agriculture in Pakistan, the Philippines, Brazil, and Chile; a relatively small modification in Mexico; and none in Malaya and Norway. The adjusted shares of the two sectors in commodity production are 6 percent for manufacturing and 88 percent for agriculture in Pakistan, 20 and 53 percent in Malaya, 24 and 62 percent in the Philippines, 28 and 26 percent in Chile, 31 and 61 percent in Brazil, 43 and 33 percent in Mexico, and 59 and 16 percent in Norway. In Chile, an upward adjustment has also been made for the mining sector that has large negative net effective protection.

Factors Affecting Economic Growth

One may attempt to explain the growth performance of a national economy from the supply side or from the demand side. In the first eventuality, we would need information on changes in the amounts of the factors of production employed as well as on technological progress. In the absence of such information, incremental capital-output ratios—defined as the ratio of new investment to the increment in output—and the share of investment in GNP are often used for this purpose.[19] For the period 1950–67, incremental capital-output ratios averaged 2.4 in Mexico and the Philippines, 2.6 in Pakistan, 3.1–3.2 percent in Malaya, Brazil, and Chile, and 7.3 in Norway (Table 2.4).[20] The interpretation of these differences is made difficult, however, because of discrepancies in the rate of growth of the labor supply and disparities in the industrial structure. In Norway, for example, the slow increase of the labor

---

[18] Since we are dealing with value added, the relevant adjustment factor is again the net effective rate of protection.

[19] By definition, the rate of growth of GNP equals the share of investment in GNP divided by marginal capital-output ratio (GNP rather than GDP is used in order to adjust for factor payments abroad). In symbols, $\Delta Y/Y = I/Y : I/\Delta Y$. Needless to say, this approach disregards the contribution of labor and land to economic growth.

[20] Data on incremental capital-output ratios and on the share of investment in GNP refer to the period 1955–67 in the case of Malaya and 1960–67 in the case of Pakistan.

TABLE 2.4:   Investment, Savings, and Capital-Output Ratios, 1950–67[a]

	Brazil	Chile	Mexico	Malaya[b]	Pakis-tan	Philip-pines	Norway
Incremental capital-output ratios[c]							
1950–55	3.2	3.3	2.3	na	na	1.4	8.1
1955–60	2.6	2.5	2.5	3.2	na	2.8	10.2
1960–67	3.6	3.6	2.3	3.1	2.6	3.4	5.8
1950–67	3.1	3.2	2.4	3.1	na	2.4	7.3
Gross domestic investment as a percent of GNP							
1950–55	17.7	10.3	14.9	na	na	12.3	33.4
1955–60	15.5	10.2	15.4	11.5	na	13.5	31.5
1960–67	13.9	18.1	15.5	17.7	14.3	16.0	30.1
1950–67	15.5	13.5	15.4	15.1	na	14.2	31.5
Gross domestic savings as a percent of GNP							
1950–55	16.3	10.3	13.9	na	na	10.6	29.5
1955–60	14.3	8.8	13.6	20.5	na	11.6	28.1
1960–67	14.1	15.4	13.7	20.1	10.1	13.0	26.8
1950–67	14.8	12.0	13.7	20.2	na	11.9	28.0
Net foreign investment and changes in reserves as a percent of GNP							
1950–55	−1.4	0.0	−1.0	na	na	−1.7	−3.9
1955–60	−1.2	−1.4	−1.8	9.0	na	−1.9	−3.4
1960–67	0.2	−2.7	−1.8	2.4	−4.2	−3.0	−3.3
1950–67	−0.7	−1.5	−1.7	5.1	na	−2.3	−3.5
Net factor incomes as a percent of GNP							
1950–55	−0.7	−1.7	−1.0[d]	na	na	−0.9	−0.3
1955–60	−0.8	−1.5	−1.1	−4.0	na	−1.1	−0.9
1960–67	−1.1	−2.1	−1.4	−3.1	−0.1	−0.5	−1.3
1950–67	−0.9	−1.8	−1.2[d]	−3.5	na	−0.8	−0.9
Balance of current accounts other than factor payments as a percent of GNP							
1950–55	−0.7	1.7	0.0[d]	na	na	−0.8	−3.6
1955–60	−0.4	0.1	−0.7	13.0	na	−0.8	−2.5
1960–67	1.3	−0.6	−0.4	5.5	−4.1	−2.5	−2.0
1950–67	0.2	0.3	−0.5[d]	8.6	na	−1.5	−2.6

Sources: U.N., *Yearbook of National Accounts Statistics;* Philippines, *The Statistical Reporter.*
[a] Data in constant prices for Chile, Norway, and the Philippines; in current prices for the other countries.
[b] 1955–67.
[c] The ratio of gross domestic investment to the increment in the gross national product.
[d] Does not include data for 1951, 1952, and 1954.

force, as well as reliance on hydroelectricity and the importance of capital-intensive industries such as aluminum smelting and chemicals, raises the incremental capital-output ratio.

To abstract from intercountry differences in the industrial structure and in the growth of the labor supply, we may compare changes in incremental capital-output ratios over time. While these comparisons are also affected by changes in the composition of output, they provide some indication of variations in effort in terms of investment per unit increases in output. The data of

Table 2.4 show a substantial decline in incremental capital-output ratios in Norway, increases in Brazil, Chile, and the Philippines, and little change elsewhere.

The rate of economic growth is further influenced by the amount invested. For the period as a whole, the share of gross investment in GNP was by far the greatest in Norway (32 percent), while it was in the 13–15 percent range in the other six countries. Intercountry variations are much greater in the share of domestic savings in GNP. During the period under consideration, this proportion was the highest in Norway (28 percent), followed by Malaya (20 percent), Brazil (15 percent), Mexico (14 percent), Chile and the Philippines (12 percent), and Pakistan (10 percent).

With the exception of Malaya, domestic investment exceeded domestic savings in all the countries under study. Differences between the two are especially large in Pakistan which received a substantial amount of foreign aid. In the 1960–67 period, foreign aid averaged over 4 percent of Pakistan's gross national product, and it financed a substantial deficit in the current account of the balance of payments. By contrast, owing to large factor payments to foreigners and the outflow of capital in the second half of the fifties, Malaya had a large surplus on the current account defined in a narrower sense, that is, excluding factor payments (8.6 percent of GNP). Factor payments to foreigners also explain that the net inflow of foreign capital was accompanied by a current account surplus in Brazil and Chile.

From the demand side, the rate of economic growth is influenced by the country's success in exporting. In the period as a whole, the dollar value of merchandise exports increased most rapidly in Norway (9.2 percent); a rate of growth of 7 percent is shown in Chile; 5.5–6.0 percent in the Philippines and Mexico; 1.6 percent in Pakistan; 1.2 percent in Brazil; and 0.7 percent in Malaya (Table 2.5). Exports were the leading sector in Norway, with their rate of growth exceeding that of national income by a considerable margin. Exports also grew faster than the gross domestic product in Chile while the opposite was the case in the remaining countries of the group. Differences between the rate of growth of GDP and that of exports were especially large in Malaya, Pakistan, and Brazil.

Changes in the volume of merchandise exports, in export and import prices, in the service account, and in the flow of capital and factor payments together determine changes in a country's import capacity. Increases in import capacity in turn affect the rate of growth of incomes, since imports provide materials, fuels, and machinery that are necessary for economic growth. Changes in the imports of the countries in question, shown in Table 2.5, are therefore of considerable interest.

The decline in the outflow of capital in Malaya, and the increase in foreign aid in Pakistan, permitted their merchandise imports to rise at a rate far exceeding that of merchandise exports. Due to rapid increases in tourism and

TABLE 2.5:   Growth Rates of Exports, Imports, and Terms of Trade, 1950–67

(*Percent*)

	Brazil	Chile	Mexico	Malaya	Pakistan	Philip-pines	Norway
Merchandise exports[a]							
1950–55	1.0	10.9	11.6	−1.9	−3.9	3.9	10.2
1955–60	−2.3	0.6	−1.1	4.3	−0.4	6.9	6.8
1960–67	3.9	9.3	6.0	0.0	7.3	6.6	10.2
1950–67	1.2	7.1	5.4	0.7	1.6	5.9	9.2
Merchandise imports[a]							
1950–55	3.8	8.8	11.7	3.3	−6.4	9.9	9.9
1955–60	2.3	5.9	6.1	6.9	17.7	2.0	6.1
1960–67	1.9	5.4	5.7	2.7	7.7	8.5	9.4
1950–67	2.6	6.5	7.5	4.1	6.1	6.9	8.6
Terms of trade							
1950–55	4.8	5.9	⎫4.3	na	na	−3.9	1.8
1955–60	−2.9	−1.4	⎭	−0.4	−4.1	0.4	−1.0
1960–67	0.4	7.5[b]	0.0	−0.8	2.9	−2.0	1.2
1950–67	0.7	4.1[b]	−2.6	−0.7[c]	−0.1[c]	−1.9	0.8

Sources: U.N., *Statistical Yearbook;* U.N., *Yearbook of International Trade Statistics;* Table 8.2 below.

[a] Values in U.S. dollars.
[b] Latest benchmark year is 1966 rather than 1967.
[c] 1955–67.

border trade and to increased foreign aid, imports also grew faster than exports in Mexico and the Philippines, respectively. By contrast, there was little import growth in Brazil where the constraint imposed by the slow growth of merchandise exports was especially important.

Export Performance

The rate of growth of exports is affected by a variety of factors, including the increase in world demand for a country's main export products, changes in a country's share in the world market, variations in export prices, and the expansion of minor exports. With major exports defined as those which accounted for at least 3 percent of a country's exports at the beginning *or* at the end of the period under review, this category includes coffee, cotton, iron ore, sugar, lumber, and cocoa beans in Brazil; copper, iron ore, and saltpeter in Chile; cotton, coffee, sugar, shellfish, maize, lead, copper, fresh fish, and tomatoes in Mexico; rubber and tin in Malaya; jute, cotton, jute textiles, cotton textiles, and sacks and bags in Pakistan; copra, sugar, hardwood, logs, abaca, coconut oil, as well as copper ores and concentrates in the Philippines; and aluminum, paper and paperboard, ships and boats, wood pulp, manufactured fertilizer, fresh fish, dried fish, and fish preparations in Norway. In making comparisons, we had to exclude, however, tomatoes in Mexico, sacks and bags in Pakistan, and copper ores and concentrates in the Philippines, because comparable data on the world exports of these commodities are not available.

Columns (1) and (4) of Table 2.6 show the average dollar value of major and minor exports in the periods 1950–53 and 1963–66. In Column (3) export values for 1963–66 are given in terms of 1950–53 prices, while Column (2) indicates the hypothetical or potential value of these exports calculated under the assumption that the country maintained its share of major export commodities in the world markets. Columns (5) to (7), labelled "market effect," "competitive effect," and "price effect" give a breakdown of the total change in exports shown in Column (8) in terms of the growth of world markets, changes in the market shares of the individual countries, and changes in export prices.[21] Finally, Columns (9) to (12) express these changes as a percentage of exports in the base period.

In 1950–53, the share of major exports in the total was 80–85 percent in Brazil, Malaya, Pakistan, and the Philippines; 75 percent in Chile; and 55–60 percent in Mexico and Norway. With the exception of Chile, however, minor exports grew faster than major exports during the period under consideration; this led to a decline in the share of the latter. The relevant figures for 1963–66 are Chile, 75 percent; Malaya, 72 percent; Brazil, 70 percent; the Philippines, 66 percent; Pakistan, 61 percent; Norway, 45 percent; and Mexico, 36 percent.

Among the countries under study, the market for the exports of Norway developed the most favorably, with world demand more than doubling between 1950–53 and 1960–63. Norway further increased its market share in aluminum to a considerable extent while the decline in its share in the world exports of wood pulp and fertilizer was more than compensated by the rise in the exports of paper products and chemicals. Throughout the period, Norway's exports increasingly shifted toward processed goods, thereby contributing to the tripling of its minor exports and a 150 percent rise in the current value of its total exports.

Apart from Norway, Chile experienced the most favorable market trends during this period, and it also benefited from an average 40 percent rise in the prices of its major exports, bringing the potential increase in export values to over 120 percent. But Chile experienced a substantial deterioration of its competitive position, as its share in the world market for copper declined from 29 percent in 1950–53 to 21 percent in 1963–66. Chile also had the smallest rise in minor exports (68 percent) among the countries of the group, so that its total exports rose by less than four-fifths.

Between 1950–53 and 1963–66, total exports more than doubled in Mexico

---

[21] The competitiveness of minor exports is evaluated in relation to changes in world exports, and variations in prices are not considered.

TABLE 2.6: Export Performance, 1950–53 and 1963–66

	Export values				Differences between actual and hypothetical exports in 1963–66							
	Actual	Hypothetical[a]	Actual	Actual	"Market effect"	"Competitive effect"	"Price effect"	Together	"Market effect"	"Competitive effect"	"Price effect"	Together
	1950–53	1963–66	1963–66	1963–66 In 1963–66 prices $ million	(2)–(1)	(3)–(2)	(4)–(3)	(4)–(1)	(5):(1)	(6):(1)	(7):(1)	(8):(1)
	In 1950–53 prices[b] $ million				$ million				percent		percent	
	(1)	(2)	(3)	(4)	(5)	(6)	(7)	(8)	(9)	(10)	(11)	(12)
Brazil												
Major exports												
Coffee	1,000.8	1,524.2	1,035.9	744.6	523.4	−488.3	−291.3	−256.2	52.3	−48.8	−29.1	−25.6
Cotton	110.9	167.8	219.4	107.3	56.9	51.6	−112.1	−3.6	51.3	46.5	−101.1	−3.2
Iron ore	16.3	62.4	78.4	88.7	46.1	16.0	10.3	72.4	282.8	98.2	63.2	444.2
Sugar	8.6	11.5	63.6	60.7	2.9	52.1	−2.9	52.1	7.6	135.7	−7.6	135.7
Lumber	38.4	74.8	46.3	48.1	36.4	−28.5	1.8	9.7	94.8	−74.2	4.7	25.3
Cocoa beans	66.2	103.3	58.3	37.1	37.1	−45.0	−21.2	−29.1	56.0	−68.0	−32.0	−44.0
Together	1,241.2	1,944.0	1,501.9	1,086.5	702.8	−442.1	−415.4	−154.7	56.6	−35.6	−33.5	−12.5
Minor exports	258.8	672.4	456.7	456.7	413.6	−215.7	0	197.9	159.8	−83.3	0	76.5
Total exports	1,500.0	2,616.4	1,958.6	1,543.2	1,116.4	−657.8	−415.4	43.2	74.4	−43.8	−27.7	2.8
Chile												
Major exports												
Copper	214.7	421.0	298.2	415.0	206.3	−122.8	116.8	200.3	96.1	−57.2	54.4	93.3
Iron ore	8.9	34.1	62.6	70.8	25.2	28.5	8.2	61.9	283.1	320.2	92.1	695.5
Saltpeter	62.6	38.3	38.3	29.1	−24.3	0	−9.2	−33.5	−38.8	0	−14.7	−53.5
Together	286.2	493.4	399.1	514.9	207.2	−94.3	115.8	228.7	72.4	−32.9	40.4	79.9
Minor exports	100.7	261.6	169.2	169.2	160.9	−92.4	0	68.5	159.8	−91.8	0	68.0
Total exports	386.9	755.0	568.3	684.1	368.1	−186.7	115.8	297.2	95.1	−48.3	29.9	76.8
Mexico												
Major exports												
Cotton	121.4	183.7	231.2	143.8	62.3	47.5	−87.4	22.4	51.3	39.1	−72.0	18.4
Coffee	49.7	75.6	77.3	67.5	25.9	1.7	−9.8	17.8	52.1	3.4	−19.7	35.8
Sugar	5.7	7.7	127.9	63.1	2.0	120.2	−64.8	57.4	35.1	2,108.8	−1,136.8	1,007.0
Shellfish	10.9	16.7	23.3	51.5	5.8	6.6	28.2	40.6	53.2	60.6	258.7	372.5
Maize	0.0	0.0	55.3	35.0	0.0	55.3	−20.3	35.0	na	na	na	na
Lead, unwrought	63.1	72.4	39.8	26.0	9.3	−32.6	−13.8	−37.1	14.7	−51.7	−21.9	−58.8
Copper, unwrought	26.7	52.4	7.7	12.8	25.7	−44.7	5.1	−13.9	96.3	−167.4	19.1	−52.1
Fish, fresh	23.4	62.6	1.6	1.9	39.2	−61.0	0.3	−21.5	167.5	−260.7	1.3	−91.9
Together	300.9	471.1	564.1	401.6	170.2	93.0	−162.5	100.7	56.6	39.9	−54.0	33.5
Minor exports	232.2	603.3	701.3	701.3	371.1	98.0	0.0	469.1	159.8	42.2	0.0	202.0
Total exports	533.1	1,074.4	1,265.4	1,102.9	541.3	191.0	−162.5	569.8	101.5	35.8	−30.5	106.9

Sources: FAO, Trade Yearbook; FAO, Yearbook of Forest Products; FAO, Yearbook of Fishery Statistics; U.N., Commodity Trade Statistics; U.N., Yearbook of International Trade Statistics; Great Britain, Institute of Geological Sciences, Statistical Summary of the Mineral Industry; Metallgesellschaft, Metal Statistics.
a Hypothetical exports have been calculated under the assumption that the countries' share in the world market remains unchanged. In the case of minor exports, the expansion of total world exports was used as a standard of comparison.
b We have assumed that the prices of minor exports, as well as the prices of ships and boats and fertilizers, have not changed during the period.

Malaya

Major exports												
Rubber	554.4	687.4	646.0	444.6	133.0	-201.4	-109.8	24.0	-7.5	-36.3	-19.8	
Tin	143.1	126.5	146.8	245.4	-16.6	98.6	102.3	-11.6	14.2	68.9	71.5	
Together	697.5	813.9	792.8	690.0	116.4	-102.8	-7.5	16.7	-3.0	-14.7	-1.1	
Minor exports	116.3	302.2	266.1	266.1	185.9	149.8	159.8	-31.0	0	128.8		
Total exports	813.8	1,116.1	1,058.9	956.1	302.3	-102.8	142.3	37.1	-7.0	-12.6	17.5	

Pakistan

Major exports												
Jute	244.4	198.5	177.8	170.6	-45.9	-20.7	-7.2	-73.8	-18.8	-8.5	-2.9	-30.2
Cotton	222.4	336.5	120.4	62.0	114.1	-216.1	-58.4	-160.4	51.3	-97.2	-26.3	-72.1
Jute textiles	0.6	1.0	70.8	36.6	0.4	69.8	-34.2	36.0	66.7	11,633.3	-5,700.0	6,000.0
Cotton textiles	0.0	0.0	55.2	43.9	0.0	55.2	-11.3	43.9	na	na	na	na
Together	467.4	536.0	424.2	313.1	68.6	-111.8	-111.1	-154.3	14.7	-23.9	-23.8	-33.0
Minor exports	85.1	221.1	196.7	196.7	136.0	-24.4	111.6	111.6	159.8	-28.7	-28.7	131.1
Total exports	552.5	757.1	620.9	509.8	204.6	-136.2	-42.7	-42.7	37.0	-24.7	-20.1	-7.8

Philippines

Major exports												
Copra	136.5	225.8	186.3	161.3	89.3	-39.6	-25.0	24.8	65.5	-29.0	-18.3	18.2
Sugar	76.4	102.7	119.6	145.2	26.3	16.9	25.6	68.8	34.4	22.1	33.5	90.1
Logs	19.0	90.6	86.7	124.0	71.6	-3.9	37.3	105.0	376.8	-20.5	196.3	552.6
Coconut oil	20.2	31.3	68.0	62.5	11.1	36.7	-5.5	42.3	55.0	181.6	-27.2	209.4
Abaca	46.2	37.1	41.8	26.7	-9.1	4.7	-15.1	-19.5	-19.7	10.2	-32.7	-42.2
Together	298.3	487.5	502.4	519.7	189.2	14.8	17.3	221.4	63.4	5.0	5.8	74.2
Minor exports	74.2	194.1	267.8	267.8	119.9	73.7	0	193.6	161.6	99.3	0	260.9
Total exports	372.5	681.6	770.2	787.5	309.1	88.5	17.3	415.0	83.0	23.8	4.6	111.4

Norway

Major exports												
Aluminium, unwrought	16.2	49.7	103.5	122.5	33.5	53.8	19.0	106.3	206.8	332.1	117.3	656.2
Paper and paperboard	62.6	135.9	142.9	114.2	73.3	7.0	-28.7	51.6	117.1	11.2	-45.8	82.4
Ships and boats	35.3	107.5	110.4	110.4	72.2	2.9	75.1	11.4	204.5	8.2	0	212.7
Wood pulp	69.2	150.2	84.5	80.6	81.0	-65.7	-3.9	24.7	117.1	-94.9	-5.6	16.5
Fertilizers	32.5	80.7	57.2	57.2	48.2	-23.5	9.1	34.0	148.3	-72.3	49.1	76.0
Fish, fresh	15.6	41.7	40.5	49.6	26.1	-1.2	9.1	-0.2	167.3	-7.7	58.3	217.9
Fish, dried	44.0	36.3	22.2	43.8	-7.7	-14.1	21.6	8.3	-17.5	-32.0	49.1	-0.4
Fish preparations	15.9	30.2	20.4	24.2	14.3	-9.8	3.8	20.9	89.9	-61.6	23.9	52.2
Together	291.3	632.2	581.6	602.5	340.9	-50.6	20.9	311.2	117.0	-17.4	7.2	106.8
Minor exports	239.2	621.3	740.1	740.1	382.1	118.8	0	500.9	159.7	49.7	0	209.4
Total exports	530.5	1,253.5	1,321.7	1,342.6	723.0	68.2	20.9	812.1	136.3	12.9	3.9	153.1

although world demand for the country's major exports increased by only one-half and there was a decline in the prices of cotton and lead. Mexico developed new exports of sugar, shellfish, and maize to replace the declining exports of lead, copper, and fresh fish. In addition, its minor exports increased threefold during this period and thereby greatly exceeded average increases in world exports.

On the whole, the Philippines achieved practically no increase in its share in the world market for its major export commodities; but it benefited from the more than 50 percent rise in the world exports of these commodities as well as from favorable price trends. The country also made above-average gains in minor exports, especially in plywood and veneer.

The slow expansion of world demand and a fall in prices led to a decline in the value of Malaya's rubber exports. Higher tin prices and increases in Malaya's share in world exports, however, contributed to an increase in the value of tin exports by approximately the same amount, so that the value of Malaya's exports remained practically unchanged. Among the countries of the group, Malaya also had one of the highest growth rates of minor exports but, given the low initial share of these commodities, total exports increased by less than one-fifth between 1950–53 and 1963–66.

The results for Brazil are by and large dominated by changes in coffee exports which accounted for two-thirds of the total in 1950–53 and for one-half in 1963–66. The fall in Brazil's share in the world coffee market nearly offset the rise in world demand, so that export volume hardly changed and the fall in prices led to a decrease in the value of coffee exports. Similar changes, entailing a decline in the value of major exports taken together, are shown for cocoa beans. This decline was barely offset by the rise of minor exports that had one of the smallest growth rates in Brazil.

The slow growth of world demand and the fall in prices would still have permitted the value of Pakistani exports of jute and cotton to remain at 1950–53 levels, had the country maintained its share in world markets. However, Pakistan's share in the world exports of these commodities declined by about 50 percent. The rapid growth in jute and cotton textiles from a small base was not sufficient to offset this decline so that the value of total exports fell by 8 percent between 1950–53 and 1963–66.

Commodity Composition of Exports and Imports

Changes in the relative shares of major and minor exports have also altered the commodity composition of total exports in the countries under study. This change has been the most pronounced in Pakistan where the share of manufactured goods rose from practically nil in the early fifties to 43 percent in 1967 (Table 2.7). Jute fabrics, sacks and bags, and cotton yarn and

TABLE 2.7: The Structure of Exports, 1950 and 1967[a]

(Percent)

Commodity group	Brazil		Chile		Mexico		Malaya		Pakistan		Philippines		Norway	
	1953	1967	1950	1967	1950	1967	1955	1967	1951/2	1967	1950	1967	1951	1967
Food, beverages, tobacco (SITC 0 + 1)	81.8	63.7	(7)	4.2	24.9	45.6	(4)	6.2	(5)	9.7	27.7	25.0	18.0	14.5
Industrial materials (2 + 4 + unwrought metals)	17.3	25.8	(90)	91.0	59.5	29.7	(93)	82.9	(94)	46.4	68.6	63.1	38.6	27.5
Fuels (3)	0.0	0.0	(0)	0.1	6.8	3.5	(1)	1.9	(0)	0.6	0.0	0.6	0.3	1.8
Total primary commodities	99.1	89.5	(97)	95.3	91.2	78.8	(98)	91.0	(99)	56.7	96.3	88.7	56.9	43.8
Chemicals (5)	0.5	1.8	(1)	0.9	1.1	5.9	na	1.6	(0)	1.0	0.2	0.6	7.0	8.0
Basic manufactures (6—unwrought metals)	0.2	5.2	(2)	3.2	5.9	10.6	na	2.9	(1)	39.0	2.7	4.8	24.2	22.0
Machinery and transport equipment (7)	0.0	2.6	(0)	0.3	0.7	2.0	na	2.1	(0)	0.5	0.2	0.1	11.0	22.2
Miscellaneous manufactured goods (8)	0.0	0.3	(0)	0.3	1.0	2.6	na	1.2	(0)	2.7	0.6	4.4	0.9	3.5
Total manufactured goods	0.7	9.9	(3)	4.7	8.7	21.1	(1)	7.8	(1)	43.2	3.7	9.9	43.1	55.7
Other (9)	0.2	0.6	(0)	0.0	0.1	0.1	(0)	1.2	(0)	0.1	0.0	1.4	0.0	0.5
All commodities (0–9)	100.0	100.0	100	100.0	100.0	100.0	100	100.0	100	100.0	100.0	100.0	100.0	100.0
Total ($ million)	1,539	1,654	371	908	469	1,145	772	953	607	608	325	875	619	1,736

Sources: U.N., Commodity Trade Statistics; U.N., Yearbook of International Trade Statistics. For Malaya in 1955, Department of Statistics, Monthly Statistical Bulletin.

[a] Figures in parentheses are based on incomplete commodity breakdowns.

fabrics dominate these exports; however, raw jute and cotton now account for less than one-half of Pakistan's exports compared with four-fifths in 1950.

In Norway, the share of manufactured goods in total exports rose from 43 percent in 1951 to 56 percent in 1967. The largest increase took place in machinery and transport equipment whose share in the total more than doubled. The relative shares of chemicals and miscellaneous manufactured goods also increased; decreases were concentrated in food (mostly fish) and industrial materials (mainly wood pulp).

Manufactured goods accounted for 9 percent of Mexican exports in 1950 and for as much as 21 percent in 1967. Textiles, thread and yarn, hormones and other pharmaceutical preparations, as well as steel products, are important in this group. Increases in the share of the food, beverages, and tobacco category (chiefly shellfish, maize, tomatoes, and sugar) were overshadowed by the decline in exports of industrial materials. The share of manufactured goods in total exports also increased in Brazil but these commodities account for less than 10 percent of export earnings and are in large part oriented toward LAFTA markets.

In 1967, manufactured goods supplied 10 percent of total exports in the Philippines, 8 percent in Malaya, and 5 percent in Chile compared with 4, 1, and 3 percent, respectively, at the beginning of the period. In the Philippines, increases in the foreign sales of plywood and veneer are noteworthy; in Malaya a variety of commodities has appeared among manufactured exports; in Chile exports of copper products and paper are important. Nevertheless, in all three countries industrial materials continue to dominate exports.

Changes in the relative proportions of primary goods and manufactures have generally been smaller on the import side. Import substitution in the manufacturing sector entailed a reduction in the share of manufactured goods in total imports in Pakistan, while the increased need for imports of chemicals and capital goods led to the opposite result in Chile, Mexico, and Malaya. Greater imports of chemicals in Brazil and of capital goods in the Philippines also contributed to increases in the share of manufactured goods in the imports of these two countries. However, the increase was the largest in Norway where intra-industry specialization associated with reductions in tariff barriers and with participation in EFTA explains the rapid rise of trade in manufactured goods (Table 2.8).

Summary

In this chapter, we have provided data for the period 1950–67 on the economic structure, growth, and trade of the seven countries under study. Apart from indicating the salient economic characteristics of these countries, the data will be utilized in the comparative evaluation of the effects of protection

TABLE 2.8: The Structure of Imports, 1950 and 1967[a]

(Percent)

	Brazil		Chile		Mexico		Malaya		Pakistan		Philippines		Norway	
	1953	1967	1950	1967	1950	1967	1955	1967	1951/52	1967	1950	1967	1951	1967
Food, beverages, and tobacco (SITC 0 + 1)	21.5	19.0	(20)	15.6	9.9	3.8	(37)	26.2	(10)	17.7	23.1	16.6	12.0	8.3
Industrial materials (2 + 4 + unwrought metals)	5.6	7.7	(11)	9.7	8.7	9.1	(15)	6.9	(5)	8.2	2.0	4.8	16.6	9.8
Fuels (3)	19.4	15.6	(10)	8.4	4.0	3.2	(8)	7.8	(7)	5.7	10.4	8.8	10.4	7.2
Total primary commodities	46.5	42.3	(41)	33.7	22.6	16.1	(60)	40.9	(22)	31.6	35.5	30.2	39.0	25.3
Chemicals (5)	6.5	13.8	(6)	10.2	12.8	13.8	na	8.8	(5)	11.0	7.9	8.9	4.4	7.5
Basic manufactures (6—unwrought metals)	13.8	10.9	(18)	10.4	19.0	12.4	na	19.9	(54)	19.5	39.8	22.8	26.0	17.5
Machinery and transport equipment (7)	31.1	28.5	(33)	41.1	39.9	51.6	na	22.2	(15)	35.7	13.3	35.5	27.6	41.8
Capital goods (7-732-733)	26.1	26.0	(27)	29.6	27.3	41.0	na	14.6	(12)	31.2	9.2	27.9	24.4	37.0
Durable consumer goods (732 + 733)	5.0	2.5	(6)	11.5	12.6	10.6	na	7.6	(3)	4.5	4.1	7.6	3.2	4.8
Miscellaneous manufactured articles (8)	1.9	3.7	(2)	4.4	5.6	6.0	na	6.0	(4)	2.2	3.5	2.4	3.0	7.7
Total manufactured goods	53.3	56.9	(59)	66.1	77.3	83.8	(40)	56.9	(78)	68.4	64.5	69.6	61.0	74.5
Other (9)	0.2	0.8	(0)	0.2	0.1	0.1	(0)	2.2	(0)	0.0	0.0	0.2	0.0	0.2
All commodities (0–9)	100.0	100.0	100	100.0	100.0	100.0	100	100.0	100	100.0	100.0	100.0	100.0	100.0
Total ($ million)	1,318	1,667	247	722	509	1,746	494	845	593	1,101	353	1,061	876	2,748

Sources: U.N., *Commodity Trade Statistics*; U.N., *Yearbook of International Trade Statistics*. For Malaya in 1955, Department of Statistics, *Monthly Statistical Bulletin*.

[a] Figures in parentheses are based on incomplete commodity breakdowns.

on resource allocation and growth (Chapter 4) as well as in the individual country studies (Chapters 6 to 12).

In view of the importance of the extent of the domestic market for both the policies of protection and their economic effects, data on market size have been shown under alternative definitions in this chapter. Among these, the most appropriate measure appears to be the domestic consumption of manufactured goods, but further account needs to be taken of the participation of the individual countries in the international division of labor. To indicate the openness of the individual national economies, import-consumption and export-production ratios in manufacturing have been used.

We have also shown changes in the share of manufacturing and agriculture in the gross domestic product and in commodity production (the latter is defined to include agriculture, mining, manufacturing, construction, electricity, gas, and water). Changes in the industrial structure are associated with the process of economic growth that is affected by supply as well as by demand factors.

While the rate of investment is a principal factor influencing the rate of economic growth from the supply side, exports have major importance from the side of demand. The chapter has provided information on the export performance of the countries in question, by separating the "market effect," "competitive effect," and "price effect," and distinguishing between major and minor exports. The rate of increase of exports and imports, changes in the terms of trade, and the transformation of the structure of exports and imports in the individual countries have also been shown.

CHAPTER 3

NOMINAL AND EFFECTIVE PROTECTION IN SEVEN COUNTRIES

Bela Balassa

Estimates of the Structure of Protection

This chapter reports on estimates of the structure of protection in the seven countries under study. We will first consider the interindustry pattern of protection on the basis of calculations made at actual exchange rates. Next, we will provide estimates of the degree of overvaluation as compared to the hypothetical free trade situation in the individual countries. The results obtained will be used to calculate net rates of effective protection and to indicate the extent of protection of import-substituting industries and the discrimination against exports. The numerical evidence given in the country studies will also be utilized to examine the bias against exports in individual industries.

In cases when direct price comparisons have been made, the results shown in the tables of this chapter are based on price comparisons (nominal implicit protection) rather than on tariffs (nominal tariff protection). Furthermore, in order to reduce the amount of numerical information, we report only the estimates of effective protection obtained by the use of the Corden formula. The estimates based on tariffs, those derived by using the Balassa formula, and the more detailed results for the individual countries are shown in the country chapters. The country tables also include estimates for 1966 and 1967 in Brazil and for 1963 and 1965 in Malaya; in this chapter we report only the estimates for 1966 and 1965, respectively, since these are more representative of the system of protection applied during the period under consideration.

49

Estimates derived by the use of domestic input-output coefficients do not permit detailed intercountry comparisons because of differences in the composition of the input-output tables of individual countries. Therefore, in Tables 3.1 and 3.2, we show averages of nominal and effective rates, calculated by using domestic and free trade input-output coefficients, for primary activities and manufacturing industries classified in ten major industry groups. Primary activities comprise agriculture, fishing and forestry, as well as mining and energy; manufacturing industries include processed food, construction materials, intermediate products at lower levels of fabrication, intermediate products at high levels of fabrication, nondurable consumer goods, durable consumer goods, machinery, and transport equipment. In contradistinction to the country chapters, we have excluded beverages and tobacco from our purview, since tariffs on them often serve primarily social and revenue objectives.

Table 3.3 provides estimates of average nominal and effective rates for export industries, import-competing industries, and non-import-competing industries; each of these categories is further divided into primary and manufacturing activities. To permit a comparative evaluation of the structure of protection in greater detail, in Table 3.4 we show estimates of nominal and effective rates of protection for the fifty-seven sectors of the free trade input-output table. The results of Tables 3.3 and 3.4 are given on a net basis, i.e., after adjustment has been made for overvaluation as compared to the free trade situation. Finally, we have calculated rank correlation coefficients between nominal and effective rates of protection estimated from domestic input-output tables (Table 3.5).

Nominal vs. Effective Protection

In Chapter 1 we have noted that, for indicating the effects of the system of protection on the national economy, the effective protection measure is superior to the traditional nominal protection measure. The question arises, however, if there are important differences between nominal and effective rates so that estimates of effective rates of protection provide information that the nominal rates do not contain.

We have seen that effective rates of protection are determined by the nominal protection of the product and its inputs, together with the share of value added in the product price. It follows that the greater are interindustry differences in output and input tariffs and in the share of value added, the more will the ranking of industries by effective rates of protection differ from ranking by nominal rates.

The similarity and dissimilarity of rankings can be measured by the rank correlation coefficient which takes values of 0 to 1 in the case of positive correlation and 0 to −1 in the case of negative correlation. Rank correlation coefficients have been calculated between nominal and effective rates derived by the use of domestic input-output coefficients under both the Balassa and the Corden formulas. For Mexico and Pakistan, as well as for non-import-competing goods in the Philippines, such calculations have been made from both tariffs and price comparisons.[1]

The results show that rank correlation coefficients between rates of nominal and effective protection, estimated from domestic input-output tables, vary between .59 in Pakistan and .97 in Brazil. For Pakistan, this result has been derived from implicit tariffs which are the relevant measure of protection. In Mexico the rank correlation coefficient is the same irrespective of whether we consider tariff or implicit protection, while in the Philippines ranking by nominal and effective protection shows greater similarity if price rather than tariff observations are used. Finally, in all cases the rank correlation coefficients are practically the same whether the Balassa or the Corden method of treating nontraded goods is applied (see Table 3.5, p. 68).

Among the individual countries, rank correlation coefficients between rates of nominal and effective protection are the highest in Brazil and in Norway. In the former, this is explained by the high degree of aggregation in the industrial classification; in the latter, the general similarity of nominal rates on products and on their inputs explains the results. Nevertheless there are substantial differences in the rankings of several industries by nominal and effective rates in these two countries.

The intercountry variation of rank correlation coefficients indicates the usefulness of estimating effective rates of protection, since without such calculations we would not know the relationship between nominal and effective rates in the individual cases. Moreover, estimates of effective rates provide information on the structure, as well as on the cost, of protection. Thus, we find that, owing to escalation in nominal rates from lower to higher levels of fabrication in the manufacturing industries of the countries in question, effective rates generally exceed nominal rates by a substantial margin. On the other hand, reverse escalation is shown in primary activities: with nominal protection on inputs generally exceeding that on output in primary activities, effective rates tend to be lower than nominal rates and are often negative.

---

[1] The reader will recall that in Mexico and Pakistan quantitative restrictions are applied to imports, and hence implicit protection derived from the comparison of domestic and foreign prices rather than tariff protection is the relevant indicator of the effects of protective measures. In turn, in the Philippines, comparisons of domestic and foreign prices show the extent of tariff protection actually utilized. In the other country studies, data for tariff protection are not shown when price comparisons have been made. For definitions, see Chapter 1, pp. 11–13.

Finally, under the assumptions stated in Chapter 1, effective rates of protection provide a measure of the cost of protection and reveal that in some instances import-substituting activities bring negative returns in terms of world market prices. These results will be discussed in detail in this chapter and the next.

The relationship between estimates of tariff and implicit protection is of further interest. The rank correlation coefficients for Mexico and Pakistan are .56 and .52 between nominal tariff and nominal implicit protection and .40 and .37 between effective tariff and effective implicit protection. The low rank correlation coefficients indicate the tenuous relationship between tariff and implicit protection and thus point to the irrelevance of tariffs for evaluating the protection of individual industries in countries that apply quantitative import restrictions.

The tables in Chapters 8 and 10 also provide information on the inter-industry pattern of differences in tariff and implicit protection in Mexico and Pakistan. In Mexico, we find that rates of tariff and implicit protection differ little in primary activities while, on the average, tariff protection exceeds implicit protection in manufacturing industries. Within the manufacturing sector, tariff protection is generally greater than implicit protection for non-import-competing goods but smaller for exports and for import-competing goods.

These results are explained if we consider that most import-competing goods, including machinery and transport equipment, consumer durables, and intermediate products with high technological requirements, are of recent origin in Mexico and the government relies on quantitative restrictions to ensure their protection. On the other hand, competition among national firms, as well as competition from the subsidiaries of foreign companies and from goods smuggled into Mexico from the United States, have contributed to the decline of domestic prices below the sum of the import price and the tariff in established industries, such as processed food, construction materials, a variety of intermediate products, and nondurable consumer goods. At the same time, in industries producing nondurable consumer goods and their inputs, low-quality products tend to be cheaper in Mexico than in the United States, whereas high-quality products are more expensive.

Similar results are observed in Pakistan. In industries where the process of import substitution has been completed and exports have begun under the Bonus Voucher Scheme, costs and prices have declined and differences between domestic and foreign prices have become smaller than the tariff. The industries in question include cotton textiles, footwear, sports goods, jute textiles, thread and threadball, leather, and sewing machines. By contrast, in virtually all remaining industries, import controls have resulted in prices well above the duty-paid price of competing imports.

Effective Protection and Substitution: A Digression

In Chapter 1 and in Appendix A, we have noted that substitution among inputs will give rise to errors in the measured values of effective protection. In the event of substitution between primary factors, taken as a unit, and material inputs, as well as among the material inputs themselves, estimates derived by using domestic input-output coefficients will overstate, and those calculated by using free trade coefficients, understate the "true" value of the effective rate of protection. Other things being equal, if these substitution effects were important, we would expect the estimated effective rates to be higher under the first alternative than under the second.

However, as the data of Table 3.1 indicate, in the majority of industries in the countries under study, the use of free trade coefficients gave higher effective rates than the domestic coefficients did. Nor can this result be explained by differences in the industry averages of nominal rates under the two alternatives. Although in the majority of cases nominal rates for individual industries are higher if weighted by world trade rather than by domestic supply, with the exception of Pakistan and the Philippines, the degree of escalation from nominal to effective rates is also generally greater if free trade rather than domestic coefficients are used in the calculations.

Differences in the rankings of effective rates calculated by the use of domestic and free trade coefficients are also of interest. This is because the extent of the bias due to substitution may vary among industries and affect their ranking by effective rates; moreover, substitution between individual primary factor and material inputs will give rise to errors of estimation whose direction is not known.

It appears that, with the exception of Malaya, the interindustry pattern of effective protection in the countries under study is roughly the same whether we use free trade or domestic coefficients. Whatever differences are shown between the two sets of estimates are due largely to considerations unrelated to the substitution issue. This can be seen if we examine the results of the seven countries in the order of their industrial development and also consider differences in weighting schemes.[2]

If the share of manufacturing output in commodity production measured at world market prices is used as an indicator of the degree of industrialization, Norway (58 percent) occupies first place in the group, followed by Mexico (49 percent), Brazil (31 percent), Chile (28 percent), the Philippines (24 percent), Malaya (20 percent) and, at some distance, Pakistan (6 percent).

The results for Norway differ little under the two alternatives, although effective rates are on the average somewhat higher, and the extent of escala-

---

[2] For information on the weights used in averaging rates of nominal and effective protection calculated by the use of domestic and free trade coefficients, see Chapter 1, pp. 18–21.

TABLE 3.1: Nominal and Effective Protection in Selected Developing Countries[a]

(Percent)

Industry group		Brazil (1966) T	Brazil (1966) Z	Chile (1961) T	Chile (1961) Z	Mexico (1960) T	Mexico (1960) Z	Malaya (1965) T	Malaya (1965) Z	Pakistan[b] (1963–64) T	Pakistan[b] (1963–64) Z	Philippines (1965) T	Philippines (1965) Z	Norway (1954) T	Norway (1954) Z
I Agriculture, forestry, and fishing	D[a]	63	53	42	49	7	3	2	0	7	(−10)	8	0	15	16
	F	50	46	53	58	7	6	17	22	8	−19	31	33	24	34
IV Mining and energy	D	27	25	8	−2	4	−5	−14	−17	na	na	3	−25	0	0
	F	23	−16	39	72	−1	−13	−2	−8	35	29	11	−9	0	−7
Primary production, total	D	59	52	28	21	6	1	−2	−6	na	na	7	−1	14	15
	F	38	18	47	64	3	−3	9	8	18	−15	22	14	13	16
II Processed food	D	82	87	82	2,884	18	6	2	0	133	−307[e]	15	46	11	6
	F	71	92	101	255	13	20	11	7	154	379	37	89	4	0
V Construction materials	D	79	86	66	64	−4	1	5	−2	54	51	25	50	5	6
	F	67	79	115	154	4	−5	7	9	91	118	42	56	6	8
VI-A Intermediate products I	D	92	110	53	70	22	37	−4	−23	44	69	13	16	1	−1
	F	68	115	60	105	14	25	4	9	71	147	18	28	3	3
VI-B Intermediate products II	D	[c]		118	159	25	38	9	8	55	188	33	85	7	11
	F	121	187	113	195	33	56	13	25	91	173	34	63	7	14
VII Nondurable consumer goods	D	140	173	204	277	25	30	25	64	100	65	22	53	12	16
	F	157	218	188	300	33	45	14	20	112	156	32	46	16	25
VIII Consumer durables	D	108	151	84	101	49	93	1	−2	234	−2,100[e]	68	1,062	25	38
	F	154	285	95	123	50	85	1	−5	247	510	52	81	27	57
IX Machinery	D	87	100	92	98	29	38	0	−6	86	139	27	103	12	18
	F	80	93	86	97	32	38	5	6	80	110	26	24	12	18
X Transport equipment	D	[d]		[d]		26	37	..	..	..	..	29	75	1	−2
	F	26	−26	16	−65	26	30	..	..	..	..	16	−3	1	−6
Manufacturing, total	D	96	113	111	182	24	26	2	−6	85	271	25	61	8	8
	F	86	127	89	158	20	32	8	11	96	188	29	53	6	9

Source: Country tables.

[a] Effective rates have been estimated by using the Corden formula. Explanation of symbols: T = nominal rate of protection; Z = effective rate of protection; D = estimates based on domestic input-output coefficients; F = estimates based on free trade input-output coefficients. For definitions, see Chapter I.

[b] In the manufacturing sector, the estimates refer only to producers receiving import privileges.

[c] Included with intermediate products I.

[d] Included with consumer durables.

[e] Denotes negative value added at world market prices.

tion from nominal to effective rates slightly greater, if free trade rather than domestic coefficients are used in the calculations. In industries where the difference in effective rates calculated by using free trade coefficients and those obtained with domestic coefficients is greater than the average, this can be explained by differences in the composition of domestic supply as compared with that of world trade. In the agriculture, forestry, and fishing group, the share of forestry and fishing products that receive no protection is much larger in domestic than in world trade; in consumer durables, automobiles subject to high tariffs have greater weight in world than in domestic trade; and in the transport equipment category, ships with negative effective protection predominate in domestic supply.

In Mexico, averages of nominal and effective protection for the manufacturing sector are remarkably similar whether free trade or domestic coefficients are used, while absolute differences in the rates of protection estimated for individual industries are generally small and fit the pattern observed in Norway. The pattern of escalation from nominal to effective protection is also similar under the two alternatives. Food processing is, however, a major exception; the negative effective protection of food exports, which have a large weight in the domestic production of processed food, reduces the industry average calculated from domestic coefficients and results in "reverse escalation."

By and large, the use of domestic and free trade coefficients also give similar results in Brazil and Chile, although the generally higher nominal protection observed in these countries leads to greater variability in the estimates. In addition, we find that in both countries, as in Norway and Mexico, somewhat higher effective rates of protection and a greater degree of escalation are shown by the use of free trade as compared to domestic coefficients. A major exception is the Chilean food processing industry where low value added at world market prices has resulted in extremely high effective rates calculated by domestic input-output coefficients, thereby raising the average obtained for the manufacturing sector as a whole. In turn, in primary activities (especially mining), we find that the large share of exports in domestic output reduces the estimates obtained by using domestic input-output coefficients in Chile, whereas the high protection of domestically produced minerals leads to the opposite result in Brazil.

In the Philippines and in Pakistan, the pattern of protection is roughly the same irrespective of whether domestic or free trade coefficients are used in the calculations. However, in both countries, the preponderance of exports reduces the averages of effective rates of protection of primary activities calculated by using domestic input-output coefficients. Conversely, averages of effective rates of protection in the manufacturing sector of the two countries are higher, and the degree of escalation from nominal to effective rates is

TABLE 3.2: Net Nominal and Effective Protection in Selected Developing Countries[a]

(Percent)

		Brazil (1966)		Chile (1961)		Mexico (1960)		Malaya (1965)		Pakistan[b] (1963–64)		Philippines (1965)		Norway (1954)	
Industry group		T'	Z'	T'	Z'	T'	Z'	T'	Z'	T'	Z'	T'	Z'	T'	Z'
I Agriculture, forestry, and fishing	D	29	21	-15	-11	-2	-6	-2	-4	(-29)[f]	(-40)[f]	-6	-13	11	12
	F	18	15	-9	-6	-2	-3	13	17	-28	-46	14	16	19	29
IV Mining and energy	D	0	-1	-36	-42	-5	-13	-17	-20	na	na	-10	-34	-4	-4
	F	-3	-34	-17	2	-9	-20	-6	-12	-10	-14	-3	-21	-4	-11
Primary production, total	D	25	20	-24	-28	-3	-7	-6	-10	na	na	-7	-14	10	11
	F	9	-7	-12	-2	-6	-11	5	4	-21	-43	7	0	9	12
II Processed food	D	44	48	8	1,676	8	-3	-2	-4	55	-238[e]	0	28	7	2
	F	35	52	20	111	4	10	7	3	69	219	20	65	0	-4
V Construction materials	D	41	47	-1	-2	-12	-7	1	-6	3	1	9	31	1	2
	F	32	41	28	51	-5	-13	3	5	27	45	24	36	2	4
VI-A Intermediate products I	D	52	66	-9	1	12	26	-8	-26	-4	13	-1	1	-3	-5
	F	33	70	-5	22	5	15	0	5	14	65	3	12	-1	-1
VI-B Intermediate products II	D	°	°	30	54	15	27	5	4	3	92	16	62	3	7
	F	74	127	27	76	22	43	9	20	27	82	17	42	3	10
VII Nondurable consumer goods	D	89	115	81	124	15	19	20	58	33	10	7	34	8	12
	F	103	151	71	138	22	33	10	15	41	71	15	28	12	20
VIII Consumer durables	D	64	98	10	30	37	77	-3	-6	123	-1,433[e]	47	915	20	33
	F	100	204	16	33	38	70	-3	-9	131	307	33	58	22	51
IX Machinery	D	48	58	14	18	18	27	-4	-10	24	59	11	77	8	13
	F	42	52	11	17	21	27	1	2	20	40	10	8	8	13
X Transport equipment	D	d	d	d	d	16	26	:	:	:	:	13	53	-3	-6
	F	-1	-42	-31	-79	16	19	:	:	:	:	1	-15	-3	-1
Manufacturing, total	D	55	68	26	68	14	16	-2	-10	23	147	9	41	4	4
	F	47	79	13	54	10	21	4	7	31	92	13	34	2	6

Source: Country tables.

[a] Effective rates have been estimated by using the Corden formula; both nominal and effective rates have been adjusted for overvaluation as compared to the hypothetical free trade situation. Explanation of symbols: T' = net nominal rate of protection; Z' = net effective rate of protection; D = estimates based on domestic input-output coefficients; F = estimates based on free trade input-output coefficients.

[b] In the manufacturing sector, the estimates refer only to producers receiving import privileges.

[c] Included with intermediate products I.

[d] Included with consumer durables.

[e] Denotes negative value added at world market prices.

[f] Approximate figure.

greater, if calculations are made by the use of domestic rather than free trade coefficients.

The observed differences in the two sets of estimates of effective rates of protection for the manufacturing sector of the two countries, however, appear to have more to do with the low level of economic development than with substitution among inputs. Thus, in the durable consumer goods, machinery, and transport equipment industries where differences are the largest, effective rates of protection calculated by using domestic input-output coefficients are relatively high because domestic output is heavily weighted by a few highly protected items[3] while weighting by world trade gives much lower estimates since it is dominated by goods that are not yet produced in the two countries and receive little protection. By contrast, estimates of effective protection based on free trade domestic coefficients are larger for intermediate products at lower levels of fabrication and nondurable consumer goods where the industries of the two countries are more fully developed.

Malaya is an exceptional case insofar as the results are greatly affected by the choice of the input-output coefficients. For several industry groups, including agriculture, forestry, and fishing, mining and energy, as well as intermediate products at lower levels of fabrication, the large share of export commodities in total supply accounts for the negative effective protection derived by the use of domestic coefficients. Averages of effective rates for primary production and for manufacturing are also negative if we use domestic coefficients; however, they are positive if free trade coefficients are employed. Nevertheless, absolute differences in the sectoral averages are small.

We have shown that, with the exception of Malaya, the interindustry pattern of effective protection is little affected by the choice of the input-output coefficients and we do not observe systematic differences in the estimates. Differences in the results obtained under the two alternatives are largely explained by considerations unrelated to substitution among inputs, such as the level of industrial development and the weighting schemes employed. These findings tend to confirm the results of empirical studies that show little substitution between primary factors and material inputs in response to price changes.[4] It appears, then, that in practical instances errors due to substitution among inputs do not substantially affect the estimates of effective rates of protection.

---

[3] In the Pakistani durable-consumer-goods industry, value added on world market prices is even negative, leading to effective rates of less than −100 percent. The reader will recall that while effective rates of protection between nil and −100 percent indicate discrimination against the industry in question, effective rates between −100 and −∞ result from the "derived" world market value added being negative; i.e., the world market value of material inputs exceeds that of output. On the latter case, see Chapter 4, p. 74.

[4] Appendix A, p. 335.

Interindustry Structure of Protection

Apart from Malaya and Norway, we find a strong tendency to discriminate in favor of manufacturing and against primary activities in the countries under study. Average nominal rates of protection of primary production and manufacturing calculated by using domestic input-output coefficients, are 59 and 96 percent in Brazil, 28 and 111 percent in Chile, 6 and 24 percent in Mexico, 7 and 85 percent in Pakistan, and 7 and 25 percent in the Philippines (see Table 3.1).[5] Owing to escalation in nominal rates of protection from lower to higher levels of fabrication, the differences are even larger in terms of effective rates. The results for the two sectors are Brazil, 52 and 113 percent; Chile, 21 and 182 percent; Mexico, 1 and 26 percent; Pakistan, −10 and 271 percent; and the Philippines, −1 and 61 percent.

It appears then that the average degree of discrimination in favor of manufactured goods and against primary activities is relatively small in Mexico; it is greater in Brazil and the Philippines; and it is the most pronounced in Chile and Pakistan. There is discrimination against the mining and energy industries also in Malaya and Norway, but the system of protection applied in these countries tends to favor agriculture. In Malaya, average effective rates of protection are nil for agriculture as compared with −6 percent for manufacturing and −17 percent for mining and energy; for Norway, the relevant estimates are 16 percent, 8 percent, and nil.

The results obtained in Malaya and Norway reflect the combined effects of a liberal trade policy for manufactures and the protection of certain segments of agriculture. However, this policy is carried out under different conditions in the two countries—Norway having the most, and Malaya one of the least, industrialized economies in the group. In Norway, trade liberalization in manufactured goods has been considered necessary to enable the country to remain competitive with other countries at similar or higher levels of development, while agricultural protection has been rationalized on income distributional and on defense grounds. Malaya, on the other hand, began to industrialize through "natural import substitution," and it is not yet clear whether it will follow the example of other developing countries in imposing high barriers on the imports of manufactures. However, it should be noted that Malaya aims at increasing its degree of self-sufficiency in various agricultural products through protection.

Interest attaches also to the pattern of protection within the manufacturing sector. If we exclude processed food from our purview and consider machinery as an input, we find the familiar pattern of escalation from inputs to final goods. Rates of effective protection are the lowest on construction materials, followed by intermediate products at lower levels of fabrication, machinery,

---

[5] In the case of Pakistan, the data exclude mining and energy.

intermediate products at higher levels of fabrication, and finally consumer goods. No definite conclusions can be reached for transport equipment, since this category is often not shown separately in the domestic input-output table.

Within the consumer goods sector, differences in the effective protection of consumer durables and nondurables seem to depend on the level of industrial development and the size of the domestic market. Consumer durables are protected relatively more heavily in countries at higher levels of industrialization, such as Norway and Mexico, since their small domestic markets provide disadvantages in producing consumer durables where economies of scale are important. By contrast, average levels of protection of consumer durables are relatively low in Chile, Malaya, and the Philippines which have not yet embarked on the domestic production of several of these commodities.

Pakistan presents a special case, inasmuch as it exports some nondurable consumer goods under a subsidy scheme while domestic production for the small home market requires the high protection of consumer durables. Finally, levels of protection of the two types of consumer goods are about the same in Brazil whose aim is self-sufficiency in both.

The degree of protection of processed foods in the countries in question does not fit any definite pattern. In Pakistan, the high protection of sugar has raised the average for this industry to a considerable extent; in Chile the desire for self-sufficiency has had a similar effect. In the Philippines, the results depend on the choice of the input coefficients; elsewhere, comparative advantage in food products (Brazil, Mexico, and Malaya) or the desire to keep food costs low (Norway) explains the relatively low levels of protection of food processing.

The Extent of Import Protection

Comparisons of effective rates calculated at actual exchange rates provide an indication of the degree of discrimination among domestic activities brought about by protection. But the imposition of protective measures also affects the equilibrium exchange rate and permits balance-of-payments equilibrium to be maintained at a lower exchange rate than under free trade. By lowering the domestic currency equivalent of the c.i.f. prices of imports and the f.o.b. prices of exports, overvaluation as compared to the hypothetical free trade situation thus reduces the extent of protection of import-competing goods and increases discrimination against exports. It has therefore been necessary to calculate *net* effective protection by adjusting the estimates made at actual exchange rates for overvaluation as compared to the hypothetical free trade situation. A further adjustment has been made in the case of Chile where balance-of-payments equilibrium was not ensured at the exchange rate applied in the year for which the calculations have been made.

The adjustment has been carried out in accordance with the methodology described in Appendix A. The estimated extent of overvaluation as compared to the hypothetical free trade situation (the percentage excess of the free trade rate over the actual exchange rate) for the individual countries is as follows: Brazil, 27 percent; Chile, 68 percent; Mexico, 9 percent; Malaya, 4 percent; Pakistan, 50 percent; the Philippines, 15 percent; and Norway, 4 percent.

Table 3.3 provides estimates of net effective rates of protection calculated from domestic input-output coefficients for export, import-competing and non-import-competing industries. Industries that export more than 10 percent of their output have generally been considered export industries; import-competing industries have been defined as those where imports provide more than 10 percent of domestic supply; industries with lower import and export shares have been classified as "non-import-competing."

These distinctions could not be made for Brazil and Pakistan. Brazil's input-output table does not provide sufficient detail to separate exports from the other categories. In Pakistan, the same commodities have often protected domestic markets and receive export subsidies, so that there is no clear distinction between import substitutes and exports. Nevertheless, some general conclusions can also be derived for these countries.

There are no industries in Norway which could not be classified as either import-competing or export industries. Also, there are only a few industries that would come into the non-import-competing category in Malaya and these usually enjoy natural protection. In the remaining countries, however, a substantial segment of industries has been considered "non-import-competing."

The non-import-competing category includes two distinct groups of industries: those on the border line between import-substitution and exports and those with prohibitive tariffs. Primary activities classified as non-import-competing, such as forestry and fishing, are borderline cases and usually have negative net effective rates of protection. By contrast, the intermediate goods and consumer goods industries included in the non-import-competing category often supply domestic needs behind prohibitive tariff walls. In these industries domestic competition has generally reduced the domestic price below the sum of world market price and the tariff. Nevertheless, calculations based on price comparisons still show substantial effective protection in Chile and the Philippines but not in Mexico.

With the exception of Norway where agriculture is protected, the net effective rate of protection is usually negative on primary activities classified as import-competing. This conclusion is of special interest since in most cases rates of effective protection calculated at existing exchange rates were positive and only the adjustment for overvaluation has revealed that the structure of protection indirectly subsidizes imports and thus penalizes the domestic production of primary goods.

TABLE 3.3: Net Nominal and Effective Protection on Export, Import-Competing, and Non-Import-Competing Industries[a]

(Percent)

Sector	Chile		Mexico		Malaya		Philippines		Norway	
	Nominal protection	Effective protection	Nominal protection	Effective protection	Nominal protection	Effective protection	Nominal protection	Effective protection	Nominal protection	Effective protection
Export industries										
Primary	-32	-36	-5	-7	-11	-11	-19	-32	-4	-8
Manufacturing	—	—	6	12	-7	-19	-2	9	-3	-6
Total	-32	-36	-3	-5	-10	-12	-14	-28	-3	-7
Import-competing industries										
Primary	-15	-11	—	—	5	1	-2	-2	13	15
Manufacturing	9	14	20	39	2	7	14	39	6	9
Total	1	0	20	39	3	3	7	8	8	12
Non-import-competing industries										
Primary	-22	-23	-1	-7	3	0	3	1	—	—
Manufacturing	39	153	10	5	-3	17	13	86	—	—
Total	38	124	6	-1	3	0	7	9	—	—
All import-substituting industries										
Primary	-15	-12	-1	-7	4	0	1	0	13	15
Manufacturing	26	68	15	16	2	7	14	57	6	9
Total	17	30	11	6	3	1	7	9	8	12

Source: Country tables.

[a] Export industries comprise industries where more than 10 percent of production is exported; import-competing industries include industries where imports provide more than 10 percent of domestic supply; and non-import-competing industries are those where international trade does not exceed 10 percent in either direction. The figures exclude beverages and tobacco. Effective rates have been estimated from domestic input-output coefficients by using the Corden formula; both nominal and effective rates have been adjusted for overvaluation as compared to the hypothetical free trade situation.

Within the manufacturing sector, the effective protection of import-competing industries is 39 percent in the Philippines and Mexico, 14 percent in Chile, 9 percent in Norway, and 7 percent in Malaya. The high figure for Mexico is rather surprising; it is largely due to the high protection of a few intermediate products and consumer durables (paper and paper products, iron and steel, and motor vehicles) that are produced domestically and are also imported. Mexico suffers in this comparison because it permits imports in some industries where other countries have achieved self-sufficiency behind high tariff walls. At the same time, the average rate of net effective protection of non-import-competing industries in the manufacturing sector is practically nil in Mexico compared with 153 percent in Chile and 86 percent in the Philippines.[6]

Since the relative shares of import-competing and non-import-competing industries in the manufacturing sector vary from country to country, special interest attaches to results derived by combining the two. We then find that average net effective protection in these import-substituting industries is 68 percent in Chile, 57 percent in the Philippines, 16 percent in Mexico, 9 percent in Norway, and 7 percent in Malaya. The corresponding figure is 68 percent in Brazil which has no manufacturing export industries and whose manufacturing industries engage in import substitution. Finally, net rates of effective protection of manufactured goods including exports average 147 percent in Pakistan.

Discrimination against Exports

Export taxes, tariffs on inputs used in export industries, and overvaluation of the exchange rate as compared to the hypothetical free trade situation—all contribute to discrimination against exports. Such discrimination, expressed by negative net effective protection, means that the industries in question have to operate with lower value added than they would under free trade. This is because tariffs on inputs increase the cost of production while export taxes reduce the price received in terms of foreign currency and overvaluation lowers the domestic currency equivalent of the foreign exchange receipts.

Tariffs on inputs increase the cost of production in export industries in all countries, especially in the Philippines. In addition, Malaya and the Philippines levy taxes on most primary exports; Pakistan and, to a lesser extent, Mexico tax primary exports and subsidize the exports of manufactured goods;

---

[6] The 17 percent effective protection shown in Malaya is greatly affected by the high protection of a single industry—joineries.

except for taxes on Brazilian coffee exports, there are, however, no export taxes or subsidies in Brazil, Chile, and Norway. Finally, the extent of discrimination against exports due to overvaluation as compared to the hypothetical free trade situation is measured by the rate of overvaluation itself.

These influences have given rise to discrimination against export industries in all the countries under consideration, with the exception of exports of manufactured goods from Pakistan.[7] Discrimination against export industries is the most pronounced in Chile, followed by Brazil and the Philippines; it is the smallest in Malaya, Norway, and Mexico.

Apart from discrimination against export industries, the system of protection also involves a bias against exporting and in favor of sales in domestic markets in industries classified as import-competing or non-import-competing. The extent of this bias has been measured by calculating the percentage excess of domestic value added in import substitution over that obtainable in exporting.

Among the countries in question, Pakistan does not have a bias against exporting in manufacturing industries that receive special privileges under the Export Bonus Scheme. Moreover, the relatively low tariffs on inputs and/or drawbacks for the tariffs paid on imported inputs reduce the extent of this bias in Norway, Malaya, and Mexico. By contrast, in Brazil, Chile, and the Philippines there is a substantial bias against exporting manufactures. This bias exceeds 100 percent in most manufacturing industries of these countries; i.e., to compete on export markets, producers would have to operate with a value added of less than one-half of that obtainable in producing for domestic markets. There are also cases where protection raises the cost of inputs to such an extent that exporting at world market prices would require negative value added domestically.[8]

Net Protection in Manufacturing and in Primary Industries

If calculations are made by the use of domestic coefficients, the net effective protection of primary activities taken together is shown to be negative in all the countries under consideration, with the exception of Brazil and Norway. In these two countries, the results are dominated by the protection of agriculture, fishing, and forestry, while there is discrimination against mining and energy industries. In all the other countries, net effective rates are negative for

---

[7] The positive average effective rates of protection in the manufacturing export industries of Mexico and the Philippines are an average of net discrimination against export products and net protection of import substitutes in these industries.

[8] For numerical estimates, see the tables included in the country chapters.

agriculture, fishing, and forestry and for mining and energy; i.e., the system of protection discriminates against both groups of industries.

In turn, the manufacturing sector is protected in all the countries in question, with Malaya providing the only exception. Net rates of effective protection for the individual countries derived by the use of domestic input-output coefficients are Brazil, 68 percent; Chile, 68 percent; Mexico, 16 percent; Malaya, −10 percent; Pakistan, 147 percent; the Philippines, 41 percent; and Norway, 4 percent (see Table 3.2, p. 56).

Within the manufacturing sector, net effective rates of protection calculated by using domestic coefficients are negative for construction materials in Chile, construction materials and processed food in Mexico, intermediate products at lower levels of fabrication in Norway, as well as for all industries other than intermediate products at higher levels of fabrication and non-durable consumer goods in Malaya. At the other extreme, net effective rates exceed 100 percent for nondurable consumer goods in Brazil, processed food and nondurable consumer goods in Chile, and consumer durables in the Philippines, and negative value added is shown at world market prices for consumer durables in Pakistan and the Philippines, as well as for processed food in Pakistan.

More detailed comparisons can be made by using estimates based on the free trade input-output table which excludes the possibility of negative value added in world market prices. We now find that, with the major exception of gas in Chile, every country strongly discriminates against mining and energy as well as against fisheries. In Malaya and the Philippines, weighting by world trade shows positive net protection for agriculture and forestry (Table 3.4).

Net effective rates of protection are high on most food processing industries in Brazil, Chile, and Pakistan. Sugar in Brazil and meat products in Chile provide a peculiar exception, inasmuch as high input costs and low domestic prices lead to negative domestic value added in the estimates based on free trade input-output coefficients. Net effective rates of protection are also relatively high on dairy products in Mexico, the Philippines, and Norway.

Construction materials generally have low rates of protection with non-metallic mineral products receiving greater protection than basic materials. Among intermediate products at lower levels of fabrication, net effective rates are usually low on chemical materials and, in the large majority of cases, negative on lumber, wood pulp, and petroleum products. These products tend to have low nominal rates of protection, probably as a result of pressure from industries that use them as inputs.

Pressure from user industries may also explain the relatively low nominal rates on pig iron, steel ingots, and nonferrous metals. But, for these products, the escalation of duties from lower to higher stages of processing—and the small share of value added in the product price—raises the effective rates of protection well above the nominal rates. Finally, net effective rates are generally high on leather, synthetic materials, and glass and glass products. High effective rates on leather are chiefly explained by the fact that the major raw material of the industry (hides and skins) is available at world market prices. The reason for the high rates in the other two cases is that most of the countries in question have only recently entered into the manufacturing of synthetic materials and of glass and glass products and accord them high rates of nominal protection.

Effective rates of protection exceed nominal rates by a considerable margin in the case of intermediate products at higher levels of fabrication, largely because nominal rates on these commodities are much higher than nominal rates on the intermediate products at earlier stages of transformation that are used as inputs. In all countries effective rates of protection are especially high on textile fabrics, rubber products, plastic goods, metal manufactures, wood products and furniture, and paper and paper products. In Malaya, however, the net effective rate of protection is practically nil on rubber goods, some of which are now exported. Moreover, Chile and Norway are internationally competitive in paper manufacturing and have negative net effective rates of protection in this industry.

Chemical products are highly protected in Brazil, Chile, the Philippines, and Malaya, as are steel products in Pakistan and Mexico. Steel products, however, receive negative net protection in Brazil and Malaya. Malaya also gives negative protection to metal castings whereas in Chile these are highly protected.

Among nondurable consumer goods, hosiery, clothing, other textile articles, leather products (other than shoes), as well as toys, sports goods, and jewelry, receive especially high protection in Brazil and Chile. Except for clothing in Mexico, and hosiery and clothing in the Philippines, net effective rates of protection on these commodities also exceed the average in the other countries. On the other hand, net protection on shoes is relatively low in most of the countries under consideration. In addition, no country other than Brazil protects the printing and publishing industry in any appreciable degree; in turn, Brazil is the only country with negative effective protection on precision instruments.

Apart from Malaya which does only assembly operations, automobiles are highly protected everywhere; high protection is provided also to bicycles and motorcycles except in Pakistan which has started to export bicycles. However, shipbuilding has negative protection everywhere, and the construction of railroad vehicles receives little, if any, protection. Finally, net effective rates of protection are generally low on both electrical and nonelectrical machinery, except in Brazil which increasingly aims at self-sufficiency in machinery industries.

TABLE 3.4: Net Nominal and Effective Protection in Individual Industries Estimated on the Basis of Free Trade Coefficients[a]

(Percent)

	Industry	Brazil (1966) T'	Z'	Chile (1961) T'	Z'	Mexico (1960) T'	Z'	Malaya (1965) T'	Z'	Pakistan (1963–64) T'	Z'	Philippines (1965) T'	Z'	Norway (1954) T'	Z'
01	Agriculture and forestry	18	16	-6	-6	-2	-3	13	18	-29	-47	15	17	20	31
02	Fishing	14	-3	-15	-4	-8	-11	-2	-13	-13	-37	-13	-13	-4	-6
03	Solid fuels	26	26	-18	-24	27	38	-4	-7	na	na	-12	-24	-4	-7
04	Gas	7	-50	51	225	-2	-11	2	12	na	na	-6	-7	-2	1
05	Iron ore mining	-21	-40	-40	-45	-27	-38	-18	-25	na	na	-20	-31	-4	-6
06	Nonferrous metal ores	-12	-48	-33	-60	-2	-6	-12	-25	7	5	-20	-45	-4	-8
07	Petroleum and natural gas	-1	-40	-12	25	-8	-24	-4	-11	-13	-17	-6	-30	-4	-14
08	Basic construction materials	18	8	29	50	-8	-13	-1	-6	na	na	7	6	-4	-6
09	Other minerals	1	-10	-5	-5	-16	-23	3	3	na	na	45	59	-4	-6
10	Meat products	85	477	-35	-101	-3	21	-4	-8	134	361	3	19	6	-10
11	Prepared food products	153	442	25	57	28	42	13	12	103	303	21	47	8	22
12	Sugar	-21	-113	-23	-33	-8	6	57	188	na	na	16	79	-4	-6
13	Confectionary	119	272	79	174	-8	-16	9	-8	na	na	17	15	2	4
14	Dairy products	40	133	10	55	39	94	0	-12	4	132	29	162	26	35
15	Cereal products	123	266	8	51	-5	-28	-2	-3	na	na	6	10	-1	2
16	Other food products	10	-96	29	165	0	-1	2	-22	na	na	25	70	-4	-10
17	Beverages	93	160	58	126	74	137	36	71	49	89	-13	-13	52	106
18	Fats and oils	59	165	-8	-36	10	-4	1	-6	35	94	14	45	-3	-4
19	Tobacco	162	372	23	13	20	45	99	12	105	191	0	20	39	-17
21	Thread and yarn	115	272	-1	32	0	5	-3	-1	-18	-22	19	73	0	1
22	Textile fabrics	153	269	85	230	18	50	20	59	37	99	14	66	9	24
23	Hosiery	157	276	214	564	39	95	22	62	51	71	-3	13	13	35
24	Clothing	157	206	153	283	1	-16	20	26	117	228	-3	12	16	30
25	Other textile articles	152	220	60	61	13	9	15	17	na	na	-3	14	15	23
26	Shoes	157	261	58	74	15	15	1	-1	7	8	-6	1	12	13
28	Lumber	-4	-42	-26	-39	-7	-9	-4	-5	15	41	-20	-29	-3	-4
29	Wood products and furniture	74	139	46	111	22	25	7	15	na	na	-4	7	6	13

No.	Industry														
31	Wood pulp	-1	-48	-11	-5	18	57	10	31	-25	-59	1	8	-4	-9
32	Paper and paper products	70	142	-5	-3	31	54	8	9	29	71	21	37	-4	-6
33	Printing and publishing	75	93	2	7	5	-7	-1	-6	-15	-32	10	3	1	3
35	Leather	58	48	58	213	8	6	11	34	-3	31	61	166	11	35
36	Leather goods other than shoes	140	243	51	57	18	26	18	30	7	11	72	99	13	18
37	Rubber products	59	89	20	48	22	51	0	1	69	165	42	87	13	30
38	Plastic goods	47	29	49	54	47	96	12	24	124	273	53	113	13	16
39	Synthetic materials	75	145	58	140	12	16	11	19	116	279	17	24	17	39
40	Other chemical materials	7	-11	11	17	4	1	4	6	10	23	8	12	0	2
41	Chemical products	44	76	39	82	15	28	17	37	10	27	32	60	6	14
44	Petroleum products	69	204	-14	38	-6	-15	-4	-8	-2	9	-1	-2	-3	-6
45	Nonmetallic mineral products	36	47	28	51	-4	-14	4	7	27	45	27	41	3	6
46	Glass and products	70	100	70	118	5	6	18	23	76	108	29	41	13	21
48	Pig iron and ferromanganese	23	111	-40	-49	17	91	-4	4	na	7	-8	-3	-4	-7
49	Steel ingots	23	69	23	651	18	53	-4	-12	-17	7	-1	19	-4	-10
50	Rolled steel products	14	-29	-8	4	18	36	-4	-9	3	77	7	34	-2	4
51	Other steel products	7	-25	-1	10	19	31	-4	-8	13	85	5	-7	0	3
54	Nonferrous metals	24	68	-18	-14	11	38	-3	4	27	149	2	14	-4	-7
55	Metal castings	23	27	24	59	22	36	-4	-6	na	na	13	21	2	5
56	Metal manufactures	51	93	21	58	19	28	4	12	30	78	17	28	6	14
57	Agricultural machinery	9	-12	-20	-42	6	0	-4	-9	na	na	0	-12	3	3
58	Nonelectrical machinery	37	44	10	13	21	27	2	3	26	50	6	-2	9	15
59	Electrical machinery	58	81	19	37	24	33	11	na	11	22	21	29	7	13
60	Shipbuilding	-2	-47	-35	-89	na	na	na	na	na	na	1	-15	-3	-11
61	Railroad vehicles	16	2	4	7	16	19	na	na	na	na	-1	-15	2	3
62	Automobiles	98	198	16	33	39	74	-4	-12	133	309	34	63	23	52
64	Bicycles and motorcycles	133	276	14	31	15	20	9	20	114	273	8	-4	17	38
65	Airplanes	na	na	na	na	na	na	na	na	na	na	na	na	na	na
66	Precision instruments	6	-8	5	5	na	na	3	4	40	63	9	7	11	16
67	Toys, sport goods, jewelry	137	218	8	114	48	80	10	13	10	12	57	95	12	17

Source: Country tables.

[a] Effective rates have been estimated by using the Corden formula; both nominal and effective rates have been adjusted for overvaluation as compared to the hypothetical free trade situation. For definitions, see Chapter 1. Explanation of symbols: T' = net nominal rate of protection; Z' = net effective rate of protection.

TABLE 3.5: Rank Correlation Coefficients between Nominal and Effective Protection[a]

Country	Estimates based on domestic coefficients	
	Balassa method	Corden method
Brazil 1966	.95	.97
1967	.94	.96
Chile 1961	.89	.91
Mexico 1960		
Tariff protection	.91	.92
Implicit protection	.91	.91
Malaya 1963	.73	.74
1965	.87	.87
Pakistan 1963–64		
Tariff protection	.88	.92
Implicit protection	.60	.59
Philippines 1965[b]		
Tariff (potential) protection	.64	.63
Implicit (realized) protection	.82	.82
Norway 1954	.93	.95

Source: Country tables.

[a] Spearman rank correlation coefficients calculated by the formula

$$r = 1 - \frac{6\Sigma d^2}{n(n^2 - 1)},$$

where n refers to the number of observations and d is the difference between ranks by nominal and effective rates of protection for individual industries calculated by the use of domestic input-output coefficients. All the results are significant at the 95 percent level.

[b] Non-import-competing goods only.

Conclusion

In this chapter, we have presented the results of the calculations on nominal and effective protection in the seven countries studied. We have shown that not only do differences in the ranking of industries by rates of nominal and effective protection vary among countries, but there are substantial differences in the absolute magnitudes of nominal and effective protection for individual industries. While these findings demonstrate the usefulness of estimating effective rates of protection, large differences between rates of tariff and implicit protection in Mexico and Pakistan indicate that tariff data will not appropriately describe the structure of protection in countries which employ quantitative restrictions to limit imports.

It further appears that the interindustry pattern of effective protection is generally little affected by the choice of the input-output coefficients. Nor do errors in estimation due to substitution among inputs seem to have appreciably affected the results. Rather, the observed differences in the two sets of estimates are largely explained by considerations relating to the level of economic development and the weighting schemes applied.

Comparing the structure of protection in the seven countries under study, we find considerable variation in the extent of net protection of domestic manufacturing. Manufactured goods are highly protected in Pakistan, Brazil, and Chile, less so in the Philippines, relatively little in Mexico, and not at all in Norway and Malaya. In the first five countries, the protection of manufacturing is accompanied by discrimination against primary activities; in the latter two, agriculture is protected while the system of protection discriminates against mining and energy.

Within the manufacturing sector, however, there is much similarity in the interindustry pattern of protection among all seven countries. The results exhibit the familiar pattern of escalation, with effective rates being generally the lowest on primary commodities, followed by intermediate goods at lower levels of fabrication, machinery, intermediate products at higher levels of fabrication, and consumer goods. By contrast, the degree of protection of food processing varies among countries.

Apart from Norway, the exports of the countries in question are mainly primary products, so that the negative protection of primary activities indicates the existence of discrimination against exports. In Brazil, Chile, and the Philippines, and to a lesser extent in Mexico, the system of protection also favors import substitution over exporting in manufacturing industries. Such a bias does not exist in Pakistan, however, where more-or-less equal incentives are provided for production in domestic and in foreign markets.

CHAPTER 4

EVALUATION OF THE SYSTEM
OF PROTECTION

Bela Balassa

Policies of Protection

In the previous chapter, we presented our findings on the structure of protection in the seven countries under study. This chapter will provide an evaluation of these findings. In the discussion, use will be made of the numerical results shown in Chapters 2 and 3 and in the country chapters.

We have seen that in Brazil, Chile, Pakistan, and the Philippines there is a considerable degree of discrimination in favor of manufacturing and against primary activities. This discrimination is the result of deliberate policies aimed at providing incentives for the expansion of manufacturing, with agriculture paying much of the cost of this expansion in the form of lower product prices and higher input prices. The extent of discrimination against primary activities is relatively small in Mexico, and the system of protection appears to slightly benefit agriculture—but not mining—in Malaya and Norway.

The discriminatory effects of the system of incentives in favor of manufacturing have entailed the protection of the domestic manufacturing sector against imports. At the same time, within this sector, protection tends to increase from lower to higher stages of fabrication. Rates of protection are the lowest on construction materials, followed in ascending order by intermediate products at lower levels of fabrication, machinery and transport equipment, intermediate products at higher levels of fabrication, and consumer goods.

71

Apart from escalation in the protective structure, we find considerable variability in rates of effective protection for individual industries. Among the countries under study, variability in effective rates appears to be correlated with the level of protection of the manufacturing sector. Thus, the inter-industry variation of effective rates of protection, measured by their standard deviation, is the smallest in Norway and in Malaya, somewhat greater in Mexico, greater again in the Philippines, and the most variation is shown in Brazil, Chile, and Pakistan.

The high variability of effective rates of protection cannot be considered the result of deliberate decisions. Rather, in the countries in question the system of protection is a historical result of actions taken at different times in response to the then existing situation and the pressures exerted by special interest groups. Furthermore, setting nominal rates, the governments have given little attention to the interdependence of these decisions. The interrelationships of tariffs and exchange rates have generally been disregarded; nor have attempts been made to evaluate how particular industries are affected by tariffs on their outputs and inputs. Yet, as we have seen, differences in nominal rates of protection are accentuated if we measure effective rates.

This situation reflects the absence of a systematic policy of protection and also indicates the lack of adequate consideration of the cost of protection for the national economy. Raul Prebisch notes in regard to Latin American countries that "the criterion by which the choice was determined was based not on considerations of economic expediency but on immediate feasibility, whatever the cost of production."[1] Moreover, one observer speaks of a policy of "import substitution at any cost."[2]

Yet protection involves a cost to the national economy on various counts. In the following, we will examine this cost under two major headings: the "static" (allocative) and the "dynamic" cost of protection. Some tentative calculations will also be made on the cost of protection in the countries under study. Furthermore, we will indicate the effects of the system of protection on the primary and manufactured exports of these countries and on their rate of economic growth.

The "Static" (Allocative) Cost of Protection

Distortions in the relative prices of inputs and outputs due to the imposition of protective measures lead to inefficiencies in resource allocation that entail a cost for the national economy. Distortions in relative prices interfere

---

[1] Raul Prebisch, *Towards a Dynamic Development Policy for Latin America* (New York: United Nations, 1964), p. 71.

[2] Santiago Macario, "Protectionism and Industrialization in Latin America," *Economic Bulletin for Latin America*, March 1964, p. 61.

with interindustry specialization according to comparative advantage between primary activities and manufacturing industries as well as within the manufacturing sector itself. Intra-industry specialization and participation in the international division of the production process are also obstructed by barriers to imports and disincentives to exports. Moreover, in individual industries, the bias against exports and in favor of production for domestic use creates a divergence between social and private profitability. Such a divergence also results from distortions in input prices that affect the choice of the input mix.

The reduced extent of interindustry specialization due to the application of protective measures involves a consumption as well as a production cost. For one thing, protection interferes with consumer choice by distorting the prices paid by consumers; for another, it leads to the movement of resources from low-cost to high-cost industries. Limiting our attention for the moment to the production cost of protection, we may express this as the excess domestic resource cost of saving or earning foreign exchange.

For the proverbial small country of international trade theory, the world market prices of both its exports and imports are given, and any deviation of domestic prices from world market prices will involve an economic loss. The nature of this loss can be indicated by an example. Assume that production takes place under constant costs and there are no excess profits (or wages) in protected industries. Effective rates of protection of, say, 100 percent on import-competing goods and nil on exports will then mean that domestic processing costs are double the world market costs in the first case and equal to world market costs in the second. Protection thus permits the profitable operation of import-competing industries that require twice as many domestic resources per unit of foreign exchange saved through import substitution as would be needed to earn a unit of foreign exchange through exports. It follows that eliminating protection would entail the transfer of resources from industries engaged in import substitution to export industries where their contribution to foreign exchange earnings and to national income is twice as large.

None of the countries under consideration fit the small country case. Although it can be assumed that they face given import prices, an expansion of their major exports would generally require reductions in export prices in terms of foreign currency while entailing increases in the domestic costs of exports. Accordingly, the elimination of protection would be associated with devaluation of the currency, and measurement at existing exchange rates would overstate the extent and the cost of protection. Under the stated assumptions, the cost of protection will then be measured by the net effective rate of protection of import-competing goods, against which we should set the gains due to the higher foreign prices and the lower domestic cost on the smaller volume of exports under protection.

Among the countries under study, net effective rates of protection of import-substituting manufacturing industries estimated by the use of domestic input-output coefficients, are especially high in Brazil (68 percent), Chile (68 percent), and the Philippines (57 percent). Import-substituting industries are much less protected in Mexico (16 percent), Norway (8 percent), and Malaya (6 percent). Finally, in Pakistan, protection also extends to manufactured exports and the average net rate of effective protection of all manufactured goods including exports is 147 percent.

Averages of net rates of effective protection conceal much variation among industries. We find a number of very high net effective rates, and in several cases (consumer durables in Pakistan and the Philippines, and processed food in Pakistan) value added in world market prices is negative; i.e., the c.i.f. value of material inputs exceeds that of output. While this seemingly paradoxical result might conceivably be due to errors in observation, there are genuine cases of negative value added at world market prices, entailing an absolute waste of resources.

There is evidence that in some instances when only assembly is undertaken domestically, the foreign purchase price of parts and components exceeds that of the assembled product. This may be explained by the monopolistic position of the seller or by the fact that the product has to be disassembled in order to ship the required parts and components—as in the case of typewriters. Parts and components may also be more costly to transport than the product itself, and this would raise the c.i.f. price of imported inputs to a greater extent than that of the final product.

Negative value added at world market prices may also be due to the waste of materials or to the substitution of materials with higher world market prices for those with lower prices. Such substitution can occur since differences in tariffs among inputs may make it profitable for the entrepreneur to utilize materials that would not be used under free trade conditions. Finally, negative value added may indicate that the country's resource endowment is not suitable to the production of a particular commodity whose manufacturing is made profitable only by protection.[3]

Efficient resource allocation also suffers if incentives for import substitution and disincentives to exporting provide obstacles to intra-industry specialization (i.e., producing—and exporting—certain varieties of a commodity and importing others) and to participation in the international division of the production process through the export and import of parts and components. In such instances, however, excess costs are principally due to the small scale of output. We will, therefore, discuss these cases below, where we consider the "dynamic" costs of foregoing economies of scale.

---

[3] On the last point, see S. E. Guisinger, "Negative Value Added and the Theory of Effective Protection," *Quarterly Journal of Economics*, August 1969, pp. 415–33.

Economies of scale are also foregone as a result of the bias in favor of production for domestic use and against exporting particular products. But this bias entails a cost to the national economy even in the absence of scale economies since private returns will not be the same on sales in domestic and in foreign markets although social returns are identical in the two cases. If we take world market prices as given—a reasonable assumption for most manufactured goods—social returns in import substitution and in exporting will be the same: the domestic production of one unit of output will save the same amount of foreign exchange in import substitution as it would earn in exporting. However, unless export subsidies are provided at the same rate as tariffs, the producer will get a higher price in domestic markets than abroad. The effects of these policies on exports will be considered below.

The "Dynamic" Costs of Protection

We have considered the so-called static or allocative costs of protection which result from distortions in relative prices due to the application of protective measures. The infant industry argument tells us that an industry should nevertheless be protected if this cost is recouped as a result of productivity improvements over time.[4] In a more general form, the infant industry argument can be reinterpreted by considering as acceptable a reallocation of resources that raises the discounted value of future national income without additional sacrifices in terms of work and/or saving. Such an allocation would lead to increases in productivity on the national economy level which offset the initial loss due to protection.[5]

Whichever formulation is chosen, the gist of the matter is that the present (static) cost of protection is accepted for the sake of future (dynamic) benefits, when it is assumed that infant industries will "grow up" and become competitive in the world market. The emphasis is on the temporary nature of protection, needed to shelter the fledgling industry, which will be removed after maturity is reached.

In developing countries engaged in import substitution, however, there are generally no expectations for the removal of protection, and governments as well as firms act on the assumption that it will be maintained ad infinitum. Policies of import substitution, then, bear only a superficial resemblance to the infant industry argument; they envisage the continuing protection of manu-

---

[4] This is the Mill-Bastable test of infant industry protection. Cf. M. C. Kemp, "The Mill-Bastable Infant Industry Dogma," *Journal of Political Economy*, February 1960, pp. 65–67. A further condition is that some of the gain accrues to other firms or that the entrepreneur attaches a lower value to this gain than does the community.

[5] Productivity growth is defined here as the ratio of increases in output to increases in the combined inputs of the primary factors of production.

facturing industry rather than a temporary deviation from the free trade norm.[6]

The continued sheltering of domestic industry from foreign competition, in turn, involves a dynamic cost to the national economy in the form of opportunities foregone for improvements in productivity. For one thing, the small size of domestic markets limits the scope of application of large-scale production methods. For another, technical change is hindered by the lack of sufficient domestic competition and the existence of sellers' markets in these countries; producers have a dominant position and users have practically no choice between domestic and foreign products nor often among domestic products.

The scale requirements of efficient production and of domestic competition represent less of an obstacle in countries of larger size; hence they can proceed further with import substitution than smaller nations. Nevertheless, the limitations of domestic markets are apparent even in large developing countries, and the absence of foreign competition also hinders improvements in production methods. Our conclusions thus apply to Brazil, too, although this country has more leeway in expanding manufacturing industries that produce only for domestic markets than, for instance, Chile does.

These considerations explain that, rather than catching up with the industrial nations, developing countries have often fallen further behind in terms of productivity levels. This is not to say that there have been no improvements in productivity in these countries; in some consumer goods industries in Mexico and Pakistan, improvements have even proceeded at a more rapid rate than in the industrial nations. Nevertheless, available evidence indicates that, on the average, productivity growth has been lower in the developing countries pursuing a policy of import substitution behind high protection barriers than in the industrial nations.[7]

Economies of Scale

The possibilities for exploiting economies of scale in manufacturing industries depend on the size of the domestic market and on the policies followed in regard to international specialization. Economies of scale can be obtained through the construction of larger plants to produce a single product (economies of scale in the traditional sense), through reducing product variety in individual plants (horizontal specialization), and through the manufacturing of parts, components, and accessories of a given product in separate establishments (vertical specialization).

---

[6] For an argument along these lines, see Hla Myint, "International Trade and the Developing Countries," in *Proceedings of the Third Congress of the International Economic Association*, ed. P. A. Samuelson (London: MacMillan and Co., Ltd., 1969), pp. 15–35.

[7] See, for example, H. J. Bruton, "Productivity Growth in Latin America," *American Economic Review*, December 1967, pp. 1099–1116.

Economies of scale in single product firms depend on the character of the product and on the degree of sophistication in production techniques. The efficient scale of operations is relatively low, and costs of production on a smaller scale are only moderately higher, in some nondurable consumer goods industries which employ relatively simple production techniques. However, the efficient scale of output is large, and costs increase substantially at lower output levels, in the production of most intermediate products, capital goods, and durable consumer goods which necessitate the use of sophisticated production techniques.

Thus, while in the production of textiles and shoes costs per unit may decline only 10 percent as output doubles, cost differences are substantially larger in most other major industries. For example, steel production costs are one-third higher in a plant producing 250 thousand tons a year than in a plant with an annual output of one million tons; a doubling of fertilizer output involves a decrease in unit costs by nearly one-half; and in pulp and paper production, unit costs are about two-thirds higher in a mill with a daily output of 50 tons than in one with 200 tons.[8] In addition, an investigation of 221 U.S. firms, mainly in the chemical industry, petroleum refining, and electric power showed investment costs as well as operating costs per unit to decline by 0.2–0.3 percent for a 1 percent increase in output.[9]

Comparisons of unit costs in domestic and foreign plants of American firms in a wide range of industries, reported in a National Industrial Conference Board study, also provide evidence of scale economies. According to this study, costs in foreign operations are on the average 29 percent higher than in the United States whenever the foreign plant's output is less than 5 percent of that of the U.S. plant; the ratio of foreign to domestic costs falls to 106 in the case of output ratios of 5 to 10 percent, it is 98 in the case of output ratios of 10 to 50 percent, and 85 if the foreign plant produces more than one-half of the U.S. factory's output.[10] While data on foreign plants combine information on plants in Western Europe and in developing countries, plants in the latter being generally smaller than in the former, they provide powerful evidence of the existence of economies of scale.

Available evidence indicates the importance of economies of scale in single product firms. Yet in developing countries where protective barriers are high and there is bias against the exports of manufactured goods, the limitations of domestic markets generally permit only the construction of plants that are much below optimum size. By contrast, the disadvantages of small national

---

[8] Bela Balassa, *Economic Development and Integration* (Mexico D.F.: Centro de Estudios Monetarios Latinamericanos, 1965), ch. 4.

[9] John Haldi and David Whitcomb, "Economies of Scale in Industrial Plants," *Journal of Political Economy*, Part 1, August 1967, pp. 373–85.

[10] T. R. Gates and F. Linden, *Costs and Competition: American Experience Abroad* (New York: National Industrial Conference Board, 1961), p. 129.

markets are surmounted in countries where low protective barriers and the lack of bias against exports permit efficient-scale operations through specialization according to comparative advantage and catering to both domestic and foreign markets.

By reducing product variety in individual plants, horizontal specialization also results in scale economies. In countries where protection levels are low, multi-product plants can specialize in a narrower range of commodities for domestic production and for exports and hence have longer production runs. The lengthening of production runs, in turn, permits improvements in manufacturing efficiency through "learning by doing"; reduces the expenses associated with resetting machines and reorganizing work; and allows for the use of specialized machinery. Horizontal specialization may bring considerable gains even in the large European industrial countries;[11] the benefits are correspondingly greater in the developing countries under consideration. Textiles, clothing, footwear, machine tools, and shipbuilding are frequently mentioned examples.

Horizontal specialization is important in the textiles, clothing, and footwear industries in Norway where imports accounted respectively for 51, 25, and 17 percent of domestic consumption in 1966, while Norwegian firms export a variety of specialty items. By contrast, in Brazil and Chile, the proportion of imports in these industries does not exceed 1 percent and exports are practically nonexistent. These results are explained by the fact that in countries with high levels of protection and bias against exporting, horizontal specialization is hampered by the incentive system; home production serves only domestic outlets and, in the absence of imports, firms produce many varieties of a particular product in conformity with the pattern of domestic demand. The lack of horizontal specialization, in turn, involves excess costs.

In industries producing durable consumer goods, machinery, and transport equipment, further gains can be derived from vertical specialization through the separation, in individual plants, of various activities leading to the production of a given commodity. Even when the final product may be produced on a large scale in a developing country, efficient-scale operations will hardly be possible in the manufacturing of parts, components, and accessories, so that the "backward integration" of the production process involves considerable costs. It has been shown, for example, that the excess cost of domestic car production in Brazil rises from 6 to 71 percent as we move from assembly to the domestic production of 99 percent of the value of the automobile.[12] Yet Brazil has required automobile manufacturers to raise the domestic con-

---

[11] Bela Balassa, *Trade Liberalization Among Industrial Countries: Objectives and Alternatives* (New York: McGraw-Hill, 1967), ch. 5.

[12] Jack Baranson, *Automotive Industries in Developing Countries*, World Bank Occasional Staff Papers No. 8 (Washington, D.C., 1969), p. 36.

tent of an automobile to 99 percent. Legal requirements on the minimum proportion of nationally fabricated components have also been progressively increased in Chile: from 27 percent in 1964 to 32 percent in 1965 and again to 45 percent in 1966.[13] By contrast, Norway has no automobile industry although it has five times as many passenger cars as Chile; rather, it participates in the international division of the production process by manufacturing parts, components, and accessories of automobiles for assembly abroad.

Competition and Technological Change

The effects of protection on competition and technical change should further be noted. In countries with high levels of protection, the smallness of domestic markets has led to the establishment of monopoly positions in some industries, and there is rarely effective competition in others, because the high profits assured by continuing protection are conducive to a "live and let live" attitude in industry. High profits, then, absorb part of the excess of domestic over world market value added that is shown by the rate of effective protection. In national firms, these profits represent a redistribution of incomes from domestic consumers to producers. However, protection will involve an additional cost to the national economy if the firms are foreign-owned since profits are now transferred abroad. Foreign investment in highly protected industries, then, may conceivably bring a loss rather than a gain to a developing country.

High profits assured by protection will tend to have further adverse effects, irrespective of whether firms are owned by the country's nationals or by foreigners. These effects relate to the firm's motivation in the "hothouse" atmosphere of sheltered domestic markets. In such a situation, firms tend to follow a policy of low turnover and high profit rates and have little incentive for product improvement and technical change. In fact, in highly protected industries, product quality has often deteriorated and firms have been reluctant to assume the risk associated with the introduction of new products, production methods, and innovating activity in general. At the same time, by maintaining prices at high levels, the lack of competition limits the expansion of domestic markets.

Brazil and Chile provide examples of the effects of continuing protection in long-established industries. In both countries, industries producing nondurable consumer goods and the intermediate products used in their manufacturing were well established by the end of World War II. Nevertheless, the industries in question receive higher protection than the newly-developed machinery and intermediate products industries. With continuing protection

---

[13] L. L. Johnson, "Problems of Import Substitution: The Chilean Automobile Industry," *Economic Development and Cultural Change*, January 1967, pp. 202–16.

assured to them, high costs observed in many of the firms of these industries appear to be the result rather than the cause of protection.

It should be added that discrimination in favor of consumer goods and the intermediate products used in their manufacture and against machinery and other intermediate products has often hindered the development of the latter industries. In addition, the relatively low prices of machinery have encouraged the expansion of capital-intensive industries and the application of capital-intensive production methods in countries such as Brazil, Chile, Pakistan, and the Philippines. Demands for new equipment increased further as high levels of protection made it possible for firms to operate profitably at less than full capacity. The priority given to new investments by the governments of these countries has also favored the imports of capital goods, while foreign exchange limitations have frequently led to shortages in imported materials, parts, and components, thereby contributing to the underutilization of existing equipment.

Measurement of the Cost of Protection

In the postwar period, several efforts have been made to measure the static or allocative cost of protection. The estimates range from 0.05 percent of gross national product for the Common Market[14] to 2.5 percent in Chile[15] and 4 percent in Canada.[16] These estimates suffer from several deficiencies. First, they consider the case when output in protected industries declines but all industries continue to operate under free trade. Second, they take no account of possible improvements in productivity following the elimination of trade barriers. Third, they are based on tariff observations and disregard the effects of quantitative restrictions and the interaction of the protection of outputs and inputs. Fourth, they do not consider the interdependence of tariffs and exchange rates.

In a criticism of Harberger's estimates for Chile, I have made calculations under alternative assumptions as to whether protected industries will continue to operate or disappear under free trade.[17] In the same paper I have also sug-

---

[14] Tibor Scitovsky, *Economic Theory and Western European Integration* (Stanford: Stanford University Press, 1968), p. 64. This estimate refers to the cost of tariffs on trade among the Common Market countries.

[15] A. C. Harberger, "Using Resources at Hand More Effectively," *Papers and Proceedings of the American Economic Review*, May 1958, pp. 134–55.

[16] R. J. and G. P. Wonnacott, *Free Trade between the United States and Canada: The Potential Economic Effects* (Cambridge, Mass.: Harvard University Press, 1967), p. 300.

[17] Cf. Bela Balassa, "Resource Allocation and Economic Integration in Latin America," (Paper presented at the Conference on the Next Decade of Latin American Development, Cornell University, April 20–22, 1966). The Spanish translation of the paper was published under the title "Integracion regional y asignacion de recursos en America Latina," *Comercio Exterior*, September 1966, pp. 672–85.

gested that estimates should be made by using effective rather than nominal rates of protection. In turn, Leibenstein has put forward the proposition that the main source of the welfare cost of protection or monopoly is not static (allocative) inefficiency but rather what he calls "X-inefficiency"—actual processing costs exceed costs that would be attainable if the best-known production and organizational methods were applied.[18] Finally, in estimating the cost of protection in the United States, Basevi has allowed for the effects of the removal of tariffs on the exchange rate.[19]

These threads have been pulled together in an unpublished paper by Joel Bergsman.[20] Bergsman assumed constant costs in protected industries and separated them into two groups, depending on whether they can be expected to disappear or to continue under free trade. The saving in costs in the first group of industries was considered to represent an improvement in static (allocative) efficiency; in the second group, production costs were assumed to decline to competitive levels under free trade, thereby representing an improvement in X-efficiency.

Bergsman's estimates had originally been made for Brazil. His method has subsequently been applied to the other countries included in this study. In addition, I have estimated the consumption cost of protection, the terms-of-trade loss due to reductions in export prices, and the cost of increased exports under free trade, the latter under the assumption that export industries are subject to increasing costs. Furthermore, I have reinterpreted the excess costs in industries whose production costs would be reduced to competitive levels under free trade to represent the dynamic costs of protection resulting from the use of backward and small-scale production methods in the framework of protected domestic markets.[21]

According to the estimates of Table 4.1, the dynamic cost of protection exceeds the static or allocative cost by a considerable margin in all the countries under consideration, except Malaya. By contrast, the terms-of-trade effect of protection is relatively large in Malaya which has a dominant position in the markets of two of its major export products, rubber and tin. The terms-of-trade effect is even greater in Chile which provides a large proportion of the world's copper, while the assumption of low export-supply elasticities explains the relatively high cost of increases in Chilean exports under free trade.

---

[18] Harvey Leibenstein, "Allocative Efficiency vs. 'X-Efficiency,'" *American Economic Review*, June 1966, pp. 392–415. Empirical evidence on the importance of X-efficiency in particular industries is provided in Leibenstein's original article as well as in W. S. Comanor and Harvey Leibenstein, "Allocative Efficiency, X-Efficiency, and the Measurement of Welfare Losses," *Economica*, August 1969, pp. 304–9.

[19] Giorgio Basevi, "The Restrictive Effect of the U.S. Tariff and Its Welfare Value," *American Economic Review*, September 1968, pp. 841–52.

[20] Joel Bergsman, "Commercial Policy, Allocative Efficiency, and 'X-Efficiency,'" mimeographed, June 1970.

[21] The formulas and their derivation are contained in Appendix B.

TABLE 4.1: The "Cost" of Protection in Individual Countries

(Percent of GNP)

	Brazil 1966	Chile 1961	Malaya 1965	Pakis- tan 1963–64	Mexico 1960	Norway 1954	Philip- pines 1965
Static (allocative) cost of protec- tion of import substitutes[a]	0.6	1.4	0.6	1.5	0.6	0.5	2.0
Dynamic cost of protection of import substitutes[b]	9.5	9.6	0.4	5.4	2.2	2.0	2.6
Consumption effect[c]	0.1	0.6	0.1	0.2	0.1	0.1	0.4
Terms-of-trade effect[d]	−0.5	3.5	−1.4	0.6	−0.3	−0.7	−0.6
Cost of increased exports under free trade[e]	−0.2	1.9	−0.1	0.3	−0.1	−0.1	−0.7
Net cost of protection	9.5	6.2	−0.4	6.2	2.5	1.8	3.7

Source: See text.

[a] Excess costs plus above-normal profits and wages in industries that would not survive under free trade.

[b] Excess costs plus above-normal profits in industries that would become competitive under free trade.

[c] Consumer surplus on the increased consumption of imports.

[d] Reductions in export prices in the event of free trade.

[e] The rise of the cost of exports under free trade under the assumption that export industries are subject to increasing costs.

Taken together, the net cost of protection as a proportion of GNP appears to be the highest in Brazil, followed by Chile and Pakistan and, at some distance, the Philippines. Terms-of-trade effects and the assumed cost increases of export expansion reduce the static and dynamic cost of protecting import substitutes in Chile, while in Pakistan and the Philippines the low share of the protected manufacturing sector in national income mitigates the relative proportion of the cost of protection in GNP. For reasons explained earlier, the cost of protection is relatively low in Mexico and Norway; it is negative in Malaya where the terms-of-trade effects more than offset the inefficiencies of resource allocation due to the application of protective measures.

It should be emphasized, however, that the method applied is subject to various limitations and hence the results obtained are indicative only of general magnitudes. To begin with, the division of industries into two groups involves an oversimplification since it disregards possible intra-industry specialization which would entail the disappearance of some lines of production and the continuation of others within both groups.

Moreover, the arbitrariness of separating industries into two groups affects the division of the measured cost of protection into that imputed to static (allocative) and to dynamic costs, and both of these cost elements include an undetermined amount of above-normal profits and wages. As noted in Chapter 1, above-normal profits may be due to monopolistic or oligopolistic market structures or to interfirm differences in the cost of protection; in turn, the bargaining power of the unions may explain above-normal wages.

Effects on Primary Exports

In examining the effects of the system of protection on the export performance of the countries in question, we consider separately the exports of primary products and manufactures. Regarding the former, it should be noted that incentives (or disincentives) to primary exports and to primary activities in general do not necessarily coincide since primary activities also include foodstuffs produced under protection.

Among the countries under study, the system of protection has entailed a substantial bias against primary exports in Brazil, Chile, Pakistan, and the Philippines. Overvaluation as compared to the hypothetical free trade situation, the protection of inputs used in export industries, and, in some instances, taxes on exports all reduce profitability in the primary export industries of these countries and result in substantial negative net rates of protection. In turn, Malaya's major export products, rubber and tin, are subject to export taxes, but there is practically no discrimination against its minor primary exports. Finally in Mexico and Norway, the extent of discrimination against primary exports is generally small.

During the postwar period, the unfavorable treatment of primary exports appears to have contributed to the decline in the shares of Brazil, Chile, and Pakistan in the world market for their major export commodities, while on the whole there has been little change in the Philippines. Among the remaining three countries, Malaya experienced a decline in its market share for major exports and an increase in minor exports; Mexico has increased its share in the world exports of most of its primary exports; and Norway has shown a decline in market shares due to supply limitations and to the shift toward exporting commodities in processed form.

Brazil's major primary export, coffee, is a rather special case; while African producers rapidly increased plantings, Brazil restricted output to mitigate the decline in prices. But Brazil has also experienced a decline in its market share for cocoa and lumber to which these considerations do not apply; at the same time, increases in its sugar exports are explained by the opening of preferential markets in the United States. Finally, very small increases or even a decline are shown in Brazil's minor agricultural exports, such as bananas, Brazil nuts, tobacco, hides and skins, wool, and processed oils and fats. Nor have the policies applied been conducive to the development of new exports.

Chile has been able to increase its market share in iron ore, but this has been far overshadowed by the decline in its share in the world market for copper. Apart from the overvalued exchange rate, contributing factors were the unfavorable tax treatment of large companies, the fear of further tax increases, and the risk of nationalization. Chile has also experienced a decline in its exports of timber and beans, and discrimination against agriculture has thwarted the development of new agricultural exports, with the exception of wine.

In Pakistan, both the volume and value of major exports declined in absolute terms. And even after adjustment for increases in exports of cotton and jute textiles, Pakistan's share in the world exports of cotton and jute is shown to have fallen to a considerable extent. Nor does the replacement of imports of cotton and jute textiles by domestic production fully compensate for this loss.

The Philippines has made gains in sugar exports under preferential arrangements with the United States; it has increased its share in the declining world exports of abaca and has expanded its timber exports, especially to Korea and Taiwan for transformation into plywood and veneer. By contrast, the share of the Philippines' copra exports in world trade in oilseeds has declined, and this loss has not been fully offset by gains made in coconut oil. At the same time, there has been little change in minor agricultural exports, and among mineral exports, only those of copper ores and concentrates show a substantial increase.

In Malaya, the imposition of export taxes may have contributed to the fall in its share in the world exports of rubber; this decline has been only partly offset by an improvement in Malaya's position in the world tin market. On the other hand, Malaya has experienced substantial increases in the exports of some other primary commodities that are subject to practically no discrimination.

Primary exports enjoy relatively favorable treatment in Mexico where few export taxes are applied and some primary exports receive subsidies. This policy may largely explain the development of a variety of new export commodities to replace lead, copper, and fish where supply limitations or restrictions in Mexico's major market, the United States, have led to a substantial decline in exports. Among new exports, sugar, shellfish, and maize have assumed a major role; substantial increases are also shown in the exports of livestock, meat, dairy products, pulses and, especially, tomatoes.

Finally, supply limitations explain the decline in Norway's market share in fish and fish preparations while the fall in its share in the world exports of wood pulp has been more than offset by increased exports of paper and paper products. More generally, we find a shift in the structure of Norwegian exports from commodities at lower to those at higher levels of fabrication.

It appears, then, that in cases where the system of protection entails a bias against primary exports, this has often led to a decline in the share of the individual countries in the world markets for their traditional export commodities. Although developing countries often emphasize the sluggishness of demand for their exports on the part of the industrial nations, our findings indicate the adverse effects of protection on the supply of these exports. Discrimination against primary exports has also hindered the development of new exports that rarely encounter market limitations.

Effects on Manufactured Exports

The cost-raising effects of the protection of inputs and the overvaluation of the currency as compared to the hypothetical free trade situation also hinder the creation of export industries in the manufacturing sector. These sources of discrimination are the most pronounced in Brazil, Chile, and the Philippines; there is also a considerable bias in favor of import substitution and against exporting in the manufacturing industries of these countries. In the majority of cases, value added in producing for domestic markets is more than double that obtainable in exporting and, in several instances, exporting would even require negative value added.

The unfavorable treatment of exports largely explains that none of the three countries export an appreciable proportion of their manufacturing output. In Brazil, the share of exports in manufacturing output remained below 1 percent during much of the period. This share rose to 1.3 percent in 1967 but nearly one-half of the exports were directed to LAFTA countries under preferential arrangements. In Chile, too, about one-half of the 2.6 percent share of exports in manufacturing output is attributable to preferential exports to LAFTA.

In the Philippines, exports account for 3.6 percent of manufacturing output, but one-half of these exports consists of embroidery and undergarments produced on consignment. Much of the remainder is plywood and veneer that provide a clear case of the sensitivity of exports to changes in the system of protection. Although plywood and veneer exports increased rapidly during the second half of the 1950s after the exchange rates applicable to exports and imports were equalized, they declined in absolute, as well as in relative, terms in the following years when the import rate consistently exceeded the export rate. Exports increased again after the 1962 devaluation, but the 1964 peak was not surpassed in later years when the real value of the export exchange rate was lower. Meanwhile, the Philippines lost ground in competition with Korea and Taiwan which produce plywood and veneer from logs imported from the Philippines itself.

There is less bias against exporting manufactured goods in Mexico where the share of such exports, consisting of a wide variety of products, reached 3 percent of the manufacturing output in 1967. An even smaller bias is shown in Malaya and Norway, both of which have markedly increased their share of exports in manufacturing output during the postwar period. In Malaya this ratio rose from practically nil to nearly 10 percent, while in Norway the increase was from 3 percent in 1950 to 22 percent in 1967. In accordance with the increases in average shares, the share of exports in the increment of manufacturing output was even larger.

Finally, in a variety of manufacturing industries, Pakistan accords by and large equal treatment to production for exports and for domestic use. The introduction of an export-bonus scheme helped Pakistan to achieve a considerable improvement in its export performance during the sixties, with exports accounting for 8 percent of manufacturing output in 1967. However, the expansion of these exports involved a cost in the form of large subsidies and has partly taken the place of the exports of jute and cotton.

Effects of Protection on Economic Growth

High levels of protection may affect economic growth in various ways. Unless protection leads to increases in profits that are in turn reinvested, the static cost of protection due to inefficiencies in resource allocation reduces the amount available for investment. Furthermore, although import substitution in nondurable consumer goods may ensure rapid growth until imports have been replaced, progress becomes increasingly difficult as the country enters the next stage of import substitution. The limitations of domestic markets do not permit the exploitation of large-scale economies and, in the absence of effective competition, there is little incentive for improvements in product quality and in technical methods. Finally, discrimination against exports unfavorably affects economic growth since the slowdown in exports restrains the increase of the country's import capacity.

We have noted above the impact of protection on the export performance of the countries under study. In the following, we will consider the effects of the system of protection on the growth of agriculture and manufacturing. Needless to say, these explanations are of a partial character; to reach more definite conclusions, a more detailed investigation than that attempted here would be necessary.

The virtual lack of discrimination against agriculture has contributed to rapid increases in per capita food production in Mexico and Malaya during the postwar period. By contrast, per capita food production has declined in Chile and Pakistan where discrimination against agriculture is the most pronounced. In the Philippines the stagnation of per capita food production until the mid-sixties gave place to increases resulting from productivity improvements associated with the so-called Green Revolution.

Brazil presents a puzzling case with a steady increase in per capita food production despite the existence of discrimination against the agricultural sector. But in this country the expansion has been largely due to an increase in the area of cultivation rather than to improvements in agricultural productivity. Finally, the relative constancy of agricultural output in Norway is explained by its unfavorable resource endowment and its desire to keep down the cost of protecting agriculture.

We have noted that protection permits a rapid expansion of manufacturing in the first stage of import substitution when imports of nondurable consumer goods are replaced by domestic production. Industries producing nondurable consumer goods and their inputs are the prime candidates for import substitution in developing countries because they employ chiefly unskilled and semi-skilled labor, do not require the application of sophisticated technology, and need few inputs from ancillary industries. In addition, the efficient scale of operations in these industries is relatively low.

The expansion of output in industries producing nondurable consumer goods and their inputs necessarily slows down, however, after imports have been fully replaced, since domestic production cannot continue to grow faster than home demand. At the same time, increasing difficulties are encountered in import substitution in regard to other intermediate products, capital goods, and durable consumer goods that have higher technological and skill requirements, need large-scale production for efficient operations, and require the availability of material, parts, and components from other industries.

In applying protective measures within their limited domestic markets, countries at the second stage of import substitution have built up an industrial structure which entails the use of small-scale and outdated production methods, inadequate specialization, and the manufacturing of products of low quality.[22] The rising cost of import substitution, in turn, necessitates increased efforts for obtaining an additional increment in output. As a result, economic growth tends to slow down unless there is a compensating rise in the share of investments in national income.

At higher stages of import substitution, adverse changes in the balance of payments due to protection also impose a limitation on the rate of economic growth. Apart from unfavorably affecting export performance, discrimination against primary activities often necessitates larger imports of food and raw materials. At the same time, the domestic production of durable goods and intermediate products requires substantial import requirements in the form of materials, parts, components, and accessories as well as machinery.

These considerations help to explain the pattern of industrial growth in the countries under study. In the postwar period, both the Philippines and Pakistan attained a rapid expansion of manufacturing output from a low base behind high protective barriers. However, in the Philippines where the first stage of import substitution was completed in the mid-fifties, the rate of increase of manufacturing subsequently declined to a considerable extent while incremental capital-output ratios more than doubled.

The example of the other countries of the group also indicates that the expansion of manufacturing output encounters increasing difficulties at the second stage of import substitution. Thus, although the manufacturing sector is strongly favored in Chile, the country's small national market has not permitted a rapid increase of output after World War II when the first stage of

---

[22] This is what Felix called the "premature widening" of the structure of production, i.e., an expansion of a large number of relatively small-scale activities rather than concentration on a few (David Felix, "Monetarists, Structuralists, and Import-Substituting Industrialization: A Critical Appraisal," in *Inflation and Growth in Latin America*, ed. W. Baer and I. Kerstenetzky [Homewood, Ill.: Richard D. Irwin, Inc., 1964], pp. 370–401).

import substitution had already been completed. This may largely explain that on a per capita basis the postwar growth of manufacturing was slower in Chile than in any of the countries studied.

Brazil, too, had completed the first stage of import substitution prior to the period under consideration. Its large domestic market, however, provided possibilities for the continued expansion of manufacturing during the fifties, mostly in industries producing intermediate products, capital goods, and durable consumer goods. But, subsequently, industrial expansion slowed down also in this country and incremental capital-output ratios rose commensurately.

By contrast, the growth of manufacturing output has accelerated in Mexico where levels of protection are considerably lower than in Brazil or in Chile. The acceleration of industrial growth has been even greater in Malaya where there is practically no discrimination against the manufacturing sector. Finally, increased outward orientation and participation in the European Free Trade Association have importantly contributed to the observed increases in the rate of growth of manufacturing output in Norway. During the sixties, the per capita rate of growth of Norwegian manufacturing was exceeded only in Malaya and Pakistan.

Summary

In this chapter we have considered the effects of the system of protection on resource allocation and economic growth. It appears that in countries with high protection a considerable burden has been imposed on the national economy in the form of static (allocative) inefficiencies. Protection has further limited the scope of introduction of large-scale production methods and provided few inducements for improvements in productivity. The cost of the resulting inefficiencies as a percentage of the gross domestic product is especially large in Brazil, Chile, and Pakistan.

High protection has also contributed to a slowdown in the production and exports of primary commodities and has hindered the expansion of the exports of manufactured goods. While import substitution in nondurable consumer goods and their inputs has permitted rapid economic growth in countries at the first stage of import substitution, growth has slowed down in countries that embarked on the production of more sophisticated commodities.

By contrast, agricultural production has grown rapidly in countries with relatively low levels of protection and these countries have also experienced improvements in their export performance. They have increased their market share in traditional exports, developed new primary exports, and been successful in expanding the exports of manufactured products. Success in exporting, in turn, has contributed to economic growth.

CHAPTER 5

GUIDELINES FOR INDUSTRIAL PROTECTION POLICY

Bela Balassa

Protection and Industrialization

In this volume we have examined the experiences of seven countries with protection in the postwar period. Since these countries cover a wide spectrum in terms of their level of development, market size, and the protective measures applied, our findings have applicability to other developing countries as well. In the following, we will utilize the findings to formulate guidelines for a policy of protection in developing countries. In so doing, we will also draw on the experiences of countries not covered in this volume[1] and will utilize the conclusions derived from the theory of international trade.[2]

Although we will discuss the desirability of using direct measures in lieu of protection in certain situations, we will exclude from our purview such instruments of industrial policy as taxes, credit, minimum wages, public planning, and incentives to foreign investment. This omission can be rationalized on the grounds that protective measures play a central role in the industrial policy of

---

[1] Cf. Bela Balassa, "Growth Strategies in Semi-Industrial Countries," *Quarterly Journal of Economics*, February 1970, pp. 24–47 and "Industrial Policies in Taiwan and Korea," *Weltwirtschaftliches Archiv*, band 105, heft 1 (1971).

[2] For a discussion of the theory of protection as it applies to developing countries, see Jagdish Bhagwati, *The Theory and Practice of Commercial Policies: Departures from Unified Exchange Rates*, Special Papers in International Economics No. 8, International Finance Section, Department of Economics, Princeton University, January 1968.

developing countries. Nevertheless, other policy instruments often modify the effects of protection, and hence their study is of considerable importance. The joint effects of protection and other policy instruments in resource allocation will be examined in the framework of the research project "Development Strategies in Semi-Industrial Countries," directed by the present author and sponsored by the World Bank.

It should be emphasized that policy formulation for individual countries would have to depend greatly on the particular circumstances of the situation. In offering policy advice, one has to take account of such characteristics of individual countries as the size of domestic markets, geographical location, preferential access to foreign markets, natural resource endowment, prospects for traditional exports, and the availability of human and physical capital. Consideration must also be given to political and social conditions in the country in question, and to the interactions of political, social, and economic factors. Finally, for countries which have already established some industries, the existing industrial structure limits the available policy choices.

A program for industrialization is conditioned first of all by the size of the country's domestic market. Thus, the relatively large home market of Brazil or India creates opportunities for the establishment of firms of efficient size in some industries, while there are few such possibilities in most African countries or in the smaller Latin American republics. On the other hand, a small country may recognize the disadvantages of import substitution sooner than a medium-sized nation, and accordingly embark on an export-oriented industrial development program. More generally, developing countries form a continuum with respect to the size of domestic markets, so that there is a need for a spectrum of policies applicable to countries of different sizes, with varying emphasis on import substitution and exports.

Geographical location affects the possibilities for exporting manufactures as well as the chances for regional integration. Nearby markets provide an advantage to the countries of Southern Europe, although Japan and, more recently, Korea and China (Taiwan) have shown that geographical distance is not an obstacle to expanding the exports of manufactured goods. In turn, regional integration can be regarded as a way of increasing the size of the domestic market; in this respect Colombia is better situated than, for example, Korea.

Preferential access to foreign markets is a related consideration. A policy of industrial development for Portugal, for instance, would have to be based on the availability of a large market in the European Free Trade Association where Portuguese exports are not subject to duty. In general, the desirability of alternative policies will depend on the extent of such preferences and the probability of their continuation. In formulating policies, one also has to be concerned with the optimal exploitation of the advantages offered by existing preferential arrangements and the possible scope of obtaining preferential access to the markets of developed nations.

A favorable natural resource endowment and good prospects for traditional exports may make the process of industrialization less painful by lessening the need for stringent measures to limit the imports of manufactured goods. But rapidly rising foreign exchange earnings can also lead to wasteful spending on prestige projects. On the other hand, as the example of Hong Kong and Singapore indicates, the lack of natural resources may mean that a country by necessity avoids costly mistakes in import substitution. Finally, a high educational level of the labor force may create the preconditions for rapid industrialization, as in Korea and Taiwan.

Notwithstanding the importance of the particular circumstances which have to be considered in individual cases, one may provide general guidelines for industrial protection policy in the developing countries. But such guidelines cannot be confined to the manufacturing sector, since the policies followed in this sector necessarily affect the other sectors of the national economy and its growth performance. In other words, industrial protection policy has to be regarded as an essential element of an overall development strategy.

Tariffs vs. Quantitative Restrictions

In the formulation of policies of protection for developing countries, the choice between price and nonprice measures of protection first needs to be considered. Absolute prohibitions to import, import quotas, and licensing have been used by a number of developing countries. Such quantitative restrictions have usually been first applied during a balance-of-payments crisis but have often been continued thereafter. And while they may have originally been imposed on only a few commodities, they were later extended to cover most of all imports.

It has often been said that quantitative restrictions permit rapid action on the part of the government and provide an easy way of translating economic priorities into concrete decisions. But while rapid action may be called for when sudden changes occur in the balance-of-payments situation, such considerations cannot provide a basis for long-term policy-making. Moreover, although it may appear promising to link import policy directly to planning, in practice the limitations of planning procedures and the administrative problems of applying quantitative restrictions create considerable difficulties in the decision-making process.

In fact, the administration of a system of import licensing imposes a great burden on the government apparatus and contributes to the growth of bureaucracy. It also introduces arbitrariness into decision-making since one can hardly devise general rules applicable to each case. At the same time, the system of case-by-case decisions, in which responsibility ultimately rests with petty bureaucrats, necessarily creates inequities as well as uncertainty for the would-be quota recipients.

Firms—both public and private—have to make decisions under uncertainty regarding quota allocations, and expend considerable effort on making applications for licenses to import equipment, spare parts, and materials. Such an effort, though profitable for the individual firm, involves a cost to national economy. Also, since licenses have a scarcity value, their recipients will get the difference between the domestic price of the product and the import price that would accrue to the government if tariffs were used.

The profit obtainable from licenses not only induces a diversion of productive effort but also provides incentives for bribery that may be looked upon as a "sharing" in this profit. Moreover, vested interests are created to perpetuate the system of quantitative restrictions. As quota recipients try to avoid sharing the spoils with new entrants, they resist changes in the system of protection. Finally, the application of quantitative restrictions makes the policy-maker's task of evaluating the effects of these restrictions on the national economy more difficult. In the absence of detailed price comparisons, it is impossible to appraise the protective effects of the quotas; ultimately, policy formulation will suffer for lack of appropriate criteria to evaluate possible alternatives.

By contrast, the effects of tariffs on domestic prices can be ascertained relatively easily; in addition, tariffs permit the replacement of case-by-case decision-making by automatic rules, reduce uncertainty for the producer and the user, and contribute to government revenue. These considerations explain why several Latin American countries have shifted from quantitative restrictions to tariffs; such changes are also under way in socialist countries such as Czechoslovakia and Hungary. It would appear desirable for other developing countries using quantitative restrictions to replace them increasingly by tariffs.

Traditional vs. Nontraditional Primary Products

Before turning to the question of relative incentives to manufacturing and primary activities, we should consider the need for differential incentives within the primary sector. Such a need arises because of differences in the potential contribution of various primary products to the growth of the national economy. Thus, an expansion of traditional exports would tend to engender a fall in export prices while nontraditional primary exports could be generally increased without encountering market limitations.

Differential incentives to the two groups of primary products could be provided by applying the basic exchange rate to nontraditional primary products while converting earnings from traditional exports at less favorable exchange rates or—what amounts to the same—imposing an export tax on them. Export tax rates on individual commodities should be set by allowing for the elasticity of world demand for the commodity in question, the country's share in the world market, and the possible reactions on the part of foreign competitors.

An extreme case is that of coffee where producing countries should set the export tax (differential exchange rate) at a level calculated to ensure that domestic supply would equal their quota allocations under the International Coffee Agreement. In this way, profits due to the price-raising effects of quotas in international markets would accrue to the government, and resources would be transferred to other activities where higher returns can be obtained. For most commodities, however, the determination of the optimum export tax is subject to uncertainty because of the lack of exact information on foreign demand and supply response.

The suggested policy measures would take account of market limitations for traditional exports, without discouraging either their production for domestic use or the development of new primary exports. The question remains, however, whether manufacturing industries should be favored over non-traditional primary production, and if so, to what extent, and by the use of what measures. A further question is whether the incentives provided should be uniform within the manufacturing sector or should vary from one industry to another.

The Infant Industry Argument

All economic arguments for the preferential treatment of manufacturing find their origin in assumed differences between social and private profitability. On the firm level, such differences may arise if the lack of credit facilities, the overestimation of the risks involved, or simply the desire to exclude the possibility of bankruptcy provide disincentives for investment, although eventual cost reductions through the learning process or through increases in the scale of operations would make the investment socially desirable. Other instances are when some of the benefits of the pioneering firm's activities are enjoyed by others who utilize the know-how generated by the firm or hire away skilled labor and technicians it has trained.

These "infant industry" arguments provide a rationale for the application of special incentives to manufacturing on a temporary basis. But, as the industry reaches maturity, the need for preferential treatment disappears. At the same time, to ensure that the industry will indeed "grow up," it appears desirable to provide incentives on a declining scale set in advance so that producers can plan in the full knowledge of future changes in the system of incentives.

It has often been said that infant industry arguments justify using production subsidies rather than tariffs since the latter limit the size of the domestic market by raising the price of the commodity. But while tariffs contribute to government revenue, production subsidies represent a claim on this revenue. Budgetary reasons, then, may explain why developing countries use tariffs in preference to production subsidies. In fact, tariffs often account for a large part of government revenue in these countries, and their replacement by other forms of taxation may encounter practical difficulties.

Employment Considerations and Provision for Overhead Facilities

The arguments for the use of subsidies in preference to tariffs gain in force when a particular distortion or cost disability needs to be corrected. This will be so if the cost of industrial labor to manufacturing enterprises exceeds its social cost in the form of the output foregone in primary activities from which labor is drawn. In some overpopulated countries, such a situation may exist on family-type farms where the contribution of the marginal worker is said to be less than his consumption. There is also the possibility that unemployment will persist at the existing wage rate which cannot be reduced lest it decline below a socially acceptable minimum. Mining industries, for example, utilize relatively little labor, and countries relying on mineral exports may be unable to fully employ their labor force without providing special incentives for labor use.

In the described cases, the appropriate measure would be to subsidize the use of labor rather than to impose tariffs. Tariffs encourage the use of labor as well as that of capital in protected industries and they favor the use of labor in such industries over other sectors of the economy. Moreover, tariffs may provide incentives for the development of industries that would not be profitable under free trade even if wages were nil. In such instances, there is a trade-off between employment and growth since resources are channeled into industries with relatively high costs. Some of these industries may also have limited possibilities for improving productivity; this situation is said to exist in the Indian cottage industry which receives considerable incentives. Finally, while employment-creating measures tend to improve the distribution of income, they may also adversely affect savings and hence the prospects for future growth. The choice between employment and growth, then, becomes a choice between present and future employment.

Subsidizing the use of labor may take the form of taxing output and rebating the tax on the basis of the number of employees. This method would encourage the expansion of labor-intensive industries and would also provide incentives for employing labor-intensive production methods in individual industries. At the same time, in an unemployment situation, it is hardly likely that such subsidies, instead of promoting employment, would be absorbed by higher wages.

Particular disabilities or handicaps of manufacturing industries owing to inadequate overhead facilities can also be best corrected by specific action rather than by protection. These cost disabilities may arise because private profitability considerations may not induce the establishment of service installations subject to economies of scale. The appropriate measures would then be for the government to build roads and ports, and to make electricity and water available at a reasonable cost. However, the provision of such facilities should not be restricted to manufacturing. Roads and electricity are needed for agricultural activities, just as an increase in the educational level of the labor force would contribute to the development of industry and the modernization of agriculture.

Further Arguments for the Preferential Treatment of Manufacturing

The question remains if, apart from temporary protection for an infant industry and the correction of a particular cost disability, manufacturing should receive preferential treatment. In support of such treatment, it has been adduced that productivity tends to rise more rapidly in manufacturing than in primary production and that the expansion of manufacturing industries provides indirect benefits by inducing investments in other branches of industry and improving the quality of the labor force. The first claim holds true if we compare manufacturing with agricultural activities that employ traditional techniques although modern advances in agriculture offer possibilities for improvements in productivity. Furthermore, linkages among industries often favor the establishment of related branches of manufacturing, but one should not condone on this basis the establishment of inefficient industries that supply inputs to other industries at a high cost. There is finally some merit to the argument that manufacturing contributes to improvements in the quality of the labor force to a greater extent than does even modern agriculture.

From the point of view of long-term policy-making, further consideration should be given to possible future changes in the supply and demand of primary products. In some developing countries, either the supply of primary commodities or foreign demand for them would eventually prove to be a limiting factor for the country's economic growth. In such a situation, the preferential treatment of the manufacturing sector, where supply and demand limitations are negligible, would be warranted not only vis-à-vis traditional primary commodities but also in comparison to the primary sector as a whole.

These considerations indicate the difficulties encountered in appraising the claims made for the superiority of manufacturing over primary production; the difficulties are compounded if we attempt to quantify these alleged advantages. Nevertheless, one may argue that manufacturing offers *some* advantages over primary production in the form of labor training and in encouraging the expansion of related industries that do not enter into the profit calculations of the firm but benefit the national economy. Moreover, manufacturing will improve the growth potential of the economy whenever supply or demand limitations would eventually impinge on primary activities.

Import Substitution and Exports of Manufactured Goods

There is some presumption, then, in favor of using direct and indirect measures to promote manufacturing industry in developing countries. The word "promote" is used advisedly since it includes protection of production for domestic markets (import substitution) as well as assistance to firms exporting manufactures. This point needs emphasis because in most developing countries protection is provided for import substitution in the form of tariffs or quotas whereas subsidies are rarely granted to exports.

Yet exports of manufactured goods can play an important role in industrial development by increasing foreign exchange earnings and enabling firms to use large-scale production methods. Instead of production on a small scale exclusively for domestic markets, the expansion of exports makes possible specialization according to comparative advantage, reduction of product variety in individual firms, and participation in the international division of the production process by the production of parts and components for assembly abroad. Finally, familiarity with foreign markets and competition abroad will provide incentives for technological change and product improvement.

Discrimination against the exports of manufactured goods thus entails an economic loss and hinders the growth of the developing economies. To remedy this situation, equal incentives would need to be provided to production for domestic and for foreign markets. This can be accomplished by granting a subsidy to the exports of manufactured goods at a rate equal to the tariff applied to the same commodity or by using differential exchange rates for the manufacturing sector. Given the cost and the uncertainties of entering foreign markets, it might even be desirable to provide additional incentives to exports of manufactured goods on a temporary basis.

Promotion of Manufacturing Activities

While the equal treatment of import substitution and exporting is desirable for each manufactured product, the question remains what are "reasonable" rates of tariffs and subsidies and whether all manufactured goods should receive equal treatment. Assuming that particular measures are used to correct special disabilities and that employment objectives are served by a direct or indirect subsidy to the use of labor, as a first approximation, one may suggest providing effective protection at equal rates to all manufacturing activities that have passed the infant industry stage. In this way, one would apply the "market principle" in the sense that firms would be established that are profitable under such conditions and existing firms would have to improve their operations, change their product composition, or disappear. At the same time, nonessential imports could be restricted by levying excise taxes that also apply to domestic production.

The choice of a "reasonable" rate of tariffs and subsidies for mature industries in the developing countries will depend on the particular circumstances of the situation and on the range of other policy measures available to a particular country. It may be suggested, however, that since most developing countries have small domestic markets, they should aim at eventually reducing the net effective protection of manufacturing to levels observed in such countries as Denmark and Norway, i.e., to approximately 10 percent.

If, as a first approximation, we wish to set identical effective rates of protection for the mature industries of the developing countries, a method needs to be devised for attaining such a result. It will be recalled that effective and nominal rates are identical if tariffs and export subsidies are applied to all inputs and outputs at equal rates. But, in many developing countries, raw materials are available at world market prices either because the country exports them or because they are not dutiable. This practice corresponds to that followed in developed nations and it should be maintained in order to avoid penalizing the relatively simple transformation of raw materials. The equalization of effective rates of protection would then require slight increases in tariffs according to the stage of fabrication.

Let us take, for example, the case where material inputs account for 60 percent of the world market price of products at every stage of processing. A 5 percent tariff on a product in the first stage would then provide 12.5 percent effective protection; the same effective protection could be ensured at the second stage by imposing a tariff of 8 percent; and at the third and fourth stages by tariffs of 10 and 11 percent, respectively. Eventually, we would get a tariff rate of 12.5 percent, i.e., the same as the effective rate.

Exceptions to the proposed equality of effective rates may be made if there is evidence that profitability on the firm level greatly understates (or overstates) the contribution of a particular industry to the national economy. But such exceptions should apply to entire industries rather than to individual firms and only in cases which are well-documented so as to avoid a "slippage" in protection. In other words, the burden of proof should be on those who request favorable treatment. This conclusion also pertains to industries that claim injury from dumping by foreign suppliers.

In view of our earlier discussion, additional protection would need to be provided to infant industries on a temporary basis. But standard rates of protection should also be applied to infant industries and one should avoid "tailor-made" tariffs. Exceptions to this rule could be made only if evidence is provided that the industry in question promises greater than average cost reductions through the learning process of scale economies.

Again, it is difficult to judge how much protection could be justified on infant industry grounds since there is little empirical evidence on the learning process in individual firms. It does not appear likely, however, that—exceptional cases aside a rate of effective protection more than double that for mature industries could be warranted.[3] Moreover, the additional protection of infant industries should be set on a declining scale so that its eventual disappearance provides incentives for improvements.

The "Ideal" System of Protection

The described scheme may be implemented by using a basic exchange rate for nontraditional primary products, export taxes on traditional primary exports, and a combination of tariffs and subsidies on manufactured goods. The same result could be achieved by applying differential exchange rates for the three groups of commodities, with further adjustments made for differences in the elasticity of foreign demand among traditional primary exports, and allowing for the temporary protection of infant industries. In other words, as long as domestic prices are the same, it is immaterial to the entrepreneur if prices have been raised (or lowered) through the application of tariffs and export subsidies (taxes) or through higher (or lower) exchange rates on the product in question. Accordingly, the choice between the two alternatives, or a combination thereof, would have to be determined on the basis of considerations of political and administrative feasibility with further account taken of reactions by foreign countries and the implications of the choice of exchange rates for the service account and capital movement.

The application of these policy recommendations assumes that the exchange rate (or rates) would be set so as to ensure balance-of-payments equilibrium. In the event of a continuing balance-of-payments deficit, however, imported goods as well as exports would be undervalued, thereby providing an incentive to import and a disincentive to export. The deficit may be financed by foreign aid or by the inflow of foreign capital; in deciding on policy changes, one should take account of possible changes in these flows.

Balance-of-payments equilibrium should be maintained continuously by avoiding the inflation-devaluation cycle which results if continuing inflation is accompanied by periodic devaluations. The existence of such an inflation-

---

[3] According to an OECD study, economies of scale and external economies can hardly justify effective protection of infant industries exceeding 20 percent even if direct subsidies to labor use are not provided. This figure declines to 10 percent if labor use is subsidized. Cf. Ian Little, Tibor Scitovsky, and Maurice Scott, *Industry and Trade in Some Developing Countries* (London: The Oxford University Press, 1970), pp. 158–59.

devaluation cycle, observed in several Latin American countries, provides disincentives to exports since the domestic currency equivalent of foreign exchange receipts is subject to uncertainty, and profits or losses are made depending on the phase of the cycle in which the country finds itself. To remedy this situation, exchange rates should be changed *pari passu* with domestic inflation in order to keep the real exchange rate—the ratio of an index of nominal exchange rates to the domestic price index—constant. This is, in fact, being done in Brazil, Chile, and Colombia where devaluation takes place every two or four weeks. But, in order to avoid a devaluation-cost-price spiral, the application of these measures should be accompanied by disinflationary policies.

Summary

In this chapter we have put forward guidelines for a policy of protection in developing countries. Compared with the policies followed today by most of these countries, the application of the suggested policy guidelines would entail providing more favorable treatment to nontraditional primary commodities, reducing the protection of manufactured products, and equalizing incentives in individual industries to produce for domestic and for export markets.

The policy guidelines call for providing differential incentives to traditional and nontraditional primary products, depending chiefly on their export prospects. It is further suggested that the manufacturing sector should receive preferential treatment, albeit to a limited extent. Apart from correcting particular cost disabilities, however, equal incentives should be provided to the individual branches of manufacturing, with additional protection to infant industries on a temporary basis. Finally, the application of the guidelines would necessitate maintaining the real value of foreign exchange constant.

For countries that have already embarked on industrialization behind high protective barriers, the application of the guidelines would necessitate revamping the structure of protection. Needless to say, such a transformation could not be undertaken instantaneously but would require a transitional period, the length of which depends on the particular circumstances of the country in question. There would also be differences in the mode of application of these guidelines, again depending on political and institutional factors. Finally, the relative importance of direct measures and the suggested tariff-subsidy scheme may differ among countries at different levels of industrialization.

PART II

CHAPTER 6

THE STRUCTURE OF PROTECTION IN BRAZIL

Joel Bergsman and Pedro S. Malan

Economic Growth and International Trade[1]

Brazil is a large country, rich in natural resources and, as a whole, not overpopulated. In area it is larger than the continental United States excluding Alaska, yet its population is over 80 million as compared to 200 million in the U.S. Although arable land is abundant, much of it lies fallow; moreover, a large portion of the cultivated area is used in ways which result in very low productivity per acre.

At the time this chapter was written, Joel Bergsman was with the University of California, Berkeley, and Pedro Malan with the Instituto de Pesquisa Economico-Social Aplicada, Rio de Janeiro; Bergsman has since joined The Urban Institute in Washington. The authors wish to acknowledge the helpful suggestions of Earl Rolph and Tibor Scitovsky, as well as those of their colleagues on this project. They also wish to express appreciation for help from Gabriel Ferreira, Jack Heller, Joaquim Ferreira Mangia, Otto Ferreira Neves, Jose Sampaio Portela Nunes, and Jose Maria Vilar de Queiroz. Credit for assistance with the tremendous amount of calculations goes to Regis Bonelli, Marcos de Carvalho, and Dag Ehrenpreis.
    [1] General sources on economic development in Brazil are Werner Baer, *Industrialization & Economic Development in Brazil* (Homewood, Ill.: Richard D. Irwin, Inc., 1965) and Celso Furtado, *The Economic Growth of Brazil: A Survey from Colonial to Modern Times*, trans. Ricardo W. DeAguiar and Eric C. Drysdale (Berkeley and Los Angeles: University of California Press, 1963). On import substitution see United Nations Economic Commission for Latin America, "The Growth and Decline of Import Substitution in Brazil," *Economic Bulletin for Latin America*, March 1964, pp. 1–59. Much useful data on prices, production, and trade are available in the monthly review *Conjuntura Econômica*, published by the Fundacao Getulio Vargas, Rio de Janeiro.

Most commonly-used metallic ores are plentiful and economically exploitable in Brazil, especially iron and manganese. Important exceptions are copper and tin, although large copper deposits have recently been discovered. Some petroleum has also been found; nevertheless, about two-thirds of consumption is imported. Only a little coal is present and it is of poor quality, i.e., not economically suited for coking for the steel industry. Hydroelectric resources that can be utilized economically are, however, plentiful.

According to official estimates, converted at exchange rates used by the U.N., per capita income was about $280 in 1967, with substantial differences shown between the two major centers of population. The Northeast, with about one-fourth of the people, has a backward social and economic structure, very little industry, and a per capita income below $100. The Center-South, with most of the remaining population, has a per capita income over $300. Its agricultural system is much more efficient than that of the Northeast. In addition, virtually all Brazilian manufacturing is located in the Center-South; centered around Sao Paulo, Belo Horizonte, and Rio de Janeiro, it is as extensive, modern, and diversified as any in the less-developed world.

Until World War I, Brazil's economy was dominated by the production and export of a few primary products; brazilwood was first, followed in approximate order by sugar, gold, diamonds, rubber, cotton, cocoa, and coffee. In providing for part of the domestic needs in food products, construction materials, and textiles, with relatively low levels of protection, the development of manufacturing industries took the form of "natural" import substitution. The interruption of supplies during the two world wars contributed to the further expansion of the manufacturing sector. Industrialization was also promoted by increasing protection and other forms of state support, although these measures assumed primary importance only after World War II. Other contributing factors were the widening of the domestic market and the availability of mineral resources. As a result of these influences, by the end of World War II, manufacturing accounted for about one-fifth of the gross domestic product in Brazil.

The rapid expansion of manufacturing continued until the early sixties, when the completion of import substitution in various industries and the adverse effects of rapid inflation contributed to a decline in the rate of growth of manufacturing from 9–10 to 3–4 percent a year. As a result, while agricultural production continued to increase at an average annual rate of about 4.5 percent, the annual rate of increase of the gross domestic product declined from nearly 6 percent during the 1950s to 4 percent after 1960 (see Table 2.2). Official data also show some decline in the share of investments in GDP and an increase in the marginal capital-output ratio from 3.0 in 1950–60 to 3.6 in the next seven years (see Table 2.4). Note, however, that the investment data particularly are subject to errors of measurement.

Brazilian national income data show manufacturing, together with mining and quarrying, construction, and electricity, gas, and water. The combined share of these sectors in the net domestic product increased from 24 percent in 1950 to 27 percent in 1965 while that of agriculture increased from 28 to 29 percent. Thus, the former group of industries gained at the expense of agriculture whose share in commodity production declined from 55 to 53 percent (see Table 2.3). These proportions would change further if comparisons were made on a gross value added basis, since the difference between gross and net figures is much smaller in agriculture than in manufacturing. The share of manufacturing is about 25 percent of GDP and 45 percent of gross value added in commodity production. But these estimates should be treated with caution, since the basic data are not on a consistent basis.

Import substitution has been crucial in Brazilian industrialization. It has been both wide and deep: virtually all final goods are now produced in Brazil, in addition to most processed inputs and components. Industrial growth was so rapid and diversified that the absolute value of imports of manufactured goods remained roughly constant though incomes grew rapidly. In 1964 only 4 percent of the domestic consumption of manufactured goods was provided by imports, and these were largely restricted to investment goods and some chemicals. The postwar Brazilian data do not show the pattern of rising imports of semi-processed products and components which is typical of countries in the early stages of industrialization.

Table 6.1 illustrates the diverse and broad nature of industrial growth in Brazil, while Table 6.2 shows the evolution of import substitution in manufacturing. Immediately before World War II, Brazilian manufacturing was heavily concentrated in food products and textiles, which accounted for one-half of the output as late as 1949. The production of metals and metal products, including machinery, started to grow rapidly during the war years; after the war, the chemical industry also expanded. By 1964, the share of metals and metal products in manufacturing output reached 31 percent, and that of chemicals 17 percent, while the share of food products and textiles, taken together, fell to 36 percent of the total.

The transformation of the industrial structure should be examined in conjunction with the import substitution process which gave its main impulse and determined its evolution. In the early postwar period, there were already few imports of nondurable consumer goods. In the first half of the fifties, import substitution was concentrated on consumer durables, with the share of imports declining from three-fifths to one-tenth of total supply. (Since exports of manufactured goods are negligible, total supply can be considered to equal domestic consumption.)

As imports of consumer goods were almost completely eliminated, the emphasis shifted to producer goods. In the second half of the fifties, domestic production, as well as imports of capital goods, increased at a rapid rate. Domestic production of intermediate products also grew rapidly, thereby permit-

TABLE 6.1: Evolution of the Structure of Brazilian Manufacturing, 1939–64

Industry group	Value added (millions of U.S. dollars)				Percentage distribution				Average annual growth rates (percent)			
	1939	1949	1959	1964	1939	1949	1959	1964	'39–'49	'49–'59	'59–'64	'39–'64
Food, beverages, and tobacco	345	612	1,118	1,859	30	27	21	22	5.9	6.2	10.6	7.0
Textiles, clothing, and footwear	307	537	815	1,164	27	23	16	14	5.7	4.3	7.4	5.5
Wood, paper, and products	79	200	456	519	6	8	8	6	9.8	8.6	2.6	7.8
Leather and rubber products	26	75	181	239	3	3	3	3	11.2	9.2	5.8	9.3
Chemicals	124	230	723	1,386	11	10	14	17	5.6	12.2	13.8	10.2
Nonmetallic mineral products	61	165	356	355	5	7	7	4	10.5	8.0	0.0	7.3
Metals and metal products	150	349	1,437	2,547	13	16	27	31	8.8	15.2	12.0	12.0
Others	54	129	247	288	5	6	4	3	9.1	6.8	3.0	6.9
Total manufacturing	1,146	2,297	5,333	8,357	100	100	100	100	7.2	8.5	9.4	8.3

Source: Industrial Censuses for 1939, 1949, and 1959; for 1964, Instituto Brasileiro de Geografia e Estatística (IBGE), Industrias de Transformacao Dados Gerais—1963/64, Rio de Janeiro, April 1966. Adjustments for comparability made by the authors.

TABLE 6.2:   Structure of Imports and Domestic Production of Manufactured Products, by Use, 1949–64[a]

| Year | Consumer goods | | Producer goods | | All manufactured products |
	Durables	Nondurables	Intermediate	Capital	
		Imports (billion cruzeiros in 1955 prices)			
1949	8.9	5.4	18.2	15.8	48.3
1955	2.1	4.5	22.6	13.7	42.9
1959	2.9	2.8	21.2	29.2	56.1
1964	1.5	3.9	18.6	8.7	32.7
		Domestic production (billion cruzeiros in 1955 prices)			
1949	4.9	140.0	52.1	9.0	206.0
1955	19.0	200.9	104.0	18.0	341.9
1959	43.1	258.0	159.6	59.5	520.2
1964	93.8	319.5	261.2	79.7	754.2
		Imports as percentages of total supply			
1949	64.5	3.7	25.9	63.7	19.0
1955	10.0	2.2	17.9	43.2	11.1
1959	6.3	1.1	11.7	32.9	9.7
1964	1.6	1.2	6.6	9.8	4.2

Source: Imports from IBGE, *Números Indices Annuais dos Precos edas Quantidades no Comércio Exterior e de Cabotagem*, Rio de Janeiro, 1965. Gross value of industrial production from Industrial Census (*Registro Industrial*) and Indices of Physical Production in *Conjuntura Econômica*. Imports of 1949 projected backward using data in United Nations Economic Commission for Latin America, "The Growth and Decline of Import Substitution in Brazil," *Economic Bulletin for Latin America*, March 1964, pp. 1–59.

[a] Data are in constant prices.

ting imports to remain at constant levels in the face of rapidly rising demand. Between 1959 and 1964, the imports of both capital goods and intermediate products decreased in absolute terms. Imports of manufactured goods as a whole fell from 19 percent of the total supply of these goods in 1949 to 10 percent in 1959 and to 4 percent in 1964. Imports of capital goods were, however, abnormally low in 1964. The average share of imports in the total supply of capital goods during the mid-sixties was about 30 percent, raising the share of imports in the total supply of manufactured goods above 6 percent.

These changes brought about a decline in the value of imports as a proportion of the gross national product, as well as the transformation of the structure of imports. The value of total imports, which was 16 percent of GDP in 1947–49, decreased to 10 percent in 1948–50 and to 8 percent in 1960–62. The share of processed products in total imports fell from 87 percent in 1953 to 58 percent in 1965; a different source shows the share of processed products falling from 90 percent in 1948–50 to 70 percent in 1959–61.[2] Within the total,

[2] Authors' calculation from Instituto Brasileiro de Geografía e Estatística (IBGE), *Números Indices Annuais dos Precos edas Quantidades no Comércio Exterior e de Cabotagem*, Rio de Janeiro, 1965, and ECLA, "The Growth and Decline of Import Substitution in Brazil." The two series overlap in part; the former starts in 1953 while the latter ends in 1961.

the imports of chemical goods increased while, apart from the high import levels of 1967, the share of capital goods declined. Within the primary product category, including some simply processed goods, the share of industrial materials rose and that of food and fuel imports fell (see Table 2.8). Among foodstuffs, wheat is most important; its share in total imports was about 12 percent in the early sixties.

Primary commodities continue to dominate Brazil's exports. In 1967, manufactured goods provided less than 10 percent of total exports, and accounted for 3 percent of the output of manufactured goods other than food, beverages, and tobacco. Among primary products, the share of coffee declined from 64 percent in 1950 to 43 percent in 1967 and that of cocoa fell from 6 to 4 percent. By contrast, large increases were shown in exports of iron ore and sugar, both of which were negligible in 1950 but reached, respectively, 6 and 5 percent of the total in 1965. During this period, however, the value of all exports increased by only 20 percent (Table 6.3).

Decreases in export prices, as well as a deterioration in Brazil's competitive position, have contributed to these results. As the data of Table 2.6 indicate, despite the approximate 50 percent increase in the world demand for coffee and cocoa between 1950–53 and 1963–66, Brazilian exports of these commodities remained unchanged in volume terms and the decline in prices led to a fall in export values. Increases in Brazil's market share in iron ore, cotton, and sugar were not sufficient to offset the deterioration of its competitive position in coffee and cocoa. Thus, the exports of the six major export commodities, measured in constant prices, rose only one-fifth while world demand increased by more than one-half. With the prices of these commodities falling by one-third, the value of Brazil's major export products declined 13 percent during the period under consideration. This decline was barely offset by a near-doubling of minor exports which did not keep pace with the rise of world exports.

TABLE 6.3:   Principal Exports of Brazil, 1950–67

(Percent of total exports)

Commodity	1950	1955	1960	1965	1967
Coffee, raw (SITC 071.1)	63.8	59.3	56.2	44.3	42.6
Iron ore (281)	0.5	2.1	4.2	6.5	6.2
Cotton, raw (263.1)	7.8	9.2	3.6	6.0	5.5
Sugar (061.1)	0.3	3.3	4.6	3.6	4.9
Lumber, conifer (243.2)	2.4	4.1	3.4	3.3	3.1
Cocoa beans (072.1)	5.8	6.4	5.5	1.7	3.6
Total principal exports	80.6	84.4	77.5	65.4	65.9
Total exports ($ million)	1,355.5	1,423.3	1,268.8	1,595.5	1,654.0

Source: U.N., *Yearbook of International Trade Statistics.*

The System of Protection

Import Policy

The exchange rate of 18.5 cruzeiros per U.S. dollar, which had been in force throughout World War II, remained unchanged until 1953, although prices in Brazil rose 144 percent between 1945 and 1953.[3] This rate had already overvalued the cruzeiro in 1945, since prices had risen about 80 percent more in Brazil than in the United States during the war while the exchange rate remained practically the same.

Two reasons are commonly given to explain the overvaluation that followed World War II. First, restrictions on imports during the war had created a large demand for both producer and consumer goods, and the authorities wanted to keep down price increases by facilitating imports financed from accumulated foreign exchange reserves. Second, the government wished to maintain the value of coffee exports at high levels.

The policy of unrestricted imports had continued for slightly more than one year before it resulted in the depletion of Brazil's foreign exchange reserves; controls on imports were then chosen as the principal means of equilibrating the balance of payments. From 1947 to 1953, a licensing system was used to allocate available foreign exchange. The categories pertaining to merchandise imports were as follows:

1. "Super-essential": agricultural equipment, fuels, oils, lubricants, metals not domestically available, and needs of government agencies
2. "Essential": other raw materials, machinery, spare parts, and producer goods in general; some pharmaceuticals
3. Other goods (i.e., most consumer goods)

Of the total amount of foreign exchange allocated to merchandise imports, about 17–19 percent went to the "super-essential" category and about 65–70 percent to the "essential."[4]

The imposition of the licensing system was principally a response to a foreign exchange crisis which called for a reduction of total imports. Protection of existing consumer goods industries was a secondary goal, and growth of new industries was not an intended result. Around 1949, the economic policy started to move toward more deliberate protectionism, with the prohibition of imports of products for which domestic substitutes existed. This

---

[3] *Conjuntura Econômica*, index No. 2.

[4] Estimated from data in ECLA, "The Growth and Decline of Import Substitution in Brazil."

was under the authority of the "Law of Similars," which had been on the books in one form or another since 1911. The Dutra government (1946–50) was economically too orthodox to use this and other means of inducing structural change very aggressively. Deliberate industrialization did not take place until Vargas (1951–54) and then Kubitschek (1956–60) first tolerated and then embraced the *desenvolvimentismo* philosophy.[5]

In October 1953, import licensing was replaced by a five-category exchange auction system. The Superintendency of Money and Credit (SUMOC) allocated available foreign exchange among these categories while the Foreign Trade Department (CACEX) of the Bank of Brazil administered the system. The import rates were set in auctions for each category.[6]

Some commodities were not subject to the auction system. These included imports for governmental agencies, wheat, newsprint, and petroleum products. The rate for these products was usually equal to the average export rate (*custo de cambio*) plus a tax which amounted to as much as 38 percent ad valorem, but which was often waived. Petroleum products were also subject to licensing. These goods accounted for about one-third of the total value of imports. All other imports were classified among the five categories, as follows:

1. Inputs to agriculture, certain pharmaceuticals and inputs to the pharmaceutical industry, and some other "essential" commodities
2. "Essential" raw materials (i.e., those for favored industries, almost all producers of intermediate goods)
3. Other raw materials and "essential" spare parts and equipment (again, those for favored industries)
4. Other spare parts and equipment, and fresh fruits
5. All other commodities (i.e., most finished consumer goods)

According to Kafka, at least 80 percent of the total foreign exchange available for auctions was allocated to the first three categories, and a maximum of 3 percent went to the fifth category.[7] But disaggregated import data for 1954–57 show finished consumer goods to be about 14 percent of all auction imports, with the remainder divided equally between capital goods and intermediate producer goods. This indicates that the fifth category was not rationed quite as strictly as Kafka suggests.

---

[5] The *desenvolvimentista* ideals seem to be economic development, modernization of production techniques and structure, and reduced dependence on foreign trade and foreign influences in general. See T. E. Skidmore, *Politics in Brazil* (New York: Oxford University Press, 1967), pp. 87–100.

[6] See International Monetary Fund, *Annual Report on Exchange Restrictions*, 1954 through 1958; Alexander Kafka, "The Brazilian Exchange Auction System," *Review of Economics and Statistics*, August 1956, pp. 308–22.

[7] Kafka, "The Brazilian Exchange Auction System," p. 310.

A rough idea of the relative price effects of the auction system can be derived from the average exchange rates shown in Table 6.4. As the exchange rate was fixed at Cr$ 18.50 per dollar, the level of the premia rose to keep pace with inflation; their general structure, however, remained roughly the same. Nor did the distribution of commodities among individual categories change much during the period the system was in effect (between October 1953 and August 1957), although new domestic availability of some goods led to the removal of such goods from the "essential" category.

The biases among different types of imports were similar in both the licensing period (1947–53) and the exchange auction period (1953–57). The magnitude of the price effects may have differed, but the ranking was almost identical: the most favored were capital and current inputs to agriculture and some favored industries; next, other producer goods; and least, finished consumer goods. There were considerable incentives to import substitution of industrial products, disincentives to export anything at all, and some compensation to agriculture in the form of cheap inputs.

In August 1957 the system of controlling imports was reformed once again. The number of product categories was reduced to two ("general" and "special") and a comprehensive set of ad valorem tariffs was introduced. Most raw materials, intermediate products, and machinery for which domestic supplies were insufficient were placed on the general category. The exchange rate in this category was set in auctions until March 1961, when the auctions were discontinued and a free market allowed to function. Most other goods, considered "inessential," were placed in the special category. These were mostly consumer goods, and some producer goods that were domestically available. The exchange rate in the special category was set in auctions, and it generally varied between two and three times the general category rate.

Imports of a few commodities (fertilizers, newsprint, wheat, petroleum, and petroleum products) again received preferential treatment. Until 1961, the

TABLE 6.4: Import Exchange Rates and Protection in Brazil, 1954 and 1956

Category	Average rate (cruzeiros per dollar)		Protection (percent)	
	1954	1956	1954	1956
Custo de cambio	30	44	−21	−38
1	42	74	10	4
2	45	81	18	14
3	58	103	52	45
4	68	116	80	62
5	111	222	190	210

Source: Average rates from EPEA, "Diagnostico Preliminar, Setor de Comercio Internacional," mimeographed (Rio de Janeiro: Ministry of Planning, March 1967).

Notes: "Protection" is the percent by which the rate exceeds the free trade rate estimated later in this chapter. The custo de cambio is equal to or slightly above the average export rate, and was usually used for imports of wheat, newsprint, and petroleum products, etc.

exchange rate applicable to these products was generally equal to the average rate for exports. The rate was, however, increased in 1961 and in 1964 these goods were shifted to the general category.

In addition to multiple exchange rates and tariffs, various forms of restrictions and exemptions were employed to reduce or to facilitate particular imports. Across-the-board surcharges, prepayment requirements, and similar devices were used from time to time, principally during 1961–65. Finally, all imports are liable to a variety of minor taxes. The effect of these instruments will be considered in estimating the nominal and the effective rates of protection below.

To oversimplify somewhat, imports in the general category were subject to tariffs and other charges up to about 80 percent, with lower rates applying to producer goods and higher rates to consumer goods. To import products in the special category, one had to buy foreign exchange at a premium of 100–200 percent, and also to pay tariffs ranging up to 150 percent. The rates were reduced in 1966 and, more importantly, in 1967 when a major tariff reform was undertaken, including the abolition of the special category of imports.[8]

The various exemptions and restrictions form a complex set of modifications to the tariffs. Enforcement is very flexible, varying through time as well as among products, and a precise description is somewhat difficult; we will try to summarize here the major characteristics of the system applied. The exemptions are principally two types. One is based on the following form: upon proof of purchase of a given quantity of domestic production, a proportional quantity may be imported at a very low tariff rate. The proportion is set in order to protect the full capacity of a domestic industry which does not produce enough to satisfy the entire domestic demand. This type of exemption usually also functions as a quantitative restriction; if the domestic product is not purchased, importing is often difficult even if the higher tariff is paid. The most important products involved were coal, lead, aluminum, and asbestos.

The second type of exemption is for important inputs (mostly capital equipment) for high-priority industries. This exemption depends not only on the type of good, but also on the identity of the user. The nature of the exemption varies, at times being limited to exemption from the tariff, and at times including a lower exchange rate; moreover, the foreign investor could often buy capital equipment abroad and import it without a foreign exchange transaction, while Brazilian investors would have to buy foreign exchange for this

[8] For a description and analysis of tariff changes over time, see Samuel A. Morley, "Import Demand and Import Substitution in Brazil," in *The Economy of Brazil*, ed. Howard S. Ellis (Berkeley and Los Angeles: University of California Press, 1969), pp. 283–313. Also Paul Clark and Richard Weisskoff, "Import Demands and Import Policies in Brazil," mimeographed, February 1967, and Paul Clark, "Brazilian Import Liberalization," mimeographed, September 1967.

purpose at a higher cost. This exemption was widely used, and for capital goods the ratio of tariff collections to the value of imports seldom exceeded 10 percent, even though the average official tariff, weighted by imports, was about 50 percent.

The restrictions are also very complicated. We have already mentioned one type of restriction: that which functioned in conjunction with the exemptions on coal, lead, aluminum, and asbestos. Other types are the Law of Similars, and monopoly or government price-setting combined with quantitative restrictions.

The Law of Similars has assumed much importance since the mid-fifties. The basic idea is that some or all importers are prohibited from importing a product which is recognized by the government as being available domestically. The practice was formally instituted in 1911; its scope of application among importers, the criteria for government recognition of domestic availability, and the strictness of enforcement have varied considerably since that time.

To register a product as a similar, the manufacturer applied to the *Conselho de Politica Aduaneira* (CPA). This body is composed of representatives of manufacturers, importers, and the government. If the CPA was satisfied that the domestic supplier(s) could furnish the product in sufficient quantity and quality (in 1967, price and time for delivery were added as elements of the criteria), the product was registered as a similar. Goods so registered cannot be imported by most public corporations, mixed (partly owned by the government) companies, and public authorities. Private importers could import general category goods even if a national similar existed, but in that case would not be granted any exemptions, government loans, or other special treatment to which they might otherwise be entitled.

Public corporations and authorities, as well as private importers who received favorable treatment such as government loans, needed a license to import anything. A license was also necessary for importing goods in the special category. This license was granted by the Foreign Trade Department (CACEX) of the Bank of Brazil. CACEX tended to be more protectionist than the CPA, and sometimes refused to grant licenses even if there was no "similar" registered with the CPA. In cases where goods were not standardized (especially capital goods), the CPA's register tended to omit many goods for which domestic similars had recently come into existence; CACEX used an informal procedure and was more restrictive on licensing. A private importer who did not receive license from CACEX could, however, forego any special privilege and import without a license if the good was in the general category. In October 1967, CACEX was given complete authority to enforce the Law of Similars. In determining if a similar exists, CACEX uses the informal and broad concepts it had employed in licensing.

Exceptions to all rules were and still are made, sometimes toward easing and sometimes toward tightening the provisions. Furthermore, there are several products for which the government grants an import monopoly, sets quantitative restrictions, or controls prices. The most important instances are salt, soda ash, steel, and rubber. Such arrangements are usually made to protect extremely high-cost domestic production (salt, soda ash, and rubber); however, domestic steel prices are not too much higher than in the major exporting countries.

Export Policy

The 1945–53 period was characterized by the maintenance of an increasingly overvalued currency. As a result, the volume as well as the value of exports declined steadily from 1946 until the Korean War. In 1949, exporters of certain products which were being priced out of the world market were allowed to sell foreign exchange directly to importers of nonessential goods. This implicit devaluation was at first severely limited in its scope among export products, but it became important just before and just after the Korean War export boom.

In 1953, different exchange rates were established for exports of various types of products. Bonuses were also used from time to time, and the system was quite complicated and variable. The average export exchange rate rose slightly faster than the domestic price level, but not until 1959 did the real rate (the ratio of an index of nominal rates and the wholesale price index) reach the level of the immediate postwar years when the exchange rate was already overvalued. In 1959 trade in more and more products was freed; by the end of the year proceeds from all exports except coffee, cocoa, mineral oil and castor oil beans could be sold on the free market.

The continuous rise in domestic prices with only occasional readjustments in export exchange rates caused wide variations and uncertainty as to the real export exchange rate. Periods of three to six months during which the real average rate for exports dropped 10 or 15 percent were not uncommon. During the 1953–59 period, the real export exchange rates for individual products fluctuated even more and were more uncertain than the average rate. These fluctuations affected exports of primary commodities and seem to have been especially prejudicial to the exports of manufactured goods.

Administrative regulations on exports also had unfavorable effects. Throughout the entire postwar period, the system of import licensing, together with the various bonuses, freedom to sell part of foreign exchange receipts from exports of certain products on the free market, and other schemes used to reduce the disadvantages of the overvalued cruzeiro, complicated matters considerably. Licenses to export primary goods were refused in various instances; the most important was when the government wanted to keep domestic food prices down and therefore prohibited the export of certain food products. Licenses to export manufactured products were rarely refused, although the exporter was required to prove that at least 70 percent of the value of the product could be attributed to domestic inputs.[9]

There were periodic official protestations that exports should be encouraged, and measures to this effect were taken from time to time. Nevertheless, Brazilian policy was never really concerned about promoting exports of anything except coffee and, to some extent, a very few other primary commodities.

Table 6.5 provides information on the average import and export exchange rates during the postwar period. The export rate does not include coffee—coffee policy will not be analyzed in this chapter. We do not show an import rate for 1947 through 1953 because estimates of the price effect of the licensing system then in force are not available. The rates include bonuses, taxes, tariffs, exchange premia, port charges, and other across-the-board surcharges, as well as the tariff equivalent of prepayment requirements.

The ratio of import to export exchange rates provides a rough indication of the extent of discrimination against export activities. During the period 1954–64, the domestic currency equivalent of a dollar of imports was, on the average, 2.7 times that of a dollar's worth of exports. This ratio declined to 2.5 in 1964 and to 2.1 in 1965; it fell again, in connection with the tariff reforms of those years, to 1.7 in 1966 and to 1.4 in 1967.

Further changes, leading back to greater protection, took place after 1967. In mid-1968, the Central Bank required importers to make prepayment for goods with an ad valorem tariff of 50 percent or more. In December 1968 the government increased tariffs by 100 percentage points on 549 items, most of which had been in the special category before 1967. This tariff increase restored the protection of these items to the 1966 level. On the other hand, duties on commodities in the general category continued to be below the 1966 rates.

Nominal and Effective Protection

Potential and Realized Protection

Our detailed numerical results on the structure of nominal and effective protection pertain to the situations in 1966 and 1967. However, since the only input-output table available is for 1959,[10] the estimates of effective protection

---

[9] For a discussion of export policies in general, see Nathaniel H. Leff, "Export Stagnation and Autarkic Development in Brazil, 1947–1962," *Quarterly Journal of Economics*, May 1967, pp. 286–301. Leff goes a bit far in describing the evils of the licensing system when he says, ". . . export licenses were denied if . . . the domestic price was rising." In a footnote he explains that this means the absolute price (p. 290). If this were true, there would have been virtually no exports from Brazil.

[10] Instituto de Pesquisa Economico-Social Aplicada, *Relacoes Interindustriais no Brasil*, Cadernos IPEA No. 2, Rio de Janeiro, Ministry of Planning, December 1967.

TABLE 6.5:   Average Exchange Rates in Brazil, 1946–67

| | Nominal rates | | | |
| | | Imports | | Ratio of total |
Year	Noncoffee exports including bonuses[a]	Basic rate[b] (cruzeiros per dollar)	Including protection[c]	import rate[d] to export rate
1946	18.40	18.60	18.60	1.0
1947	18.40	na	na	na
1948	18.40	na	na	na
1949	18.40	na	na	na
1950	18.40	na	na	na
1951	18.40	na	na	na
1952	18.40	na	na	na
1953	22.50	na	na	na
1954	27.00	41.80	62.30	2.3
1955	41.30	63.80	91.90	2.2
1956	44.90	73.80	173.00	3.9
1957	53.00	65.60	173.00	3.3
1958	65.40	149.00	173.00	2.6
1959	114.00	202.00	291.00	2.6
1960	160.00	223.00	321.00	2.0
1961	245.00	268.00	611.00	2.5
1962	370.00	390.00	1,040.00	2.8
1963	553.00	575.00	1,670.00	3.0
1964	1,210.00	1,284.00	3,000.00	2.5
1965	1,874.00	1,899.00	3,930.00	2.1
1966	2,200.00	2,220.00	3,750.00	1.7
1967[e]	2,700.00	2,730.00	3,730.00	1.4

[a] Average export rate does not include adjustments for proceeds from hard-to-export goods being sold on the free market prior to 1953. Source: EPEA, "Diagnostico Preliminar, Setor de Comercio Internacional."

[b] Basic import rate from *ibid.*

[c] Includes tariffs, the tariff equivalent of prepayment requirements, port charges, and across-the-board surcharges. The basic source for the series of protection is Paul Clark and Richard Weisskoff, "Import Demands and Import Policies in Brazil," mimeographed, February 1967. We have added an adjustment for advance deposits and surcharge during 1961–65, taken from EPEA, "Diagnostico Preliminar, Setor de Comercio Internacional." Furthermore, the time series of protection weighted by actual imports were adjusted by weighting with total supply. On the basis of data for the year 1967, an upward adjustment of 76 percent was made in the entire series. The results for 1966 are not the same as those shown elsewhere in this study because Clark's estimates show a different change between 1966 and 1967 than do our estimates.

[d] Import rate including protection.

[e] Data for 1967 are for April–December only, to show the effects of the February–March reforms.

are based on the input structures of that year. The table provides information on twenty-four industries; tariffs on individual items have been weighted by domestic supply in 1959 for the purpose of deriving averages according to the industrial classification of the input-output table. All flows in the table have been adjusted to producer prices by deducting trade and transport margins.

The tariff equivalent of various price measures, such as exchange auction premia, port charges, other across-the-board surcharges, and adjustments for prepayment requirements have been added to tariffs. Exchange auction premia have been expressed as a percentage of the basic exchange rate; port charges and other across-the-board surcharges have been estimated at 13 percent of the c.i.f. value of imports; and the tariff equivalent of prepayment requirements has been calculated at the real interest rate applicable to the period. Tariff rates have in turn been adjusted downward for excise taxes levied on domestic production but not on imports. Finally, protection has been assumed to be nil on major export products other than coffee, for which it was calculated from the ratio of the price received by the producer to the export price.

Before we present detailed numerical results, some words of caution are necessary. First, the basic data for the analysis are imprecise. The exact tariff rate is known for each commodity, and the effects of surcharges, auction premia, prepayment requirements, etc., can be calculated without much error. But other factors that affect the ratio of domestic to import prices are harder to quantify. These include the effects of restrictions and exemptions which have been noted earlier; we have attempted to make adjustments for these, as well as for other factors which have not been taken into account. Second, as noted in Chapter 1, the averaging of tariffs involves conceptual as well as empirical difficulties, and estimating the effective rate of protection requires further assumptions and approximations which may not be realistic. Third, the use of the 1959 input-output table in conjunction with tariff and price information for 1966 and 1967 may give rise to considerable error.

The estimates of protection should be interpreted as the maximum which governmental regulations, legally constituted and actually adminsitered, allow. This raises the problem of redundancy (excess protection); i.e., domestic prices may not be as high as permitted by the system of protection. There are various possible reasons for redundancy. Domestic competition may force prices below levels permitted by protection. A further complication is caused by the continuous inflation and only occasional exchange rate adjustments which characterized the postwar period in Brazil. In such a situation, the tariff-inclusive price of imports remains constant from one devaluation to the next while the price of the domestic product increases by small steps. Correspondingly, the degree of protection actually utilized tends to increase with the inflation and to decrease sharply when the next devaluation takes place.

In dealing with the problem of redundancy, we have used different methods for capital goods, intermediate products, and consumer goods, Capital goods have been divided into two groups: imports and domestically produced goods. The tariffs on the former have been calculated as the ratio of actual tariff collections to the actual value of imports which take account of average exemptions on each item. In the absence of quantitative information, however, we could not allow for the effects of the differences in tariff exemptions granted to the various users of imported capital equipment. For domestically produced capital goods, which are mostly simpler types than those imported and are to some extent protected by the Law of Similars, we have assumed that no exemptions were available and that the difference between domestic prices and world market prices equaled the tariff.

For particular standardized intermediate products where restrictions or exemptions are important, the ratio of domestic factory prices to c.i.f. prices has been estimated directly. This has been done for the following products: soda ash, caustic soda, eight different petroleum products, natural rubber, automotive tires and tubes, aluminum, lead, tin, copper and zinc ingots, coal, various steel products, and cement. Most of these prices are set administratively, either by government agencies and government-controlled corporations, or in close consultation with the government. Prices are adjusted (to the inflation) irregularly, and often not in conjunction with devaluations. We have calculated averages of internal prices for several months if data were available and if this seemed to give a reasonable estimate of the implicit tariff. For a few products (notably cement and tin) we have not been able to get reasonable price comparisons, and have used an indirect estimate of the price effect of the official tariff plus any restrictions or exemptions. For coal we have used an estimate of blast furnace productivity as an index of quality to adjust for differences in quality.

The adjustments discussed cover most products affected by the Law of Similars. For the few products not covered, the following procedure has been applied. For 1966, we have used the 100 percent special category premium plus the high tariffs on these products. For 1967, when the special category was abolished, we have accepted the provision of the Brazilian regulations that no additional protection would be given if the domestic price exceeds the c.i.f. price plus the tariff, and thus simply used the tariff. On some similars, these methods may have overestimated the protection actually utilized in 1966, but not in 1967.

With these adjustments, our measures of realized nominal protection for capital goods and for intermediate goods are likely to be quite close to the actual price differentials between Brazilian and world prices. For consumer goods, however, where we were unable to make analogous adjustments, there probably is substantial redundancy in our estimates of protection for consumer goods for 1966. For the estimates pertaining to 1967, however, various considerations suggest that redundancy was small or even nonexistent. These include the relatively low levels of protection in 1967, the behavior of imports, and some crude price comparisons made on the retail level (see below).

Average protection was reduced to very low levels by the reforms of February and March, 1967, and the largest decrease is shown for consumer goods (see Tables 6.7 and 6.12 below). Partly as a result, imports of consumer goods rose sharply. For example, in 1967, automobiles were imported at the rate of roughly 1,000 units per month; in 1961–65 imports had averaged 340 per year. The dollar value of imports of manufactured consumer nondurables grew 23 percent in 1966 and 44 percent in 1967.[11] In his study of changes in protection, Clark concluded that "about a third of the large increase (in all imports combined) in 1966 was attributable to import liberalization, the remainder being due to the sharp recovery of gross investment."[12] Finally, we made some price comparisons at the retail level in Rio de Janeiro which showed domestic prices of consumer goods to approximate U.S. prices, converted at the import exchange rate including tariffs. For these reasons, we conclude that redundancy was very small or nonexistent in 1967.

Redundancy is more of a problem in calculating the *effective* rate of protection. For one thing, the method of calculation amplifies differences in the nominal rates of protection on outputs and inputs; for another, redundancy in the protection of material inputs would lead to an understatement of the extent of effective protection. Since we have made direct price comparisons for most of the intermediate products, however, the latter problem is unlikely to be important.

All in all, we conclude that the estimates of effective protection in 1967 are generally nonredundant, while there was some redundancy in the estimated structure of protection in 1966, chiefly for consumer goods. Nevertheless, these last estimates are also of interest, partly because they indicate the extent of potential protection before the 1967 reforms, and partly because after increases in tariffs in 1968, average protection was roughly halfway between the 1966 and 1967 levels.

The Pattern of Effective Rates

Having discussed these qualifications, we present our estimates of nominal and effective protection for 1966 and 1967 in Table 6.6. The effective rates apply to gross value added, since we have no data on depreciation. Results are presented under both the "Balassa" method (nontradeable inputs treated as tradeable with zero effective protection) and the "Corden" method (the value-added part of nontradeable inputs treated as value added by the using sector, and the tradeable part treated as tradeable inputs with the relevant tariffs). The extent of discrimination against exports and in favor of import substitution in individual industries is also shown.

It should be emphasized, however, that the estimates of Table 6.6 do not indicate changes in the extent of *net* protection of domestic industries, since calculations have been made at existing exchange rates and there was a devaluation between the two dates. Changes in net protection can be shown only if adjustment is made for overvaluation as compared to the free trade situation,

---

[11] Ministry of Finance, *Mensario Estatistico*, various issues and unpublished worksheet data.

[12] Clark, "Brazilian Import Liberalization," p. i.

TABLE 6.6: Nominal and Effective Protection in Brazil, 1966 and 1967

(Percent)

Industry	1966				1967			
	Nominal protection	Effective protection		Bias against Exporting[a]	Nominal protection	Effective protection		Bias against Exporting[a]
		Balassa	Corden			Balassa	Corden	
Primary vegetable products	36	36	35	...	10	8	8	...
Primary animal products	137	169	164	...	17	17	17	...
Mining	27	28	25	...	14	14	13	...
Food products	82	110	87	*	27	55	40	52
Beverages	205	1,529	447	*	83	602	173	632
Tobacco	193	373	313	*	78	147	124	151
Nonmetallic mineral products	79	103	86	138	40	47	39	57
Metallurgy	54	68	58	135	34	44	36	48
Machinery	48	48	41	106	34	38	32	40
Electrical equipment	114	382	215	*	57	172	97	176
Transport equipment	108	233	151	1,640	57	115	75	118
Wood products	45	50	45	91	23	27	25	29
Furniture	132	401	239	9,430	68	208	124	211
Paper and products	93	157	118	674	48	78	59	84
Rubber products	101	167	136	295	78	142	116	145
Leather products	108	156	117	*	66	113	85	133
Chemicals	53	67	59	198	34	48	42	51
Pharmaceuticals	48	50	39	103	37	48	35	51
Perfumes, soaps, etc.	192	−919	8,480	*	94	−415	3,670	*
Plastics	122	315	183	1,060	48	99	58	103
Textiles	181	939	379	*	81	412	162	427
Clothing	226	457	337	*	103	193	142	195
Printing and publishing	122	198	142	528	59	93	67	94
Miscellaneous	104	181	128	251	58	101	72	104

Source: See text.
[a] Calculated by using the Corden formula.
* Denotes negative value added.

as will be done in the next section. Nevertheless, the estimates provide information on changes in the *structure* of protection; this is not affected by adjustment for overvaluation.

There is a high degree of correlation between the ranking of industries by nominal and by effective protection. The Spearman rank-correlation coefficient between the two series is .95 for both years. Furthermore, a considerable escalation of the tariff structure is shown, with effective rates exceeding nominal rates in both 1966 and 1967 by a wide margin. Differences between effective and nominal rates are the largest for perfumes and soaps, beverages, textiles, and furniture, where tariffs on inputs are relatively low. Effective and nominal rates are approximately equal for primary product industries which include a variety of export products.

The escalation of the tariff structure also increases the dispersion of the effective rates of protection. While nominal rates varied between nil and 226 percent in 1966 and between nil and 103 percent in 1967, effective rates often exceeded 300 percent in 1966 and 150 percent in 1967. In both years, the ratio of the standard deviation to the arithmetic mean is 0.6 for nominal rates as against 1.0 for effective rates.

Averages of nominal rates of protection, weighted by total supply, were 85 percent in 1966 and 37 percent in 1967, while averages of effective rates, weighted by "derived" free trade value added were 96 or 83 percent in 1966 and 43 or 36 percent in 1967, depending on whether the Corden or the Balassa method was used (see Table 6.8). Among individual industries, reductions in nominal rates were largest for primary animal and vegetable products, beverages, tobacco, and manufactured consumer goods in general; they were smallest for pharmaceuticals and rubber products. Changes in effective rates show a similar pattern.

The classification scheme used in the Brazilian input-output table often groups together components, semi-finished goods, finished producer goods, and finished consumer goods in the same industry. To estimate the average protection of commodities in these categories, it has been necessary to estimate nominal protection for subsectors, and reaggregate these results according to the major product categories by use. The results, shown in Table 6.7, indicate that before the 1967 reform nominal rates on manufactured products were lowest on capital goods. Next came intermediate goods, then construction materials, parts and components, and finally nondurable and durable consumer goods. Intermediate goods dropped slightly below capital goods in 1967, and tariffs on consumer durables and nondurables were reduced more than the average. Nevertheless, the general structure of rates remained similar.

The combination of different types of goods by use in the same industries of the input-output table makes it difficult to estimate effective rates of protection according to the commodity breakdown in Table 6.7. Also, because of the

TABLE 6.7: Nominal Protection by Use of Product in Brazil, 1966 and 1967

(Percent)

Industry group	Use of product	1966	1967
	A. Disaggregation		
Nonmetallic mineral products	Construction materials	76	41
	Consumer durables	91	24
Machinery	Parts and components	46	33
	Capital goods	35	27
	Consumer durables	86	46
Electrical equipment	Parts and components	75	47
	Capital goods	70	61
	Consumer durables	216	92
Transport equipment	Parts and components	103	69
	Capital goods	74	47
	Consumer durables	202	88
Paper and products	Intermediate goods	69	40
	Consumer nondurables	161	65
Rubber products	Intermediate goods	80	59
	Consumer durables	106	79
Chemicals	Intermediate goods	47	33
	Fertilizers	22	6
	Consumer nondurables	58	32
Textiles	Threads and yarns	168	60
	Fabrics	226	101
	B. Reaggregation		
All 21 manufacturing sectors	Capital goods	56	40
	Construction materials	76	42
	Intermediate goods	70	37
	Parts and components	88	59
	Consumer durables	132	67
	Consumer nondurables	114	46

Source: See text.

high degree of aggregation in the industrial breakdown of the Brazilian input-output table, the ten categories used in the other country studies could be established only in an approximate fashion. The results for both nominal and effective rates are shown in Table 6.8.

With few exceptions, there is a correspondence between the estimates derived from domestic input-output coefficients and those based on free trade coefficients. Apart from primary producing industries, the differences between the averages of nominal and effective rates of protection are small and the results for the individual commodity categories are generally consistent.

Nominal and effective rates of protection are by far the highest on consumer goods—nondurables as well as durables; the rates are the lowest on agriculture, mining and energy, and transport equipment. Construction materials, intermediate products, processed food, and machinery are between the two groups; if we also separate intermediate products at different levels of fabrication, the ranking (from low to high) by effective protection within this category is the following: construction materials, processed food, machinery,

TABLE 6.8: Nominal and Effective Protection for Major Product Categories in Brazil, 1966 and 1967

(Percent)

	Industry group	Estimates based on domestic coefficients						Estimates based on free trade coefficients					
		1966			1967			1966			1967		
		Nominal protection	Effective protection		Nominal protection	Effective protection		Nominal protection	Effective protection		Nominal protection	Effective protection	
			Balassa	Corden		Balassa	Corden		Balassa	Corden		Balassa	Corden
I	Agriculture, forestry, and fishing	63	55	53	12	10	10	50	50	46	18	13	11
II	Processed food	82	110	87	27	55	40	71	122	92	26	16	12
III	Beverages and tobacco	201	795	406	81	334	155	152	313	252	61	115	90
IV	Mining and energy	27	28	25	14	14	13	23	−15	−16	19	−4	−4
V	Construction materials	79	103	86	40	47	39	67	98	79	34	41	31
VI-A	Intermediate products I	na	na	na	na	na	na	68	160	115	48	136	98
VI-B	Intermediate products II	na	na	na	na	na	na	121	232	187	62	128	103
VI	Intermediate products I and II	92	141	110	49	94	67	84	182	137	53	134	100
VII	Nondurable consumer goods	140	246	173	70	156	101	157	248	218	74	109	94
VIII	Consumer durables	108	233	151	57	115	75	154	341	285	80	163	133
IX	Machinery	87	134	100	47	87	60	80	110	93	48	67	56
X	Transport equipment	a	a	a	a	a	a	26	−28	−26	16	−17	−17
I-X	All industries	85	96	83	37	43	36	67	108	85	35	56	43
I + IV	Primary production	59	54	52	12	10	10	38	21	18	18	5	4
II, III, V-X	Manufacturing	99	155	118	48	94	66	87	165	129	46	89	68
VI-X	Manufacturing less food, beverages, tobacco, and construction materials	101	162	122	53	105	73	93	182	123	55	121	93

Sources: Tables 3.1 and 6.6.
a Included with consumer durables.

intermediate products at lower levels of fabrication, and intermediate products at higher levels of processing.

Aggregation to twenty-four sectors hides a lot of variation. Many sectors include some items which are not yet produced domestically and receive little protection, and others which are produced domestically and receive high protection. This occurs in producer goods sectors such as chemicals and metallurgy, and in the machinery and equipment sectors which include both consumer and producer goods. Thus the data of Tables 6.6, 6.7, and 6.8 tend to understate the actual range of variation in protection.

We have considered so far the differential effects of the structure of protection on individual industries and on product categories. These effects entail an overall discrimination in favor of industries producing import-competing goods at the expense of export-oriented industries. Further indications of the discrimination against exports (as opposed to domestic sales) in individual sectors[13] are shown in the last column of Table 6.6. In 1966, in eight out of twenty-one manufacturing sectors, no margin for value added was available for sales in foreign markets. In 1967 there was still one such case, and in eleven other sectors the bias still exceeded 100 percent; i.e., producing for the domestic markets ensured firms a value added more than double that obtainable through exporting.

Overvaluation and Net Effective Protection

The analysis presented so far has dealt with nominal and effective protection relative to Brazil's "basic" exchange rate. This rate, however, is dependent on tariff protection itself, in the sense that equilibrium in the balance of payments can be attained by a variety of combinations of exchange rates, tariffs, and other protective measures. To estimate net protection against imports— and net discrimination against exports—the calculations made under the existing exchange rate need to be adjusted for overvaluation as compared with the free trade situation.

Such an analysis is inherently hypothetical. To estimate the equilibrium free trade exchange rate, we need information on the response of exports and imports to drastic changes in commercial policy. The usual way to do this, through estimates of the price elasticities of supply and demand for imports and exports, presents many problems, both conceptual and empirical. The elasticity of demand for imports, for example, depends on the magnitude, direction, and duration of the price change. It also depends on changes in the structure and level of domestic industrial production; these, in turn, are

---

[13] This has been estimated by assuming no drawbacks for tariffs paid on inputs used in export production in 1966, and full drawbacks in 1967. While these assumptions somewhat exaggerate differences between the two periods, they can be useful as an approximation to the actual situation which is too complex to represent with great precision.

affected by policy changes other than commercial policy that might be taken in response to the new situation. Such potential changes could not, however, be considered in our calculation.

In estimating the free trade exchange rate which would compensate for the removal of all protective measures, we have assumed no change in governmental policy concerning coffee. Sales of coffee take place under the International Coffee Agreement, which sets quotas for each producing country. Coffee sales thus being predetermined, the export tax on coffee needs to be set so as to equate domestic supply to the quota. The resulting "free trade" exchange rate is therefore really a "quasi-free-trade" rate in the sense that coffee exports are still taxed. We have further assumed that the price of coffee, and hence the value of coffee exports, would remain unchanged.

The derivation of the free trade exchange rate is described in Appendix C. The free trade exchange rates chosen for estimating net protection show a 27 percent overvaluation as compared with the free trade situation in 1966 and 14 percent in 1967. We have further estimated the free trade exchange rate for the years 1954–65, as well as average protection and export taxes expressed as a percentage of this rate. The results are shown in Table 6.9, together with index numbers of real values of the free trade, import, and export exchange

TABLE 6.9: Net Protection, Implicit Export Taxes, and the Free Trade Exchange Rate in Brazil, 1954–67

Year	Free trade rate (cruzeiros per dollar)	Import[a] protection	Implicit[b] export taxes	Indices of real values[c]		
		(percent of free trade rate)		Import rate	Free trade rate	Export rate
				(free trade rate for 1954 = 100)		
1954	38	64	29	164	100	71
1955	57	61	28	204	126	92
1956	71	144	37	314	129	81
1957	81	114	35	275	129	84
1958	95	82	31	240	132	91
1959	160	82	29	283	156	111
1960	210	53	24	238	155	118
1961	350	75	30	322	185	129
1962	550	89	33	366	193	130
1963	830	101	33	333	166	110
1964	1,700	76	29	330	187	133
1965	2,500	57	25	281	179	134
1966	2,800	34	22	190	142	112
1967[d]	3,100	20	13	150	125	109

Source: Table 6.5 and text.

[a] The import rate including protection shown in Table 6.5 divided by the free trade rate, less one.

[b] One, minus the export rate (Table 6.5) divided by the free trade rate. Coffee exports are not included.

[c] Nominal rates deflated by the index of wholesale prices excluding coffee (Conjuntura Econômica, index No. 45).

[d] Data for 1967 are for April–December only, in order to show the effects of the February–March reforms.

rates, calculated by deflating the nominal values by the wholesale price index excluding coffee.

The results indicate the extent of the discrimination against imports (net protection) and the implicit discrimination against exports, by comparing the actual situation to a free trade equilibrium. On this basis, net protection averaged 86 percent during the period 1954–64. Net protection declined in subsequent years, falling to 34 percent in 1966 and 20 percent in 1967. Results obtained by adjusting nominal exchange rates for changes in domestic prices show the same general picture: levels of protection were the highest during 1956–64, with deflated values of net protection later declining to a considerable extent.

Discrimination against exports remained at roughly constant levels in the 1954–65 period, irrespective of whether we consider nominal or deflated implicit taxes on exports. The average rate of export taxes implicit in the structure of protection varied between 24 and 47 percent during this period, falling to 22 percent in 1966 and 13 percent in 1967.

As a result of the combined influences of these changes, the index of the deflated value of the free trade exchange rate rose more or less regularly from 100 in 1954 to 193 in 1962 and declined thereafter; it was 142 in 1966, and 125 in 1967. This behavior of the free trade rate is consistent with the growth performance of the Brazilian economy. The rate rose during the period of rapid growth that increased the demand for imports while exports were sluggish. It declined, however, during the subsequent slowdown.

The figures of Table 6.9 provide information on nominal protection but do not allow for changes in tariffs on inputs which influence the effective protection of both import-competing goods and exports. We have estimated the extent of this net protection for 1966 and 1967 only. The results are shown in Tables 6.10, 6.11, 6.12, and 6.13.

When adjusted for overvaluation as compared to the hypothetical free trade situation, the range of nominal protection in the 24 sectors becomes nil to 160 percent in 1966 and −4 to 77 percent in 1967. Even if we disregard the perfumes industry which shows extremely high effective protection, there are three industries (textiles, clothing, and tobacco) with effective rates of protection exceeding 240 percent in 1966 and 110 percent in 1967. If we assume that protection is nonredundant in 1967, such rates indicate considerable inefficiencies and high costs in these industries.

We can get some idea of the relative size of the sectors enjoying different levels of protection from Table 6.11. Considering only the twenty-one manufacturing industries and protection levels as of 1966, we find that over 50 percent of value added (at unadjusted domestic prices) was in sectors that had, on the average, less than 50 percent of net effective protection.

As suggested above, redundancy in our estimates for 1967 is likely to have

TABLE 6.10:   Net Nominal and Effective Protection in Brazil, 1966 and 1967[a]

(*Percent*)

Industry	1966		1967	
	Nominal protection	Effective protection	Nominal protection	Effective protection
Primary vegetable products	8	7	−4	−5
Primary animal products	88	109	2	2
Mining	1	0	−1	−1
Food products	44	48	10	23
Beverages	142	333	59	139
Tobacco	132	227	55	96
Nonmetallic mineral products	42	47	22	22
Metallurgy	22	25	17	19
Machinery	17	12	17	16
Electrical equipment	69	149	37	73
Transport equipment	65	99	37	53
Wood products	15	15	7	10
Furniture	84	168	46	96
Paper and products	53	73	29	39
Rubber products	59	87	55	89
Leather products	65	72	44	62
Chemicals	21	26	17	25
Pharmaceuticals	17	10	19	18
Perfumes, soaps, etc.	131	6,710	69	3,210
Plastics	76	124	29	39
Textiles	123	279	57	130
Clothing	158	246	77	112
Printing and publishing	76	92	38	46
Miscellaneous	62	81	37	51

Source: Table 6.6 and text.

[a] Effective rates of protection have been estimated by using the Corden formula; both nominal and effective rates have been adjusted for overvaluation as compared to the hypothetical free trade situation.

been small. The small differences in rates of net nominal protection between 1966 and 1967 for major product categories suggest that the situation was similar in 1966 for capital goods and parts and components (Table 6.12). By contrast, nominal rates have declined from 84 to 45 percent on consumer durables, from 70 to 27 percent on consumer nondurables; large reductions are also shown for textile materials. These commodity groups are the prime

TABLE 6.11:   Number of Manufacturing Sectors in Given Ranges of Net Effective Protection

Range	Number of industries		Percent of 1964 value added
	1966	1967	1966
Less than 50%	7	10	54
Between 50 and 100%	6	7	17
Between 100 and 200%	3	3	10
200% and above	5	1	19
Total	21	21	100

Sources: Table 6.10 and IBGE estimates of industrial output for 1964.

candidates for redundancy, and it can be assumed that the reductions show a combination—in unknown proportions—of declines in realized protection *and* in redundancy.

Table 6.13 provides estimates of net nominal and effective rates of protection for ten industry groups, as well as for all industries, for manufacturing, and for primary production. From calculations based on the domestic input-output table, average net nominal protection was 46 percent in 1966 and 20 percent in 1967; the corresponding results from the free trade input-output table are 32 and 18 percent, respectively. Again, the differences are explained by the smaller weight given to high tariff items under the second method.

The estimates derived from the domestic input-output table show net effective protection in all sectors averaging 44 percent in 1966 and 19 percent in 1967. For primary production the results are 20 and −4 percent, and for manufacturing 72 and 45 percent. Finally, for manufacturing industries other

TABLE 6.12: Net Nominal Protection by Use of Product in Brazil, 1966 and 1967

(*Percent*)

Industry group	Use of product	1966	1967
	A. Disaggregation		
Nonmetallic mineral products	Construction materials	40	23
	Consumer durables	51	8
Machinery	Parts and components	16	16
	Capital goods	7	10
	Consumer durables	47	27
Electrical equipment	Parts and components	39	28
	Capital goods	35	40
	Consumer durables	151	67
Transport equipment	Parts and components	61	47
	Capital goods	38	28
	Consumer durables	139	63
Paper and products	Intermediate goods	34	22
	Consumer nondurables	107	43
Rubber products	Intermediate goods	43	38
	Consumer durables	63	56
Chemicals	Intermediate goods	17	16
	Fertilizers	−3	−8
	Consumer nondurables	25	15
Textiles	Threads and yarns	113	39
	Fabrics	159	75
	B. Reaggregation		
All 21 manufacturing sectors	Capital goods	24	22
	Construction materials	40	23
	Intermediate goods	35	19
	Parts and components	49	38
	Consumer durables	84	45
	Consumer nondurables	70	27

Source: Table 6.6 and text.

TABLE 6.13: Net Nominal and Effective Protection for Major Product Categories in Brazil, 1966 and 1967[a]

(Percent)

| | Estimates based on domestic coefficients | | | | Estimates based on free trade coefficients | | | |
| | 1966 | | 1967 | | 1966 | | 1967 | |
Industry group	Nominal protection	Effective protection	Nominal protection	Effective protection	Nominal protection	Effective protection	Nominal protection	Effective protection
I Agriculture, forestry, and fishing	29	21	-2	-4	18	15	3	-3
II Processed food	44	48	11	23	35	51	10	-2
III Beverages and tobacco	138	299	58	123	99	177	41	67
IV Mining and energy	0	-1	0	-1	-3	-34	4	-16
V Construction material	41	47	23	22	32	41	17	15
VI-A Intermediate products I	na	na	na	na	33	69	30	74
VI-B Intermediate products II	na	na	na	na	74	126	42	78
VI Intermediate products I and II	52	66	28	46	45	87	34	75
VII Nondurable consumer goods	89	115	44	76	103	150	52	70
VIII Consumer durables	64	98	37	53	100	203	58	104
IX Machinery	48	58	26	40	42	52	30	37
X Transport equipment	b	b	b	b	-1	-42	2	-27
I-X All industries	46	44	20	19	32	46	18	25
I + IV Primary production	25	20	-2	-4	9	-7	3	-9
II, III, V-X Manufacturing	57	72	30	45	46	80	28	47
VI-X Manufacturing less food, beverages, tobacco and construction material	59	75	34	51	52	91	36	69

Source: Table 6.8.

[a] Effective rates of protection have been estimated by using the Corden formula; both nominal and effective rates have been adjusted for over- valuation as compared to the hypothetical free trade situation.

[b] Included with consumer durables.

than food, beverages, tobacco, and construction materials, we get 71 percent for 1966 and 51 percent for 1967 (Table 6.13). The figures thus indicate a substantial reduction in net effective protection between 1966 and 1967, only part of which can be explained by reductions in tariff redundancy.

Among industry groups, apart from alcoholic beverages and tobacco, nondurable consumer goods and consumer durables are the most highly protected, with net effective rates in 1967 averaging 76 percent in the first case and 53 percent in the second.[14] Average net effective rates were 46 percent on intermediate products, 40 percent on machinery, and slightly over 20 percent on processed food and construction materials. These estimates have been derived by using domestic input-output coefficients; the range becomes wider if free trade coefficients are used. On the one hand, net effective protection will now be about 50–90 percent on consumer goods; on the other, it becomes negative on transport equipment. Finally, protection is considerably greater on intermediate products at higher levels of transformation than on those at lower levels.

Evaluation and Policy Recommendations[15]

The results of this study show that the structure of protection in Brazil strongly favored production for the domestic market, and discriminated against exports during the postwar period. Average import taxes, adjusted for overvaluation, were mostly in the 50–100 percent range between 1954 and 1965, and export taxes implicit in the structure of protection were around 30 percent. However, net nominal protection declined to 34 percent in 1966 and to 20 percent in 1967 while export taxes decreased to 22 percent and then to 13 percent.

In manufacturing, average net effective protection was 72 percent in 1966 and 45 percent in 1967. Nominal and effective rates of protection were highest on consumer goods—durables as well as nondurables. Effective protection was low or negative on construction materials, processed food, and transport equipment. Among the remaining industry groups, the ranking in ascending order is machinery, intermediate products at lower levels of fabrication, and intermediate products at higher levels of processing.

Discrimination against exports is a further consideration. As noted above, there was approximately a 30 percent implicit tax on noncoffee exports in the period 1954–65, 22 percent in 1966, and 13 percent in 1967. Most of these

---

[14] Estimates on consumer durables in Tables 6.8 and 6.13 are understated because they include all transport equipment, some of which is capital goods bearing lower duties.

[15] For a more extensive analysis, see Joel Bergsman, *Brazil: Industrialization and Trade Policies* (New York: Oxford University Press, 1970), parts 3 and 4.

exports are primary goods where value added accounts for about four-fifths of the output. The system of protection was roughly neutral with respect to inputs; therefore net effective discrimination against these exports was roughly 37 percent during 1954–65, 27 percent in 1966, and 16 percent in 1967.

The bias against exports of manufactured goods was very large. Even if we assume full drawbacks of tariffs on inputs in more than half of the manufacturing industries in 1967, value added available for domestic sales exceeded value added obtainable through exporting by 100 percent or more. This bias was even greater in earlier years, when there was a larger difference between import and export exchange rates. In 1966, there were eight sectors in which, on the average, exporting would have required negative value added.

Discrimination against exporting in traditional as well as nontraditional industries contributed to Brazil's poor export performance during the postwar period. In the bias against exports we find a self-confirming prophecy: policy-makers assumed that export promotion would not be productive; policies discriminated against exports, and exports stagnated. Since the ratio of imports to GNP is already quite low in Brazil, and cannot be reduced indefinitely, in the long run the growth of exports limits the rate of economic growth. Even in the presence of protection in other countries, therefore, it does not make sense for Brazil to adopt policies which discriminate against her own exports.

On the other hand, protection has contributed to growth through import substitution. But for various reasons the relationship between protection and import substitution in the postwar period is far from simple. First, import substitution in many manufacturing industries was already virtually complete at the start of the period. Second, the industrial classification which had to be used often combined products and processes which are very different, and which received very different levels of protection. Third, the measures of the structure of protection relate to only 1966 and 1967 and are not completely representative of the entire period. Fourth, the estimates of the structure of protection do not take into account the differences between the using sectors in costs of capital equipment, or other subsidies and special treatment; yet these were important influences on structural change within manufacturing. Fifth, the estimates of effective protection based on the domestic input-output table pertain to gross value added. A better measure for estimating the effects of the structure of protection on resource allocation would have been the protection of net value added. Data to estimate this measure were, however, not available.

In spite of all these problems, it turns out that there is a relationship between the structure of protection and the structure of import substitution. In this analysis, the measure of import substitution used is the ratio of imports to domestic production for 1949, divided by that same ratio for 1962. This measure will be called the "import substitution ratio."[16] Higher or lower import substitution ratios indicate that much or little import substitution has taken place. To represent the structure of protection, our estimates of protection for 1966, adjusted for overvaluation, will be used.

We have classified only wood products and food products as export industries. These industries increased the ratio of exports to output to a considerable extent, approaching 20 percent in 1962. Also, they had a low share of imports in total supply and enjoyed relatively low protection throughout the postwar period. Three other manufacturing industries (leather products, textiles, and chemicals) export 5–10 percent of their production. But their exports fell in absolute terms, as well as in relation to output, between 1949 and 1962, and therefore have not been included in the export category.

In an analysis of import substitution in the remaining sectors, it should be noted that for a number of industries any measure of import substitution is meaningless because the initial share of imports in total supply was very low. These "mature" industries were already well-established at the beginning of the postwar period. The exact definition of these industries is necessarily somewhat arbitrary. We have included in this group all industries where imports were less than 13 percent of domestic production in 1949. This rule enables us to divide all nonexport industries into three groups:

1. Mature industries: imports accounting for less than 13 percent of domestic production in 1949
2. Highly protected infant industries: net effective protection exceeding 98 percent in 1966, and the import substitution ratio above 11
3. Less-protected infant industries: net effective protection below 98 percent and import substitution ratio less than 11

There are no industries among the "infants" with high protection and low import substitution, or vice versa. This means that if industries with very little scope for import substitution in 1949 are excluded, a relationship exists among those remaining: high protection is associated with high import substitution, and vice versa. The results are shown in Table 6.14.

The differences among the four groups are brought out clearly in Table 6.15 which shows average values for each of them: a low export ratio for all but the export industries, a low initial import ratio and very high protection for the mature sectors, and a greater reduction in the import ratio for the highly protected infant industries than for the less-protected infants. In 1949 the

---

[16] These data are based on calculations by Samuel A. Morley and Gordon Smith, "On the Measurement of Import Substitution," *American Economic Review*, September 1970, pp. 728–35.

TABLE 6.14: Relation between Protection and Import Substitution in Brazilian Manufacturing

Industry	Export-production ratio,[a] 1962	Import-production ratio,[b] 1949	Import-substitution ratio, 1949 relative to 1962	Net effective protection, 1966 (percent)
Export industries: low initial import ratio and low protection				
Wood products	0.193	0.122		15
Food products	0.185	0.060		48
Mature industries: low initial import ratio and high protection				
Furniture	0.000	0.025		168
Rubber products	0.002	0.127		87
Leather products	0.069	0.104		72
Perfumes, soaps, etc.	0.000	0.007		6,710
Textiles	0.097	0.084		279
Clothing	0.001	0.002		246
Beverages	0.000	0.118		333
Tobacco	0.001	0.000		227
Highly protected infants: high protection and much import substitution				
Electrical equipment	0.001	5.400	21.7	149
Transport equipment	0.008	4.470	37.0	99
Plastics	0.000	0.965	41.7	124
Less-protected infants: lower protection and less import substitution				
Nonmetallic mineral products	0.002	0.270	3.52	47
Metallurgy	0.001	1.160	2.31	25
Machinery	0.009	1.860	2.95	12
Paper and products	0.004	0.471	1.90	73
Chemicals	0.076	8.730	10.31	26
Pharmaceuticals	0.004	0.277	2.73	10
Miscellaneous	0.003	0.399	2.33	81

Source: Joel Bergsman, *Brazil: Industrialization and Trade Policies* (New York: Oxford University Press, 1970).
[a] Ratio of the value of exports to that of domestic production.
[b] Ratio of the domestic value added that would have been necessary to produce the actual imports to value added in domestic production.

import ratio for the highly protected infant industries had been much higher than for the less-protected infants, but by 1962 this relationship was reversed.

The mature industries, which were already well established at the end of World War II, generally received even higher protection than the infant industries[17] and also failed to export. But these industries had no inherent disad-

---

[17] Some qualifications should be noted: the consumer durables parts of electrical and transport equipment were "infants," and received very high protection. Rubber products, on the other hand, included automotive tires and tubes, a real infant; imports were low in 1949 because the Brazilian motor vehicles industry had not yet been started, but imports of finished automobiles were already extremely expensive and therefore quite limited.

TABLE 6.15: Protection and Import Substitution in Four Groups of Industries

Group	Ratio of exports to domestic production, 1962	Ratio of imports to domestic production		Import substitution ratio, 1949 relative to 1962	Net effective protection, 1966 (percent)
		1949	1962		
Export industries	0.186	0.070	0.036		44
Mature industries	0.055	0.074	0.017		244
Highly protected infants	0.005	4.536	0.145	31.3	120
Less-protected infants	0.024	1.504	0.346	4.4	30

Source: Table 6.14.

vantages—there are firms in leather products, textiles, and tobacco which export regularly. So not only the justification but also the need for high protection for these sectors is doubtful. Indeed, it would appear that the high costs observed in many firms of these industries are probably the *result* rather than the cause of high protection.

The infant industries are generally those producing capital goods and intermediate products. They also tend to be the industries where foreign private investment is most important. Finally, they were the recipients of investment subsidies in the form of low interest loans and special treatment of imported capital equipment. This helps to explain why import substitution proceeded rapidly even in industries with relatively low protection such as machinery and transport equipment.

On the whole, Brazilian import substitution in the postwar period proceeded by way of "backward linkages," encompassing many intermediate products and capital goods. Imports do, however, continue to play an important role in these groups of commodities. Among capital goods, imports are technologically more advanced than domestic production and have a much higher content of engineering design. Among intermediate products, the bulk of imports are products of processing industries where economies of scale are especially important.

In evaluating the system of protection in Brazil, one is struck by the fact that the greatest protection was provided for the established, mature industries where infant industry arguments do not apply. Protection also appears to have been excessive in a number of industries producing intermediate products and capital goods.

In international trade theory, the costs of protection are usually defined in terms of losses caused by misallocations arising from the price-distorting effects of protection. These costs appear to be relatively minor in Brazil as compared with other sources of inefficiency which have also been due to protection. Protection has probably cost Brazil far more by permitting inefficiencies in industries which *could* be efficient, than by helping to establish industries which are at an inherent comparative disadvantage.[18]

Protection is a powerful instrument for creating domestic industry. It is not useful for making that industry efficient. Tariffs help to induce investment by increasing the profitability of domestic operations, but also reduce the motivation for improvements in efficiency. Efficiency has been of secondary importance as a goal of Brazilian industrialization policy, which has aimed at import substitution without appropriate consideration of its cost. But, as protection reduces the search for better production methods, better organization, improved quality, and technological progress, the national economy suffers a continuing and increasing cost. This last effect seems to be particularly important in Brazil.

Brazil's relatively large domestic market has been both a help and a hindrance to the development of its manufacturing industries. The larger Brazilian market has made import substitution less uneconomical than in smaller developing countries and has facilitated the backward integration of Brazilian industry to capital goods and intermediate products. But the large domestic market has also made most Brazilian manufacturers content with their home market, and has contributed to a live-and-let-live attitude that breeds inefficiencies and does not provide inducements for technological progress. Such attitudes have been especially prevalent in the mature industries, which are the most protected.

If Brazilian manufacturing is to become modern and efficient, it must be given both the opportunity and the motivation to reduce costs. Indiscriminate tariff-cutting alone is not the answer. Better physical infrastructure, better education, and more industrial experience can contribute to the ability to reduce costs. Lower protection can increase the motivation. Future competitiveness and reductions in current inefficiencies should be emphasized and high-cost production should not be supported indefinitely.

Further reductions in the escalation of tariffs would also be advisable. This would bring effective rates of protection closer to nominal rates; it would reduce existing disparities in effective rates, and lessen the very high protection for those industries which need it least. The reductions in escalation would be accomplished by moving to a more uniform set of nominal rates. One such system would be as follows: there could be a minimum tariff of 10 to 15 percent applied for revenue purposes to all imports without exception, a higher rate of perhaps 30 percent for all manufactured products, and a special, temporary higher rate to protect infant industries where the government determines higher protection to be advisable. Such reductions in tariffs would be

---

[18] See Chapter 4.

associated with a higher (devalued) exchange rate—perhaps halfway between the 1967 level and the free trade equilibrium level. In addition, exports of manufactured goods should receive subsidies in order to remove the existing bias against such exports. Sale of manufactured goods should be at least as profitable in export markets as in the domestic market.

Removing the bias against exports of manufactures could be one of a number of changes needed to make Brazilian industry more cost-conscious, less inward-looking, and more modern and efficient. The almost complete lack of contact with competitors in domestic or export markets can only harm the Brazilian economy. Increasing the profitability of exports of manufacturers, increasing competition from imports, and providing better infrastructure, education, etc., would all be useful steps toward lower costs and improved quality in domestic production.

CHAPTER 7

THE STRUCTURE OF PROTECTION IN CHILE

Teresa Jeanneret

Economic Growth and International Trade[1]

Natural Resource Base

Chile is a comparatively thinly populated country and its population is unevenly distributed, with more than 85 percent of its 9 million inhabitants concentrated in the central provinces that extend from Aconcagua to Llanquihue and cover one-fourth of the national territory. Chile's small population, long transportation routes (the country's length is about 2,650 miles; its average width, 110 miles), and rather unevenly distributed per capita income of about $500 make it a country with a small market, with all the consequences that this entails for its development process. It should be added that Chile's long coast-

Teresa Jeanneret is a research associate and lecturer at the Institute of Economics at the University of Chile; her work on the study was carried out in the framework of the Institute's research program and was partly financed by the Institute.
    [1] Extensive use has been made in this section of the information contained in the following publications: P. T. Ellsworth, *Chile: An Economy in Transition* (New York: Macmillan Co., 1945); O. Muñoz, "Long-run Trends in the Manufacturing Industry in Chile since 1914" (Ph.D. diss., Yale University, 1967) which was published in Spanish under the title *Crecimiento Industrial de Chile, 1914–65* (Santiago: Instituto de Economia, 1968); and P. Cabezón, "An Evaluation of Commercial Policy in the Chilean Economy" (Ph.D. diss., The University of Wisconsin, 1970).

line opens it toward the sea but formidable natural barriers separate it from neighboring countries.[2]

Chile has abundant arable land and a broad climatic range. Almost the entire northern region covering two-fifths of the national territory is, however, desert; the growing of rubber, coffee, bananas, and other tropical crops is therefore impossible. The southern part of the country is, however, amenable to the cultivation of temperate zone products. The importing of such products into Chile during recent decades has resulted not so much from any shortage of natural resources as from a combination of adverse factors relating to policy-making. These include discrimination against agriculture through tariffs and exchange rates, the structure of farm ownership, and poor farming techniques and marketing.[3]

Chile's lengthy coastline gives it considerable fishery potential. Neither this nor its abundant forestry resources have so far been adequately exploited. Nor has its considerable hydroelectric potential, the exploitation of which could reduce production costs in certain mining and manufacturing industries, been fully utilized.

It is Chile's enormous mineral resources, mainly in the north, but also in parts of the center and the south, that have set the pattern for the Chilean economy practically since it gained independence. Since 1844, exports first of silver, then of copper and saltpeter, and later of copper alone, have provided the country with at least three-fifths and at times almost nine-tenths of its foreign exchange earnings. Moreover, taxes on the mining industry have continued to account for a substantial part of the government's tax revenues.

An essential feature of Chile's mineral wealth is the large size of the deposits, which has made it possible to use modern, highly mechanized techniques requiring little labor and to attain high productivity per worker. In large-scale copper mining, dominated by two giant American companies, Kennecott and Anaconda, the annual output of copper per worker reached 40 tons in the mid-sixties as against 17 tons in 1929. Restricting our attention to the postwar period, we find that in 1944, 490 thousand tons of copper were produced in large-scale mining with a working force of 20 thousand; in 1965, 480 thousand tons were produced by only 13 thousand workers. In the latter year, the entire mining industry employed 100 thousand workers out of 2.4 million in the economy as a whole. This phenomenon partially explains the country's wish to become industrialized. Even if Chile had fully exploited its

---

[2] The Andes separate it from Argentina and Bolivia; the Atacama desert, from Peru; and the Pacific Ocean, from the rest of the world.

[3] Imports of temperate zone agricultural products, which amounted to about $36 million a year between 1942 and 1944, rose to an annual average of $132 million between 1960 and 1964. Over the same period the foreign trade gap in farm products widened from $10 million to $92 million.

possibilities in developing the mining industry, in which it enjoys a comparative advantage, this would not have absorbed a high proportion of its entire
labor force.

Patterns of Growth and Structural Change

While Chile has much unexploited copper and iron ore, its saltpeter is
limited by world market conditions. Chilean saltpeter could not withstand
competition from synthetic nitrates discovered during World War I, and its
production has been declining more or less continuously from the record levels
reached in the mid-twenties. Correspondingly, Chile's share in the world
supply of nitrogen fell from 64 percent in 1910 to 1.5 percent in 1960 (Table
7.1).

Copper output rose by one-half between 1929 and 1945, and by one-third
between 1945 and 1965. Following a decline during the depression of the
1930s, the growth of production accelerated at the time of World War II, and
Chile's share in the world copper supply reached 21 percent in 1945 as against
15 percent in 1929. Production fell, however, in the years immediately following the war, and by 1950 Chile accounted for less than 14 percent of the world
output of copper. Despite the rise in production in subsequent years, Chile's
share in world supply declined further and it was below 12 percent in 1965.

Increases in Chile's share during World War II, and its decline in the years
immediately following, are explained by the fact that during the war copper
from other exporting countries was not available or was available in limited
quantities. More recently, however, the overvalued exchange rate, the unfavorable tax treatment of the large companies, together with the actual or
imagined risk of nationalization and the fear of further increases in taxes,
appear to have been the major factors contributing to the decline of Chile's
share in world copper production.

By contrast, the production of iron ore, which was comparatively small
until the end of World War II, has risen spectacularly following the discovery
of rich new deposits. Between 1955 and 1965, output increased more than
seven times, and the value of exports rose from $6 million to $73 million.
Finally, petroleum production, which began early in the 1950s, can now meet
practically all domestic consumption needs, although the deposits so far discovered provide no assurance that this will remain so.

Manufacturing production showed an upward trend during much of the
period under consideration. Between 1929 and 1940, output in manufacturing
nearly tripled, that of agriculture rose by only 23 percent, and mining output
did not recover its 1929 level; the greatest proportional increase—due largely
to the growth of public administration—was in government and public util-

TABLE 7.1: Copper and Nitrate: Chile's Share in World Production and Chilean Export Prices, 1910–65

| | Copper | | | | Nitrate[a] | | | |
Year	Chilean production (million pounds) (1)	World production (2)	Chilean share in world production (percent) (3)	Chilean export price (U.S. cents per pound) (4)	Chilean production (thousand tons of nitrogen) (5)	World production (6)	Chilean share in world production (percent) (7)	Export price (U.S.$ per ton) (8)
1910	8	na	na	15.0	382	590	64.3	60.6
1920	176	2,165	8.1	16.7	391	1,160	33.6	91.4
1929	634	4,236	15.0	17.5	509	2,130	23.9	67.7
1932	206	1,974	10.4	5.6	170	1,580	10.7	41.1
1940	732	5,010	14.6	11.2	na	na	na	21.2
1945	994	4,808	20.7	11.5	na	na	na	27.1
1950	760	5,556	13.7	21.0	271	4,730	5.7	41.2
1955	864	6,777	12.7	34.1	250	7,960	3.1	38.5
1960	1,173	9,006	13.0	29.4	191	12,310	1.5	32.9
1965	1,291	10,846	11.9	35.2	na	na	na	na

Sources: (1) Until 1955, Dirección de Estadísticas y Censos; for 1960 and 1965, Corporación del Cobre. (2) American Bureau of Metal Statistics, Yearbook. (4) S. Reynolds, Essays on the Chilean Economy (Homewood, Ill.: Richard D. Irwin, Inc., 1965), and direct information. (5) and (6) 1910 to 1934, Ministerio de Hacienda, "La Industria del Salitre en Chile," 1935; 1950 to 1965, Dirección de Estadísticas y Censos, "Annuario Mineria" 1961, 1962. (8) Corporación de Ventas de Salitre y Yodo de Chile.

[a] Since 1929, data refer to production year (from the previous July to the month of June in the year indicated).

ities. With public services increasing nearly fivefold, the output of these sectors combined rose 37 percent during the period (Table 7.2).

In the following years agriculture remained the lagging sector while mining recorded an annual rate of growth of 5.6 percent between 1950 and 1967. By contrast, the expansion of the manufacturing sector slowed down, with its rate of growth hardly exceeding that of the net domestic product. As a result of these changes, agriculture's share in the net domestic product fell from 14.0 percent in 1950 to 9.1 percent in 1967, that of mining rose from 5.3 to 8.1 percent, and manufacturing's contribution increased from 17.3 percent to 19.0 percent. In the same period, there was a slight decline in the share of services, with transportation and communications in the lead (see Table 2.3).

Rates of growth in the individual manufacturing industries showed substantial differences between the 1920–50 and 1950–65 periods. Between 1920 and 1950, the output of chemical and petroleum products, metal products (including machinery), and textiles rose nearly ten times while in the manufacturing sector the increase was not quite threefold. The lagging sectors—with output less than doubling—were food products, beverages, tobacco products, and clothing and shoes. Chemical and petroleum products and metal products maintained their lead after 1950, and were joined by beverages and by paper and printed matter. By contrast, between 1950 and 1965, the output of tobacco products, and that of clothing and shoes, declined in absolute terms (Table 7.3).

The industrialization process, which began during the last century, was given impetus by the depression of the thirties. On the one hand, the catastrophic decline in the prices of mineral exports reduced the advantages of this sector over manufacturing industries; on the other, it necessitated the imposition of import restrictions and successive devaluations (from 8.26 to 25.07 pesos to the dollar between 1931 and 1934) which improved the competitive position of domestic manufacturing industry vis-à-vis imports. In addition to this, and closely linked with the depression, was the idea that development was

TABLE 7.2:   Sectoral Production Indices in Chile, 1909–51

(Index, 1929 = 100)

Year	Agriculture	Mining	Manu- facturing industry	Government and public utilities	Together
1909–11	56.3	40.4	55.0	60.6	46.1
1919–21	70.0	41.3	68.0	58.7	48.3
1929	100	100	100	100	100
1932	88.3	30.4	85.0	105.1	54.2
1929–31	97.4	76.0	91.6	104.6	87.8
1939–41	108.3	94.5	146.0	203.5	102.2
1949–51	123.0	95.4	272.1	461.5	136.7

Source: Marto Ballesteros and Tom Davis, "The Growth of Output and Employment in Basic Sectors of the Chilean Economy," *Economic Development and Cultural Change*, I, 1960.

TABLE 7.3: Manufacturing Production in Chile, 1919–65

(Million escudos in 1950 prices)

Annual averages	Manu-facturing total	Food products	Bever-ages	Tobacco products	Textiles	Clothing and shoes	Wood products and furniture	Paper and printed matter	Leather and rubber products	Chemical and petroleum products	Nonmetal mineral products	Metal products[a]
1919–21	17.4	8.1	0.9	0.8	0.9	3.1	0.9	0.6	0.8	0.4	0.3	0.7
1929–31	na	7.8	na	0.9	1.3	na	na	na	na	0.7	0.4	na
1939–41	31.3	9.2	1.1	1.5	5.0	4.6	2.7	1.4	1.2	1.5	1.0	2.0
1949–51	47.2	12.8	1.7	1.3	7.3	6.0	2.2	2.0	1.8	3.5	2.0	6.7
1954–56	55.1	14.9	2.2	1.4	8.7	5.6	1.8	2.1	1.7	3.9	2.1	10.9
1959–61	72.7	19.4	3.8	1.2	11.2	5.1	2.1	4.1	2.1	7.9	3.1	12.8
1964–65	97.3	24.3	4.9	1.1	16.1	5.2	2.7	5.4	2.7	10.1	4.3	20.4

Source: Oscar E. Muñoz, "Long-run Trends in the Manufacturing Industry in Chile since 1914" (Ph.D. diss., Yale University, 1967). This was published in Spanish under the title *Crecimiento Industrial de Chile, 1914-65* (Santiago: Instituto de Economía, 1968).

[a] Includes basic metals, metal products, and machinery and transport equipment.

synonymous with industrialization and that this, in turn, called for state intervention in the economy. Consequently, a vigorous policy of industrial protection and direct governmental promotion was undertaken. By the time when, following World War II, the price of copper more than regained its pre-depression level and reestablished its relative position vis-à-vis manufacturing products, the trend toward industrialization and state intervention was firmly established.

Import Substitution and Export Structure

The policy of protection in Chile falls into two distinct stages: the first comprises the emergency measures taken to alleviate the immediate effects of the depression; the second, those adopted afterward. In the first period, general and nondiscriminatory measures, such as across-the-board increases in tariffs and devaluations, had been applied. Subsequently, however, particular industries were encouraged by the use, in addition to customs tariffs, of quotas, subsidies, loans, multiple exchange rates, exemptions, and direct state investments. As a result, effective protection was probably increased in these industries but was reduced in others. Thus, for example, the protection of the iron and steel industry and of petroleum undoubtedly stimulated the expansion of their production and penalized the users of these commodities.

Across-the-board protection during the thirties importantly contributed to the acceleration of the process of import substitution. Although it took thirteen years to reduce the share of imports in the domestic supply of manufactured goods from 51.5 percent in 1914–15 to 43.8 percent in 1927, a decline from 43.8 to 29.9 percent was accomplished in the following decade. By the late thirties, the import share for manufacturing fell below the level indicated for an "average" country possessing Chile's characteristics in Chenery's well-known study.[4]

The decline was the largest for nonmetallic products where Chile had been behind other countries in the process of import substitution. In paper and printed matter, and in leather and rubber products, the share of imports fell more than the average, bringing it by the end of the period well below that observed in other countries at similar levels of industrialization (Table 7.4).

Haphazardness in the structure of protection and the difficulties encountered at a higher stage of import substitution have contributed to a slowdown in the process of import substitution since World War II, and Chile has returned to the status of Chenery's "normal" country. Import substitution has been the most pronounced in chemicals, nonmetallic materials, and metal

---

[4] H. B. Chenery, "Patterns of Industrial Growth," *American Economic Review*, September 1960, pp. 624–54.

TABLE 7.4: Share of Imports in Domestic Supply in Chile, 1914–15 to 1963–64[a]

(Percent)

Industry group	1914–15	1927	1937–38	1952–53	1963–64
Food, beverages, and tobacco	22.5 (12.2)	11.4 (11.2)	7.2 (10.5)	11.6 (9.3)	12.2 (8.3)
Textiles, clothing and shoes	57.6 (55.7)	50.3	35.5	6.1	6.6
Wood products	23.2 (30.8)	4.9 (26.8)	3.2 (24.0)	1.5 (20.0)	2.0 (17.7)
Paper and printed matter	40.0 (52.9)	42.0 (45.1)	23.9 (39.3)	29.6 (30.6)	13.9 (25.6)
Leather and rubber products	24.6 (57.4)	36.5 (48.3)	16.3 (41.3)	31.1 (31.6)	17.3 (26.2)
Chemical products	91.3 (72.8)	71.3 (66.2)	60.6 (60.6)	51.8 (51.5)	38.5 (45.0)
Nonmetallic products	81.0 (34.2)	75.5 (27.7)	29.5 (23.5)	14.3 (17.9)	11.1 (15.2)
Metallic products	87.0 (86.3)	85.0 (79.0)	71.1 (71.7)	53.3 (58.8)	46.9 (51.3)
Total	51.5 (44.4)	43.8 (39.1)	29.9 (35.1)	26.0 (30.8)	24.6 (25.1)

Source: O. Muñoz, "Long-run Trends in the Manufacturing Industry in Chile since 1914." concept in "Patterns of Industrial Growth," American Economic Review, September 1960, pp. 624–54.

[a] Figures in parentheses are "normal" values, according to the Chenery

products, and has contributed to the high growth rates observed in these industries.

Whereas import substitution in nonmetallic minerals and metals has led to a substantial decline in the share of industrial materials in total imports, the increased need for base chemicals has had the opposite effect on the imports of chemicals. In turn, the rise in the domestic production of intermediate products has both entailed a decline in the share of basic manufactures in total imports and necessitated an increase in that of capital goods. Finally, as noted before, the expansion of the domestic production of fuels has reduced the need for fuel imports (see Table 2.8).

Exports continue to be dominated by copper which accounted for three-fourths of export earnings in 1967. Iron ore comes next with a share of 8 percent, showing a considerable increase over the 2 percent share in 1950. By contrast, exports of saltpeter (nitrates) continued to decline in absolute as well as in relative terms, with their contribution to total exports falling from 25 percent in 1950 to 2 percent in 1967 (Table 7.5).

Chile exports approximately 96 percent, 90 percent, and 79 percent, respectively, of its copper, iron ore, and nitrate output. Agricultural exports are small and declining. In manufacturing only the exports of copper products and paper are of importance and this, too, is a recent development, due largely to the establishment of LAFTA. Export possibilities for pulp and paper are excellent, although they have not yet been sufficiently exploited.[5]

We have further compared data for the 1950–53 and 1963–66 periods on changes in the major factors which affect Chile's export performance. The

TABLE 7.5: Principal Exports of Chile, 1950–67

(Percent of total exports)

Commodity		1950	1955	1960	1965	1967
Unwrought copper	(SITC 682.1)	50.0	65.2	68.9	59.1	75.1
Copper products	(682.2)	na	4.2	0.2	8.0	1.0
Iron ore	(281.3)	2.4	1.3	7.2	11.4	7.5
Saltpeter	(271.2)	24.9	11.8	5.3	4.4	1.8
Molybdenum ore and concentrates	(283.9)	na	na	1.3	1.7	na
Fishmeal	(081.4)	na	na	0.3	1.2	1.5
Newsprint	(641.1)	na	na	0.8	1.1	0.9
Wool	(262.1)	3.3	0.5	1.1	0.8	0.6
Timber	(243)	2.0	3.5	0.3	0.5	0.0
Total principal exports		82.6	86.5	85.4	88.2	88.4
Total exports ($ million)		283.3	474.6	490.1	687.8	907.7

Source: U.N., *Yearbook of International Trade Statistics.*

---

[5] The insignis pine, which is a species of conifer suitable for cellulose manufacture, grows in Chile almost twice as quickly as in other countries that produce and export cellulose and paper. This advantage has, however, been neutralized by inadequate utilization of economies of scale, and the comparatively high cost of electric power.

figures of Table 2.6 show that while Chile benefited from increases in world demand for copper and the concomitant rise in copper prices, it experienced a substantial decline in its share in world copper exports. Still, copper export values nearly doubled during this period and the eightfold rise in iron ore exports further helped Chile's balance of payments. In spite of the fall in the exports of saltpeter, Chile's major exports, including copper, iron ore, and saltpeter, rose by three-fourths; its minor exports rose by only slightly less. But had Chile maintained its share in world markets, exports would have been one-third higher.

The System of Protection

Development until 1955

Until 1928, protection in Chile was confined to general and comparatively modest tariffs on imports (25–30 percent) and to specific taxes on exports, notably on saltpeter. Their main purpose was to raise revenue for the government. By 1928, however, the manufacturing sector was fairly well developed and it brought increasing pressure on the government to raise tariffs. This was accomplished in the Tariff Law of 1928 which served as the basis of Chilean tariff legislation until 1966.

As noted before, the depression of the thirties intensified the trend toward protection and ultimately led to the application of a variety of measures which discriminated among individual industries, regions, and suppliers. The result was a complicated system of regulations, which gave rise to a rather chaotic situation. Without claiming to describe in full the system prevailing from 1928 to 1955, we outline its six main features.

Tariffs. The Tariff Law of 1928 provided for specific duties on imports. From 1928 to the middle of the thirties, various adjustments were made in these duties, with the overall effect of raising them to more than twice their 1928 levels in ad valorem terms.[6] Subsequently, in 1936, 1941, and 1942, for various commodity groups, ad valorem tariffs of 30 percent, 3 percent, and 62 percent were added to the specific duties. There were many other amendments to the Tariff Law but these related to particular products and are difficult to evaluate.

Exchange control. The decline in exports that occurred in the early thirties led to the introduction of exchange control, operated first by the Exchange Control Committee and later by the National Board of Foreign Trade and the Central Bank. This control was exercised by means of multiple exchange rates and import licenses. During the first few years it was designed to minimize fluctuations in exchange rates and to ensure a supply of essential

---

[6] Ellsworth, *Chile: An Economy in Transition.*

imports; subsequently, its major objectives were to minimize the effects of successive devaluations on domestic prices (in particular on the prices of prime necessities) and to maintain or increase the taxes levied on the large-scale mining firms.

Multiple rates of exchange. At the outset, three rates of exchange were employed but their number increased to seven by 1955. The situation developed along familiar lines. Owing to the rapidity of inflation[7] and the fact that rates of exchange were fixed, the balance of payments ran into periodic crises, which, coupled with the pressure exerted by the exporters who were hardest hit, compelled the government to introduce a new rate of exchange, called "free," "temporary," or otherwise. This was originally applicable only to certain exports and some of the luxury imports but little by little it was extended to other products, and the lowest rates of exchange fell into disuse.

Quotas and import licenses. Quotas were imposed to protect home industries from foreign competition and to ration the expenditure of foreign exchange on luxury goods. In some instances quantitative restrictions were applied to imports of goods from certain countries to force them to import from Chile. Closely bound up with quotas of this type were the bilateral trade agreements concluded to secure markets for Chilean goods, and governed by ad hoc clauses.

Special regimes. Mainly from the end of the forties, a number of special customs regimes were introduced to promote the development of specific industries, companies, or regions. With various amendments, these regimes have remained in force up to the present time. In view of their impact on effective protection, they are examined in considerable detail in Appendix D.

Lobbying. Like any other system of licenses and controls, Chile's foreign trade control machinery lent itself readily to lobbying. Although impossible to measure, such pressures existed throughout and served to heighten the confusion already inherent in the system.

The 1955 Reform and Subsequent Changes

The system of protection underwent changes in 1955. At that time a team of foreign experts, the Klein-Saks mission, was invited to advise the government on the formulation of a stabilization policy. Apart from the adoption of a series of measures on fiscal, monetary, wage, price, and administrative policies, a reorganization of the foreign trade system was also undertaken.[8]

---

[7] Inflation reached its peak in 1954–55 when prices rose by more than 75 percent.

[8] For a detailed discussion see D. Felix, "Structural Imbalance, Social Conflict, and Inflation: Appraisal of Chile's Recent Anti-Inflationary Effort," *Economic Development and Cultural Change*, January 1960, pp. 113–47, and "Chile's Economy in the Period 1950–63," mimeographed (Santiago: Institute of Economics of the University of Chile, 1963).

Its basic features may be summarized as follows: (*a*) the elimination of the system of import quotas and licenses; (*b*) the establishment of a list of permitted imports; (*c*) the consolidation of the system of multiple exchange rates into two rates of exchange, a banking rate for merchandise exports and imports and a brokers' rate for invisible transactions; and (*d*) the introduction of advance deposits on imports.

The stabilization policy introduced in 1956 made widespread use of foreign loans, both for financing public investments undertaken to maintain the level of employment and for increasing the supply of imported goods to curb price increases. Because of the increase in foreign exchange supply, in the late fifties "permitted imports" included virtually all commodities. But the loans substantially increased Chile's external debt, the servicing of which contributed to the exhaustion of the country's foreign exchange reserves in 1961. Another factor contributing to this result was that although exchange rates had originally been intended to fluctuate freely, they were in practice regulated by the Central Bank and in fact remained fixed from 1959 until the end of 1961. Two exchange rates were in effect during this period: a banking rate applicable to merchandise transactions and approved capital exports and a brokers' rate applied to invisibles and some capital flows.

Following the balance-of-payments crisis in January 1962, practically all imports were suspended and devaluation ensued, although only for the brokers' rate; payments on merchandise imports were postponed. By the end of 1962, the list of permitted imports had been greatly curtailed and the banking rate of exchange had been finally devalued. Payments for permitted imports, however, were still being effected about six months late.

In 1963 a new, higher rate of exchange, the "forward" rate was introduced for essential imports, which permitted these to be paid for with a delay of only three or four months. In 1964, practically all import transactions were effected at the "forward" rate of exchange, as were all exports, except those of the large-scale copper-mining industry. Finally, as a result of the Copper Agreements[9] concluded between the large copper companies and the government, the banking rate of exchange was devalued more rapidly until, in the midsixties, it was brought into line with the "forward" rate of exchange, thus marking a return to two exchange rates (Table 7.6). These rates have since been devalued at monthly and, subsequently, semimonthly intervals in accordance with increases in domestic prices.

Mention should also be made of the introduction of advance deposits (prepayment requirements) on imports, which need to be made for a period of one or three months at rates that vary among commodities. These deposits are

---

[9] Under these agreements, the companies undertook to expand production in return for substantial tax reductions and nondiscriminatory exchange treatment.

TABLE 7.6:   Exchange Rates in Chile, 1928–67[a]

(Pesos per U.S. dollar)[b]

1928	8.22
1930	8.26 (until July 1931)
1934	Official 9.66 (Exports of large-scale mines; government imports; 1 to 20 percent other exports) Export draft rate *25.07* (Other exports, most imports) Free 25.09 (Invisibles, more or less forbidden by the law)

1940   Official   19.37 (id.)
       Exports   *24.98* (id.)
       Free   32.82 (id.)
       Free disposal   *30.95* (official invisibles, luxury imports, some exports)
       Special (ex official)   19.37 (Exports of large-scale mines, very few imports, and other exports)

1950   Official   *31.0* (Diverse imports and exports)
       Banks   *43.0* (Diverse imports and exports)
       Special commercial *50.0* (Diverse imports and exports)
       Provisional   *60.0* (Diverse imports and exports)
       Brokers   90.0   (Invisibles)

1955   Special (until May 1955) 19.37 (id.)
       Banks   *200* (Most exports and imports)
       Others   31 (Some exports and imports)
                                43 (Some exports and imports)
                                60 (Some exports and imports)
                                110 (Some exports and imports)
       Brokers   730 (Invisibles)

	Banks	Brokers
1956[c]	*453*	534
1957	*621*	694
1958	*793*	1,000
1959	*1,047*	1,055
1960	*1,051*	1,051
1961	*1,051*	1,051
1962	*1,142*	1,751

	Forward	Cash	
1963	na	1,875	3,011
1964	*2,741*	2,373	3,204
1965	*3,310*	3,131	3,739
1966	*4,000*	3,948	4,645
1967		5,031	5,689

Sources: "Estadistica Chilena," *Dirección General de Estadísticas;* "Boletin Mensual," *Banco Central de Chile.*
   [a] Rates in italics are those at which the larger proportion of exports and imports were carried on, except for exports of the great mining enterprises in 1934, 1940, 1950, and 1955 (until May).
   [b] 1,000 pesos = 1 escudo
   [c] In August 1956, multiple exchange rates were eliminated.

tantamount to an additional customs tariff, with rates depending on the cost of their financing. The task of determining the rate and the duration of prior deposits was assigned to the Central Bank.[10]

---

   [10] Initially, the rates of these deposits varied from 5 to 200 percent of the c.i.f. value, but the upper limit subsequently climbed to as much as 10,000 percent in certain cases. During recent years, however, the rates have seldom exceeded 1,000 percent.

Whereas, prior to 1959, advance deposits had been made in national currency, between 1959 and 1964 they had to be effected in dollar bonds issued by
the government. These dollar bonds, which earned interest in dollars at the
rate of about 7 percent per annum, were introduced as a means of securing the
repatriation of Chilean capital abroad. Since their issue was limited, they
became increasingly scarce, and their owners received, besides the 7 percent
interest, an additional income (which sometimes reached 30 percent a year) by
leasing them to importers. To put an end to this situation, deposits in escudos
were reintroduced in 1964.

In 1959, the intention had been gradually to replace the advance deposits
by import tariffs, and with this object in view, an "additional tax" on the c.i.f.
value of imports was imposed, to be fixed by the Central Bank.[11] This, however, proved to be a slow process, and in 1961 a large number of products
were still subject to the advance deposit requirement rather than to the additional tax. As a result of the crisis that occurred in December of that year, not
only was the list of permitted imports curtailed, but all the products that were
admitted were made subject to both prepayment requirements and an additional tax.

At the end of 1964, a new attempt was made to eliminate the prior deposit
by replacing it with a tax termed the "added additional tax";[12] but such a
substitution did not in fact take place so that by 1966 permitted imports were
subject to customs tariffs at specific and ad valorem rates, a prior deposit, an
additional tax, and an added additional tax.[13]

Finally, in January 1967, the proliferation of protective measures was
brought to an end by the introduction of a new customs tariff schedule classified according to the Brussels Tariff Nomenclature (BTN). In this tariff
schedule an attempt was made to combine in a single ad valorem duty the
specific and ad valorem duties of the old tariff, as well as the additional and
added additional taxes, in such a way that their incidence on the c.i.f. value of
imports remained unchanged. (In other words, the new tariff schedule did not
seek to alter the level of protection, but aimed at administrative simplification.) As a result, imports are currently subject to an advance deposit, an ad
valorem duty, and, in a few exceptional cases, the payment of a specific duty.

The 1955 restructuring of the system of protection did not affect the special
regimes applied in Chile. Several new regimes of this kind have been created
since then, particularly between 1958 and 1960. However, there were no

---

[11] The additional tax ranges from 0 percent to 200 percent of the c.i.f. value, depending
on the commodity.

[12] The added additional tax varied between 0 percent and 300 percent of the c.i.f. value.

[13] It should be noted that, apart from its protective effect, the prior deposit scheme has
also reduced inflationary pressures. At the outset, this scheme led to a decrease in the supply of active money; subsequently, its effect varied with the total value of imports, their
composition, and the rates at which prior deposits had to be made. Finally, during the
period when deposits were made in dollars, it induced a return flow of short-term capital.

important changes in the scope and application of special regimes at the time of the 1967 reform.[14]

It is not easy to assess the net effect of the described changes in protective measures and exchange rates in the postwar period. In broad outline, however, it is clear that a general liberalization of imports was in progress between 1958 and 1961, with 1961 being a record year in this respect. During this period, the rate of exchange declined in real terms (Table 7.7) and practically all products were included in the list of permitted imports, while a good number of prepayment requirements and additional taxes were reduced.

Severe restrictions were imposed in 1962, and were gradually relaxed by 1964. In 1962 itself there was a devaluation, the list of permitted imports was reduced to a minimum, and not only were the advance deposit rates and the additional taxes increased, but both were levied simultaneously on all products. After 1966, as the high copper prices gave some relief, the exchange policy aimed not merely at keeping the value of the currency constant but at restoring the real exchange rate to a level similar to that prior to the foreign exchange crisis of 1961. Furthermore, Chile has introduced a system of drawbacks for duties paid on imported inputs used in the exports of manufactured goods.

The favorable balance-of-payments situation has also made it possible to pursue a more selective protection policy, without having to make adjustments on account of short-term balance-of-payments or tax revenue problems. This policy of selectivity, favoring imports of raw materials and capital goods and discouraging imports that compete with domestic products, has been applied in part by manipulating the rates of the additional tax and of the prior deposits.

It should be added that the Chilean economy is subject to a considerable degree of state intervention. The incentives provided to productive activities are thus determined not only by the measures of protection but also by other factors such as the credit system, the social security system, profit taxes, and indirect taxation.

The bank rate of interest, as fixed by the government, has often and sometimes for lengthy periods been negative in real terms; i.e., it has been lower than the rate of inflation. Correspondingly, credit has been rationed; those given access to credit have been mainly the most attractive customers of the private banks or the recipients of government loans provided through the state development institutions. These individuals and firms, then, have received a subsidy through low interest rates while others have not had access to bank credit at any price.

Chile's labor legislation is among the most "advanced" in the world. Because of the social security levies, each worker costs his employer approxi-

---

[14] See Appendix D.

TABLE 7.7: Nominal and Real Exchange Rates in Chile, 1956–66

(Index, 1960 = 100)

Year	Nominal exchange rate[a] (1)	Wholesale prices[b] (2)	Consumer prices[c] (3)	Real exchange rate (1)/(2)	Real exchange rate (1)/(3)
1956	43.1	40.9	38.5	105.4	111.9
1957	59.1	58.3	51.3	101.4	115.2
1958	75.5	73.1	64.6	103.3	116.9
1959	99.6	95.0	89.6	104.8	111.2
1960	100	100	100	100	100
1961	100	100.7	107.7	99.3	92.9
1962	108.7	109.1	122.6	99.6	88.7
1963	178.4	167.6	176.9	106.4	100.8
1964	260.8	252.3	258.2	103.4	101.0
1965	314.9	314.0	332.9	100.3	94.6
1966	380.6	385.5	408.5	98.7	93.2
1967	478.7	459.9	482.9	104.1	99.1

Sources: "Estadistica Chilena," *Direción General de Estadísticas;* "Boletin Mensual," *Banco Central de Chile.*

[a] The exchange rates in italic in Table 7.6 were considered as representative of each year. A simple average was used when there is more than one rate in italic for a single year.

[b] Weights of 1947 index.

[c] Weights of 1958 index.

mately twice what he actually receives, and the circumstances in which the law allows a worker to be dismissed are so specific and the cost is so great that they sometimes prevent old companies from modernizing or compel new ones to mechanize more than would otherwise be necessary. Although firms pass on part of these costs either to the workers themselves or to consumers by lowering money wages or raising prices, there is a certain amount of discrimination against labor-intensive industries as well as against the use of labor-intensive production methods. These social security levies vary among industries as well as among labor categories.

An assessment of the effect of credit policy, social security legislation, or profit taxes on effective protection would go beyond the scope of this study. Rather, we will concentrate on measures that directly affect international trade. In making calculations, we will also take account of indirect taxes and subsidies, although their relative unimportance does not justify their being discussed in any detail.

Nominal and Effective Protection

Data Sources and Estimation Procedures

Although the only available input-output table for Chile reflects the productive structure of the economy in 1962,[15] the rates of nominal and effective protection calculated in this study refer to 1961, or, more accurately to the

---

[15] *Chilean National Accounts, 1960–65: Study of Intersectoral Transactions in the Chilean Economy, 1962*, National Planning Office (ODEPLAN), 1967.

period July–September 1961.[16] Because of the successive and varied emergency measures adopted in 1962 to alleviate the balance-of-payments crisis of December 1961, it seemed inadvisable to use the protective measures applied in 1962 in estimating the extent of protection. Furthermore, while the 1962 productive structure is bound to some extent to reflect the foreign trade difficulties of that year, it probably does not differ substantially from that of 1961. Nevertheless, to the extent that the increased protection of domestic activities has been translated into changes in relative prices, the method applied will tend to underestimate the rates of protection of import-competing industries.

The Chilean input-output table distinguishes 54 sectors, 28 of which produce goods that can be traded internationally and 26 of which produce nontradable goods or services. Value added is broken down into factors: salaries, wages, employers' social security charges, and other payments. The table also shows indirect taxes net of subsidies, and it is estimated at user prices; hence it has to be adjusted to approximate a table based on producer prices.[17]

In carrying out the adjustments, we have first deducted indirect taxes net of subsidies from the value of output. The average rates of indirect taxes varied from −42 percent for the highly subsidized railroad transportation to 85 percent for tobacco. But, most average sectoral rates were in the 0 to 6 percent range, with higher rates applying to a few products, such as gasoline, beer, and tobacco. It should further be added that special regimes often authorized exemptions from indirect taxes, thus necessitating a further adjustment in the results.

In an input-output table expressed in user prices, the value of output includes trade and transportation markups, as well as the cost of warehousing and storage associated with transportation. This means that to estimate the value of output at producer prices, and the protection of value added, it has been necessary to deduct trade and transportation costs from both the output and the input side. No adjustment has been made, however, in regard to the cost of material inputs.[18]

After these adjustments were made, the procedure followed in estimating rates of nominal protection in Chile has involved several steps. It has been necessary (1) to classify the approximately 5,000 import items in the tariff schedule in conformity with the U.N. Standard International Trade Classification and to group these SITC categories in accordance with the industrial

---

[16] While there were no substantial changes in the protective measures during 1961, some did take place and this has made it necessary to pinpoint more exactly the measures that were applied in the July–September period.

[17] The basic assumption needed to estimate the actual protection, namely that the domestic price is equal to the international c.i.f. price plus nominal (or implicit) tariffs, is, of course, relevant only at the producer level.

[18] On this point, see Appendix A, pp. 320–21.

classification scheme of the input-output table; (2) to determine the tariff equivalent of the various protective measures on the products contained in each item of the 1961 customs tariff; (3) to give separate consideration to the so-called special regimes; (4) to identify prohibitive tariffs and to estimate the corresponding implicit tariffs; (5) to distinguish between the nominal protection of the output of a given industry and that of its products used as inputs the latter including imports of items not produced domestically; and (6) to average nominal rates of protection for each four-digit SITC category and then for each sector of the input-output table.

Before each of these steps is considered, however, it is useful to indicate briefly which tariffs and taxes affected Chilean imports in 1961. Imports were generally subject to (*a*) a specific duty; (*b*) an ad valorem tax of 3, 30, or 62 percent;[19] (*c*) a prior deposit in dollar bonds ranging from 0 to 1,500 percent of import value and required for periods of one or three months; and (*d*) an additional tax of 0 to 200 percent of the c.i.f. value, depending on the product.[20]

The classification of the items in the tariff schedule in accordance with the SITC posed certain difficulties. The tariff schedule, compiled in 1928, is based on a scheme of classification that is ill-suited to modern conditions. It is very detailed for some types of products and overly general for others. In the former event, it has been necessary to average several tariff items to arrive at four-digit SITC categories. At this stage, averages have been calculated by using Chilean imports as weights. In the latter case, items covering several products had to be classified into two and sometimes more four-digit SITC categories. Since the relative importance of the items in the different SITC categories is not known, a degree of arbitrariness is introduced into the calculations.

A different classification scheme is used by the Central Bank for setting prior deposits and additional taxes. This has caused difficulties in cases where different deposit requirements or additional taxes were applied to products within a given tariff item, since no information exists on the value of the imports subject to the different additional taxes or deposits within individual items of the tariff classification. Thus, we had no other choice than to calculate the simple average of these measures for each tariff item. It should be added that the error due to the procedures applied is lessened by the fact that

---

[19] The 62 percent ad valorem tariff was applied mainly to "luxury" goods, the 3 percent tariff to some raw materials and prime necessities and the 30 percent tariff to the remaining items.

[20] The prior deposits scale included 0.5, 100, 200, 400, 1,000, and 1,500 percent and the additional tax 0, 10, 20, 50, 100, and 200 percent rates. Deposits of less than 100 percent were for one month, those in excess of 100 percent for 3 months, and those of 100 percent for one or three months, depending on the case.

the tariff items have been averaged further in groups that are subject to broadly similar rates of prior deposits and additional taxes.

Having determined the rates of specific duties, ad valorem tariffs, prior deposits, and additional taxes pertaining to each tariff item, we have calculated their combined tariff equivalent for the c.i.f. value of the individual items. To begin with, specific duties have been converted to their ad valorem equivalent by relating them to the average value of imports per physical unit. Moreover, since ad valorem tariffs are applied to the sum of the c.i.f. value and the specific duty, it has been necessary to calculate their equivalents on c.i.f. value only.

There are also several small import surcharges in Chile; a consular fee of $5 for each shipment and a consular duty of 2.5 percent on the f.o.b. value. Using the data from a sample of imported goods in 1961, we have estimated that these items, plus the fees of the customs brokers, were equivalent to a surcharge of about 5 percent on the c.i.f. value; this has been added to the tariff figures.

The tariff equivalent of advance deposits has been estimated on the basis of the financial cost of maintaining such deposits. In 1961, the average rental rate of dollar bonds used in making deposits was 18.6 percent per year,[21] so that the tariff equivalent of deposits of 100 percent for one month is 1.55 percent and for three months 4.65. The highest advance deposit obligation, 1,500 percent for three months, had a tariff equivalent of 70 percent. Finally, additional taxes presented no problem since these have already been expressed as a percentage of the c.i.f. value of imports.

Exceptions to the general procedure noted above have been made in a variety of special cases. In 1961, Chile levied lower specific duties on some commodities imported from member countries of GATT, and luxury imports from these countries were liable to a 50 percent instead of a 62 percent ad valorem duty. It was observed that, whenever the average c.i.f. price of any such imports from GATT countries was lower than or on a par with the average price from third countries, more than 70 percent of the total amount imported was purchased from GATT countries. Where the third country price was lower, however, the bulk of the imports came from third countries.

For most products, the GATT countries were the cheapest suppliers, and we have used the tariffs applicable to imports from these countries. In a few instances (mainly raw materials) the opposite was the case, indicating that the tariff preference to GATT members did not fully compensate for the price differentials; we then used the general duties in the calculations. Similar procedures have been followed in regard to imports from some countries, such as

---

[21] This rate rose to 30 percent at the time of the foreign exchange shortage in 1962–63. Information on the rates has been obtained from banks and from importers.

Ecuador and Cuba, that were subject to special arrangements. Since LAFTA was not yet in operation in 1961, adjustments for trade with LAFTA countries did not have to be made.

Another special case came to light when it was found that the average price of the imports of certain items varied substantially according to whether the imports entered through the free ports or through dutiable ports. In the latter case the average price was much higher, reflecting differences in quality[22] and even in products if the tariff item was very broad. Whenever imports through dutiable ports were large, the price of these imports has been used to estimate the tariff equivalent of the specific duty under the assumption that the degree of nominal protection was similar for inferior grades. In turn, whenever most of the imports (roughly over 85 percent) entered through free ports or came under other special regimes, it was assumed that the tariffs were prohibitive and direct price comparisons have been made.[23] Such comparisons have not been made, however, for commodities with a dutiable value of less than $2,000 in 1961.

The separation of imports entering through duty-free ports or under other special regimes from those coming through dutiable ports has been possible because the Chilean import statistics indicate the ports of entry, as well as the amount of duty paid in each case. It is conceivable, however, that some imports with prohibitive tariffs have escaped our attention because they were not imported under the special import regimes. Nevertheless, given the importance of special regimes in Chile, it is not likely that there were more than a handful of such cases.

Free ports represent one of the several varieties of special regimes. The principal special regimes discussed in Appendix D are as follows: the Department of Arica; the Provinces of Chiloé, Aysén, and Magallanes; the Provinces of Tarapaca, and Antofagasta; the Department of Iquique, Pisague, Taltal, and Chañaral; nitrate, coal, iron, and copper mining; the iron and steel industry; the sugar industry and fishing; petroleum; certain capital goods; and, lastly, the donations received from various countries to help the victims of the great earthquake of 1960.

The great majority of the items with prohibitive tariffs are concentrated in industries producing nondurable consumer goods, such as textiles, clothing and certain foodstuffs, beverages, and agricultural products. In estimating the ratio of domestic to import prices (the nominal implicit rate of protection), we have followed the following procedure:

---

[22] For cheap products of low quality the ad valorem equivalent of the specific duty became very high when they were imported through the dutiable ports.

[23] Duties applicable under the special regimes (mostly zero tariffs) could not be taken as representative of the nominal rate of protection in the country as a whole, partly because they applied only in specific regions and partly because transshipping to other parts of the country was subject to duties.

1. In each four-digit category, we have eliminated all tariff items that had very small import values as compared with the total imports having non-prohibitive rates.
2. In certain cases when the products contained in an item with a prohibitive tariff for which price information was not available, were very similar to the products contained in a given tariff item with a nonprohibitive tariff (or in a tariff item for which it was possible to make direct comparisons between domestic prices and c.i.f. prices), we have assumed that the margin of nominal implicit protection was also similar in the two cases.
3. In the remaining cases, we have made direct comparisons between domestic and average c.i.f. prices of imports from domestic price statistics (or direct information could be obtained from some producers) and import statistics. In cases when domestic prices were given on the retail level, we have deducted marketing margins as well as indirect taxes. In addition, whenever commodities were expressed in different units in the domestic and in the import statistics, we have converted the latter to comparable units.
4. If comparable price observations were not available, we have calculated the average "safety margin" provided by nominal tariffs for comparable products—i.e., the excess tariff protection granted over and above the amount needed to equate the 1961 domestic price with the c.i.f. import price plus the "implicit" tariff—and applied this margin in estimating the rate of nominal protection.

In the industries where most of the prohibitive tariffs were found (notably textiles, and clothing and footwear) the estimates of implicit tariffs are not entirely satisfactory. This is especially the case for products that entered only through the free ports, since some of them are of extremely poor quality or very cheap rejects. For example, the average price of men's shirts imported through Arica was about $0.76 apiece, and that of ladies' nylon stockings less than $0.17 a pair.

These considerations illustrate the difficulties of making meaningful price comparisons and raise doubts about the representativeness of the implicit tariffs. The results should therefore be interpreted with caution. In the case of clothing and footwear, the error is less serious because the nominal implicit rate of protection of the industry affects only its own effective protection. In textiles, however, it also affects the effective protection of other industries, especially clothing.

In 1961 not all imported products had domestic counterparts. This means that not all the nominal tariffs were relevant for determining the nominal protection of the goods produced by individual industries. Some of these products, however, were imported and used as inputs in other industries. Their tariffs therefore affected the cost of inputs, and the effective protection of the industries in which they were used. Correspondingly, it has been necessary to calculate two sets of nominal rates of protection for each industry; one pertaining to the industry's output, and another relating to the use of the industry's products as inputs.[24] With few exceptions it has not been possible, however, to calculate tariff averages for individual input categories separately for all user industries.

We turn next to the problems of averaging. Ideally, domestic supply weights should be used in the averaging of both output and input tariffs, but information on domestic supply was not available in the appropriate breakdown. We were left, therefore, with the choice between unweighted and weighted averages. The first alternative was rejected because the Chilean tariff classification system, established in 1928, bears no relationship to the relative importance of individual commodities in 1961, and the choice has been made for using weighted averages.

Up to the four-digit SITC level, nominal rates of protection for output and inputs have been averaged by using domestic import weights. However, in order to avoid the downward bias inherent in this procedure, average rates of nominal protection for four-digit SITC groups have been averaged further by the use of world trade weights to arrive at the industry level. World imports have also been employed in weighting the nominal rates of protection on the machinery and equipment portion of depreciation while construction has been assumed to have zero protection.[25]

The Pattern of Effective Rates

Nominal and effective rates of protection are shown in Table 7.8 for three export industries, twelve import-competing industries, and thirteen non-import-competing industries. All industries included in the first group export at least four-fifths of their production; this ratio does not reach 10 percent in any of the other industries. Next, we have classified industries whose imports exceed one-tenth of output as import-competing and those with a lower import share as non-import-competing.

Effective rates of protection have been estimated by the use of both the Balassa and the Corden formulas. Differences between the results obtained under the two alternatives are small, and in the following discussion we will concentrate our attention on the latter. Table 7.8 also includes estimates on

---

[24] This was of some importance for products that require a technological process beyond the country's technical and economic capabilities as, for example, precision instruments, machinery, and transport equipment. The differences are also large for agriculture and food processing that include a variety of noncompeting industries, but they are smaller for chemical products and metal products, and they are negligible elsewhere.

[25] The relative importance of the two major components of depreciation for individual industries has been estimated by ODEPLAN.

TABLE 7.8:   Nominal and Effective Protection in Chile, 1961

(*Percent*)

Industry	Nominal protec- tion	Effective protection Balassa	Corden	Bias against exporting[a]
Export industries				
(4) Iron ore	0	−6	−7	...
(5) Copper	2	−5	−5	...
(6) Nitrates	0	−14	−14	...
Average	1	−6	−6	...
Import-competing industries				
(1) Agriculture	43	51	50	78
(8) Other mining	46	55	40	105
(17) Printed matter	72	93	82	226
(19) Rubber products	102	122	109	*
(20) Chemicals	94	111	89	*
(21) Petroleum and coal products	50	48	45	194
(23) Basic metals	66	262	198	*
(24) Metal products	59	46	43	264
(25) Nonelectrical machinery	84	89	85	3,125
(26) Electrical machinery and equipment	105	117	111	790
(27) Motor vehicles and other transport equipment	84	107	101	568
(28) Other industries	125	175	164	1,230
Average	69	72	68	246
Non-import-competing industries				
(2) Fishing	21	26	25	34
(3) Coal mining	37	32	31	64
(7) Stone, clay, and sands	66	65	64	87
(9) Food processing	82	5,350	2,884	*
(10) Beverages	122	827	609	*
(11) Tobacco	106	146	141	2,720
(12) Textiles	182	864	672	*
(13) Clothing and shoes	255	418	386	*
(14) Wood and cork	35	22	21	233
(15) Furniture	129	224	209	*
(16) Paper and paper products	55	46	41	4,720
(18) Leather products	161	1,094	714	*
(22) Nonmetallic products	139	248	227	*
Average	130	324	288	*
Nonexport industries, together	98	140	125	*

Source: See text.

[a] Calculated by using the Corden formula.

* Denotes negative value added in case of exporting; thus the extent of discrimination against exporting is infinite.

the bias against exporting in individual industries, estimated by the Corden formula.

Among the three export industries, nominal rates of protection are zero on iron ore and nitrates (saltpeter) and 2 percent on copper; in the latter case, tariffs on copper alloys explain the result. The nitrate industry imports three-fourths of its inputs duty-free, but the remaining one-fourth is purchased at domestic prices; this results in a negative effective protection of 14 percent for this industry. By contrast, the special regimes have reduced input costs for iron ore and copper to the extent that the negative effective protection of these industries is relatively small (7 and 5 percent, respectively). Another factor contributing to these differences has been the relatively high proportion of value added in the output of iron ore (65 percent) and copper (68 percent) as against nitrates (49 percent).

Among import-competing industries, both nominal and effective rates of protection are the lowest in agriculture (43 and 50 percent, respectively). This average, however, conceals a considerable degree of variation among individual products. Nominal rates of protection vary from nil for maize and rice to about 100 percent for temperate zone fruits and vegetables, and differences in effective rates are likely to be even larger. In the absence of a more detailed breakdown of the input-output table, however, it has not been possible to estimate the extent of protection of agricultural subsectors.

In import-competing manufacturing industries, both nominal and effective rates of protection are generally in the 50–120 percent range. Exceptions are basic metals and the miscellaneous group of other industries, both of which show a considerable degree of escalation. In the case of the former, the effective rate of protection is 198 percent as against a nominal rate of 66 percent, partly because steel producers, who account for about one-half of the industry's output, benefit from a special regime providing for duty-free entry of inputs and partly because value added is a relatively small part of output value. Finally, the products in the "other industries" group receive above-average nominal protection (125 percent) while their inputs are not subject to high tariffs.

Effective rates also exceed 100 percent for chemicals (under the Balassa formula), rubber products, electrical machinery, and transport equipment (to a large extent, motor vehicles). In the absence of export subsidies, in these industries there is also a considerable degree of discrimination against exporting. Exporting rubber products and chemicals, as well as the basic metals mentioned earlier, would even require negative domestic value added; i.e., the domestic value of material inputs exceeds the prices at which the commodities in question could be sold abroad.

There are finally two instances of "reverse" escalation with nominal rates exceeding effective rates—petroleum and coal products and metal products. In the first case, duties on petroleum products are less than on some of the inputs; in the second, basic metals receive much greater nominal protection than the products utilizing these metals. Furthermore, in the "other mining" industry, effective rates are higher or lower than nominal rates depending on whether the Balassa or the Corden formula is used.

The range of variation in nominal and effective rates, as well as the escalation of the structure of protection, are generally greater for non-import-competing industries than for those competing with imports. There are, nevertheless, a few instances of low protection and reverse escalation within this group. Effective rates of protection are below nominal rates for coal mining, stone, clay and sand, wood and cork, and paper and paper products. Tariffs are relatively low on the first three which are important inputs in a number of industries, while some paper and paper products are exported by Chile albeit in rather small quantities. Tariffs are also low (21 percent) on fishery products which, however, enjoy natural protection.

Nominal rates of protection in Chile are the highest in the remaining non-import-competing industries which include processed foods, beverages, tobacco, textiles, and nondurable consumer goods. These industries are characterized by relatively simple technical processes, and they all reached self-sufficiency behind high tariff walls in the early postwar period. At the same time, price comparisons indicate that domestic competition has failed to reduce internal prices much below the sum of world market prices and the tariffs.

Differences between nominal and effective rates of protection in these industries are also large. Effective rates are approximately double nominal rates for clothing and shoes, furniture, and nonmetallic products and even larger differences are observed in regard to food processing, beverages, textiles, and leather products. In the latter industries, the availability of major inputs at only slightly above world market prices, together with the low share of value added, raises the effective rate of protection to a considerable extent. Particularly in the case of food processing, since value added expressed in world market prices is very small, the measured effective rate of protection is far out of line with the results for the other industries. On the other hand, due to the high tariffs on raw tobacco, there is little escalation in the case of tobacco products. Tobacco products also provide an exception to the finding that in all these industries exporting would require negative domestic value added.

The average rate of nominal protection for the group of non-import-competing industries is 130 percent while the corresponding averages of effective rates are 324 percent under the Balassa formula and 288 percent under the Corden formula. The corresponding averages for import-competing industries are 69, 72, and 68 percent. Finally, if all nonexport industries are combined in one group, the relevant figures are 98 percent for nominal protection, and 140 and 125 percent for the effective rate. The 98 percent average rate of nominal protection will be used below in estimating the extent of overvaluation as compared to the hypothetical free trade situation.

It is of further interest to consider the extent of protection for industry groups classified by use. The estimates of Table 7.9 show effective rates of protection to be highest for processed food, followed by beverages and tobacco, nondurable consumer goods, intermediate products at higher levels of fabrication, durable consumer goods, machinery, intermediate products at lower levels of fabrication, construction materials, agriculture and forestry, and mining in this order.

TABLE 7.9: Nominal and Effective Protection for Major Product Categories in Chile, 1961

(Percent)

	Industry group	Estimates based on domestic coefficients			Estimates based on free trade coefficients		
		Nominal protection	Effective protection		Nominal protection	Effective protection	
			Balassa	Corden		Balassa	Corden
I	Agriculture, forestry, and fishing	42	50	49	53	62	58
II	Processed food	82	5,350	2,884	90	332	200
III	Beverages and tobacco	120	395	427	161	326	264
IV	Mining and energy	8	−2	−2	39	75	72
V	Construction materials	66	65	64	115	184	154
VI-A	Intermediate products I	53	71	70	60	139	105
VI-B	Intermediate products II	118	179	159	113	234	195
VI	Intermediate products I and II	99	135	127	76	168	132
VII	Nondurable consumer goods	204	315	277	188	339	300
VIII	Consumer durables	84	107	101	95	146	123
IX	Machinery	92	103	98	86	111	97
X	Transport equipment	a	a	a	16	−74	−65
I-X	All industries	89	96	84	73	160	121
I + IV II, III,	Primary production	28	22	21	47	68	64
V-X	Manufacturing	111	208	190	90	221	159
VI-X	Manufacturing less food, beverages, tobacco, and construction materials	120	162	150	88	173	140

Source: See text.
a Included with consumer durables.

The same ranking is obtained if we group estimates obtained by the use of free trade coefficients, except that nondurable consumer goods now show slightly higher levels of protection than processed food or beverages and tobacco. Furthermore, averages of nominal and effective protection are lower for the manufacturing sector but higher for primary activities if free trade rather than domestic coefficients are used in the calculations.

In Chile's case, special interest attaches to the results obtained by using the free trade input-output table since this has a considerably more detailed breakdown than the domestic table. In the following, we consider these estimates (see Table 3.1) in some detail, with comparisons made, whenever possible, with the results obtained by the use of domestic input-output coefficients.

In agriculture and fishing, the nominal and effective rates derived by the two alternative methods are remarkably similar. By contrast, substantial differences are shown for mining and energy: the large weight in world trade of the relatively highly protected natural gas and petroleum raises the average obtained by the use of free trade coefficients while domestic supply is dominated by copper which receives negative protection. These considerations also explain the differences observed under the two alternatives in regard to the primary sector taken as a whole.

While food processing activities are combined in one category in the domestic input-output table, they are separated into eight groups in the free trade table. Among these, the high nominal protection of its major inputs and low tariffs on the output give rise to negative domestic value added in meat processing, and reduce the effective rate of protection below the nominal rate in the case of sugar and for fats and oils. For all other food processing industries, however, effective rates of protection calculated by the use of free trade coefficients are well above the average for the manufacturing sector taken as a whole. Effective protection is also high on beverages and tobacco where the results obtained by the use of domestic and free trade coefficients are very similar.

Both construction materials and intermediate products at lower levels of fabrication show a considerable degree of escalation if we use free trade, but not if we use domestic, input-output coefficients. For construction materials, this is a consequence of differences in input composition under the two alternatives; for intermediate products, the large weight in world trade of some industries with a high degree of escalation (leather, synthetics, glass, and steel ingots) largely explains the results. In these industries, nominal duties on the major inputs are low compared with tariffs on the final products, thereby giving rise to high effective protection. These industries do not, however, appear separately in the domestic input-output table.

Intermediate products at higher levels of fabrication show smaller differences in the results obtained under the two alternatives, although the extent of escalation is again greater if free trade rather than domestic coefficients are used. Among the industries in this category, the level of effective protection and the degree of escalation from nominal to effective rates is the highest for textiles, irrespective of whether we use domestic or free trade coefficients.

In manufacturing taken in a narrower sense (i.e., excluding food, beverages, tobacco, and construction materials), nondurable consumer goods appear most heavily protected under both alternatives, with nominal rates averaging about 200 percent and effective rates about 300 percent. This group of industries is dominated by clothing which shows nominal rates of 250–300 and effective rates of 400–500 percent. In the consumer durables group where automobiles are dominant, nominal rates of protection are slightly below, and effective rates above, 100 percent under both alternatives. Effective rates are only slightly lower on machinery, while transport equipment shows negative protection on the basis of free trade coefficients and it does not appear separately in the domestic input-output table.

Overvaluation and Net Effective Protection

The results presented so far have been calculated at the official exchange rate applicable in 1961 which was 1,050 escudos per U.S. dollar. Given the high tariffs and other protective measures, however, this rate was considerably lower than what it would be in a free trade situation. Moreover, as noted earlier, the exchange rate applied did not equilibrate the balance of payments in 1961. Indeed, the deficit was the largest Chile ever experienced, although the price of copper was not abnormally low and there was an inflow of foreign private capital. As a result, by December 1961, Chile's foreign exchange reserves were exhausted and import operations practically stopped until March 1962.

The estimates of nominal and effective rates of protection thus had to be corrected for both the overvaluation as compared to the free trade situation and the overvaluation at the existing set of protective measures which led to a foreign exchange loss. The adjustment has been made by the use of equation (12a) of Appendix A. The assumptions underlying the calculations are briefly described below.

Given Chile's size and the relative importance of the foreign trade sector, we have taken the elasticity of supply of imports to be infinite while the elasticity of demand for imports has been assumed to be 3. On the export side, we have separately considered copper (66 percent of Chile's exports in 1961), iron ore (9 percent), nitrates (7 percent) and all other exports, taken together.

On the basis of available information on the elasticity of demand for the world exports of these commodities and on Chile's share in these exports, we have derived the following values for the elasticity of demand for exports from Chile: copper, 1–1.5; iron ore and nitrates, 4–6; and all other exports,

15–20. This gave a range of 4.2–5.8 for all exports, and we have used the midpoint of the range in estimating the equilibrium exchange rate under free trade conditions. Finally, taking account of differences among the main export products, we have assumed the elasticity of supply of exports in Chile to be 3.

In 1961, the deficit in the balance of payments amounted to approximately 20 percent of Chilean exports while the average nominal protection of nonexport goods was 98 percent and that of exports 1 percent. If these data are inserted, together with the assumed elasticity values in the formula referred to above, an overvaluation of 68 percent is obtained. Tables 7.10 and 7.11 pro-

TABLE 7.10:   Net Nominal and Effective Protection in Chile, 1961[a]

(*Percent*)

Industry	Nominal protection	Effective protection
Export industries		
(4) Iron ore	−40	−45
(5) Copper	−39	−43
(6) Nitrates	−40	−49
Average	−40	−44
Import-competing industries		
(1) Agriculture	−15	−11
(8) Other mining	−13	−17
(17) Printed matter	2	8
(19) Rubber products	20	24
(20) Chemicals	15	13
(21) Petroleum and coal products	−11	−14
(23) Basic metals	−1	77
(24) Metal products	−5	−15
(25) Nonelectrical machinery	10	10
(26) Electrical machinery and equipment	22	26
(27) Motor vehicles and other transport equipment	10	20
(28) Other industries	34	57
Average	1	0
Non-import-competing industries		
(2) Fishing	−28	−26
(3) Coal mining	−18	−22
(7) Stone, clay, and sands	−1	−2
(9) Food processing	8	1,676
(10) Beverages	32	322
(11) Tobacco	23	43
(12) Textiles	68	360
(13) Clothing and shoes	111	189
(14) Wood and cork	−20	−28
(15) Furniture	36	84
(16) Paper and paper products	−8	−16
(18) Leather products	55	385
(22) Nonmetallic products	42	95
Average	37	131
Nonexport industries, together	18	34

Source: Table 7.8 and text.
   [a] Effective rates of protection have been estimated by using the Corden formula; both nominal and effective rates have been adjusted for overvaluation as compared to the hypothetical free trade situation.

TABLE 7.11: Net Nominal and Effective Protection for Major Product Categories in Chile, 1961[a]

(Percent)

	Industry	Estimates based on domestic coefficients		Estimates based on free trade coefficients	
		Nominal protection	Effective protection	Nominal protection	Effective protection
I	Agriculture, forestry, and fishing	−15	−11	−9	−6
II	Processed food	8	1,676	20	111
III	Beverages and tobacco	31	214	55	117
IV	Mining and energy	−36	−42	−17	2
V	Construction materials	−1	−2	28	51
VI-A	Intermediate products I	−9	1	−5	22
VI-B	Intermediate products II	30	54	27	76
VI	Intermediate products I and II	18	35	5	38
VII	Nondurable consumer goods	81	124	71	138
VIII	Consumer durables	10	30	16	33
IX	Machinery	14	18	11	17
X	Transport equipment	[b]	[b]	−31	−79
I–X	All industries	13	10	3	32
I + IV	Primary production	−24	−28	−12	−2
II, III V–X	Manufacturing	26	73	13	54
VI–X	Manufacturing less food, beverages, tobacco, and construction materials	31	49	12	43

Source: Table 7.9 and text.

[a] Effective rates of protection have been estimated by using the Corden formula; both nominal and effective rates have been adjusted for overvaluation as compared to the hypothetical free trade situation.

[b] Included with consumer durables.

vide estimates of net protection in Chile, adjusted for overvaluation as compared to the free trade equilibrium exchange rate.

Adjustment for overvaluation alters the results for Chile to a considerable extent. Thus, the average effective rate of protection will now be −44 percent for export industries, nil for import-competing industries, 131 percent for non-import-competing industries, and 34 percent for all nonexport industries, taken together. It is especially noteworthy that in a variety of industries, the apparent protection measured at the official exchange rate gives place to a net disincentive if the exchange rate is appropriately adjusted. This result obtains for agriculture, other mining, petroleum, and coal products, and metal products among import-competing industries, as well as for fishing, coal mining, stone, clay and sand, wood and cork, and paper and paper products among non-import-competing industries.

By contrast, five industries receive net effective protection exceeding 100 percent. They are—in order of the effective rate of protection—food processing, leather products, textiles, beverages, and clothing and shoes. Rates of net effective protection are between 50 and 100 percent for nonmetallic mineral products, furniture, basic metals, and the miscellaneous group of other industries while machinery and transport equipment and a few industries producing intermediate products have less protection (Table 7.10).

Taken together, average net effective protection of primary activities in Chile was −28 percent in 1961 as against 73 percent for the manufacturing sector; the latter figure falls to 49 percent if we exclude food, beverages, tobacco, and construction material. Among the major industry groups the average rate of net effective protection exceeds 100 percent for processed food, beverages and tobacco, and nondurable consumer goods while it is in the zero to 50 percent range for others. These estimates have been derived by using domestic coefficients; the results based on free trade coefficients are practically the same for the manufacturing sector defined in a narrower sense while differences are shown for food processing, beverages and tobacco, and construction material. However, for reasons noted earlier, the estimates for mining, food, beverages, tobacco, and construction material differ under the two alternatives.

Evaluation and Policy Recommendations

Although the relatively high degree of aggregation of the domestic input-output table used in this study does not permit deriving conclusions in a detailed industrial breakdown, some conclusions of a general nature can be drawn. It is apparent that the structure of protection in Chile entails a substantial degree of discrimination among economic activities, against exporting, as well as against imports. The brunt of discrimination is borne by the mining sector, but agriculture and some potential export sectors in manufacturing also have negative net effective protection. By contrast, processed food and nondurable consumer goods are the most protected.

The high protection of industries that use relatively simple technical methods and have a long history in Chile, points to the existence of considerable inefficiencies and/or excess profits. Although in the absence of data on the capital stock one cannot determine the relative importance of the two, the fact remains that the high protection of these industries isolates them from the world market and provides no incentives to technological improvements. At the same time, the continuing "infant industry" protection for industries that have long passed the infant stage entails differences between social and private profitability while competition is restricted by the limited size of the domestic market.

The extent of discrimination against exports should also be emphasized. Except for copper, the demand for Chilean exports is fairly elastic and a more rational protection policy would have permitted higher export growth by increasing Chile's share in the world market and/or by developing new exports.

Among manufacturing industries, the protective measures applied favor import substitution against potential new exports. We have seen before that in ten out of twenty-one manufacturing industries, firms could export only if they operated with negative value added. Yet the resources available in Chile provide good opportunities to export copper products, paper and paper products, as well as some iron products. Furthermore, among nonmanufacturing activities, exports of fishery and forestry products and some agricultural products appear promising.

All in all, inefficient import substitution and discrimination against exports are likely to have adversely affected the growth of the Chilean economy. On the one hand, within the limits of the small domestic market, import substitution has become increasingly difficult as Chile moved from nondurable consumer goods to durable goods and to intermediate products. On the other hand, discrimination against exports has not allowed rapid growth of export earnings, thereby limiting the expansion of import capacity. This in turn has led to recurrent balance-of-payments crises, increased import restrictions, and slowed down the growth of the Chilean economy.

It appears then that improvements in Chile's growth performance would require radical changes in the structure of protection. There is need to reduce discrimination among economic activities, to improve the relative position of exports, especially of manufactured goods, and to allow greater competition in manufacturing industries. These purposes could be served by the simultaneous reduction and leveling of tariffs, accompanied by a devaluation of the exchange rate. Export subsidies could further be employed to promote exports of manufactured goods while export taxes could be utilized to siphon off excess profits from devaluation accruing to producers of traditional exports. For optimal effect, such measures would have to be taken simultaneously and without having recourse to case-by-case decisions.

The example of Argentina indicates that the "compensated" devaluation suggested here can be undertaken without serious effects on employment. But further reductions and leveling of tariffs cannot be made overnight. Thus, in order to avoid unemployment resulting from rapid resource shifts, policy changes would have to be gradual. Nonetheless, to reduce uncertainty, it would be advisable to make public a timetable on changes in tariffs and other protective measures.

CHAPTER 8

THE STRUCTURE OF PROTECTION IN MEXICO

Gerardo Bueno

Economic Growth and International Trade

Sources of Economic Growth

In examining the structure of protection in Mexico, one should bear in mind three principal features of the Mexican economy that distinguish it from some some of the other countries studied. The first is its proximity to the United States, which has the most highly developed economy in the world; they have a common border some 2,000 miles long. This restricts Mexico's freedom of action in commercial and industrial policy, since for many types of goods large differentials between the Mexican and U.S. prices of the same article can result in smuggling. The second feature is Mexico's long period of rapid growth which now places it, with a per capita income of about $500, ahead of most developing countries. The third feature is its relative price stability which has helped to keep the exchange rate unchanged since 1954. All these aspects are considered below in greater detail.

Between 1940 and 1967 the gross domestic product in Mexico rose at an

Gerardo Bueno is manager of the Nacional Financiera, Gerencia de Programacion Industrial. The author wishes to acknowledge the valuable comments received from Leopoldo N. Solis, Victor L. Urquidi, David Ibarra, Donald Keesing, and Miguel Alvarez Uriate. He is also indebted to Ignacio Coss who carried out most of the statistical calculations.

average annual rate of 6.4 percent (Table 8.1). Growth rates declined slightly from 1940–50 to 1950–60 but increased to a considerable extent after 1960. As a result of accelerating population growth, the situation is somewhat less favorable in per capita terms. Between 1940 and 1950, the population rose at a rate of 3.0 percent, and per capita incomes at 3.4 percent a year; the growth rate of population reached 3.2 percent between 1950 and 1960 with incomes per head rising 2.6 percent a year; finally, during the sixties the population was increasing at an average annual rate of 3.4 percent, and per capita incomes at 3.7 percent. Among developing countries, Mexico has had one of the highest rates of growth of per capita incomes.

Solis has argued that there is no fully satisfactory explanation for the continued growth of the Mexican economy. Explanations range from those emphasizing the gradual resolution of conflicts between three social groups—politicians, technicians, and businessmen—to those invoking fortunate accidents, political pragmatism, and lucky dilettantism.[1] At the risk of oversimplification, we suggest that the following economic and social factors have been of chief importance.

Among economic factors, the vitality of the agricultural sector should be noted; it has developed fast enough not only to meet the food requirements of a rapidly growing population without appreciable price increases but also to generate substantial surpluses. At the same time, the stability of prices and exchange rates reduced uncertainty in investment decisions and contributed to the relatively high share of domestic saving and investment in the gross national product (about 14 to 15 percent during the sixties). In addition, public investment, especially in infrastructure,[2] played an important role as did the favorable treatment of the inflow of foreign capital that brought with it modern technology.

Mexico also benefited from rapid increases of external demand for its exports of both goods and services, especially tourism, which helped to maintain the share of exports and imports in the gross domestic product at relatively high levels. The buoyancy of exports was helped by realistic exchange rates and by policies promoting export diversification. Meanwhile, the large

---

[1] Leopoldo N. Solis, "Hacia un analisis general a largo plazo del desarrollo economico de Mexico," *Economia y Demografia*, vol. 1, no. 1 (1967), pp. 40–91. The two points of view referred to in the text are illustrated by Raymond Vernon's *The Dilemma of Mexico's Development: The Roles of the Private and Public Sectors* (Cambridge, Mass.: Harvard University Press, 1963), and by Miguel Wionczek's "Incomplete Formal Planning: Mexico," in *Planning Economic Development*, ed. E. E. Hagen (Homewood, Ill.: Richard D. Irwin, Inc., 1963), pp. 150–82.

[2] Public investment in infrastructure has been given much emphasis by the United Nations Economic Commission for Latin America. See "El Desequilibrio Externo en las Economias Latinoamericanas: El Caso de Mexico," mimeographed (Mexico, 1958).

TABLE 8.1: Changes in the Industrial Structure of Mexico, 1940–67

(Percentages based on data valued at 1960 prices)

Industry group	1940	1950	1960	1967	Average annual rates of growth			
					1940–50	1950–60	1960–67	1940–67
Agriculture, forestry, and fishing	19.3	18.2	15.2	12.8	5.6	4.5	4.0	4.8
Mining	4.2	2.5	1.5	1.0	0.6	2.3	0.3	0.8
Manufacturing	17.2	20.8	22.6	23.9	8.5	6.6	8.1	8.1
Food, beverages, and tobacco		(36.7)	(36.7)	30.0		6.1	5.3	5.8*
Processed food		(26.5)	(27.6)	22.9		6.6	5.4	6.1*
Beverages and tobacco		(10.2)	(9.1)	7.1		3.2	4.7	4.8*
Petroleum	2.3	2.2	3.4	3.3	7.0	9.2	9.2	7.9
Other manufacturing		(63.3)	(63.3)	(70.0)		6.2	9.9	7.7*
Construction materials		(3.6)	(4.1)	(4.4)		7.7	9.4	8.3*
Intermediate products I		(10.4)	(12.1)	(13.3)		7.8	9.8	8.6*
Intermediate products II		(26.9)	(25.3)	(27.0)		5.6	9.4	7.1*
Nondurable consumer goods		(15.9)	(12.7)	(11.9)		3.8	7.3	5.3*
Consumer durables		(3.8)	(5.3)	(9.9)		9.6	18.6	13.2*
Machinery		(1.7)	(1.9)	(1.7)		7.4	4.3	6.9*
Transport equi ment		(1.0)	(1.9)	(1.8)		13.1	5.9	10.5*
Construction	3.8	3.5	4.1	4.4	5.4	7.4	6.8	6.9
Electricity	0.7	0.5	1.0	1.5	4.1	12.5	14.1	9.5
Services	54.7	54.5	54.9	56.4	6.3	5.9	6.6	6.6
Gross domestic product	100.0	100.0	100.0	100.0	6.6	5.7	7.2	6.4
Index (1960 = 100)	30.5	57.5	100.0	163.5				
Population (million)	19.7	26.3	36.1	45.7	3.0	3.2	3.4	3.2
Per capita incomes, index (1960 = 100)	53.0	77.9	100.0	123.7	3.4	2.6	3.7	3.1

Source: Annual Reports of Banco de Mexico, S.A.; *Cuentas Nacionales y Acervos de Capital Consolidadas y por Tipo de Actividad,* Banco de Mexico, S.A.

Note: Figures in parentheses are expressed as a percentage of value added in manufacturing.

* Data cover only the period 1950–1967.

and rapidly growing home market, together with policies of import substitution, led to the expansion of industries producing for domestic use.

Among social factors, the agrarian reform should first be mentioned. The reform brought about a radical redistribution of wealth and has contributed to the transfer of labor from agriculture to industry.[3] Note should further be taken of Mexico's continuing political stability[4] and the rapid improvements made in education. The literacy rate rose from 34 percent in 1930 to around 70 percent in 1965, and in recent years the annual rate of increase of skilled labor has been approximately 9 percent.[5]

Against these factors benefiting the growth performance of the Mexican economy, one should set some of the obstacles to growth which have impeded this process and may assume increased importance in the future. One of these is Mexico's regressive tax system which, together with rising public expenditures, meant growing deficits in the government budget. In addition, there is little coordination between policies of protection and of industrial development, with too much emphasis on import substitution per se and inadequate attention to efficiency aspects.[6] The dual character of Mexican agriculture has also become increasingly pronounced, with a widening gap between a highly productive sector using modern agricultural techniques and the *ejido* sector which scarcely rises above subsistence level and has little access to credit, to well-organized markets, or to technical know-how.[7] Finally, despite rapid increases in technically qualified personnel, demand for such personnel tends to outrun supply, since professional training in Mexico is not of sufficiently high quality.

Structural Change

As noted above, agriculture has been growing at a rapid rate in Mexico; between 1940 and 1967, value added in agriculture rose at an average annual rate of 4.8 percent, which is rather high among developing countries. Nevertheless, with value added in manufacturing increasing 8.1 percent a year, the

---

[3] On this point, see Solis, "Hacia un analisis general a largo plazo del desarrollo economico de Mexico," in particular pp. 86–91.

[4] The political stability of the country was stressed by V. L. Urquidi. See in particular his "El desarrollo economico de Mexico," *Cuadernos Americanos* (Mexico, 1960) and, more recently, "An Overview of Mexican Economic Development," *Weltwirtschaftliches Archiv*, band 101, heft 1 (1968), pp. 2–19.

[5] The figure comes from an unpublished paper by Donald Keesing who kindly made it available to me.

[6] See P. Garcia Reynoso, "La politica mexicana de fomento industrial," *Comercio Exterior*, November 1968, pp. 959–75; D. Ibarra, "Mercados, Desarrollo y Politica Economica," mimeographed, 1969; and G. M. Bueno, "Las perspectivas de la política de desarrollo industrial en Mexico," *Comercio Exterior*, November 1967, pp. 891–94.

[7] See Banco de Mexico, Oficina de Proyecciones Agricolas, "Perspectivas de Oferta y Demanda de Productos Agropecuarios" (Mexico, 1964).

share of agriculture in the gross domestic product fell from 19.3 percent in 1940 to 12.8 percent in 1967 whereas that of manufacturing rose from 17.2 to 23.9 percent. The shares of construction and electricity, gas, and water have also risen and services have gained at the expense of the commodity-producing sectors (Table 8.1).

Within the manufacturing sector, there has been a decline in the share of food processing, tobacco, and nondurable consumer goods while increases have been the most rapid in consumer durables and transport equipment. During the sixties, the share of intermediate products also increased with chemicals, basic metals, and metal products in the lead.

Changes in the composition of imports and exports were related to those in the structure of production. Since Mexico's experience during World War II was much affected by the rapid expansion of wartime demand, developments in the 1950–67 period are of especial interest. During this period, the dollar value of merchandise exports rose at an average annual rate of 5.4 percent while the increase in terms of domestic currency was 7.0 percent (Table 8.2; see also Table 2.5). Service exports, including tourism as well as border trade, grew even faster, and their share in the combined exports of goods and services increased from 34.2 percent in 1950 to 48.0 percent in 1967 (Table 8.3).

Services also assumed increasing importance in the import bill, with their proportion in the combined imports of goods and services rising from 25.9 percent in 1950 to 35.6 percent in 1967 (Table 8.4). Nonetheless, the dollar value of merchandise imports increased, on the average, at an average annual rate of 7.5 percent, and their domestic value at a rate of 8.8 percent. In the same period, Mexico's terms of trade deteriorated at an annual average rate of nearly 3 percent.

The share of merchandise imports in the gross domestic product of Mexico declined little between 1950 and 1967. But Mexico's "qualitative dependence" on imports increased during this period. This is seen in the rise in the share of the imports of capital goods and, to a lesser extent, of raw materials and basic chemicals necessary to maintain and to increase domestic productive capacity. By contrast, the share of foodstuffs and intermediate products in merchandise imports declined (Table 8.4; see also Table 2.8).[8]

A detailed study by Nacional Financiera, comparing the input-output tables of the Mexican economy for 1950 and 1960, highlights this situation even more clearly. It shows that although in most manufacturing industries the share of imported inputs in production value fell, the import dependence of Mexico's manufacturing sector taken as a whole increased, owing to the

---

[8] The changes in the composition of foreign trade have been examined in greater detail in several studies. See in particular, ECLA, "El Desequilibrio Externo en las Economias Latinoamericanas: El Caso de Mexico"; Ibarra, "Mercados, Desarrollo y Politica Economica"; and C. Reynolds, "Mexican Commercial Policy," mimeographed, 1968.

TABLE 8.2: Merchandise Exports, Imports, and the Terms of Trade in Mexico, 1940–67

(Percent)

Category	1940	1950	1960	1967	Average annual rates of growth			
					1940–50	1950–60	1960–67	1950–67
Merchandise exports (1950 = 100)								
At current prices	20.4	100.0	196.4	315.0	17.2	7.0	5.9	10.4
At 1950 prices	86.9	100.0	166.8	250.3	1.5	5.3	5.9	4.0
Merchandise imports (1950 = 100)								
At current prices	13.0	100.0	287.3	422.0	22.0	11.1	5.7	13.5
At 1950 prices	34.9	100.0	157.4	216.0	11.1	4.6	4.6	6.9
Terms of trade (1950 = 100)	63.3	100.0	64.5	64.5	4.7	−4.3	…	0.1
Share of taxes on foreign trade in federal fiscal revenue	27.0	29.5	24.8	15.8				
Taxes on imports	17.8	14.1	16.2	12.8				
Taxes on exports	9.2	15.4	8.6	3.0				

Source: For exports, imports, and the terms of trade, Mexican trade statistics; for the share of taxes in federal fiscal revenue in 1940–60, Rafael Izquierdo, "Protectionism in Mexico," Table 5, in *Public Policy and Private Enterprise in Mexico*, ed. Raymond Vernon (Cambridge, Mass.: Harvard University Press, 1964), pp. 241–89; in 1967, same as in Table 8.1.
Note: Original data in Mexican currency.

TABLE 8.3: Changes in the Structure of Exports of Goods and Services in Mexico, 1940–67[a]

(Percent)

Exports	1940		1950		1960		1967	
Exports of commodities and services	100.0		100.0		100.0		100.0	
Commodities		72.5		59.7		53.8		50.0
	100.0		100.0		100.0		100.0	
Agriculture and forestry	19.6		46.9		41.6		38.5	
Livestock and fishing	4.1		4.4		11.0		11.5	
Ores, concentrates, and unwrought metals	62.4		24.6		18.6		14.6	
Petroleum and its products	11.5		5.3		2.7		3.5	
Manufactured goods	2.4		6.7		18.4		21.3	
Food			1.4		9.6		9.9	
Textiles			3.8		4.6		3.0	
Chemicals			0.7		2.3		4.4	
Other manufacturing industries			0.8		1.9		4.0	
Unclassified exports			12.1		7.7		10.6	
Services		27.5		34.2		42.7		48.0
	100.0		100.0		100.0		100.0	
Tourism	32.0		39.2		26.5		34.2	
Border trade	60.8		43.1		62.5		56.6	
Other	7.2		17.7		11.0		9.2	
Gold and silver		na		6.1		3.5		2.0

Source: See Table 8.1.
[a] Exports are valued in current prices.

TABLE 8.4: Changes in the Structure of Imports of Goods and Services in Mexico, 1940–67[a]

(Percent)

Imports	1940	1950	1960	1967
Imports of commodities and services	*100.0*	*100.0*	*100.0*	*100.0*
I. Commodities	*80.9*	*74.1*	*71.0*	*64.4*
	100.0	*100.0*	*100.0*	*100.0*
A. Consumer goods	27.7	23.3	18.6	16.4
a) Nondurable	14.0	12.6	6.0	5.4
b) Durable	13.7	10.7	12.6	11.0
B. Producer goods	71.5	75.8	81.3	83.6
a) Raw materials	44.1	37.6	34.0	33.5
1) Nonprocessed	8.9	7.0	4.9	4.3
2) Processed	35.2	30.6	29.1	29.2
b) Capital goods and intermediate products (by sector of destination)	27.4	38.2	47.3	50.1
1) Agriculture	na	0.1	0.9	1.0
2) Construction	na	6.9	5.8	5.0
3) Tools, fittings, repairs and spare parts	na	8.1	9.1	8.2
4) Machinery, equipment and articles	na	23.1	31.5	35.9
(a) Agriculture	na	3.6	3.6	2.1
(b) Transports and telecommunications	na	5.3	9.8	10.7
(c) Industry, consumptions and others	na	14.2	18.1	23.1
C. Nonclassified articles	0.8	0.9	0.1	…
II. Services	*19.1*	*25.9*	*29.0*	*35.6*
	100.0	*100.0*	*100.0*	*100.0*
A. Tourism and border trade	23.2	45.1	52.7	54.1
B. Payments on foreign investment	60.5	34.8	28.5	22.4
C. Interest payments on official debts	…	5.9	6.1	12.6
D. Others	16.3	14.2	12.7	10.9

Source: See Table 8.1.
[a] Imports are valued at current prices.

rising share of the chemical, electrical, and nonelectrical machinery and transportation equipment industries which use imported inputs more intensively than the other industries.

The structure of merchandise exports also changed to a considerable extent. Between 1940 and 1950, the share of metallic mineral products and fuels in exports declined, with corresponding increases in agricultural products and manufactured goods. These trends continued after 1950, except that the share of agricultural products in exports stabilized at 40 to 50 percent, with foodstuffs gaining at the expense of industrial materials (Table 8.3; see also Table 2.7).

Changes in the relative importance of individual export products are also of interest. In Table 8.5, we list separately all products which accounted for more than 2 percent of Mexico's merchandise exports in any of the benchmark years—1950, 1955, 1960, and 1967. The data show that a number of new exports developed and assumed importance in Mexico since 1950. They include cattle, wheat, maize, fresh tomatoes, sugar, sulfur, and salt, as well as a variety of manufactured goods. In turn, the share of commodities that dominated Mexican exports in 1950—cotton, coffee, silver, and petroleum and its products—declined in varying degrees. It may be added that, as late as 1940, silver and nonmonetary gold accounted for nearly half of Mexican exports; however, they are no longer exported in metal form.

TABLE 8.5: Principal Exports of Mexico, 1950–67

(*Percent of total exports*)

Commodity	1950	1955	1960	1965	1967
Bovine cattle (SITC 001.1)	0.0	1.3	4.4	3.3	3.3
Fish—fresh, chilled, or frozen (031.1)	7.6	0.1	0.2	0.1	0.0
Shellfish (031.3)	2.0	2.3	4.6	3.8	5.4
Wheat (041)	0.0	na	0.0	3.6	1.8
Maize (044)	0.0	0.6	2.9	6.7	6.3
Tomatoes, fresh (054.4)	na	na	3.3	3.1	4.3
Raw sugar (061.1)	0.6	0.5	1.8	5.1	5.9
Coffee, green or roasted (071.1)	8.2	12.7	9.4	6.6	5.5
Raw cotton, other than linters (263.1)	19.2	28.6	20.7	18.5	12.5
Henequen (265)	4.1	1.2	1.7	0.4	0.6
Sulfur, crude or refined (274.1)	na	0.8	3.7	2.9	4.2
Salt (276.3)	na	na	0.1	0.4	0.6
Zinc ores and concentrates (283.5)	2.9	2.1	2.9	3.3	3.2
Zinc and alloys, unwrought (686.1)	2.4	1.7	1.0	0.5	0.7
Silver, unworked or partly worked (681.1)	6.6	4.6	3.2	2.7	3.6
Lead, unwrought (685.1)	12.9	8.1	4.1	2.4	2.1
Copper, unwrought (682.1)	4.5	6.0	3.3	0.7	0.6
Petroleum, crude and partly refined (331)	4.0	1.2	0.2	1.2	1.7
Petroleum products refined (332)	2.8	6.7	1.6	1.5	1.0
Textile yarn and thread (651)	1.4	1.9	2.5	1.6	1.5
Total principal exports	79.2	80.4	71.6	68.4	64.8
Total exports ($ million)	466	805	763	1,120	1,145

Source: U.N., *Yearbook of International Trade Statistics.*

Declining exports of silver and gold resulted mainly from the exhaustion of mines and rising operating costs. Government policies undertaken to conserve domestic resources affected developments in lead and copper where Mexico's share in world exports decreased very considerably between 1950–53 and 1963–66 (see Table 2.6). Exports of fresh fish also declined while Mexico succeeded in increasing its share in the world exports of cotton, coffee, sugar, shellfish, and maize. Combining the results for these commodities, we find that Mexico improved its competitive position in its major exports in the period under consideration. But this improvement was more than offset by the decline in prices (especially of cotton and sugar) so that the more than doubling of Mexican exports between 1950–53 and 1963–66 was chiefly due to rapid increases in minor exports.

From Table 2.7 it further appears that there has been a substantial increase in the share of manufacturing in total exports—from 8.7 percent in 1950 to 21.1 percent in 1967.[9] Among chemicals, the most important export products are hormones, pharmaceuticals, and some colorants; in recent years, exports of petrochemicals have also gained in importance. Among basic manufactures, steel and copper products are in the lead followed by tiles and pottery; in the machinery and transport equipment category, exports consist mostly of railroad cars. Finally, among miscellaneous manufactures, the most important items and those increasing most rapidly during recent years are textiles, shoes, and books.

The System of Protection

Stages in Policy

Trade policies played an important role in the changes that occurred in the Mexican economy during the last decades, although their importance has often been exaggerated and the influence of other factors neglected.[10] Among the latter we may mention increases in the size of the domestic market; increasingly qualified and relatively cheap labor; tax policies which encouraged refinancing with a company's own resources; a policy which made low-cost fuel, electric power, and rail transport available to industry; and finally, the orientation of monetary and credit policy which, by setting up financial devel-

---

[9] It will be observed that there are some discrepancies between the figures relating to the exports of manufactured goods that appear in Tables 8.3 and 2.7. These discrepancies are due to differences between the Mexican classification scheme and the U.N. Standard International Trade Classification. For one thing, the Mexican classification includes food under the category of manufactured goods; this appears under primary commodities in the SITC. For another, the group of unclassified exports in Table 8.3 comprises some manufactured goods that are shown as such in Table 2.7.

[10] See, for example, Reynolds, "Mexican Commercial Policy."

opment institutions and using selective credit controls, gave the industrial sector greater access to the money market than other sectors had.

A consideration of these factors, however, falls outside the scope of this study and we will concentrate on Mexico's trade policy. Broadly speaking, we may distinguish three stages in the development of this policy and in the principal objectives it was to serve.

1. Between 1940 and 1945 the principal objective was tax collection; export and import duties represented a very large part of fiscal revenue since they were easy to collect (Table 8.2). During this period, Mexico had a current account surplus in every year and accumulated sizable reserves, so that the objective of balance-of-payments equilibrium received little attention. Apart from creating foreign demand for raw materials, World War II also provided a stimulus to the home production of a variety of manufactured goods which were then difficult to obtain from abroad. Nevertheless, tariffs were raised slightly to protect domestic manufacturing industries.[11]

2. The situation changed radically between 1946 and 1955. Although tax collection remained an objective, balance-of-payments equilibrium and the protection of domestic industry began to assume increasing importance in decision-making. This was a period characterized by rapid inflation which originated largely in budgetary deficits and led to balance-of-payments problems. To achieve equilibrium in the balance of payments, at first tariffs were increased; later when it was seen that these did not have the desired effects, the country's currency was devalued three times, in 1948, 1949, and 1954. Import licenses were introduced at this time as an additional instrument of trade policy; subsequently, they were increasingly used for protecting industry.[12]

3. Since 1955, the main objective of trade policy has been the protection of domestic industry, while the tax collection and the balance-of-payments objectives of trade policy have become less important. In a document presented by the government of Mexico to the Latin American Symposium on Industrialization it was stated that tariffs "should be considered as mechanisms for regulating trade rather than as sources of revenue."[13] At any rate, with a better organized and flexible fiscal system, the share of tariffs in budgetary revenue has declined to a considerable extent.

---

[11] For a very good description of these events see V. Urquidi, R. Ortiz Mena, A. Waterston, and J. Haralz, *The Economic Development of Mexico: Report of the Combined Mexican Working Party* (Baltimore: published for the International Bank for Reconstruction and Development by the Johns Hopkins Press, 1953).

[12] Mexican commercial policy is discussed more extensively in Reynolds, "Mexican Commercial Policy" and in R. Izquierdo, "Protectionism in Mexico," in *Public Policy and Private Enterprise in Mexico*, ed. R. Vernon (Cambridge, Mass.: Harvard University Press, 1964), pp. 241–89.

[13] See "El Desarrollo Industrial de Mexico," mimeographed (prepared by the Mexican Government for the Latin American Symposium on Industrialization, Santiago, March 14–25, 1966).

Finally, although balance-of-payments equilibrium remains one of the government's principal objectives, it has achieved this by monetary policy and foreign borrowing rather than by tariff increases, exchange controls, and devaluation. As Clark Reynolds expressed it in a recent study, the government considers in general "that devaluation *per se*, owing to the uncertainty and speculation it creates and its effects on the capital account, is a greater evil than the illness it is supposed to cure."[14]

Main Instruments of Trade Policy

Since World War II, the main instruments of Mexico's trade policy have been tariffs, licenses, import and export subsidies, export drawbacks, and the institution of "official prices" as a basis for setting tariffs. The importance of each of these and their special features have gradually changed with the objectives of trade policy. Their use for relatively well-defined protectionist purposes and for the promotion of rapid industrialization seems to have begun in the second stage of the development of trade policy referred to above. The industrialization achieved in previous years was rather the result of unusual external conditions and a by-product of policies designed to safeguard the balance of payments and to provide tax revenue.

In 1947 the tariff system, hitherto expressed in terms of specific duties, was modified by the introduction of ad valorem duties levied on the basis of "official prices" that differed from the prices at which trade actually took place. In 1949 the Executive Committee on Tariffs, with representatives from the public and private sectors, was set up with the task of defining a tariff policy and submitting recommendations on tariff levels to the Department of Finance. In practice, however, its activities were limited. Not until 1966 was a new start made by the creation of a new National Committee on Tariff Policy.

In 1954 duties on all imports were raised 25 percent for balance-of-payments reasons. After the devaluation later in that year, this additional tax was removed on some imports but retained on many others, especially luxury consumer goods. In the same year, a new tariff policy was instituted which remains in force. Its main features are (*a*) for goods produced in Mexico the tariff is fixed by agreement between the Department of Finance and the manufacturers, taking into account (in reality only occasionally) the opinion of the National Committee on Tariff Policy; (*b*) for goods not produced in Mexico there is a double standard: low tariffs for raw materials, machinery and equipment, and certain types of essential consumer goods, and high tariffs for luxury consumer goods; and (*c*) finally, the price differential between domestic and foreign products should not encourage smuggling.

---

[14] Reynolds, "Mexican Commercial Policy."

Since 1947, import licenses have been used in addition to tariffs, and licensing has assumed increasing importance in the years following. The simultaneous use of tariffs and licensing is characterized by a lack of coordination, since they are handled by two different government departments: tariffs by the Ministry of Finance and import permits by the Ministry of Industry and Commerce. A manufacturer seeking protection can thus turn to one or the other, depending on where he encounters less resistance. There have been cases, for example, when one Ministry, under pressure from other manufacturers, agreed to reduce tariffs or to waive the prior permit requirement only to find that the other Ministry, under pressure from the producer, has made the importation of the commodity in question subject to prior permit or has raised the tariff.[15]

The import license system is now the main instrument of trade policy. Whereas initially it was used to restrict importation of luxury consumer goods, it now covers about 80 percent of all the items in the tariff classification. Two main arguments are advanced for continuing to use import licenses. First, it is claimed that through the combined use of tariffs and import licenses industry obtains imported raw materials and capital goods at low cost while national production is protected from foreign competition. According to the second argument, whatever the tariff level, if consumers in developing countries can choose between the imported and the domestic varieties of a particular product they will tend to choose the former for reasons of prestige, or because they consider them better, even if it means paying more.[16]

Neither argument is convincing. For one thing, the licensing of capital goods imports tends to discourage the domestic production of these commodities; for another, it is unrealistic to assume that demand for imported consumer goods would be completely inelastic. Moreover, the system of licensing creates administrative difficulties that entail a cost for the national economy.

Administrative difficulties arise because of both the large number of applications for import licenses and the large number of criteria involved in deciding whether they should be granted. Each application has to be submitted to the Ministry of Industry and Commerce with a statement of why the import is required, which often means wasting the best administrative talent in a company on this task, although there is considerable likelihood that the application will be rejected.

The following figures indicate what the system means in administrative terms: about 30,000 applications are received every month, of which only

---

[15] In fact, this lack of coordination gave rise, especially in the past, to frequent complaints by the organizations of industrialists.

[16] See "El Desarrollo Industrial de Mexico." This point is also made in several speeches by government officials.

about one-third are approved; in the judging of the requests, thirty-seven criteria are used which are so varied that the element of uncertainty for the would-be importer is enormous.[17] It seems clear that, in a system of this kind, inefficiencies, arbitrary actions, and unfair distribution of profit opportunities among importers are inevitable.

There are also other costs. Some of these are measurable—like the inventory charges after the license has been granted—and may amount to 1 or 2 percent of the value of the imports; others are difficult to quantify, although they may amount to more. It has happened, for example, that a firm's entire importation of machinery has been held up because the machinery incorporated simple motors which were also manufactured domestically. The same has happened repeatedly when there was uncertainty about whether particular goods had domestically manufactured substitutes.

Administrative problems also hinder the manufacturer in obtaining export subsidies and drawbacks. This partly explains why, except for textiles and a few other manufactured goods, little use has been made of them so far. Other reasons are the government's apparent aversion to the fiscal expenditure involved in granting subsidies and the availability of a protected domestic market.

The exchange rate in Mexico has changed only once since 1950. The devaluation in 1954 reflected the government's concern with losses in foreign exchange reserves and the low export prices after the Korean war. The devaluation raised Mexico's real exchange rate, calculated by dividing the exchange rate by the Mexican wholesale price index, beyond the 1950 level (Table 8.6).

Mexican prices continued to rise after 1954, and thus the real exchange rate fell. This conclusion is not affected if we adjust for changes in the wholesale price index of the United States, Mexico's major market and supplier. The adjusted real exchange rate fell from 8.64 in 1950 to 7.18 in 1953; it rose to 9.59 after the devaluation in 1954 but declining again in subsequent years, it reached 7.00 in 1964 and 6.95 in 1967. Yet, a devaluation has not been necessary, largely because of the equilibrating effect of tourist flows.

Nominal and Effective Protection

Data Sources and Estimation Procedures

Rates of nominal and effective protection for Mexico in 1960 have been calculated on the basis of the tariff classification and input-output matrix for that year. However, subsequent changes in tariffs and technical coefficients would hardly modify the results to any important degree. Thus, the 1965

---

[17] See S. L. Cano, "Politica sobre el otorgamiento de permisos de importacion," *El Mercado de Valores*, January 1966, pp. 103–7.

TABLE 8.6: Nominal and Real Exchange Rates in Mexico, 1950–67

(Pesos per U.S.$)

Year	Nominal exchange rate (1)	Goods whole-sale price index (2)	Real exchange rate (3) (1)/(2)	U.S. whole-sale price index (4)	Adjusted real exchange rate (5) (3) × (4)
1950	8.64	100	8.64	100	8.64
1951	8.65	124	6.98	111	7.75
1952	8.60	129	6.67	107	7.14
1953	8.60	127	6.77	106	7.18
1954	12.49	138	9.05	106	9.59
1955	12.49	158	7.91	106	8.38
1956	12.49	165	7.57	111	8.40
1957	12.49	172	7.26	114	8.28
1958	12.49	180	6.94	115	7.98
1959	12.49	182	6.86	115	7.89
1960	12.49	191	6.54	115	7.52
1961	12.49	192	6.51	115	7.49
1962	12.49	196	6.37	115	7.33
1963	12.49	198	6.31	115	7.26
1964	12.49	205	6.09	115	7.00
1965	12.49	209	5.98	117	7.00
1966	12.49	214	5.84	121	7.07
1967	12.49	219	5.70	122	6.95

Source: IMF, *International Financial Statistics.*

modifications in the tariff classification scheme seem to have left tariff levels practically unchanged. Nor has the structure of production undergone substantial changes.

The input-output table of the Mexican economy in 1960 provides information on forty-five branches of the economy: four in agriculture, forestry, and fishing, two in mining, one in oil, twenty-seven in manufacturing, and the rest in services. A recent Bank of Mexico publication has made it possible, however, to calculate rates of protection for some industries in greater detail.

Various adjustments had to be made in the calculation of effective rates of protection from the Mexican input-output table. First, we have deducted from the value of output indirect taxes which in Mexico are important mostly for consumer goods.[18] Second, we have excluded depreciation from value added. As information on depreciation of furniture, machinery, construction, and vehicles was available separately for most industries, it has been possible to calculate the average tariff on depreciation with considerable accuracy. Rental payments have been handled in the same way as depreciation.

Third, in order to express output in producer prices we have deducted trade and transport margins from both inputs and outputs. Fourth, we have excluded repairs from the value of production in the machinery industry, and

---

[18] This is especially the case for processed food, beverages, and tobacco. In the other commodity categories indirect taxes are of importance only for petroleum.

have treated them in the same way as other services. Fifth, although no separate import matrix is available, we have been able to estimate this on the basis of information on major inputs in individual industries provided in the Bank of Mexico publication referred to above.

It has further been necessary to reclassify the 5,000 Mexican tariff sections in conformity with both the Standard International Trade Classification and the classification of the Mexican Catalogue of Economic Activities on which the input-output table is based. Moreover, we have combined ad valorem tariffs and specific duties for each particular item, and made additional adjustments for differences between actual prices and the so-called "official prices."

These "official prices" (for which a parallel exists in the United States in the "American Selling Price") were originally devised by the Treasury to insure that importers could not reduce duties by lower price declarations. But, in actual practice, official prices have served as an additional measure of protection. As changes in nominal tariffs generally involve cumbersome administrative procedures, the Treasury has often resorted to the relatively simple device of augmenting official prices to attain the desired increase in the tariff rate.

Export subsidies, as noted before, have not been very important in Mexico. Exceptions are textiles and some agricultural products. These have been considered in the calculations on protection, and, in the relevant instances, we added averages of tariffs and subsidies.

Rates of Nominal and Implicit Protection

An assumption underlying much of the theoretical work on effective protection is that domestic prices equal the sum of world market prices and the tariff. This assumption cannot, however, be made in a country like Mexico, partly because imports are often constrained by quantitative restrictions rather than by tariffs and partly because of the existence of prohibitive duties. These considerations, then, call for measuring effective protection from direct price observations which provide us with an estimate of nominal implicit protection.

This does not mean, however, that an analysis of nominal and effective protection based on tariffs would be useless. To begin with, the tariff structure provides an indication of the policies the tariff-setting agency intends to apply. Furthermore, it is useful to compare the results of calculations based on tariffs and on price comparisons, and to show the margins of protection provided by tariffs and licensing. Finally, the calculations can be helpful in establishing criteria for an eventual restructuring of the tariff schedule.

For purposes of this study, price comparisons have been made for 400 commodities. The main sources of information on prices were the following.

1. A survey, carried out by the Bank of Mexico at the request of the World Bank, compared the 1957 and 1962 prices of some 300 articles in Mexico and in the United States, the main supplier. These were converted to a common base (c.i.f. Mexico), and in derivation of 1960 figures it was assumed that between 1957 and 1962 the relationship between Mexican and U.S. prices changed at a constant rate. As the changes between 1957 and 1962 were relatively small, the margin of error that this assumption might introduce is negligible.
2. Another survey on the structure of Mexican industry was carried out jointly by the Bank of Mexico and Nacional Financiera in 1960 and 1961. This has provided a great deal of information on the domestic levels of producer prices for a wide range of products.
3. Direct information is available from firms on the prices of their products. In some cases it was possible to obtain this for 1960, but in others, information for the nearest year was used and deflated by the price indices calculated by the Bank of Mexico.
4. Specialist journals often quote prices for articles produced by different industries in the United States and in some European countries.
5. Average import prices are shown in the trade statistics.

Obtaining information on the domestic and foreign prices of comparable goods was the most difficult part of the work on the structure of protection and its effects in Mexico. In general, to establish appropriate criteria for the comparisons and to eliminate inconsistencies in the results, it called for close contacts with industrial firms and with specialist technicians. It has further been necessary to deal with the problem of quality differences between domestic and foreign products. In this connection, we have considered separately intermediate products, nondurable consumer goods, durable consumer goods, and machinery and equipment.

Quality differences do not appear to be important for intermediate products, most of which are manufactured according to standard specifications. Nondurable consumer goods, however, presented difficulties in ascertaining quality differences. We have attempted to minimize these difficulties by making price comparisons for goods with very similar characteristics, but—as expected—have found divergent opinions among consumers. They varied from statements claiming that there were no quality differences to those stating that they were substantial. The issue could not be satisfactorily resolved and the assumption has been made that quality differences were not important enough to warrant adjustment.

Durable consumer goods present a similar situation. However, although the question was not entirely settled, our discussion with industrialists and wholesalers has led to the conclusion that the differences in quality are not so marked as to warrant an adjustment in the results of the price comparisons. In general it has been suggested that manufacturers (almost exclusively subsid-

iaries of foreign corporations) adhere to the standards set by the parent company and that quality differences are not shown for the final product but rather
in the greater rejection rate of the components, which raises the cost of production and is reflected in the observed price differentials.

The only case where an adjustment has been considered essential was for
machinery and equipment where the difference in quality between imported
variants and the domestic product is quite marked. On the basis of information received from the users of equipment on maintenance costs, we have
adjusted the prices of domestic machinery and equipment by 10 to 15 percent
to make them comparable to foreign prices.

Concerning export products, we have assumed that the difference between
the export price and the price of the same article in the United States reflects
the quality differential. Finally, for products in the "limbo" between imports
and exports (i.e., due to transportation costs, neither imports nor exports are
profitable), the domestic price differential between Mexico and the United
States is very small and we have assumed that nominal implicit protection is
zero.

To arrive at levels of nominal implicit protection for each branch of manufacturing industry, we have used a recent Bank of Mexico publication on the
industrial structure in 1960.[19] Rates of implicit protection have been weighted
by the share of the products in domestic supply within each branch and sub-
branch for which calculations have been made. Nominal tariffs have been
averaged in the same manner.

The results shown in Table 8.7 indicate that, for the primary sector as a
whole, averages of both nominal tariffs and implicit rates of nominal protection are 6 percent; for agriculture, forestry, and fishing, the relevant figures
are between 6 and 7 percent; for mining and energy, between 4 and 5 percent.
Differences between nominal tariffs and implicit rates are only slightly larger
if we separate the major primary industries, with the exception of fishing
where tariffs average 6.2 percent while implicit rates are nil.

Within agriculture, there are some negative rates of nominal tariff protection, inasmuch as export taxes apply to cotton (20 percent), coffee (10 percent), and sugar (8 percent). Implicit rates are roughly the same for cotton and
coffee; however, for sugar, prices are substantially lower in Mexico than in the
United States where they are bolstered by quotas. By contrast, government
subsidies to small farmers raise the price of corn by 42 percent and that of
wheat by 14 percent above the U.S. price.[20] Wheat and corn are purchased by
the government at support prices, and if they are sold abroad, this is done at

---

[19] Banco de Mexico, Departamento de Investigaciones Industriales, "La Estructura
Industrial de Mexico, 1960" (Mexico, 1968).
[20] These figures are not shown in the tables where agriculture has been taken as a single
category.

world market prices. Accordingly, the products in question receive, in effect, an export subsidy.

For manufacturing as a whole, average nominal tariffs (33 percent) exceed averages of implicit rates of nominal protection (25 percent) by a considerable margin. But these averages conceal substantial variations among industries and industry groups. Nominal rates are higher than implicit rates for processed food, beverages and tobacco, construction materials, intermediate products, and nondurable consumer goods, and lower for durable consumer goods, machinery, and transport equipment. Differences are especially large for construction materials where Mexican prices are slightly lower than U.S. prices, yet tariffs average 26 percent. By contrast, in the machinery industries, price differences are, on the average, 29 percent as against tariffs of 11 percent.

The relationship between nominal tariffs and implicit rates of nominal protection also depends on whether the industry is classified as import-competing (imports exceeding 10 percent of domestic consumption); an export industry (exports exceeding 10 percent of domestic production); or non-import-competing (international trade in either direction is negligible). In the four manufacturing export industries (tiles and pottery, sawn wood, cotton textiles, and other textiles), implicit rates of nominal protection are relatively low, and in two out of three cases are below the rate of duty. For non-import-competing goods, too, tariffs usually exceed implicit rates while they are lower for import-competing industries (Table 8.8).

Among individual commodity groups, foodstuffs show generally small differences between nominal tariffs and implicit rates of protection. The only exception is meat and dairy products where the rates are respectively 38 and 47 percent. On the other hand, implicit rates of nominal protection on beverages are much lower than tariffs, since soft drinks and beer are much cheaper in Mexico than in the United States; domestic prices equal the sum of the import price and the tariff only for alcoholic beverages. Domestic prices of tobacco, too, are lower than the tariff-inclusive prices of imports.

Among construction materials, implicit rates of protection are much below nominal tariffs for tiles and pottery and for cement. Mexico has a cost advantage over the United States in glazed tiles and in cement but this is not yet reflected in exports, partly because of high transportation costs and technical problems and partly because of capacity limitations and unfamiliarity with export possibilities. However, since 1960 a large cement plant has been installed catering largely to exports and, following improvements in technical standards, exports of glazed tiles have picked up, too.

Among the remaining manufacturing industries, tariffs exceed implicit rates of protection in industries characterized by relatively simple technological requirements—intermediate products and nondurable consumer goods. Most such industries have a long history in Mexico and they have

TABLE 8.7: Nominal and Effective Protection in Mexico, 1960

(Percent)

Industry	Classification[a] (1)	Nominal tariff protection[a] (2)	Nominal implicit protection (3)	Effective tariff protection		Effective implicit protection		Bias against exporting[b] (8)
				Balassa (4)	Corden (5)	Balassa (6)	Corden (7)	
I Agriculture, forestry, and fishing								
Agriculture	X	6.2	4.7	4.4	4.3	1.7	1.6	...
Livestock	NIC	7.6	9.8	3.0	2.6	6.2	6.2	14
Forestry	NIC	6.6	3.5	5.5	5.4	2.5	2.5	4
Fishing	X	6.2	0	−1.4	−1.3	−10.4	−9.7	...
Average		6.7	6.5	3.9	3.7	3.1	3.0	9
II Processed food								
Meat and dairy products	NIC	37.5	46.8	119.9	106.0	195.7	166.3	558
Grain mill and bakery	NIC	8.2	4.0	−9.5	−8.5	−23.2	−20.9	11
Other food products	NIC	26.6	20.9	25.6	50.4	16.7	16.2	...
Average		21.2	18.3	23.0	23.0	4.7	5.7	71
III Beverages and tobacco								
Beverages	IC	75.3	28.2	292.0	228.0	45.4	39.9	83
Tobacco	NIC	49.7	30.9	124.8	109.8	58.4	52.3	87
Average		69.8	28.8	257.8	204.5	48.1	42.4	84
IV Mining and energy								
Metallic mining	X	3.0	3.5	−2.0	−1.9	−0.9	−0.8	...
Nonmetallic mining	X	1.9	−4.2	−3.4	−3.2	1.0	1.0	...
Petroleum and coal	NIC	5.0	6.0	−9.0	−8.0	−7.9	−7.6	13
Average		4.2	4.4	−6.6	−5.9	−5.1	−4.9	13
V Construction materials								
Cement	NIC	28.0	−10.0	108.4	69.2	−2.3	−1.8	−16
Bricks	IC	3.9	9.0	1.5	1.4	8.4	8.1	14
Tiles and pottery	X	74.7	8.0	239.3	218.6	−4.9	−4.7	−13
Average		26.3	−3.6	97.0	72.6	0.6	0.6	−6
VI-A Intermediate products I								
Sawn wood	X	16.7	13.8	29.7	28.9	25.7	24.8	33
Leather	NIC	49.1	20.1	145.0	126.2	28.0	26.6	64
Fertilizers and insecticides	IC	6.6	8.9	5.9	4.7	10.9	8.6	30
Synthetic fibers	IC	21.4	21.7	21.4	19.5	17.2	15.8	86

Industry	Class[a]							
Iron and steel	IC	28.3	28.8	72.8	59.5	73.7	60.1	105
Copper	NIC	17.3	18.5	48.5	44.6	57.9	53.0	...
Aluminum	IC	14.0	24.3	41.0	36.7	85.0	70.1	96
Glass	NIC	13.3	11.3	21.7	18.6	19.3	16.6	18
Average		24.4	21.8	58.0	49.8	42.2	37.1	67
VI-B Intermediate products II								
Basic chemicals	IC	16.7	23.1	23.5	20.6	48.5	41.6	88
Cotton textiles	X	56.3	12.1	120.6	111.2	14.9	14.0	26
Wool textiles	IC	36.2	42.5	67.0	63.1	90.9	84.9	160
Artificial fiber textiles	NIC	41.0	55.8	96.5	86.0	194.5	164.2	429
Other textiles	X	36.3	25.0	62.6	57.0	50.2	46.0	...
Worked timber	NIC	40.4	18.0	57.4	56.0	45.7	44.7	29
Pulp and paper	IC	40.4	35.1	81.9	65.0	95.4	74.5	166
Rubber	NIC	24.3	32.5	34.1	31.3	52.9	48.1	89
Other chemicals	IC	19.2	25.6	34.8	31.3	72.1	63.2	184
Metal manufactures	IC	40.6	30.6	62.3	55.1	49.5	44.2	108
Soaps and detergents	NIC	33.0	10.1	94.8	75.9	0.6	0.5	38
Pharmaceutical products	IC	13.0	12.4	9.1	8.1	10.0	8.9	29
Perfumes and cosmetics	IC	22.0	22.0	52.1	46.1	65.0	58.2	53
Average		33.5	24.6	67.0	59.3	42.0	37.8	75
VII Nondurable consumer goods								
Knitwear and hosiery	NIC	120.0	50.5	52.6	49.8	111.3	103.2	195
Clothing	NIC	88.0	10.0	236.6	203.1	3.1	2.9	20
Shoes	NIC	63.1	24.5	83.4	81.0	32.8	32.2	52
Printing	NIC	37.8	13.3	55.2	50.9	8.6	8.1	29
Other manufactures	IC	31.8	31.8	52.9	48.5	70.8	64.1	115
Average		63.9	25.4	129.2	112.0	31.9	29.9	65
VIII Consumer durables								
Electrical appliances	IC	41.2	45.2	95.8	87.7	57.5	53.5	211
Motorcycles and bicycles	IC	36.4	25.0	104.7	97.6	55.2	48.0	60
Motor vehicles	IC	40.8	51.7	52.9	48.5	254.7	212.0	*
Average		40.8	49.0	86.7	78.3	100.9	93.0	953
IX Machinery								
Nonelectrical equipment	IC	10.3	29.7	7.5	7.3	44.7	42.8	74
Electrical machinery	IC	11.7	25.0	13.0	11.9	36.0	32.4	41
Average		10.6	28.8	10.1	9.5	40.6	37.8	59
X Transport equipment								
Railroad equipment	IC	18.0	26.0	29.6	26.3	41.8	37.0	74

Source: See text.

a X = export industries; IC = import-competing industries; NIC = non-import-competing industries.

b Calculated by using the Corden formula.

* Denotes negative value added in case of exporting; thus the extent of discrimination against exporting is infinite.

TABLE 8.8: Nominal and Effective Protection in Mexico, 1960

(Percent)

Sector	Nominal tariff protection	Nominal implicit protection	Effective tariff protection		Effective implicit protection		Bias against exporting[a]
			Balassa	Corden	Balassa	Corden	
Primary production							
Exports	6	4	3	3	1	1	...
Import-competing goods	—	—	—1	—1	—	—	13
Non-import-competing goods	7	8	—1	—1	1	1	13
Nonexport activities, together	7	8	—1	—1	1	1	13
Total	6	6	2	2	1	1	13
Manufacturing							
Exports	43	15	94	88	23	22	...
Import-competing goods	31	31	88	73	56	49	118
Non-import-competing goods	34	20	59	53	15	15	65
Nonexport activities, together	33	25	69	60	29	27	87
Total	33	25	72	63	28	27	87
Manufacturing goods, other than tobacco and beverages							
Exports	43	15	94	88	23	22	...
Import-competing goods	27	31	49	43	58	51	123
Non-import-competing goods	33	20	58	52	14	14	66
Nonexport activities, together	30	25	55	49	27	26	89
Total	31	24	59	53	27	26	89
All commodities (except beverages and tobacco)							
Exports	13	6	13	13	4	4	...
Import-competing goods	27	31	49	43	58	51	123
Non-import-competing goods	23	15	28	25	7	8	35
Nonexport activities, together	24	21	31	28	16	16	58
Total	22	17	24	22	11	11	58

Source: Table 8.7 and text.
a. Calculated by using the Corden formula.

exhibited a rise in productivity over time. *Pari passu*, with increases in productivity, in many instances domestic prices have declined below the sum of the import price and the tariff.

Various factors have contributed to the fall of domestic prices below the sum of the import price and the tariff. First, there has been an increase in domestic competition in these groups of industries. Second, there has been competition from the subsidiaries of foreign firms located in Mexico. Third, as mentioned above, smuggling has had a restraining effect on prices. Finally, the demonstration effects of U.S. product promotion and managerial practices might have influenced Mexican industry. The last two factors can be ascribed to the proximity of Mexico to the United States.

Nonetheless, tariffs have been maintained at relatively high levels on nondurable consumer goods, with the ad valorem equivalent of duties exceeding 50 percent for knitwear and hosiery, clothing, and shoes. High tariffs on these products are probably the result of the pressure these industries exert on the government usually by arguing that a lowering of tariffs would adversely affect employment.

Duties are lower on most intermediate products where the users exert pressure for reducing tariffs. Exceptions are leather and cotton textiles, which are used in industries that themselves enjoy high protection, as well as artificial fibers, pulp and paper, and metal manufacturers which are of relatively recent origin in Mexico. Moreover, in these industries, nominal implicit rates of protection are also higher than the average.

Price differentials exceed tariffs in recently established industries requiring sophisticated technology. In these industries, tariffs serve only a revenue function and imports are effectively limited by licensing. Distinction should be made, however, between machinery and transport equipment where tariffs are in the 10–20 percent range, and consumer durables where tariffs average 40 percent. In the former case, tariffs are kept low to reduce the cost of production to the user, who is often a licensee enjoying quota profits. Such considerations do not, however, apply to durable consumer goods, where high tariffs siphon off the quota profits that would otherwise accrue to the importer.

Among intermediate products at lower rates of fabrication, Mexico exports some sawn wood to the United States, especially from the northern region which is advantageously situated from the point of view of transportation costs. Nevertheless, the industry as a whole is protected and domestic prices are on the average higher than prices in the United States.

The copper industry as defined here includes only the manufacturing of wrought metal and copper products; Mexico's exports of unwrought copper are shown under mining. Apart from leather, which has been discussed above, nominal tariffs on iron and steel (28 percent) are the highest in this group and are equal to implicit rates of protection. Pressure groups in the industry have succeeded in obtaining relatively high levels of protection on the grounds that this is needed for the industry's survival. Finally, nominal implicit rates of protection exceed tariffs by a substantial margin on aluminum which has been produced in Mexico only relatively recently.

Within the next commodity category—intermediate products at higher levels of fabrication—cotton textiles and other textiles are classified as export industries. A survey by the Bank of Mexico and Nacional Financiera has revealed that Mexico has a cost advantage over the United States in low-quality fabrics, but this advantage disappears and Mexican prices exceed U.S. prices, as we move to high-quality fabrics. On poplin, for example, the nominal implicit rate of protection is 38 percent. This would appear to indicate that in countries such as Mexico costs tend to be high in the production of higher quality goods that require more qualified personnel and are produced in smaller quantities.

It may be of interest to mention that in recent years exports of cotton textiles (yarn and low-quality fabrics) have been greatly bolstered by the use of subsidies. These subsidies have been paid out of the proceeds of taxes on cotton exports and, on the average, they account for 20–25 percent of the price of the exported products. This may largely explain the increase in exports of cotton textiles from only $2 million in 1964 to more than $25 million in 1967. The "other textiles" group also qualifies as an export industry. It includes hard fiber yarns, ropes, and cords where Mexico has a cost advantage due to the availability of the raw material (henequen). Nevertheless, partly because of some imported products in this group and partly because of subsidies to exports, the average nominal rate of protection on this group of products is 25 percent.

Among non-import-competing intermediate goods, implicit rates of protection are much lower than nominal tariffs on worked timber and on soap and detergents but not on rubber. Finally, among import-competing industries, nominal tariffs as well as implicit rates of protection exceed 30 percent on wool textiles, textiles made of artificial fibers, pulp and paper, and metal manufactures.

Most nondurable consumer goods industries are classified as non-import-competing and bear high tariffs far exceeding the price differential between domestic and foreign goods. The situation in clothing is similar to that observed in cotton textiles, with clothes made of low-quality fabrics being cheaper, and those made of artificial fibers and poplin more expensive, in Mexico than in the United States. This relationship between quality and relative prices is also shown for hosiery and for shoes.

Consumer durables industries have been established relatively recently in Mexico and their products compete with imports. Implicit rates of nominal protection exceed tariffs on electrical appliances and motor vehicles. The difference is especially marked for motor vehicles and, within this group, it is greater for cars than for trucks; this partly reflects the government policy of keeping the prices of luxury goods high and those of producer goods low. By comparison, the prices of relatively simple appliances differ little from those in the United States, but price differences increase as the equipment becomes more complex. Prices of bicycles and motorcycles also conform to this pattern.

In the machinery group, tariffs average 11 percent while the average price differential is 29 percent. The low tariffs have given the users of machinery considerable incentives to apply for import licenses. Implicit rates of protection also exceed tariffs on transport equipment (mainly railroad equipment), but nominal tariffs are higher here than on machinery.

The Pattern of Effective Rates

In manufacturing activities, the excess of tariff protection over implicit protection tends to increase if we consider *effective* rather than *nominal* rates. For manufacturing as a whole, averages of effective tariff protection are 72 percent under the Balassa method and 63 percent under the Corden method, while averages of effective implicit protection are 28 and 27 percent, respectively. Such differences are not shown for primary activities where the effective rate of protection is between 1 and 2 percent under both alternatives (Table 8.8).

We further find that averages of effective tariff protection on all import-competing goods (primary as well as manufactured) are 49 percent under the Balassa definition and 43 percent under the Corden formula as against effective rates of implicit protection of 58 and 51 percent under the two alternatives, respectively. Differences between effective tariff and implicit protection are even larger for exports and for non-import-competing goods. For exports, effective tariff rates average 13 percent and effective implicit protection 4 percent; for non-import-competing goods, the corresponding results are 25–28 percent and 7–8 percent.

The average bias against exports is 123 percent in import-competing industries and 35 percent in industries producing non-import-competing goods. This bias exceeds 100 percent for meat and dairy products, iron and steel, wool textiles, textiles made of artificial fibers, pulp and paper, miscellaneous chemicals, metal manufactures, knitwear and hosiery, miscellaneous manufactures, and electric appliances, Thus, in these industries, value added obtainable in exporting is less than half that obtained in production for domestic use. There is even one industry, motor vehicles, where the domestic cost of material inputs exceeds the price obtainable in exporting; i.e., exporting would require negative value added.

For individual industries, estimates derived by the use of domestic input-output coefficients are shown in Table 8.7, while averages for industry groups are given in Table 8.9. In the following, we will restrict our attention to effective implicit rates, and will compare estimates derived by the use of domestic and free trade input-output coefficients.

Effective rates exceed nominal rates in the case of manufactured goods while the opposite conclusion pertains to primary products. The results indicate the effects of escalation in nominal tariffs from primary products to intermediate goods and again to consumer goods. Within the manufacturing sector, however, effective rates of protection do not rise from one stage of fabrication to another. This result is explained if we consider that, starting with intermediate products at lower levels of fabrication that use largely unprotected inputs, nominal rates of protection have to increase from one processing stage to the next just to get identical effective rates.

Among primary activities, effective rates of protection are negative for metallic and nonmetallic mining and for petroleum and coal, and hence also for the mining and energy sector taken as a whole. This is hardly surprising, given the preponderance of export activities in this sector. Negative effective protection is also shown for fishing and a small positive protection for agriculture, livestock, and forestry.

In the processed food group, grain milling and bakery have negative effective protection due to the relatively high implicit protection of cereals that are the major input. By contrast, low input prices raise the effective rate of protection for meat and dairy products. For the processed food category as a whole, effective implicit protection is approximately 5 percent, irrespective of whether we use the Balassa or the Corden definition. The corresponding averages are in the 40–50 percent range for beverages and tobacco. Finally, among construction materials, negative effective protection is shown for tiles and bricks and for cement which are actual or potential export industries.

Effective rates of protection on intermediate products at lower levels of fabrication average 42 percent under the Balassa procedure and 37 percent under the Corden method. Among individual industries, the effective protection of steel, aluminum, and copper exceeds the average since these industries use inputs subject to low tariffs. Levels of effective protection are lower than the average for sawn wood, fertilizers and insecticides, synthetic fibers, leather, and glass. As noted above, sawn wood is increasingly exported by Mexico; the relatively low protection of fertilizers and insecticides is due to government policy measures favoring agriculture; domestic competition and price regulations under the petrochemical law have kept protection relatively low on synthetic fibers; and leather and glass are traditional industries in Mexico.

Among intermediate products included in the second group, the highest level of effective protection (over 150 percent) is that for artificial fiber textiles whose main input is synthetic fibers. High protection seems to be largely ab-

TABLE 8.9: Nominal and Effective Protection for Major Product Categories in Mexico, 1960[a]

(Percent)

	Industry group	Estimates based on domestic coefficients			Estimates based on free trade coefficients		
		Nominal protection	Effective protection		Nominal protection	Effective protection	
			Balassa	Corden		Balassa	Corden
I	Agriculture, forestry, and fishing	7	3	3	7	6	6
II	Processed food	18	5	6	13	24	20
III	Beverages and tobacco	29	48	42	85	190	149
IV	Mining and energy	4	−5	−5	−1	−15	−13
V	Construction materials	−4	1	1	4	−6	−5
VI-A	Intermediate products I	22	42	37	14	41	25
VI-B	Intermediate products II	25	42	38	33	70	56
VI	Intermediate products I and II	24	42	38	20	50	34
VII	Nondurable consumer goods	25	32	30	33	49	45
VIII	Consumer durables	49	101	93	50	105	85
IX	Machinery	29	41	38	32	45	38
X	Transport equipment	26	42	37	26	34	30
I–X	All industries	18	12	12	14	25	19
I + IV	Primary production	6	1	1	3	−4	−3
II, III, V–X	Manufacturing	25	28	27	21	45	33
VI–X	Manufacturing less food, beverages, tobacco, and construction materials	28	43	39	24	52	38

Source: Table 8.7 and text.

[a] Estimates refer to implicit rates of protection.

sorbed by high profits in this case, indicating that the effects of price control on the principal input are lost on the next stage of manufacturing. It should be added that the high levels of protection exclude virtually all imports.

Within the same group of intermediates, most import-competing activities, such as basic chemicals, wool textiles, pulp and paper, other chemicals, metal manufactures, and perfumes and cosmetics, bear relatively high levels of effective protection. The only exception is pharmaceutical products (9–10 percent) where prices are controlled by the government. Effective rates of protection are also low on cotton textiles, which are largely export products, and on soaps and detergents where domestic competition has led to a decline in prices. Finally, slightly above average effective protection (45 percent) is shown for the "other textiles" industry that includes export activities as well as some highly protected products.

In the nondurable consumer goods group, knitwear and hosiery have effective protection exceeding 100 percent, miscellaneous manufactures 65–70 percent, and shoes 32 percent. However, the average for the group is reduced to about 30 percent because clothing and printing have practically no protection.

Among consumer durables, motor vehicles show the highest effective protection in Mexico—over 200 percent. The reason is relatively simple: although some high-cost domestic components were incorporated in the vehicles manufactured in Mexico in 1960, their "manufacture" was still by and large limited to assembly. Among the other industries included within this group, electrical appliances and motorcycles and bicycles also receive effective protection in excess of 50 percent, bringing the average for the consumer durables category to 100 percent under the Balassa definition and 93 percent under the Corden formula.

We next compare the results obtained by the use of the domestic and the free trade input-output coefficients. With the principal exception of beverages and tobacco, there is considerable similarity in the two sets of estimates. Whenever discrepancies are shown, these are largely explained by differences in weighting and in the classification schemes.

Discrimination against mining and energy appears greater if we use estimates based on the free trade input-output table than if we use domestic coefficients; this is mainly because petroleum with high negative protection has a much larger weight in world trade than in the Mexican economy. By contrast, for processed food, the large weight in world trade of the highly protected meat and dairy products explains why the effective rate calculated by the use of free trade coefficients is higher; for beverages, the large weight of highly protected alcoholic beverages has the same effect.

Differences between the two sets of estimates are relatively small for agriculture, forestry and fishing, construction materials, and manufactured goods taken in a narrower sense (i.e., excluding food, beverages, tobacco, and construction materials). Within the latter group, however, averages of effective rates of protection for intermediate products at higher levels of fabrication are greater if calculations are made by the use of free trade rather than domestic coefficients.

Overvaluation and Net Effective Protection

The results shown in Tables 8.7 to 8.9 have been calculated at the official exchange rate in the year 1960 (12.49 pesos per U.S. dollar). This rate kept Mexico's balance of payments in equilibrium given the measures of protection applied in that year. However, to estimate the rate of net effective protection, we have had to adjust the results for the difference between the actual exchange rate and that corresponding to the free trade situation.

Nominal implicit rates of protection on nonexport industries averaged 21 percent in Mexico in 1960 and this figure has been used in calculating the extent of overvaluation as compared to the free trade situation. For exports the situation is more complicated: cotton, coffee, and sugar were subject to taxes while some products, especially manufactured goods, received export subsidies. The average of nominal implicit rates shown in Table 8.8 (6 percent) could not be used in the calculations because some of the export industries also include protected products that were not exported. We have instead assumed zero nominal implicit protection for exports as a whole.

As in the other country studies, the elasticity of supply of imports has been assumed to be infinite, while import demand elasticities have been derived by following the method applied in an article by Bela Balassa.[21] For Mexico, this gives an import demand elasticity of 3.

Mexico's share in the markets for most of its major exports is rather small: less than one percent for copper and fresh fish, between 2 and 3 percent for coffee, sugar, and maize, 10 percent for cotton, and 16 percent for shellfish and lead. But coffee exports are regulated under the International Coffee Agreement, so that the foreign demand elasticity for these products is nil. This assumption has also been made for sugar that is exported to the United States under quotas.

Coffee and sugar account for only 13 percent of Mexican exports, and products with a world market share of over one-tenth for another 7 percent. At the same time, the share of manufactured goods in Mexican exports is relatively large (21 percent in 1967) and rising, and the elasticity of demand for these products is very high. Taking account of the excellent export possibilities

---

[21] Bela Balassa, "Tariff Protection in Industrial Countries—An Evaluation," *Journal of Political Economy*, December 1965, pp. 573–94.

on U.S. markets, we have calculated with an export demand elasticity of 10 in Mexico. Finally, the elasticity of export supply has been assumed to be 3.

Under these assumptions, the extent of overvaluation as compared to the free trade situation is 9 percent in Mexico. This adjustment is relatively small and a recalculation of Table 8.7 providing results on an industry-by-industry basis does not appear necessary. However, it is of interest to consider the extent of net effective protection of export activities and of import-competing and non-import-competing industries.

The estimates of Table 8.10 indicate that there is a slight discrimination against primary commodities irrespective of whether these belong to one category or another. Among manufacturing activities, export industries seem to have a small net protection but this is due to the fact that these industries comprise import-competing goods in addition to exports. Finally, the net effective protection of import-competing goods greatly exceeds that of non-import-competing goods. This result reflects the fact that the commodities

TABLE 8.10:   Net Nominal and Effective Protection in Mexico, 1960[a]

(Percent)

Sector	Nominal tariff protection	Nominal implicit protection	Effective tariff protection	Effective implicit protection
Primary production				
Exports	−3	−5	−6	−7
Import-competing goods	...	...	...	...
Non-import-competing goods	−2	−1	−9	−7
Nonexport activities, together	−2	−1	−9	−7
Total	−3	−3	−6	−7
Manufacturing				
Exports	31	6	72	12
Import-competing goods	20	20	59	37
Non-import-competing goods	23	10	40	6
Nonexport activities, together	22	15	47	17
Total	22	15	50	17
Manufactured goods, other than tobacco and beverages				
Exports	31	6	72	12
Import-competing goods	17	20	31	39
Non-import-competing goods	22	10	39	5
Nonexport activities, together	19	15	37	16
Total	20	14	40	16
All commodities (except beverages and tobacco)				
Exports	4	−3	4	−5
Import-competing goods	17	20	31	39
Non-import-competing goods	13	6	15	−1
Nonexport activities, together	14	11	17	6
Total	12	7	12	2

Source: Table 8.8.
[a] Effective rates of protection have been estimated by using the Corden formula; both nominal and effective rates have been adjusted for overvaluation as compared to the hypothetical free trade situation.

TABLE 8.11: Net Nominal and Effective Protection for Major Product Categories in Mexico, 1960[a]

(*Percent*)

	Industry group	Estimates based on domestic coefficients		Estimates based on free trade coefficients	
		Nominal protection	Effective protection	Nominal protection	Effective protection
I	Agriculture, forestry, and fishing	−2	−6	−2	−3
II	Processed food	8	−3	4	10
III	Beverages and tobacco	18	30	70	128
IV	Mining and energy	−5	−13	−9	−20
V	Construction materials	−12	−7	−5	−13
VI-A	Intermediate products I	12	26	5	15
VI-B	Intermediate products II	15	27	22	43
VI	Intermediate products I and II	14	27	10	23
VII	Nondurable consumer goods	15	19	22	33
VIII	Consumer durables	37	77	38	70
IX	Machinery	18	27	21	27
X	Transport equipment	16	26	16	19
I–X	All industries	8	3	5	9
I + IV	Primary production	−3	−7	−6	−11
II, III, V–X	Manufacturing	15	17	11	22
VI–X	Manufacturing less food, beverages, tobacco, and construction materials	17	28	14	27

Source: Table 8.9.
[a] Effective rates of protection have been estimated by using the Corden formula; both nominal and effective rates have been adjusted for overvaluation as compared to the hypothetical free trade situation.

included in the import-competing category have been recently introduced in Mexico and require relatively high levels of protection, while in non-import-competing industries prices have fallen over time as a result of improvements in productivity.

Evaluation and Policy Recommendations

In summarizing the findings of the study, the following points should be noted. First, there is relatively little correspondence between the levels of nominal and effective protection, irrespective of whether calculations are made from tariff observations or from price comparisons. In general, implicit protection is greater than tariff protection for import-competing industries but less for non-import-competing and export industries.

Second, whether we consider tariff or implicit protection, a large diversity of rates of both nominal and effective protection is found, although this diversity is much greater if we use tariffs. This result may be interpreted as evidence for the lack of a consistent set of criteria in setting tariff rates.

Third, effective rates of protection are higher than nominal rates on manufactured goods but lower on primary products. These results reflect the effects of escalation in nominal tariffs from lower to higher degrees of fabrication. However, in the manufacturing section, effective rates of protection do not rise with the degree of fabrication, except for consumer durables.

Fourth, and most importantly, net effective protection is on the average lower than in most other developing countries and there is less discrimination against exports. This fact, as well as the stability of the exchange rate during the last 15 years, has undoubtedly contributed to Mexico's favorable export performance which, in turn, has been instrumental in reaching a high growth rate.

One should not assume, however, that there is no need for changes in the system of protection in Mexico. Changes are required partly because the structural transformation of the economy has made the present system obsolete and partly because of the shortcomings of this system we have discussed earlier.

In the postwar period, industrialization policy was oriented toward import substitution. The fiscal instruments applied under the Law for New and Necessary Industries and the National Programme for Mexicanization, as well as import licensing, were used to this effect. Protection was often granted without consideration of the excess cost of domestic products relative to imports. The system of protection also lacked downward flexibility to reduce tariffs and to eliminate import permits.

It seems, however, that the situation is changing. There is growing concern for the high cost the continuation of import-substituting industrialization entails and the limits to which it is subject. In addition, a reappraisal of industrial policy is in process, with import substitution being increasingly replaced by other objectives such as improvements in the efficiency of industry, decentralization, and increase in employment.

Of these objectives, the one that appears to be most relevant from the point of view of the system of protection is the increase in efficiency. This is sought for two major, and largely interconnected, reasons. For one thing, improved efficiency means better utilization of productive factors and widening domestic markets; for another, it would create greater possibilities for augmenting the exports of manufactured goods. The latter consideration in turn is of importance for both improving the balance of payments and maintaining a high growth rate of national income.

With external indebtedness pressing on the country's debt-servicing capacity, improvements in the balance of payments are necessary to provide for the imports needed to maintain a high rate of economic growth. And apart from increasing import capacity, exports contribute to economic growth directly by raising incomes and providing demand for domestically produced inputs. All these considerations then call for accelerating the expansion of exports.

At the same time, further prospects for Mexico's traditional exports are not very bright. Demand for such traditional export commodities as coffee, cotton, sugar, and various minerals is not rising by more than 3–4 percent, and the possibilities for continuing diversification in primary exports also appear to be limited. In addition, Mexico's good performance in manufacturing exports notwithstanding, the existing system of protection tends to discriminate against such exports.

The changes that seem to be required in the system of protection to serve the described objectives cannot come overnight. Correspondingly, it seems appropriate to distinguish between short-term and long-term policy changes. For the short-term, there is need for providing greater incentives for the exports of manufactured goods and for increasing competitive pressures in Mexican industry. For the long-term, policies should be devised to reduce discrimination among industrial activities as well as against exports and to improve resource allocation in the national economy. These will be considered below in greater detail.

The measures of export promotion presently applied—subsidies to exports, a program for the establishment of so-called "border industries," and the provision of information on export markets—do not appear to be adequate. This is apparent if we contrast these measures with the incentives that protection provides for production for the domestic markets. Our calculation of the bias against exporting in particular industries illustrates this. As a result of this bias, most industrialists do not even consider the possibilities of selling abroad or regard external markets as marginal outlets.

To increase incentives to export, it would be necessary to abolish export permits as well as to increase and to generalize the system of export subsidies. The original rationale for export permits—that of guaranteeing that the Mexican market is adequately supplied—has since disappeared and requiring export permits only serves to impress upon industrialists the idea that exports are of secondary importance.

Export subsidies show a more complex picture. We have noted that their use has been largely limited to textiles and a few other products. This situation reflects the administrative difficulties of obtaining subsidies and the government's apparent aversion to the fiscal expenditure involved. Yet higher exports create new revenue by contributing to the growth of incomes, and the expenditure involved can replace some of the fiscal incentives given to import substitution. In addition, with the transformation of the system of protection, export subsidies could be eventually reduced.

Subsidies are likely to especially help the exports of intermediate products and nondurable consumer goods. But subsidies should be accompanied with a lowering of protection—however cautiously this is to be undertaken. The government could appropriately start with eliminating excess tariff protection and gradually liberalize quotas so as to induce high-cost, marginal firms to improve their operations or to cease producing.

In the long run, there is clearly need for a general reduction in the level of protection. In addition, it appears advisable to reduce existing disparities in effective rates and to establish a "reference point" for protection, perhaps around 15 to 20 percent on a net basis. While greater protection might be given to specific industries, this should be done on a temporary rather than on a permanent basis.

CHAPTER 9

THE STRUCTURE OF PROTECTION
IN WEST MALAYSIA

John H. Power
with the assistance of Cristina Crisostomo and Eloisa Litonjua

Economic Growth and International Trade

Malaysia comprises West Malaysia, Sabah, and Sarawak. In the present study, we will deal only with West Malaysia which accounted for 80 percent of the 10 million population of Malaysia in 1968. As a short-hand expression, we will use the designation "Malaya" instead of West Malaysia throughout the study.

Malaya reached independence in 1957, but its ability to implement an independent development policy had to await the return of internal security at the end of the fifties when the struggle against organized guerrillas was successfully completed. In 1963, Malaysia was formed with the participation of Malaya, Singapore, Sabah, and Sarawak. Two years later, however, Singapore ceased to be a member.

Malaya's economy is heavily dependent on exports, chiefly those of rubber and tin. Traditionally, the pace of economic activity had been determined by the world markets for these two commodities, not only through the generation of income but also via the inflow of foreign capital for investment. Following World War II there were four main cycles of economic activity, peaking in

John H. Power is Visiting Professor of Economics at the University of the Philippines.

1951, 1956, 1960, and 1965, each deriving from a boom in Malaya's principal exports.[1]

Since 1955, however, exports have tended to lag behind the growth of incomes, with the share of exports in the gross domestic product declining from 49 percent to 40 percent in 1966. The interruption of the downtrend in the share of exports in 1959–60 by a sharp rise in rubber prices, followed by a decline, has made the problem of export lag appear especially sudden and dramatic in the early sixties.

Nevertheless, the growth of the economy accelerated after 1960. The impetus was an investment boom encouraged by a bold public infrastructure spending program and by tax, tariff, and other incentives to private investment in manufacturing industries. The leading role played by manufacturing is shown by the fact that the annual rate of growth of production in this sector increased from 3.2 percent in 1955–60 to 12.2 percent in 1960–66, while the gross domestic product grew at a rate of 3.6 percent a year in the first period and 5.8 percent in the second (see Table 2.2). Moreover, foreign capital, as well as domestic, shifted toward import substitution in manufacturing and away from the traditional export sector.

While export growth lagged, imports grew more-or-less in line with income. The result was a sharp decline in the current account surplus, expressed as a percentage of the gross national product. With the rise in gross investment roughly matching this decline, both the share of domestic savings in GNP and the marginal capital-output ratio remained, however, approximately the same (see Table 2.4).

Although manufacturing has become the leading sector in Malaya's economic growth, agriculture shared in the accelerated pace of growth, with value added rising at an annual rate of 2.9 percent in 1955–60 and 4.2 percent in 1960–66. Still, the share of agriculture in the gross domestic product declined from 40.2 percent in 1955 to 29.2 percent in 1966, while that of manufacturing and construction taken together rose from 11.2 percent to 16.1 percent. Finally, the share of mining (mainly tin) fluctuated greatly during the period in question and the relative contribution of services to GDP increased slightly (see Tables 2.2 and 2.3).

Imports of manufactured goods rose as a proportion of both the gross domestic product and total imports. At the same time, the composition of these imports changed with intermediate products and capital goods assuming greater, and consumer goods lesser, importance, In fact, between 1962 and 1966 the absolute value of imports of consumer goods remained unchanged

---

[1] G. B. Hainsworth, "Background Notes on Malaysian Economic Growth," unpublished.

(Table 9.1). This pattern is characteristic of countries at the early stage of import substitution.

An important question is the extent to which the beginnings of industrialization in Malaya depended on tariff protection and on other government policies such as tax exemptions, as opposed to the natural encouragement provided by the rapid growth of the domestic market. It would appear that in Malaya's case, the latter has been of principal importance. Contrary to the experience of many developing countries, the initial impetus to industrialization did not come from a sudden and drastic attempt to control imports in the face of a severe balance-of-payments crisis. Nor did tariff protection play a primary role in encouraging industrialization during the period in question. As will be shown below, the average level of protection in 1965 was modest, and several manufacturing industries had by then developed with no protection at all. Moreover, exports of manufactures, while small, grew rapidly during the sixties, approaching 8 percent of total exports in 1967 with the processing of domestic materials in the forefront (see Table 2.7). This suggests that the changing pattern of comparative advantage and the growth of the domestic market played a larger role in initiating industrial growth in Malaya than in most other developing countries.

Notwithstanding these developments, rubber and tin continued to account for over two-thirds of Malayan exports; rubber's share declined from 65 percent in 1950 to 42 percent in 1965 and that of tin rose from 17 to 26 percent. But data for particular years are greatly affected by fluctuations in prices and volumes. We have, therefore, compared averages of export volumes and prices for the years 1950–53 and 1963–66, and have examined changes in Malaya's share in world exports.

In the period under consideration the volume of world exports of rubber grew at a slow rate while exports of tin declined slightly. By increasing its share in the world tin market, Malaya was able, however, to maintain its tin exports constant in volume terms and, despite a small decline in its world market share, showed a one-fifth increase in the volume of its rubber exports.

Export values were further affected by changes in prices, with a substantial decline in rubber prices being only partly offset by increases in tin prices. On balance, unfavorable developments in prices completely wiped out the gain experienced in the volume of Malaya's exports of the two commodities between 1950–53 and 1963–66 (see Table 2.6).

Meanwhile, Malaya's minor exports grew at a rapid rate. Among primary commodities, increases were especially pronounced in exports of iron ore, palm oil, and tropical timber, whereas a decline is shown for copra and coconut oil (Table 9.2). Moreover, as noted above, exports of manufactured goods also grew rapidly. Despite the 130 percent increase in minor exports, however, the value of total exports rose by less than one half between 1950–53 and

TABLE 9.1: Malayan Manufactured Imports, 1962–66

Year	Total manufactured goods (Thousands of Malaysian dollars)	(Percent)	Intermediate products (Thousands of Malaysian dollars)	(Percent)	Inputs into construction (Thousands of Malaysian dollars)	(Percent)	Capital goods (Thousands of Malaysian dollars)	(Percent)	Consumption goods (Thousands of Malaysian dollars)	(Percent)
1962 A	1,124.3	100	218.5	19	149.5	13	333.3	30	423.0	38
1963 A	1,168.9	100	194.5	17	149.6	13	386.2	33	438.6	37
B	1,088.4	100	180.5	17	146.1	13	353.3	32	408.5	38
1964 A	1,184.4	100	303.4	26	140.7	12	314.3	26	425.9	36
B	1,105.8	100	291.2	26	136.7	13	279.6	25	398.3	36
1965 A	1,318.3	100	361.6	27	141.4	11	366.7	28	448.6	34
B	1,236.8	100	351.9	29	136.4	11	324.7	26	423.8	34
1966 A	1,380.2	100	333.3	25	142.8	10	472.5	34	428.6	31
B	1,299.2	100	327.9	25	138.1	11	428.1	33	405.1	31

Source: Department of Statistics, States of Malaya Annual Statistics of External Trade, 1962–1966.
Notes: A includes re-exports. B excludes re-exports.

TABLE 9.2:   Principal Exports of Malaya, 1950–67

(Percent of total exports)

Commodity	1950	1955	1960	1965	1967
Copra (SITC 221.2)	3.1	0.9	1.2	0.3	0.1
Coconut oil (422.3)	2.1	2.2	0.8	0.5	0.8
Palm oil (422.2)	1.2	1.5	2.1	3.4	3.8
Rubber (231.1)	69.3	66.8	61.2	44.1	41.7
Tropical timber (242.3 + 243.3)	0.7	1.1	1.9	2.9	4.4
Tin (687.1)	16.9	18.3	17.3	27.9	25.5
Total principal exports	93.3	90.8	83.9	79.1	76.3
Total exports ($ million)	852	775	956	1,014	953

Sources: Department of Statistics, *Federation of Malaya Annual Statistics of External Trade, 1962; Malaysia Official Yearbook, 1963;* Department of Statistics, *States of Malaya Annual Statistics of External Trade, 1965.*

1963–66 and, with rapid increases in imports, Malaya's trade balance has deteriorated.

The trade balance more or less stabilized during the sixties and the deterioration of the balance of payments finds its origin in adverse changes in the capital account. Both declines in rubber prices and changes in the cash holdings of foreign-owned firms have led to a reduction in the net inflow of capital. At the same time, the sharp rise in "errors and omissions," shown in Table 9.3, is likely to reflect private capital outflow. On the whole, overall deficits occurred in the years 1963, 1964, 1966, and 1967.

The System of Protection

Until the sixties, tariffs in Malaya served mainly revenue purposes and protected the industries of other British Commonwealth countries rather than Malayan industry. This situation began to change after 1959 with the trend toward elimination of Commonwealth preference and the rise in the proportion of imports from non-Commonwealth countries. However, the level of tariff protection has remained low by comparison with other developing countries.

There have been some important interests opposing industrialization behind protection in Malaya.[2] One such influence has been the fear of the effect of a rise in the cost of living on the wages of rubber workers. The large import houses have also been inclined to defend their vested interests in distribution, although some have recently begun the transformation to a role in industrial capitalism. Furthermore, the Treasury has apparently preferred using tariffs for revenue purposes rather than for protection. Finally, the numerically and

---

[2] E. L. Wheelwright, "Industrialization in Malaya," in *The Political Economy of Independent Malaya*, ed. T. H. Silcock and E. K. Fisk (Singapore: Eastern Universities Press, 1963), pp. 231–33.

TABLE 9.3: Malaysian Balance of Payments, 1961–67

(*Malaysian dollars*)

Category	1961	1962	1963	1964	1965	1966	1967
Merchandise							
Exports	3,212	3,232	3,296	3,346	3,752	3,808	3,679
Imports	−2,641	−2,892	−3,010	−3,071	−3,226	−3,254	−3,149
Balance	571	340	286	275	526	554	530
Services (net)	−353	−294	−324	−360	−395	−453	−438
Transfers (net)	−195	−204	−181	−74	−71	−109	−146
Private long-term capital							
(net)	180	235	270	205	190	160	135
Official long-term capital							
(net)	21	48	87	19	94	7	126
Official short-term							
liabilities (net)	...	...	−5	71	116	−11	−183
Errors and omissions	−131	−93	−210	−274	−326	−319	−271
Overall surplus (+) or							
deficit (−)	+93	32	−77	−138	+134	−171	−247

Sources: Bank Negara Malaysia, *Annual Reports;* Department of Statistics, *West Malaysia Annual Statistics of External Trade.*
Note: Data include Sabah and Sarawak.

politically dominant Malays may have been reluctant to favor urban (predominantly Chinese) interests at the expense of rural (predominantly Malay) interests.

The first important step toward protection, occurring in 1959, was a reclassification of the tariff schedule that had the effect of eliminating Commonwealth preferences in a number of categories. In the meantime, a Tariff Advisory Committee had been established as a part of the new industrial development policy. Nonetheless, the government continued to follow a cautious approach toward tariff protection which can be appreciated from the following quotation from its "Notes for the Guidance of Applicants for Tariff Concessions" (October 1961).

> The margin of protection granted will in no case be greater than that which will obtain for the local manufacturer the market for goods which can be economically produced in the Federation within a reasonable period. . . . The Government will not grant exemption or protection to an extent which would permit the marketing of goods of inferior quality or at excessive prices in comparison with imported goods. It will not grant tariff concessions to industry to an extent which would materially affect public revenue.[3]

The Tariff Advisory Board, which succeeded the Committee, was instrumental in establishing modest protective duties on more than 200 items by 1963. Since then it has been moderately active in considering and in some

---

[3] Quoted by Wheelwright, *ibid.*, p. 220.

cases granting tariff protection to applicant industries. Meanwhile, Commonwealth preferences disappeared altogether in 1967.

Still, as the evidence of the next section demonstrates, tariffs generally were at low levels in 1963 as well as in 1965. The few very high rates had been imposed for revenue purposes on goods such as tobacco and liquor. While by 1965 the government made a more definite commitment to use tariffs as a device for stimulating industrialization, this commitment was tempered by a concern to avoid excesses of protection. This is evident from the following statement of policy contained in the First Malaysia Plan (1966–70).

> In recognition of the problems of infant industries and those which arise from the limited industrial experience of the country, major attention will be given to the imposition of protective tariffs. . . . The government, however, is intent on ensuring that no more protection than is necessary will be accorded, for the cost of industrialization to the domestic consumer must be minimized. The government is also intent that tariff protection will not be afforded for periods longer than are absolutely necessary. The growth of the industrial sector in the long run will demand that eventually production be extended to supply not only the domestic market but also markets overseas. This makes it essential that domestic enterprise be constantly prodded to increase efficiency so that there will be progressive reductions in production costs.[4]

Some firms receive duty exemptions on imported inputs as a part of the government's industrial promotion program. Unfortunately, it proved impossible to take these exemptions into account in estimating effective tariff rates because they are granted to individual firms on an ad hoc basis, with no uniformity even within industries and the data is kept confidential. Because these exemptions usually pertain to inputs of equipment and materials not produced in Malaysia, the duties exempted are generally very low. This, together with the fact that the input coefficients for these goods are also low, means that the estimates of effective rates of protection are not likely to be much affected as a result of this omission.

Another omission in the analysis of the protection system is the lack of consideration of Commonwealth preferences. By 1963 these were rather unimportant and imports from non-Commonwealth countries generally predominated. Hence it is likely that the remaining preferences simply enabled high-priced Commonwealth products to compete with, for example, Japanese goods, and did not significantly reduce protection.

Note further that excise taxes are levied on only a very few commodities, mainly liquors, cigarettes, petroleum products, and matches and that they played a very minor role in the system of protection.

---

[4] Pp. 132–33.

Finally, as the results of the next section show, export taxes were responsible for negative protection in a number of industries. The following ad valorem rates were calculated from the ratio of taxes to export value: copra (5 percent), palm oil (5 percent in 1963, 7.5 percent in 1965), iron and iron ore (10 percent), and tropical logs (10 percent). Rubber, however, was taxed on a sliding scale in relation to price, and tin exports were taxed at an even higher rate.

The exchange rate of 3.06 Malaysian dollars to the U.S. dollar remained practically unchanged between 1954 and 1966. Nor did the rate vary much in real terms since the domestic price level remained stable during the period in question.[5] The import price index fluctuated somewhat more although data for the year 1965 may involve a considerable error. By contrast, the export price index varied substantially, and in the mid-sixties it was much below the high level reached in 1955–56 and 1959–60. The time pattern of the nominal and real exchange rates, with further adjustment for changes in export and import prices, is shown in Table 9.4.

Nominal and Effective Protection

With this background, we may direct our attention to the structure of protection in Malaya as it appeared in 1963 and 1965. There was a Census of Manufacturing in 1963, while 1965 is the last year for which the less comprehensive Survey of Manufacturing Industries was available. A detailed breakdown of outputs and inputs for 44 manufacturing industries was obtained for 1963 as compared with 28 for 1965. Industries common to both years numbered 27.

Nonetheless, rates of protection have been estimated for a total of 45 industries for each year. This has been done by assuming that physical input-output relationships were unchanged between the two years and by adjusting the 1963 value coefficients for changes in levels of protection of outputs and inputs. The industries for which this procedure has been followed are noted with an asterisk in Table 9.5. There is, however, one industry where the opposite procedure has been applied—for soaps and cleaning compounds, 1963 coefficients have been derived from 1965 data.

While no officially published input-output table exists for Malaysia, it has been possible to obtain nearly complete interindustry data for 1965 interrelating 18 manufacturing sectors, agriculture, rubber planting, forestry, fishing, and mining. The data make it possible to estimate effective rates of protection for the five nonmanufacturing sectors. These are shown in Table 9.6.

Since Malaysia is a very open economy it has been possible to deduce

---

[5] In the absence of a suitable wholesale price index, we have used the retail price index for indicating changes in domestic prices.

TABLE 9.4: Nominal and Real Exchange Rates in Malaya, 1954–66

(Malaysian dollars per U.S. $)

Year	Retail price index 1	Export unit value 2	Import unit value 3	Export rate			Import rate		
				Nominal 4	Real 5	Adjusted real rate 6	Nominal 7	Real 8	Adjusted real rate 9
					(4)/(1)	(5) × (2)		(7)/(1)	(8) × (3)
1954	100.0	100.0	100.0	3.08	3.08	3.08	3.08	3.08	3.08
1955	96.1	144.3	91.6	3.06	3.18	4.59	3.06	3.18	2.91
1956	97.0	133.0	94.4	3.08	3.18	4.23	3.08	3.18	3.00
1957	102.0	126.1	98.1	3.05	2.99	3.77	3.05	2.99	2.93
1958	101.0	114.8	93.4	3.06	3.03	3.48	3.06	3.03	2.83
1959	98.0	138.6	91.6	3.06	3.12	4.32	3.06	3.12	2.86
1960	97.8	145.5	94.4	3.06	3.13	4.55	3.06	3.13	2.95
1961	97.6	120.5	92.5	3.05	3.13	3.77	3.05	3.13	2.90
1962	97.7	118.2	90.6	3.06	3.13	3.70	3.06	3.13	2.84
1963	100.8	113.6	94.4	3.06	3.04	3.45	3.06	3.04	2.87
1964	100.4	115.9	100.0	3.07	3.06	3.55	3.07	3.06	3.06
1965	100.3	119.3	86.9	3.06	3.05	3.64	3.06	3.05	2.65
1966	101.2	114.8	96.2	3.08	3.04	3.49	3.08	3.04	2.92
1967	107.0	125.0	85.8	3.07	2.87	3.59	3.07	2.87	2.46

Sources: Department of Statistics, *Monthly Statistical Bulletin of West Malaysia;* IMF, *International Financial Statistics* and *Supplement.*

value added in free trade prices from the system of tariffs and excise taxes on the assumption that, with imports competing in significant volume with domestic production, nominal tariffs appropriately express the difference between domestic and foreign prices. In a few cases, however, where imports accounted for less than 10 percent of total supply, direct price comparisons have been made to estimate the level of protection. These are joineries and soft drinks for 1965 and tobacco products and refined coconut oil for 1963 and 1965. Motor vehicle (i.e., truck) bodies also had less than 10 percent competing imports, but since the industry had no protection, price comparisons have not been made. An industry has been considered an export industry if more than 15 percent of its production is sold abroad *and* the value of exports is at least double that of imports.

In the estimation of effective rates of protection, both the Balassa and Corden procedures have been used, with the latter but not the former including in domestic value added the sum of direct and indirect value added from nontraded inputs. The differences between the results are small, largely because tariffs on outputs and inputs are generally low.

Nominal and effective rates of protection for the 95 manufacturing industries covered are shown in Table 9.5. The first group includes six export industries: rubber-milling, latex processing, crude coconut oil, sago and tapioca, soaps and cleaning compounds, as well as lumber and plywood. Among these, the first three were subject to export taxes in both 1963 and 1965; all six experienced negative effective protection, averaging −20 percent in 1965 (Table

TABLE 9.5: Nominal and Effective Protection in Malayan Manufacturing, 1963 and 1965[a]

(*Percent*)

Industry	1963			1965			Bias against exporting[b]
	Nominal protection	Effective protection		Nominal protection	Effective protection		
		Balassa	Corden		Balassa	Corden	
Exports							
Rubber remilling	−6	−52	−50	−5	−41	−40	...
Latex processing	−7	−38	−36	−7	−49	−47	...
Crude coconut oil	−5	−14	−13	−5	−11	−10	...
*Sago and tapioca	0	−2	−2	0	−2	−2	...
*Soaps and cleaning compounds	0	−2	−2	0	−2	−2	...
Lumber and plywood	0	−2	−2	0	−2	−2	...
Rubber products	16	48	40	1	−9	−9	3
Import-competing industries							
Industrial machinery	0	−7	−6	0	−7	−6	0
*Hardware, tools, cutlery	6	11	10	6	10	10	14
Structural clay products	1	−7	−7	3	−5	−5	6
Structural cement	3	−7	−6	5	0	0	15
Architectural metal	0	−1	−1	3	9	8	12
Iron foundries	0	−6	−5	0	−4	−3	0
Truck parts	0	−5	−5	0	−5	−4	0
Prepared animal feeds	0	−4	−3	0	−6	−6	0
Tin cans and metal boxes	0	−2	−2	0	−3	−3	0
Wire and wire products	6	29	27	5	25	23	28
Wooden boxes	15	30	29	19	58	55	59
*Leather and products	19	54	52	19	54	52	205
Tobacco products	86	−37	−36	107	10	10	**
	(177)			(180)			
*Coffee	5	−22	−21	5	−28	−27	38
Biscuit factories	6	−9	−9	7	1	1	39
*Soybean products	0	−8	−8	0	−10	−9	0
Dairy products	5	−4	−4	5	−2	−2	17
Large rice mills	0	−2	−2	0	−2	−2	0
Pottery and chinaware	12	14	14	13	19	18	28
Bicycle and trishaw	9	17	16	8	12	11	25
*Paper and paper products	15	19	18	15	19	18	73
*Carpentry shops	15	20	19	15	20	19	74
*Pickles and sauces	15	22	21	20	35	34	103
Brass, pewter products	15	46	44	19	60	57	62
Paints, varnishes, lacquers	14	59	58	15	51	49	54
*Glass and products	25	64	57	25	64	57	336
*Clothing factories	25	65	61	25	65	61	**
*Footwear	25	67	63	25	70	66	153
*Furniture and fixtures	20	69	65	21	72	67	108
*Spice and curry mills	9	81	55	10	92	63	86
*Plastic products	22	93	83	22	93	83	88
*Chocolate and confectionery	21	133	120	24	141	128	**
*Meehon and noodles	19	146	132	19	146	132	207
*Textiles	24	337	212	24	337	212	5,825
Non-import-competing industries							
Joineries	0	−3	−3	14	39	37	44
				(20)			
Truck bodies	0	−11	−10	0	−9	−9	0
Refined coconut oil	0	−1	−1	0	−1	−1	0
Soft drinks and carbonated beverages	22	16	16	31	42	40	109
				(73)			

Source: See text.

[a] For industries denoted by an asterisk, 1965 values have been estimated from 1963 input-output coefficients. Values in parentheses indicate potential rates of protection differing from protection actually utilized.
[b] Calculated by using the Corden formula.
** Denotes negative value added in case of exporting.

9.6).[6] Rubber products did not belong to this group in 1963 when they were protected by tariffs but joined the export industries in 1965 with an effective protection of −9 percent.

---

[6] Estimates derived by using the Corden formula.

TABLE 9.6:   Average Rates of Protection by Major Sectors in Malaya

(*Percent*)

Sector	Nominal protection	Effective protection	
		Balassa	Corden
Agriculture	6	2	2
Without tobacco	4	−1	−1
Rubber planting	0	0	0
Fishing	2	1	1
Forestry	−14	−17	−16
Mining	−14	−17	−16
Manufacturing	13	−4	−4
Excluding tobacco procucts	3	−6	−5
Exports	−4	−21	−20
Rubber products	1	−9	−9
Import-competing goods other than tobacco	7	12	12

Sources: Table 9.5 and text.

All remaining industries have been classified as import-competing, although several of them have begun exporting and in two instances (joineries,
and paints and lacquers) exports exceed imports. But, given the existence of
product differentiation, tariffs continue to limit imports in both cases. Excluding tobacco, nominal rates of protection on these products in 1965 averaged 7
percent and effective rates 12 percent.

Despite the low average level of protection, the range of nominal and effective rates is rather wide. In 1965, five import-competing industries had nominal rates exceeding 20 percent, and fourteen had effective rates of 40 percent
or higher—four of them above 100 percent. These results provide evidence of
distortions in the price system and bias in resource allocation within the manufacturing sector. But there are no industries for which value added at free
trade prices would be negative, so that cases of possible absolute waste of
resources are absent.

A number of manufacturing industries warrant special comment. The
joineries industry, producing wooden flooring and frames for doors and win-
dows, had more than 10 percent competing imports in 1963 with a zero tariff.
By 1965, however, the tariff was raised to 20 percent and imports were virtually
nil. Accordingly, the potential rate of effective protection was 64 percent, as
compared to −3 percent in 1963. The absence of competing imports, however, necessitated making direct price comparisons and this gave a realized
effective rate of 39 percent, considerably below the potential rate.

A similar situation exists in regard to soft drinks. Domestic production
competed with imports at a relatively low duty prevailing in 1963, so that the
realized rate can be taken to have equaled the realized effective rate of protection. By 1965, however, a prohibitive duty had virtually eliminated imports
and the potential effective rate of protection was above 200 percent. Again,

price comparisons yielded a much lower rate—42 percent—although above that for 1963.

Tobacco products present an unusual case insofar as a high nominal rate of protection was approximately offset by high protection of the principal input, raw tobacco. The effective rate of protection was negative in 1963 and positive in 1965 but the differences in absolute magnitudes are small. For both the final product and for the raw tobacco input, effective rates have been calculated from direct price comparisons.

Refined coconut oil presented the puzzling case of zero tariff and the highest potential rate of protection of any industry. This is explained by the 5 percent export tax on the principal input, crude coconut oil, and the very low margin of value added in refining. Since Malaya does not supply a large proportion of world exports of coconut oil, it seems reasonable to assume that the export tax was absorbed by lowering the domestic price of crude oil. At the same time, price comparisons for 1963, 1964, and 1965 showed no evidence that the price of crude oil to domestic refiners was lower than the export price. The realized effective rate of protection, calculated on this basis, turned out to be −1 percent, in contrast with the potential rate of 328 percent.

Finally, chocolate and confectionary, meehon and noodles, and textiles had estimates of effective rates exceeding 100 percent, far above the nominal rates of protection because of low margins of value added. For textiles, which had the highest effective rate of protection of any industry, the ratio of value added to input on free trade prices was less than four percent.

Table 9.7 shows average rates of protection—nominal and effective—for the major product categories. Apart from beverages and tobacco, there appears to have been little change in the averages between 1963 and 1965; the change shown in the protection of the manufacturing sector, taken as a whole, is due almost exclusively to the apparent reduction in the protection of tobacco products. In the following, we will restrict our attention to the results pertaining to 1965.

If we consider the average protection of the principal sectors, we find little evidence of bias in the structure of protection in favor of manufacturing industries. But the picture changes if estimates are made by the use of free trade coefficients; the average level of protection of manufacturing is then 13 percent as against −4 percent by the use of domestic input-output coefficients. The differences are explained by the large weight given to export industries in calculations made by domestic coefficients.

In the manufacturing sector, the incentives provided to export and import-competing industries differ to a considerable extent. Using domestic coefficients, we find that, in 1965, average effective protection on export goods was −19 percent, on rubber products that joined the export category in that year −9 percent, and on import-competing goods other than tobacco 14 percent.

TABLE 9.7: Nominal and Effective Protection for Major Product Categories in Malaya, 1963 and 1965

(Percent)

		Estimates based on domestic coefficients						Estimates based on free trade coefficients					
		1963			1965			1963			1965		
			Effective protection			Effective protection			Effective protection			Effective protection	
	Industry group	Nominal protection	Balassa	Corden	Nominal protection	Balassa	Corden	Nominal protection	Balassa	Corden	Nominal protection	Balassa	Corden
I	Agriculture, forestry, and fishing	2	0	0	2	0	0	15	21	20	17	24	22
II	Processed food	2	−1	−1	2	0	0	9	6	6	11	7	7
III	Beverages and tobacco	80	−31	−30	100	15	15	21	22	17	46	91	73
IV	Mining and energy	−14	−17	−17	−14	−17	−17	−2	−9	−8	−2	−9	−8
V	Construction materials	3	−6	−6	5	−2	−2	6	8	7	7	11	9
VI-A	Intermediate products I	−4	−23	−22	−4	−23	−23	4	12	8	4	14	9
VI-B	Intermediate products II	13	29	26	9	9	8	14	33	27	13	30	25
VI	Intermediate products I and II	3	−3	−3	2	−10	−10	7	18	14	7	19	14
VII	Nondurable consumer goods	25	66	62	25	68	64	14	22	19	14	22	20
VIII	Consumer durables	1	−2	−3	1	−3	−2	1	−12	−11	1	−6	−5
IX	Machinery	0	−7	−6	0	−7	−6	5	7	6	5	7	6
X	Transport equipment	...	...	...	...	...	...	...	...	...	...	...	...
I-X	All industries	3	−6	−6	3	−5	−5	8	11	9	9	12	10
I+IV	Primary production	−2	−6	−6	−2	−6	−6	8	8	7	9	9	8
II, III, V-X	Manufacturing	11	−8	−8	13	−4	−4	8	13	10	9	15	12
VI-X	Manufacturing less food, beverages, tobacco, and construction materials	3	−3	−3	2	−9	−8	7	16	12	7	17	13

Sources: Table 9.5 and text.

While the average protection of import-competing goods in Malaya is still modest by the standards of most developing countries, the familiar pattern of escalation from lower to higher stages of fabrication is already evident. Levels of protection are the highest for nondurable consumer goods (64 percent) but are low for consumer durables which are defined to include bicycles as well as motor vehicle parts and bodies. The latter are not subject to duties, and while motor vehicle bodies are supplied exclusively by domestic firms, parts are almost exclusively imported. This, then, appears to provide an example of natural import substitution.

By contrast, machinery industries, like exports, are penalized by having to purchase protected inputs while enjoying little or no protection for their products. The industrial machinery industry included in this category produces mainly parts and spares rather than complete machinery units. The results for this industry are nevertheless interesting: they indicate the obstacles inherent in the structure of protection, hindering the establishment of machinery industries.

Intermediate goods of lower levels of fabrication include several export industries, such as rubber remilling, latex processing, as well as lumber and plywood. These industries, as well as foundry products, have negative effective rates of protection while glass and leather have positive rates. Given the importance of export industries, the average effective rate of protection for the group calculated by the use of domestic input-output coefficients is −23 percent. However, the average rate is slightly positive if free trade coefficients are applied, for these give small weight to Malaya's semi-manufactured export products.

Intermediate products at higher levels of fabrication include an export industry (soap and cleaning compounds) and a number of import-competing industries subject to low and medium protection, but the high protection accorded to a few industries—notably textiles—raises the average for the whole category. The average level of effective protection for this category did, however, decline between 1963 and 1965, largely because export industries have become more important.

Defining the manufacturing sector in a narrower sense, we exclude processed food, beverages and tobacco, and construction materials. Of these, beverages and tobacco have been previously considered. Construction materials are subject to negative effective protection, while the average effective protection of foodstuffs is practically zero. However, we find great variation within the latter category, from negative protection on rice, soybean, and dairy products to high rates of protection on spice and curry mills, chocolate and confectionary, meehon and noodles, and sugar. Estimates derived by using free trade coefficients show an average effective rate of protection of 7 percent on food processing, mainly because of the greater weight given to the highly protected sugar. At the same time, the high average effective rate shown for tobacco and beverages is explained by the fact that the high protection of alcoholic beverages has a large weight in the calculations made by free trade coefficients.

Among the nonmanufacturing sectors, the high negative effective protection on forestry and mining is explained by export taxes on these predominantly export industries. Rubber planting is shown separately from other agriculture because of its special importance in the Malayan economy. As land has alternative uses, we have assumed that the incidence of the export tax was on the processing of rubber or on world buyers, rather than on the growers. Admittedly, this is a long-run view and if in the short run the incidence was partly on the growers, the effective rate of protection would be negative.

The average effective rate of protection on agriculture is −1 percent if we exclude tobacco-growing. The latter is subject to a duty of more than 400 percent, while domestic prices exceeded foreign prices for raw tobacco by 280 percent in 1963 and 236 percent in 1965. Still, given the low share of tobacco-growing in agriculture, its inclusion raises the average effective rate of protection to only 2 percent. On the other hand, the average effective rate on agriculture will be 24 percent if free trade coefficients are used, largely because tobacco-growing has a weight 22 times as high as the weight used in calculations made from domestic coefficients.

In summary, it appears that the system of protection in Malaya discriminates against primary, as well as against manufactured, exports and favors import substitution in manufacturing. Agriculture and fishing come in between the two groups. But the protection of import-substitutes is generally modest; for some it is nil or even negative. Negative protection is shown for machinery and transport equipment while, at the other extreme, some nondurable consumer goods are highly protected.

Overvaluation and Net Effective Protection

Since in 1965 there were no restrictions on current account convertibility and the foreign exchange reserves of Malaysia were adequate, the overvaluation of the Malaysian dollar could have meaning only in relation to an alternative set of policies that would have implied a different equilibrium rate. The extent of overvaluation in this sense has been estimated in comparison with both a policy of free trade and a policy combining duty-free imports with an optimal tax on exports. For each alternative, we have estimated the extent of devaluation necessary to maintain the original trade balance.

Average import duties, weighted by the total supply of importables, were about 10 percent in 1965. Export tax rates, weighted by exports, averaged 5 percent. Among the relevant elasticities, the supply of Malayan imports has been assumed to be infinite as in the other country studies. Malaya accounts for one-third of world rubber exports and over two-thirds of tin exports; because of substitution by synthetic rubber, the world demand elasticity for natural rubber is fairly high although it is lower for tin. Taking account, however, of actual and potential minor exports, we have used a range of 5 to 10 for the average demand elasticity for Malaya's exports while the export supply elasticity has been assumed to be between 1 and 4. Finally, the assumed range for the import demand elasticity, 3 to 5, has been derived from assumed domestic elasticities of demand and supply and the share of imports in domestic supply.

The results are not sensitive to the assumptions made. The highest estimate of overvaluation as compared to the free trade situation is 7.6 percent and the lowest is 2.4 percent. The estimate corresponding to the highest elasticities in every case (perhaps the best long-run guess) is about 4 percent. The small dispersion of the results is explained by the low-average import duties and export taxes. At the same time, the expected improvement of the trade balance following the removal of export duties has reduced the degree of devaluation that would be necessary if free trade policies were adopted.

The elasticities for exports on both the supply and demand side may seem high for a country so heavily dependent on a few agricultural and mineral export products. Our viewpoint here is a long-term one—its implication being a different economic structure, with a greater diversification of exports. This is not to say that Malaya could avoid balance-of-payments difficulties in the short term if policies of free trade, together with a small devaluation, were suddenly adopted.

We have also considered the case of duty-free imports, accompanied by a tax on exports designed to bring the marginal terms of trade into line with domestic price ratios. This can be accomplished by setting the export tax equal to the reciprocal of the foreign demand elasticity for Malayan exports. This means raising the average export tax from its present level of 5 percent to 10 or 20 percent, depending on whether the foreign demand elasticity is assumed to be 10 or 5. The corresponding range of estimates is between 7 and 11 percent, again indicating very little overvaluation. Ideally, of course, the export tax should be applied to only a few exports with low demand elasticities.

In Tables 9.8 and 9.9, rates of net protection, calculated by assuming an overvaluation of 4 percent as compared to the free trade situation, are shown for the principal sectors and the major commodity groups. The results are practically identical to those shown earlier except that they are scaled down slightly. Their detailed discussion is thus not warranted.

TABLE 9.8: Average Net Rates of Protection by Major Sectors in Malaya[a]

(Percent)

Sector	Nominal protection	Effective protection
Agriculture	2	−2
Without tobacco	0	−5
Rubber planting	−4	−4
Fishing	−2	−3
Forestry	−17	−19
Mining	−17	−19
Manufacturing	9	−8
Excluding tobacco products	−1	−9
Exports	−8	−23
Rubber products	−3	−12
Import-competing goods other than tobacco	3	8

Sources: Table 9.6 and text.

[a] Effective rates of protection have been estimated by using the Corden formula; both nominal and effective rates have been adjusted for overvaluation as compared to the hypothetical free trade situation.

Evaluation and Policy Recommendations

The results show little discrimination among the principal sectors of the Malayan economy. There is, however, a bias in favor of import substitution and against exporting in the individual sectors. Moreover, within manufacturing, we observe the familiar pattern of the escalation of protection from lower to higher degrees of fabrication with the highest levels of protection shown for nondurable consumer goods. The bias against exports, capital goods, and intermediate goods is typical of countries that are at the early stages of industrialization.

In the case of Malaya, these biases are of lesser magnitude than in most developing countries, and import substitution has not yet begun to approach the limits of the domestic market in consumer goods. Eventually, however, as these limits are approached, the pace of industrialization could not continue to exceed the rate of growth of domestic demand for consumer goods unless investment were encouraged in the area penalized by the present system of protection—intermediate goods and exports. Moreover, since protection tends to generate self-perpetuating forces by spawning new activities and institutions, the biases may later prove more difficult to remove. Thus it might be fruitful to consider alternatives to continuing the biases that the protection of manufacturing now entails.

Hirschman has distinguished four types of import-substituting industrialization.[7] One of these was prominent in the nineteenth century; it is led by exports (often of primary goods) and gives rise to natural import substitution

[7] A. O. Hirschman, "The Political Economy of Import-Substituting Industrialization in Latin America," *The Quarterly Journal of Economics*, February 1968, pp. 1–32.

TABLE 9.9: Net Nominal and Effective Protection for Major Categories in Malaya, 1963 and 1965[a]

(Percent)

	Industry group	Estimates based on domestic coefficients				Estimates based on free trade coefficients			
		1963		1965		1963		1965	
		Nominal protection	Effective protection	Nominal protection	Effective protection	Nominal protection	Effective protection	Nominal protection	Effective protection
I	Agriculture, forestry, and fishing	-2	-4	-2	-4	11	15	13	17
II	Processed food	-2	-5	-2	-4	5	2	7	3
III	Beverages and tobacco	73	-33	92	11	16	13	40	66
IV	Mining and energy	-17	-20	-17	-20	-6	-12	-6	-12
V	Construction materials	-1	-10	1	-6	2	3	3	5
VI-A	Intermediate products I	-8	-25	-8	-26	0	4	0	5
VI-B	Intermediate products II	9	21	5	4	10	22	9	20
VI	Intermediate products I and II	-1	-7	-2	-14	3	10	3	10
VII	Nondurable consumer goods	20	56	20	58	10	14	10	15
VIII	Consumer durables	-3	-7	-3	-6	-3	-14	-3	-9
IX	Machinery	-4	-10	-4	-10	1	2	1	2
X	Transport equipment	...	...	...	...	...	...	...	...
I-X	All industries	-1	-10	-1	-9	4	5	5	6
I + IV, II, III,	Primary production	-6	-10	-6	-10	4	3	5	4
V-X	Manufacturing	7	-12	9	-8	4	6	5	8
VI-X	Manufacturing less food, beverages, tobacco, and construction materials	-1	-7	-2	-12	3	8	3	9

Source: See text.

[a] Effective rates of protection have been estimated by using the Corden formula; both nominal and effective rates have been adjusted for overvaluation as compared to the hypothetical free trade situation.

as incomes and markets grow, so that investment allocation tends to be deter-mined by comparative advantage. And while wars create unnatural scarcities that encourage the domestic production of substitutes for imports, they tend to affect all imports equally, and hence are generally neutral in their impact on investment choice among alternative import substitutes.

A third, and perhaps most common, type of industrial import substitution receives its impetus from a balance-of-payments crisis. Here the tendency is to restrict imports by criteria of essentiality of the use of foreign exchange and to neglect the protective effect. The resulting system of protection is often strongly biased against backward linkages and exports,[8] both of which are crucial to sustaining rapid industrial growth beyond the first easy stage. The structure of Malayan protection shows some such biases, but only to a minor degree.

A key question facing Malaysia is whether its primary exports are in a temporary slump or a long-run decline. If it is the former, Malaysia may elect to continue to enjoy export-led growth with import substitution following the growth of demand. A policy of protection, beyond a very modest level, would be a mistake in this case, since it would unnecessarily penalize exports and encourage a less efficient pattern of industrialization.

But the export prospects for rubber and tin are not favorable. A substantial rise of rubber prices from their present low level is not foreseen, and high tin prices are less encouraging than they might appear; exports are limited under the International Tin Agreement and, more important, the exhaustion of known reserves is anticipated. In fact, low rubber prices and dwindling tin reserves have given rise to a certain amount of pessimism about Malaya's continued dependence on its traditional exports. This pessimism is not sur-mounted by the growing importance of new exports such as palm oil and timber.

What form, then, should the promotion of manufacturing activities take? The alternatives include Hirschman's fourth type, rational planned import substitution and the development of manufacturing industries based on ex-ports. It would be difficult to point to a single example of rational planned import substitution, while in Latin America and Asia, there are a number of countries that allowed themselves to be deluded by quick and easy successes in the first stage of import-substituting industrialization. On the other hand, Korea, Taiwan, and Singapore—which is closer to Malaysia—provide exam-ples of industrial development through the promotion of exports of manufac-tured goods.

Malaysia has the opportunity to learn from the mistakes made in import-

---

[8] *Ibid.*, pp. 18, 27. See also my "Import Substitution as an Industrialization Strategy," *Philippine Economic Journal*, Second Semester 1966, pp. 173–74.

substituting industrialization elsewhere. The principal lesson is to avoid excessive protection that encourages inefficiencies, as well as a complacent attitude toward innovation and growth. In addition, the biases against new exports and backward-linkage import substitution should be avoided.

A possible solution is to aim at roughly uniform rates of protection at all stages of the production process and also for exports. This could be achieved either through free trade combined with a higher price of foreign exchange, or through uniform tariff rates and matching subsidies to exports, since the two are equivalent. In either case, exceptions should be made for those export products (rubber, tin) where terms-of-trade effects might be significant. Such goods should be taxed or receive lower subsidies, depending on estimates of export demand elasticities. This, incidentally, would remove the principal argument against devaluation as a means of encouraging domestic industry.

While this policy would avoid the usual biases in the system of protection, the question arises as to what special inducement should be given to manufacturing industries. The answer is that a favorable enough exchange rate can give whatever level of protection is desired, with a lower rate applied to primary activities. In addition, infant industry protection could be given to newly-established industries. But the logic of the infant industry argument calls for protection of a limited duration.

The logic of the infant industry argument also calls for protection against foreign competition in the world market, as well as at home—i.e., for matching subsidies to exports. In a country the size of Malaya the eventual development of mature, efficient manufacturing industries can hardly be expected if the export market is neglected. This again emphasizes the desirability of an exchange rate policy as a weapon to achieve industrialization goals, for it protects industries simultaneously in domestic and foreign markets.

Finally, we should admit that commercial policy is partly an international problem. We must face the possibility of a "reactive" protectionism of the advanced countries in the face of competition from new manufacturing industries in the less developed countries. This, together with the obvious difficulties of basing an industrialization on limited demand in the home market, points to the case for preferential trade among less developed countries. Regional integration could help to achieve import substitution in a wider market, so as to take mutual advantage of the gains from concentration and scale. A country the size of Malaya cannot afford to neglect this option.

CHAPTER 10

THE STRUCTURE OF PROTECTION IN PAKISTAN

Stephen R. Lewis, Jr., and Stephen E. Guisinger

Economic Growth and International Trade[1]

Transformation of Economic Structure

Pakistan was created in 1947 by the Partition of former British India. This new nation, now the fifth largest in the world with a population of nearly 110 million in 1967, is split geographically into two parts separated by over 1,000 miles of land or a 3,000-mile sea voyage. Its per capita income, measured at official exchange rates, was about $120 in 1967.

Income per head was falling in the years immediately following the Partition; it hardly increased at all during the fifties, but owing to the combination of a series of favorable circumstances, it grew at a rate of over 3 percent in the period 1960–67 (see Table 2.2). During this period, substantial changes oc-

Stephen Lewis, Jr., is Associate Professor of Economics and Provost of Williams College; Stephen Guisinger, a Teaching Fellow at Harvard University when this study was written, is now Assistant Professor of Economics at the Southern Methodist University. They are indebted to the other contributors to this volume and their colleges at Williams College and Harvard University for comments on earlier drafts and for fruitful discussion.

[1] This section and the next draw heavily on the data and analysis in S. R. Lewis, Jr., *Economic Policy and Industrial Growth in Pakistan* (London: George Allen & Unwin, Ltd., 1968), and *idem*, "Effects of Trade Policy on Domestic Relative Prices: Pakistan, 1951–1964," *American Economic Review*, March 1968, pp. 60–78. Most of the other issues treated briefly here are more thoroughly discussed in these two sources.

curred in Pakistan's economic structure; the most important were a rapid increase in the share of manufacturing in the gross national product, a rise in the rates of investment, foreign aid, and domestic saving, and a shift in the commodity composition of exports and imports. The principal factors contributing to these changes have been the Partition that destroyed the customs union in which Pakistan provided food and raw materials for the rest of the Indian subcontinent, and the restrictive trade policy adopted after the Partition and strengthened after the foreign exchange crisis in 1952.

Partition left Pakistan with much less manufacturing capacity than would be expected in a country with so large a domestic market, notwithstanding the low level of per capita income.[2] A part of its rapid industrial growth occurred in response to the unusually profitable situation created by the separation of India and Pakistan. More important, however, was the trade policy which, adopted in the late forties and early fifties, combined quantitative restrictions on imports and a low exchange rate on exports. This policy aided manufactures and discriminated heavily against farmers, since manufactured goods were primarily imported while agricultural goods were either exported or competed against exports.

Table 10.1 shows the sectoral distribution of the gross national product for the period 1949/50–1964/65.[3] The most dramatic change has been the increasing share of large-scale manufacturing industry in total value added. The relative share of the "other activities" category—largely construction and modern services—also increased, with a corresponding decline in agriculture's contribution, from three-fifths of GNP in 1949/50 to less than one-half in 1964/65.

TABLE 10.1:   Industrial Origin of the Gross National Product in Pakistan, 1949/50–1964/65

(In 1959/60 factor cost)

Sector	1949/50 Million rupees	1949/50 Per-cent	1954/55 Million rupees	1954/55 Per-cent	1959/60 Million rupees	1959/60 Per-cent	1964/65 Million rupees	1964/65 Per-cent
Agriculture	14,669	60.0	15,654	56.0	16,753	53.3	19,895	49.1
Manufacturing	1,433	5.8	2,220	8.0	2,930	9.3	4,440	10.9
Large scale	346	1.4	1,002	3.6	1,565	5.0	2,888	7.1
Small scale	1,087	4.4	1,218	4.4	1,365	4.3	1,552	3.8
Other activities	8,364	34.2	10,034	36.0	11,756	37.4	16,190	40.0
Gross national product	24,466	100.0	27,908	100.0	31,439	100.0	40,525	100.0

Source: Planning Commission, Government of Pakistan, *Third Five-Year Plan, 1965–70*, Karachi, 1965, p. 2

---

[2] This question is discussed in Lewis, *Economic Policy and Industrial Growth in Pakistan*, ch. 3, where comparisons have been made with Indian economic structure at Partition and with the "normal" pattern of output calculated from Chenery's cross-section regression results in "Patterns of Industrial Growth," *American Economic Review*, September 1960, pp. 624–54.

[3] Fiscal year, beginning July 1.

These changes reflect the rapid growth (15 percent a year) of large-scale manufacturing and the very slow growth (2 percent a year) of agriculture. In fact, in per capita terms, agricultural output failed to rise.

The transformation of the economic structure of Pakistan is in part related to the changes in the composition of aggregate expenditure shown in Table 10.2. Major developments were (*a*) a quadrupling of the share of investment (from 4.4 to 18.9 percent of GNP), (*b*) a substantial increase in the domestic saving rate (from 4.4 to 12.1 percent of GNP), (*c*) an increased share of foreign aid (from nil to 6.8 percent of GNP), and (*d*) a rapid rise in the share of imports in GNP after 1954/55. Greater investment activity brought about increased demand for manufactured goods and for construction, and in both industries value added as a share of the gross national product rose rapidly.

Composition of Exports and Imports

Changes in Pakistan's industrial structure are also reflected by shifts in the composition of exports and imports. The pattern of manufacturing growth was characterized by the replacement of simple goods previously imported by domestic production, followed by exports.[4] At the same time, exports of domestic materials used in these industries, such as cotton and jute, declined. The pattern of import substitution followed by exportation is also observed in the case of leather, footwear, sports goods, and a variety of other products, such as soap, utensils, and fans.

While manufacturing was expanding rapidly, agriculture virtually stagnated. As a result, the domestic demand for foodstuffs exceeded the domestic

TABLE 10.2: Composition of Aggregate Expenditure in Pakistan, 1949/50–1964/65
(*Percent of GNP, in current market prices*)

Category	1949/50	1954/55	1959/60	1964/65
Gross domestic saving	4.4[a]	6.6[a]	8.6	12.1
Gross domestic investment	4.4[a]	7.6[a]	11.7	18.9
Current government expenditure	11.0	9.1	8.6	10.2
Private consumption	84.6	84.3	82.8	77.7
Exports of goods and services	6.0[b]	5.5[b]	6.4	6.2
Imports of goods and services	6.5[b]	5.0[b]	9.5	13.0

Sources: Planning Commission, *Third Five-Year Plan, 1965–70*, p. 7; Pakistan, Ministry of Finance, *Pakistan Economic Survey, 1966/67*, Rawalpindi, 1967, p. 28; Pakistan, Planning Commission, *Final Evaluation of the Second Five-Year Plan*, Karachi, December 1966, p. 144; Pakistan, Ministry of Finance, *The Budget in Brief, 1966–67*, Rawalpindi, 1966, Section II.

[a] 1959/60 prices.

[b] Merchandise exports and imports only.

---

[4] See, for example, S. R. Lewis, Jr., and R. Soligo, "Growth and Structural Change in Pakistan's Manufacturing Industry, 1954–1964," *Pakistan Development Review*, Spring 1965, pp. 94–139, and S. R. Lewis, Jr. and S. M. Hussain, *Relative Price Changes and Industrialization in Pakistan, 1951–64* (Karachi: Pakistan Institute of Development Economics, 1967).

supply at prices that prevailed in the early and mid-fifties. This excess demand necessitated the importation of food grains, mainly under the PL 480 program. Despite substantial imports of foodstuffs, however, the relative prices of agricultural goods rose over the decade from 1954/55 to 1964/65.[5]

The data of Tables 2.7 and 2.8 on the composition of exports and imports support these conclusions. To begin with, the domestic manufacturing of cotton and jute goods contributed importantly to the decline in the share of basic manufactures in total imports from about 54 percent in 1951/52 to 20 percent in 1967. The expansion of domestic manufacturing also necessitated increasing imports of capital goods whose share in total imports rose from 12 to 31 percent. The share of food imports also increased, from 10 to 18 percent, as domestic agriculture was unable to provide for the rise in demand. A smaller rise, from 5 to 8 percent, is shown in imports of industrial materials.

In exports, there was a shift from raw materials to processed goods. The share of industrial materials (mostly cotton and jute) in total exports declined from 94 percent in 1951/52 to 47 percent in 1967 while basic manufactures increased their share from practically nil to 39 percent. Within the latter category, exports of jute fabrics and bags, cotton yarn and fabrics, leather, and carpets are of importance (Table 10.3).

Since fluctuations in the harvest and in world market conditions greatly affect the outcome for individual years, five-year averages of annual data have been calculated. These are shown in Table 10.4 for the five-year period pre-

TABLE 10.3:   Principal Exports of Pakistan, 1950–67

(Percent of total exports)

Commodity	1950	1955	1960	1965	1967
Raw jute (SITC 264)	39.4	46.6	43.0	33.7	29.6
Raw cotton (263.1)	44.0	26.9	11.3	12.2	na
Raw wool (262.1)	3.0	4.5	4.1	2.2	na
Hides and skins (211)	2.2	2.1	3.7	1.5	0.4
Rice (042.2)	na	4.4	na	4.7	5.3
Fish, fresh (031)	0.2	1.9	3.0	2.4	1.9
Tea (074.1)	0.8	2.3	0.5	0.5	0.0
Jute fabrics (653.4)	na	1.3	5.3	7.1	7.6
Jute bags (656.1)	na	3.1	7.1	9.5	na
Cotton fabrics (652)	na	0.0	2.8	5.4	5.8
Cotton yarn (651.3 and 0.4)	na	0.5	7.3	4.7	na
Carpets, carpeting, and rugs (657.5)	na	na	na	1.2	1.1
Total principal exports	89.6	93.6	88.1	85.1	51.7
Total exports ($ millions)	489	401	393	528	608

Source: U.N., Yearbook of International Trade Statistics.

---

[5] See Lewis and Hussain, *Relative Price Changes and Industrialization in Pakistan.* An interesting discussion of agricultural-industrial interactions is given by W. P. Falcon, "Agricultural and Industrial Interrelationships in West Pakistan," *Journal of Farm Economics,* December 1967, pp. 1139–54.

TABLE 10.4: Annual Averages of Pakistan's Major Exports, 1950/51–1964/65

Commodity	Pre-Plan 1950/51–1954/55		First Plan 1955/56–1959/60		Second Plan 1960/61–1964/65	
	$ million	Percent	$ million	Percent	$ million	Percent
Raw jute	230.7	45.3	158.4	47.3	171.7	38.6
Raw cotton	196.9	38.7	59.2	17.7	53.5	12.0
Raw wool	16.1	3.2	15.7	4.7	15.0	3.4
Hides and skins	12.1	2.4	10.4	3.1	11.0	2.5
Rice	6.1[b]	1.7[b]	6.3	1.9	22.5	5.1
Fish, fresh	5.0[a]	1.1[a]	6.5	1.9	17.7	4.0
Tea	11.5	2.3	7.0	2.1	1.6	0.4
Jute textiles	2.6[a]	0.6[a]	28.2	8.4	65.0	14.6
Cotton goods	0.3[a]	0.1[a]	18.8	5.6	29.8	6.7
Leather	0.0[a]	0.0[a]	1.1	0.3	6.1	1.4
Carpets	0.0[b]	0.0[b]	0.4	0.1	4.1	0.9
Footwear	0.0[b]	0.0[b]	0.4	0.1	1.7	0.4
Sport goods	1.8[b]	0.5[b]	2.4	0.7	3.1	0.7
Others	19.2	5.4	20.1	6.0	42.3	9.5
Total	509.2	100.0	334.9	100.0	445.1	100.0

Sources: Ministry of Finance, *Pakistan Economic Survey, 1966/67,* pp. 29–30; *Statistical Yearbook 1964,* pp. 194–95, 212–13; Pakistan, Department of Commercial Intelligence, *Foreign Trade of Pakistan July 1950–June 1951,* Karachi, 1952, pp. 34, 44.

[a] Average of 1951/52–1954/55 only.

[b] 1954/55 only.

ceding the First Plan (1950/51–1954/55) as well as for the First Plan (1955/56–1959/60) and the Second Plan periods (1960/61–1964/65). These data show the transformation of the export structure of Pakistan. They also reveal, however, that the combined exports of raw jute and jute textiles were roughly the same in the last five-year period as in the first, while the sum of raw cotton and cotton textile exports fell by about three-fourths. As regards the latter, a decline by one-half is shown even if we consider net exports by deducting from export value the amount of cotton goods imported.

Changes in export values can be explained by trends in world demand, changes in Pakistan's competitive position, and changes in prices. As the data of Table 2.6 indicate, the combined exports of raw jute and jute textiles, expressed in 1950–53 prices, were the same in 1963–66 as in 1950–53 while there was a small decline in terms of current value chiefly because the prices of jute textiles fell.

Pakistan's poor performance in cotton exports is explained by the fact that the cotton needs of the newly established domestic cotton-textile industry substantially exceeded increases in the production of raw cotton during the period under consideration. The loss in cotton exports was only partly offset by exports of cotton textiles, so that although world demand for cotton rose by one-half between 1950–53 and 1963–66, the combined exports of cotton and cotton textiles, expressed in 1950–53 prices, fell by one-fourth. Because of the sharp drop in cotton prices, the decrease was even larger in terms of current prices. The doubling of minor exports notwithstanding, these changes brought about a one-tenth decline in Pakistan's total exports in terms of current value while an increase of similar magnitude took place in terms of 1950–53 prices.

While in the mid-sixties exports were below the levels reached in the early fifties, the massive inflow of foreign aid permitted a rapid rise in imports during the First and Second Plan periods. This is shown in Table 10.5 which provides annual data on total exports and imports, together with two series of index numbers on the terms of trade. One of these uses as weights the composition of exports and imports in 1948/49 and the other the corresponding data for 1954/55; for comparability, they have both been expressed on a 1959/60 base.

Because of the changing composition of imports and exports referred to earlier, the movements in Pakistan's terms of trade are difficult to interpret; the data in the last two columns of Table 10.5 show considerable differences between the indices for the overlapping years. Nevertheless, the conclusions about changes between Plan periods are reasonably straightforward. If we use the earlier index, the terms of trade declined by almost 40 percent from the pre-Plan period to the First Plan period, largely because of falling export prices. In turn, according to the later index, increases in export prices led to an improvement in Pakistan's terms of trade by approximately 20 percent from the First Plan period to the Second.

It should be added, however, that the increase of roughly 30 percent shown by the volume index of exports from the First Plan period to the Second is

TABLE 10.5: Exports, Imports, and the Terms of Trade in Pakistan, 1948/49–1965/66

Year	Exports ($ million)	Imports ($ million)	Terms of trade, index Original base of 1948/49	Original base of 1954/55
1949/50	360.9	392.0	213.2	....
1950/51	771.8	489.6	239.1	....
1951/52	607.1	676.2	226.2	....
1952/53	456.4	418.2	162.3	....
1953/54	388.7	337.9	144.4	....
1954/55	369.7	333.4	158.6	124.7
1955/56	373.1	278.3	129.9	107.3
1956/57	336.2	488.3	121.5	96.1
1957/58	298.5	430.5	113.2	106.1
1958/59	278.3	331.5	102.1	99.1
1959/60	387.0	516.8	100.0	100.0
1960/61	377.9	669.4	157.7	137.4
1961/62	387.1	652.9	129.3	121.3
1962/63	471.9	801.9	114.0	106.6
1963/64	482.8	930.3	....	110.5
1964/65	505.6	1,128.6	....	139.2
1965/66	570.7	883.8	....	118.0

Sources: Ministry of Finance, Pakistan Economic Survey, 1966–67, pp. 28–31; Statistical Bulletin, May 1967, p. 757; Statistical Bulletin, March 1965, pp. 617–18.

probably an underestimate, since the weights for the fiscal year 1954/55 understate the importance of newer exports. Part of the apparent improvement in export unit values, derived as a ratio of export value and volume indices, may therefore simply reflect the growing volume of new exports, particularly manufactures.

The System of Protection

Instruments of Import Protection

Since Partition, a variety of devices has been used to make domestic relative prices differ from the prices that exist in world markets. An often-used measure of the protection of import-competing goods, and of the relative rewards to domestic production in import substitution and in exports, is the level of import duties. Table 10.6, based on Radhu's studies,[6] allows a comparison over time of the level of tariffs on goods classified by principal end-use.

The data show that the average level of duties and the spread of the tariff structure increased over time. Higher levels of duties, as well as the increased "cascading" or escalation of the tariff structure, are particularly marked after 1960/61, the first budget year of the Second Five-Year Plan. The tariff structure, however, remained roughly the same throughout; this conforms to patterns observed in many developing countries: the lowest duties are levied on machinery and equipment, higher duties on unprocessed raw materials, higher still on processed raw materials, and the highest on nondurable consumer goods, particularly semi-luxury and luxury goods, and consumer durables.

Even though their level remained quite high throughout the period under study, tariffs were not the principal determinant of the extent of protection, as measured by the excess of domestic over world market prices. Evidence on this point is given in Table 10.7 which compares the exchange rates implied by foreign and domestic wholesale prices of comparable goods, and the exchange rate that would have prevailed if tariffs had been the sole determinant of the relationships between these prices.

In the early years, after the balance-of-payments crisis and the subsequent adoption of strict exchange controls and import licensing in 1952, tariffs substantially understated the extent to which domestic prices exceeded world prices of manufactured goods. As time passed, however, in some industries home production became dominant in total supply, and efficiency improved so that domestic prices fell below the tariff-inclusive price of comparable imports. This happened in most consumer goods industries; in industries producing

---

[6] See G. M. Radhu, "The Rate Structure of Indirect Taxes in Pakistan," *Pakistan Development Review*, Autumn 1964, pp. 527–51.

TABLE 10.6: Average Rates of Import Duty Classified by End Use of Goods in Pakistan, 1955/56–1965/66

(Percent)

Commodity group	1955/56	1956/57	1957/58	1958/59	1959/60	1960/61	1961/62	1962/63	1963/64	1964/65	1965/66
Nondurable consumer goods											
Essentials	35	35	35	35	35	55	55	55	56	56	70
Semi-luxuries	54	54	54	54	54	111	111	111	116	118	148
Luxuries	99	99	99	99	99	140	140	140	142	144	180
Raw materials for consumer goods											
Unprocessed	26	26	26	26	26	27	27	27	30	31	39
Processed	43	43	43	43	43	50	50	48	51	65	81
Raw materials for capital goods											
Unprocessed	23	23	23	23	23	28	28	28	31	32	40
Processed	38	38	38	38	38	40	40	39	42	55	69
Capital goods and consumer durables											
Consumer durables	71	71	71	71	81	85	85	85	89	91	114
Machinery and equipment	14	14	14	14	14	17	17	17	17	22	34

Sources: For 1955/56–1964/65, G. M. Radhu, "The Rate Structure of Indirect Taxes in Pakistan," Pakistan Development Review, Autumn 1964, pp. 527–51, and P. S. Thomas, "Import Licensing and Import Liberalization in Pakistan," Pakistan Development Review, Winter 1966, pp. 500–544.

TABLE 10.7: Implicit Exchange Rates Derived from Price Comparisons Compared
with Rates Implied by Tariffs in Pakistan, 1954/55–1963/64

(*Rupees per U.S. dollar*)

Industry group	Exchange rate implied by tariffs	Exchange rate implied by price comparisons
1954/1955		
Consumer goods	5.43	8.90
Intermediate goods	4.83	8.61
Investment and related goods	3.94	8.07
All manufactures	5.34	8.94
1959/1960		
Consumer goods	7.84	8.88
Intermediate goods	6.38	8.65
Investment and related goods	6.34	9.39
All manufactures	7.61	8.96
1963/1964		
Consumer goods	10.58	7.72
Intermediate goods	6.97	9.25
Investment and related goods	6.37	9.27
All manufactures	10.02	8.08
1963/1964, Imported goods only		
Consumer goods	8.12	12.59
Intermediate goods	6.37	10.97
Investment and related goods	5.89	9.60
All imports in sample	6.79	11.16

Sources: Computed from S. R. Lewis, Jr., *Economic Policy and Industrial Growth in Pakistan*
(London: George Allen & Unwin, Ltd., 1968). West Pakistan rates weighted twice East Pakistan
rates. Averages for each industry are weighted according to purchases by agriculture, as described
in S. R. Lewis, Jr., and S. M. Hussain, *Relative Price Changes and Industrialization in Pakistan,
1951–64* (Karachi: Pakistan Institute of Development Economics, 1967). Import goods data from
M. L. Pal, "The Determinants of the Domestic Prices of Imports," *Pakistan Development Review*,
Winter 1964, pp. 597–622.

intermediate products and investment goods, domestic production remained
small relative to imports, and differences between domestic and foreign prices
continue to exceed the tariff. Price differentials also exceeded tariffs in all
major categories of goods actually imported, with average differences amount-
ing to 60 percent in 1963–64. It follows that tariffs alone would substantially
misstate the degree of nominal protection accorded to individual industries.

The ratios of domestic to foreign prices for individual commodities reflect
the relative scarcity of individual commodities due to the import licensing
system. Import licenses were issued for fairly detailed specifications of goods,
and their use for goods other than those specified was not permitted. The
system controlled both the total level and the composition of imports, and it
led to the maintenance of the official exchange rate at a level far below the rate
that would have resulted in the absence of restrictions.[7]

---

[7] Several articles examine Pakistan's import licensing system. P. S. Thomas, "Import
Licensing and Import Liberalization in Pakistan," *Pakistan Development Review*, Winter

There are two basic types of import licenses. The first are issued to commercial importers, who can legally resell the goods after they enter the country; the second, to industrialists for their own raw material and spare parts needs, as well as for their initial imports of capital equipment. The commercial (legally-resold) imports are a substantial part of the total supply of raw materials and capital goods, so that the markups implied in Table 10.7 are not simply the scarcity margin on a small amount of black or grey market goods. At the same time, since not all producers receive licenses for their capital goods and raw material imports, in many industries there are some favored firms which pay for scarce imports a price well below the opportunity cost to the economy, while others pay scarcity prices for both capital goods and raw materials. Some effects of this difference will be brought out later.

Since at the time of Partition, virtually all manufactures were imported and agricultural goods were primarily exported, the restrictive trade policy adopted in the early fifties turned the terms of trade sharply against the agricultural sector, and benefited the domestic producers of manufactures as well as the import licensees who were permitted to import and sell manufactured goods. Table 10.8 gives the picture from the point of view of the agricultural sector; it compares the terms of trade facing the farmers in exchanging agricultural goods for manufactures with the terms of trade they would have obtained had they been able to trade directly in world markets.

Because of import duties on manufactured goods, particularly cotton cloth, and heavy export duties on raw jute and cotton, at the height of the Korean boom (1951/52) the farmers received less than half the value that their produce would have brought at world prices. The relative position of the farmers worsened after the collapse of export prices and the tightening of import restrictions in 1952 so that, in the three-year period 1953/54 to 1955/56, farmers received just over one-third of the world market value of their produce when it was exchanged for manufactured goods in domestic markets. The situation improved through the mid-sixties; nevertheless, in 1961/62 to 1963/64, farmers still received only three-fifths of the value they would have obtained in world markets.

1966, pp. 500–544, deals with the entire system and its impact, as well as the attempts to liberalize the system in the 1960s. M. L. Pal, in "The Determinants of the Domestic Prices of Imports," *ibid.*, Winter 1964, pp. 597–622, and in his "Domestic Prices of Imports: Extension of Empirical Findings," *ibid.*, Winter 1965, pp. 547–88, dealt with the effects of the licensing policy on domestic relations prices of imports. S. N. H. Naqvi has written two articles of interest here: "Import Licensing in Pakistan," *ibid.*, Spring 1964, pp. 51–68, and "The Allocative Biases of Pakistan's Commercial Policy," *ibid.*, Winter 1966, pp. 465–99. Finally, Nurul Islam has made a study from reports of the Pakistani Tariff Commission on a large number of industries ("Comparative Costs, Factor Proportions, and Industrial Efficiency in Pakistan," *ibid.*, Summer 1967, pp. 213–46).

TABLE 10.8: Implicit Exchange Rates for Industrial and Agricultural Goods and Agriculture's Relative Terms of Trade in Pakistan, 1951/52–1963/64

(Rupees per U.S. dollar)

Years	Implicit exchange rates		Agriculture's domestic terms of trade relative to world price standards (percent)
	Manufactured goods (weighted by agricultural purchases)	Agricultural goods (weighted by marketings)	
1951/52	7.18	3.33	46.4
1952/53	8.20	3.58	43.7
3-year averages			
1951/52–1953/54	8.62	3.43	39.8
1952/53–1954/55	9.21	3.38	36.7
1953/54–1955/56	9.39	3.40	36.2
1954/55–1956/57	8.94	3.84	43.0
1955/56–1957/58	8.98	4.38	48.8
1956/57–1958/59	8.87	4.78	53.9
1957/58–1959/60	8.81	4.77	54.1
1958/59–1960/61	8.58	4.94	57.6
1959/60–1961/62	8.55	5.05	59.1
1960/61–1962/63	8.37	5.19	62.0
1961/62–1963/64	8.27	5.12	61.9

Source: S. R. Lewis, Jr., "Effects of Trade Policy on Domestic Relative Prices: Pakistan, 1951–1964," *American Economic Review*, March 1968, pp. 60–78.

It appears, then, that the import licensing system and the overvaluation of the currency were the major factors in the incentive system that developed in Pakistan in the years following Partition. The Tariff Commission investigated requests for protective tariffs, and made reports on over 100 industries, covering over 1,000 firms. But most major industries, including cotton, jute, and woolen textiles, fertilizers, and automobiles, were not subject to Tariff Commission inquiries. These industries received subsidies or protection from (*a*) the revenue tariffs applied after Partition, (*b*) the import-licensing system (and the tendency of the licensing authorities to restrict imports when domestic production was "adequate" to meet demand), (*c*) the taxes on exports of principal raw materials, which kept the domestic prices of these materials well below their opportunity cost to the economy, and (*d*) the direct importation at low duties and no scarcity premium of capital equipment needed in industry. Moreover, in recent years, several of these industries have received export subsidies.

The Export Bonus Scheme

The institution of an export bonus scheme explains a substantial part of the recent expansion of manufactured exports which is somewhat unusual for a low-income country. Table 10.9 shows the official exchange rate, which changed only once, in 1955, and a second series obtained by adjusting the official exchange rate for the Export Bonus Scheme, introduced in 1959.[8] The Scheme allowed exporters to retain import rights equal to a certain percentage of the f.o.b. value of their exports. These import rights were applicable to a specified list of commodities, and the license to import was transferable. As a result, an active market has developed in Bonus Vouchers, as the certificates are called. The combination of the proportion of f.o.b. value of exports the exporter received in the form of Vouchers, and the premium at which the Vouchers were selling in the open market accordingly determined the returns in terms of rupees the exporter received in addition to the official price of the foreign exchange receipts he sold to the State Bank.[9]

The data in Table 10.9 pertain to a firm entitled to the highest percentage of exports in the form of Vouchers, assuming that all the Vouchers were sold

TABLE 10.9:   Nominal and Real Export Exchange Rates in Pakistan, 1951/52–1963/64

(Rupees per U.S. dollar)

Year	Nominal exchange rate	Nominal exchange rate adjusted for export bonus	Real exchange rate[a]
1951/52	3.31	3.31	3.54
1952/53	3.31	3.31	3.65
1953/54	3.31	3.31	3.35
1954/55	3.31	3.31	3.79
1955/56	4.76	4.76	5.33
1956/57	4.76	4.76	5.11
1957/58	4.76	4.76	4.85
1958/59	4.76	4.76	5.07
1959/60	4.76	7.83	7.83
1960/61	4.76	7.14	6.99
1961/62	4.76	7.46	7.34
1962/63	4.76	7.75	7.63
1963/64	4.76	7.67	7.59

Sources: Bonus voucher premia taken from the *Economic Survey*, various issues. Manufacturing price data from Lewis and Hussain, *Relative Price Changes and Industrialization in Pakistan, 1951–64*. Appendix tables C-IW and C-IE, West Pakistan weighted twice East Pakistan. For method of calculation, see text.

[a] Adjusted nominal exchange rate divided by price index of manufactured goods, 1959/60 = 100.

---

[8] On the Export Bonus Schemes, see H. J. Bruton and S. R. Bose, *The Pakistan Export Bonus Scheme* (Karachi: Pakistan Institute of Development Economics, 1963); and Q. K. Ahmad, "The Operation of the Export Bonus Scheme in Pakistan's Jute and Cotton Industries," *Pakistan Development Review*, Spring 1966, pp. 1–37.

[9] For example: A firm exports $100 of footwear, and receives Rs. 476.00 from the State Bank *plus* Bonus Vouchers to import $40.00 of imports. The premium on the Vouchers in the open market is 50 percent, so it can sell the Vouchers for: $40.00 × Rs. 4.76/$1.00 × 1.50 = Rs. 285.60. This represents 60 percent more domestic currency than it would have received from the State Bank if it had only been given the official exchange rate. The total bonus is a product of the Bonus rate (40 percent) and the value of the Vouchers (150 percent in this case), or 60 percent in the example chosen.

at the average premium that obtained during the year.[10] The data show substantial increases in the rupee returns per dollar of manufactured exports during the period in which the rate of growth of exports of manufactures was high. In the last column of the table, we have further adjusted the current price of rupee receipts for the changes in the manufacturing price index. The domestic prices of manufactured goods changed very little over the period, however, and most of the increases in rupee returns to exporters represented higher real returns as well.

In addition to the increase in the official exchange rate in 1955 and the Bonus Scheme in 1959, other inducements were provided to exporters, including rebates on import duties, additional import licenses based on the f.o.b. value of exports, easier access to regular import licenses for firms heavily engaged in the export business, and deductions for export earnings from the corporate income tax.[11] All of these privileges were increased substantially in the sixties, so that there has been an even greater increase in the incentives to export than is suggested by the figures of Table 10.9.

Nominal and Effective Protection

Rates of Nominal Tariff and Implicit Protection

Any evaluation of the system of subsidizing or protecting manufacturing industry in Pakistan must deal with (*a*) the tariff structure, (*b*) the indirect tax system, (*c*) the multiple exchange rate system for exports, and (*d*) the system of quantitative controls on imports. Indirect taxes account for a growing share of total tax revenue in Pakistan,[12] since the government imposed sales taxes on import-substituting industries after such industries had been in production for a certain period of time. The pattern of imposing and, subsequently, increasing domestic indirect taxes has been followed in cotton and jute textiles, sugar, matches, soaps, tires and tubes, paints and varnishes, paper products, and

---

[10] From 1959 to 1964, the highest Bonus rate was 40 percent. This was lowered to 30 percent in June 1964. Cotton and jute textiles were subject to less than the maximum rate, and cotton yarn has been below cotton cloth and has been off the Bonus List at times. Certain primary goods (for example, chromite ore, fine quality rice, fresh fish) are entitled to bonus receipts, but "traditional exports" (jute and cotton, tea, wool, hides and skins), are not given export bonus privileges.

[11] Many of these, particularly the "export performance" licensing of imports are discussed by W. E. Hecox, *The Use of Import Privileges as Incentives to Exporters in Pakistan*, Research Report No. 30 (Karachi: Pakistan Institute of Development Economics, 1965); and Thomas, "Import Licensing and Import Liberalization in Pakistan."

[12] Indirect taxes provided over two-thirds of combined Central and Provincial direct and indirect tax revenue in the past decade. See S. R. Lewis, Jr., and S. K. Qureshi, "The Structure of Revenue from Indirect Taxes in Pakistan," *Pakistan Development Review*, Autumn 1964, pp. 491–526.

cement. These taxes also apply to imports but nevertheless reduce the extent of protection by raising the cost of material inputs to the domestic producer.[13]

The multiple pricing system for foreign exchange has been a substantial source of subsidy to industry. While the raw materials for cotton and jute textiles and leather tanning are exported at or below the official exchange rate, the processed goods are sold at a preferential exchange rate. Furthermore, some other industries receive drawbacks or refunds on import duties paid on raw materials, so that they obtain inputs at the official price of foreign exchange but export their products effectively at a much higher exchange rate.

The impact of the various policies on the protection or subsidy of individual industries are summarized in Table 10.10. The table compares, for the fiscal year 1963/64, the levels of protection implied by the tariff structure with levels of protection calculated on the basis of actual differentials between domestic and world market prices (the implicit tariff or nominal implicit protection).[14] Some industries (for example, cigarettes, beverages) have not been included in the table because price data could not be obtained for comparable domestic and international goods. All comparisons use the official exchange rate as the base; adjusted rates of protection, after being corrected for overvaluation, are given later.

As mentioned in the previous section, the tariff structure has not been the principal determinant of protection in Pakistan. In industries where the process of import substitution has been completed and exports have begun under the Bonus Voucher Scheme, costs and prices have declined and differences between domestic and foreign prices have become smaller than the price differentials implied by tariffs. Examples are cotton textiles, footwear, sports goods, jute textiles, thread- and threadball-making, tanning, and sewing machines.

Paper products present an interesting case. The domestic producers apparently act as discriminating monopolists (there is no more than one producer of each major type of paper and board), and sell in the export market for lower prices (including export Bonus Receipts) than they charge in the domestic market, which is protected through controls. This is a clear case where improved economic policy could both reduce inefficiency and remove windfall profits from privileged industries.

In virtually all the remaining industries, supply restrictions stemming from import controls have resulted in prices well above the duty-paid price of com-

---

[13] For a discussion, see Chapter 1, pp. 13–14.

[14] The rates of protection from the tariff system alone were computed by S. R. Lewis, Jr., and G. M. Radhu, in Lewis, *Economic Policy and Industrial Growth in Pakistan*, ch. 4. The rates of tariff protection reported in Table 10.10 are the Lewis-Radhu estimates adjusted for the treatment of nontraded goods as explained in Appendix E. The sources of information for direct price comparisons and the limitations of the data are also discussed in Appendix E.

TABLE 10.10: Levels of Nominal and Effective Protection from All Sources Compared with Levels of Tariff Protection in Pakistan, 1963/64

(Percent)

Industry	Nominal tariff protec- tion	Nominal implicit protec- tion	Effective tariff protection		Effective implicit protection	
			Balassa	Corden	Balassa	Corden
Consumer and related goods						
Sugar	55	208	400	133	−198	−329
Edible oils	45	104	22	9	−125	−189
Tea	−2	23	−59	−43	−10	−6
Cotton textiles	127	30	−555	1,900	733	213
Silk and silk textiles	174	304	9,900	488	−626	9,900
Footwear	76	60	138	89	85	59
Wearing apparel	223	218	−725	669	−470	1,900
Printing and publishing	0	28	−22	−18	22	16
Soaps	35	60	1	1	178	223
Matches	33	0	37	28	11	9
Plastic goods	94	223	245	170	669	335
Sports goods	72	60	138	108	92	75
Pens and pencils	46	140	52	45	245	186
Electrical appliances	82	286	194	144	−3,433	72
Motor vehicles	78	234	−282	150	−164	−2,100
Average	78	103	477	136	−350	883
Intermediate goods						
Jute textiles	51	27	317	133	406	183
Thread and threadball	84	60	43	28	163	82
Saw milling	61	73	426	72	1,150	92
Tanning	61	56	−2,100	150	567	96
Rubber products	25	137	28	18	−555	525
Fertilizer	0	15	14	6	−688	186
Paints and varnishes	23	60	20	15	257	133
Chemicals	24	65	12	9	300	113
Petroleum products	−23	27	−49	−40	−7	−5
Paper products	62	79	138	75	376	144
Average	29	47	22	15	187	88
Investment and related goods						
Nonmetallic mineral products	49	134	64	54	355	72
Cement	38	44	37	30	64	49
Basic metals	9	58	−1	−1	525	194
Metal products	59	88	330	100	−869	270
Nonelectrical machinery	13	89	10	8	355	170
Sewing machinery	85	60	1,330	257	138	82
Electrical machinery and equipment	22	60	18	15	89	72
Average	31	71	43	30	423	155
Average for all industries	59	85	120	65	...	271
Median	51	60	58	50	365	139

Sources Tariff data based on Lewis and Radhu calculations, in Lewis, *Economic Policy and Industrial Growth in Pakistan*, adjusted for changes in the input-output coefficients as discussed in Appendix E. Direct price comparisons are explained in Appendix E.

peting imports.[15] In addition to imports of competing goods, imports of raw materials and capital goods by these industries have also been restricted. This partly explains the excess capacity observed in many such industries, and has also led to substantial windfalls to individuals who receive import licenses for raw materials and capital goods.

Among industries where domestic prices exceed the sum of the import price and the tariff, there is considerable variation in the extent to which imports dominate in total supply. Sugar, silk and artificial silk textiles, edible oils, and plastic goods are supplied largely by domestic producers, but import restrictions on these products and their raw materials (and in the case of sugar, restrictions on plant capacity) keep domestic prices high. Imports, however, dominate total supply of consumer durables (electrical appliances and motor vehicles) and many intermediate and investment goods (rubber goods, chemicals, nonmetallic mineral products, basic metals, metal products, nonelectrical and electrical machinery and equipment); for these the scarcity of imports, together with demand conditions, determines the domestic prices. Such evidence as exists, however, suggests that these latter industries also suffer from excess capacity due partly to shortages of raw material supplies.

The Interindustry Pattern of Effective Rates

Table 10.10 also shows the effective rate of protection, or the rate of subsidy to value added; for comparison, it shows separately both the protection implied by the tariff structure and that implied by relative prices. In both instances, estimates have been made by using the Balassa as well as the Corden formula.

Two principal findings deserve mention before we discuss the extent of protection in particular industries. First, while the ranking of industries by nominal and effective rates of protection is roughly comparable in calculations made from tariff rates, this is not so for nominal and effective implicit rates that have been derived from price observations. The rank correlation coefficient is .92 in the former case and .59 in the latter. Second, when we compare the rankings of industries according to effective tariff protection, with those according to effective protection from all sources (effective implicit protection), there are so many differences that the rank correlation between the two measures is practically nil.

The results of Table 10.10 also show that both the tariffs and the price differentials understate the degree of protection given to individual industries, and that in industries with higher levels of nominal protection (subsidy) this understatement is quite substantial. If we use the Balassa formula, the effective rate

---

[15] The analysis and assertions in this and the following paragraphs are based on Lewis, *Economic Policy and Industrial Growth in Pakistan*, ch. 6.

of protection from all sources implies negative value added at world market prices for nine industries; i.e., the world market value of material inputs exceeds that of output. The number of such industries is reduced to three when nontraded inputs are included in value added under the Corden formula. Indeed, the entire structure of rates falls substantially when nontraded inputs are treated as Corden suggests. Thus, the median industry had protection of 365 percent under the Balassa method and only 139 percent under the Corden method. These results compare with median price differentials (nominal implicit rates of protection) of 60 percent.

We have already discussed the reasons for the observed differences between the percentage excess of domestic over world market prices and the tariff rates. Next, we will seek answers to the following questions: (*a*) why do some industries show much larger than average differences between effective and nominal rates of protection; (*b*) what are the reasons for the extraordinarily high rates of protection (implying "negative" value added) in certain industries; and (*c*) why do the export industries in Pakistan show high rates of effective subsidy. In dealing with these questions we will utilize the rate of effective protection or subsidy computed by the Corden formula.[16]

As noted above, in three industries (edible oils, sugar refining, and motor vehicle assembly) the value of output at world market prices appears to be less than the value of material inputs at world market prices. Two others (silk and artificial silk textiles and wearing apparel) have virtually no value added when both output and material inputs are valued at world market prices. In all five industries domestic prices of inputs and outputs are affected by a variety of supply restrictions, such as (*a*) import licensing of competing products (all five industries), (*b*) licensing of the capacity to produce domestic products (particularly in sugar refining), and (*c*) licensing of raw material inputs into the industry (all except sugar refining). Producers generally receive their inputs at well below opportunity cost to the economy, since they are direct licensees of imported goods and, therefore, pay only duties, not scarcity markups on imports.

---

[16] Including or excluding nontraded goods from value added in a processing industry understates or overstates the protection to that industry, since it is unlikely that protection to an industry is fully shared by suppliers of nontraded inputs, nor is it likely that protection has no effect on the prices of nontraded inputs. However, for reasons discussed in Appendix E and elsewhere, the value of inputs of nontraded goods in Pakistan are probably overstated, and some economists feel that these inputs may contain an allocation for profits earned by the industry. (See G. F. Papanek, "Industrial Production and Investment in Pakistan," *Pakistan Development Review*, Autumn 1964, pp. 462–90.) Thus, for practical reasons, Corden's method of treating nontraded goods appears useful in Pakistan. In addition, the value added in nontraded inputs and in the processing industry itself measures the economy's contribution to the value of the product; the extreme cases where the contribution (measured at world market prices) is negative are sharply diminished by using Corden's measure in Pakistan.

The question should be raised, however, if the accuracy of observed prices permits the conclusion about negative value added to stand unchallenged. To explore this question we assume that the input structure and the prices of inputs have been accurately observed, and we limit our discussion to the accuracy of the output prices.

Domestic producer prices exceeded world market prices for refined sugar in 1963/64 by at least 208 percent. Price differentials are even larger if comparisons are made with some low-cost producers abroad. At the same time, if the input structure is correctly estimated, the domestic price would have had to be less than 118 percent above the c.i.f. price in order for the value of domestic output to be just equal to the value of inputs. In other words, we would have to be wrong by almost 100 percent in our price observations in order for the industry to have even zero value added at world prices. Thus, even allowing for considerable error, sugar refining does not appear to be a profitable industry from the point of view of the national economy. The same concern has been voiced by several other authors and official commissions since the early 1950s. This conclusion is strengthened if sugar cane production is included in the comparison, as is discussed below.

In the edible oils (hydrogenation) industry, the margin for error is also large, and there are fluctuations in input and output prices. Price comparisons for the year 1963/64 suggest that domestic prices of hydrogenated vegetable oils were approximately twice the c.i.f. import price at the official exchange rate. In order for the output of the industry to exceed the value of material inputs when both are valued at world market prices, the domestic price of vegetable oils would have to be no more than 38 percent above world market prices. Thus, even if the observed price differential were overestimated by some 50 percent, the industry would still be unprofitable.

The motor vehicle industry is a much more difficult case because of the complexity of the product and its inputs, and the output mix of the industry (automobiles, trucks, and buses). It is a favorite example for tariff analysts, however, since in the early stages of automotive manufacturing, virtually all parts are imported (usually from the parent company abroad) and only the assembly is done domestically.[17] In some instances, automobiles are fully assembled by the parent company, then knocked down and shipped to the country of destination, where they are reassembled. In such a case, it is quite likely that the value of imports in knocked-down form exceeds the import price of a fully assembled vehicle.

The existence of price control gives rise to further complications in the

---

[17] See, for example, L. L. Johnson, "Problems of Import Substitution: The Chilean Automobile Industry," *Economic Development and Cultural Change*, January 1967, pp. 202–16.

evaluation of the motor vehicle industry in Pakistan. The differentials for motor vehicles are likely to overstate the cost of domestic production. But, at least for automobiles, value added at world market prices would be negative even if we used the tariff and sales tax on imports to represent the price differential. Given the input structure of the motor vehicle industry, the value of output would just equal the value of material inputs if the domestic price were no more than 121 percent above the world market price, while the tariff and sales tax on automobiles assembled domestically came to 130 percent for 1963/64. For trucks and buses, the tariff and sales tax in 1963/64 came to 55 percent, implying a rate of effective protection of 92 percent if nontraded inputs are treated as Corden suggests. Under the Balassa formula, however, there would be negative value added in the industry even at a 55 percent price differential. Such information strongly suggests that the assembly of motor vehicles in Pakistan in 1963/64 was not socially profitable.

A more detailed analysis of industries with negative value added at "world market" prices, including studies on the firm level, might conceivably modify these conclusions. Yet, even major changes in input composition would still show these industries to be highly inefficient. Indeed, automobiles and sugar are the second and third most highly protected industries according to the calculations made from the free trade input-output table, and fats and oils are not far behind.

It should be added, however, that negative value added at world market prices need not be explained solely in terms of the physical wasting of resources, including the failure to use by-products, although these may be very important.[18] Some of the industries that we have found to be very highly subsidized, or protected, may in fact be using processes that are not very inefficient technically, but which, when judged in the light of trade opportunity costs or world market prices of inputs and output, are found to be economically inefficient. When domestic prices become greatly distorted from world trade prices, such economically inefficient choices of processes and techniques may indeed become a real, not merely a theoretical, possibility.

Five more industries, including cotton textiles which is the single most important industry in Pakistan, showed rates of effective protection at existing exchange rates to be in excess of 200 percent. Three of the industries (rubber goods, plastic goods, and metal products) are in the situation described earlier, where the principal determinants of their output prices are restrictions on competing imports and, particularly in the case of plastic goods, on inputs into the industry itself. Rubber and plastic goods, which have effective rates of protection of 525 and 335 percent, respectively, have domestic producer prices 137

---

[18] S. E. Guisinger, "Negative Value Added and the Theory of Effective Protection," *Quarterly Journal of Economics*, August 1969, pp. 415–33.

percent and 223 percent above the world market prices. Metal products and soaps (the latter are exported) show smaller differences between domestic and world market prices, and the high rate of effective protection is largely explained by the relatively low prices paid for imports of raw materials used by these industries.

Cotton textiles and jute textiles, with effective rates of protection of 213 and 183 percent, respectively, have a number of features in common. Both have become export industries and both receive a price of foreign exchange higher than the official rate in the form of Bonus Vouchers. In addition, the principal raw materials used by the two industries are exported at a price *below* the official price of foreign exchange, since both raw jute and raw cotton have been subject to export duties. As a result, the nominal subsidy in the form of the Bonus Voucher receipts for exports is compounded by the subsidy in the form of very cheap raw materials.

It should be added, however, that given the nominal rate of subsidy for the export of the finished product, the rate of estimated effective protection or subsidy to domestic processing is quite sensitive to the level of export duty on the major raw material input. For example, the calculation given in Table 10.10 for the jute textile industry is based on the comparison of export prices f.o.b. Chittagong with the domestic price in Narayangang for the grade of jute (B-bottoms) used heavily in Pakistan's jute textile industry. If one assumed instead that the 5 percent export duty provided an appropriate indication of the price difference,[19] the rate of effective subsidy would decline to around 70 percent. Nevertheless, if there were no export tax on raw jute, the effective rate of subsidy to the industry would still be 59 percent. Also, for cotton textiles, using a 5 percent export duty instead of the actual price comparison for raw cotton would only lower the rate of effective subsidy to 197 percent. If there were no export tax on raw cotton, the rate of effective subsidy would still be 93 percent.[20]

---

[19] Jute and cotton are subject to specific duties equaling about 5 percent of the f.o.b. value for each product in 1963/64, based on the average unit value of exports. Since Pakistan uses substantially lower quality jute for her jute products than she exports in raw form, however, the ad valorem rate of export duty on the lower quality jute would be higher since the specific rate does not vary with the quality of jute.

[20] If the effective rates of protection (subsidy) to the jute and cotton textiles industries were expressed in the form Soligo and Stern used, one could say that under the most optimistic assumptions (i.e., that there was no export duty on the exports of raw materials) 37 percent of the domestic value added in the jute textile industry and 48 percent of the value added in the cotton textile industry was "due to" the subsidy inherent in the multiple pricing system for foreign exchange (R. Soligo and J. J. Stern, "Tariff Protection, Import Substitution, and Investment Efficiency," *Pakistan Development Review*, Summer 1965, pp. 249–70). Their article, which caused considerable debate when it appeared, came to the conclusion that most of Pakistan's important industries might have had negative value added when inputs and output were valued at world prices. Since they used tariff rates to represent the difference between world and domestic prices, and since they made no adjustment for the

In the face of these results, one has reports of expert groups from international agencies and institutions suggesting that, while improvements could be made, the technical efficiency of the exporting textile industry is quite good by international standards. The conclusion one might draw from this, and from casual evidence on the enthusiasm of investors to enter these industries in Pakistan, is that the high rate of effective protection (effective subsidy) to the cotton and jute processing industries in Pakistan entails not so much the inefficient use of resources through improper choice of techniques or input mix, as an extremely high rate of profits. Thus, to the extent that prices include large profits, the high rate of protection of the two industries cannot be taken as an indication of a comparative disadvantage. Unfortunately, however, there is no accurate way of assessing how much of the effective subsidy goes into profits, and how much entails a waste of resources.

There are eight industries with rates of effective protection between 100 and 200 percent; of these we have already considered jute textiles. In four of the remaining seven, high rates of effective protection are explained chiefly by the escalation of nominal rates of protection, with relatively low rates of duty on inputs. This is particularly true of basic metals and of fertilizers. For pens and pencils, however, the 186 percent rate of effective protection is largely a consequence of a 140 percent rate of nominal implicit protection. Finally, both of these considerations are relevant for nonelectrical machinery, where the scarcity due to import licensing raises domestic prices above the tariff-inclusive import price, while material inputs are priced relatively low for firms with import licenses.

The case of the paper products industry has been mentioned above. Domestic prices of paper products are determined by a combination of import licensing and the policies of price discrimination followed by the monopolistic domestic producers—they export similar products at lower prices than those charged domestically. The high rate of effective protection is a result both of some escalation in the tariff structure and of the relatively high rate (79 percent) of domestic producer price differential above world prices that results from licensing.

Paints and varnishes are exported with a 60 percent nominal subsidy. The relatively low duties on inputs used by this industry, however, result in an effective rate more than double the nominal rate of subsidy. Similar consid-

---

overstatement of nontraded inputs in the input-output table, their estimates were of questionable value in judging actual losses from price distortions. But they did contribute a useful concept to the analysis of tariffs. If one calculates the value added at "world market" prices and then expresses the difference between the actual value added and the value added at world market prices as a percent of actual value added, the resulting measure gives the percent of value added "due to" protection, which is a useful concept. This figure can be negative only for industries that are truly discriminated against by the tariff system.

erations apply to chemicals. The licensing of imported inputs raises the effective rate of protection as compared with nominal rates; although producers are able to purchase inputs at their duty-paid prices, they sell their products at the full scarcity price of competing imports. In this case, however, production takes place mainly for the domestic market.

Of the eighteen industries with effective rates of protection above 100 percent, four (soaps, cotton textiles, jute textiles, and paints and varnishes) export a substantial part of their output—albeit at a better exchange rate than the official one. In addition, some parts of the metal products, paper, and non-electrical machinery industries have been able to export at the more favorable Bonus Voucher exchange rate, even though there are imports competing with other products manufactured by these industries. All other industries of the group produce almost exclusively for the domestic market.

Eight industries have effective rates of protection between 69 and 100 percent. Five of these industries (saw milling, thread- and threadball-making, sewing machinery, sports goods, and electrical machinery and equipment) have effective rates only slightly above the nominal rates of protection, indicating a mild degree of escalation of nominal rates. In the leather-tanning industry, however, the effective rate of protection (96 percent) is considerably above the nominal rate (56 percent). This result is explained in the same way as it was for cotton and jute textiles: the principal raw material is exported at the official exchange rate while the manufactured product receives the bonus exchange rate. Finally, two industries (electrical appliances and nonmetallic mineral products) have effective rates of protection well below the nominal rates. These industries use as inputs the products of protected industries, and show reverse escalation. It should be added that the products of the tanning, thread, sports goods, and sewing machinery industries and, to a lesser extent, those of the electrical equipment industry are exported at the Bonus Voucher exchange rate.

The remaining six industries (footwear, printing and publishing, petroleum products, tea, matches, and cement) had effective rates of protection below 60 percent, and had nominal price differentials close to the effective rate of protection in the industry. For footwear (which is now exported), both output and the major input (leather) are priced at the Bonus Voucher exchange rate. Printing and publishing firms must use domestically produced, and therefore high-priced, paper since direct imports of paper inputs are restricted by licensing.

Petroleum products and tea processing show small negative effective rates of protection, since taxes on imported inputs more than offset the nominal protection of the final product. Petroleum refining expanded substantially during the sixties, and there are few competing imports left. Tea processing is a unique case in Pakistan, since it is the industry where domestic consumption has increased much faster than production, with the result that the export surplus of the fifties had disappeared by the mid-sixties.

The footwear industry, which has the highest rate of effective subsidy in the group, is the only industry which is a substantial exporter. By contrast, the cement industry is dominated by import supplies, and it is much behind its production targets in the Second Five-Year Plan (1960–65). Finally, printing and publishing has few competing imports, and matches have had virtually no recent import competition.

Protection of Privileged and Nonprivileged Firms

An important aspect of differential protection in Pakistan has not been accounted for in the above discussion. The import licensing system, as explained earlier, discriminates among producers. Some firms receive import licenses for all their imported raw materials to be purchased at the official exchange rate, with tariffs and sales taxes added to the c.i.f. price. There are, however, firms, particularly small ones, which do not receive any import licenses and must purchase all imported raw materials on the domestic market at prices well above the landed cost inclusive of duties. It would appear that most firms are at or very near these two extremes, although there are some which receive raw materials from each source.[21] Obviously, when firms in the same industry receive their inputs at widely differing costs, they must differ in profitability, use a different input mix, or both.

The calculations of effective rates of protection shown in Table 10.10 and discussed above have been based on the assumption that all firms in an industry are privileged importers, and that they receive their imported raw materials at the official exchange rate plus import duties and sales taxes. There are two reasons for this assumption. For one thing, the input-output table utilized in the calculations has been based on data from the Census of Manufacturing Industries, which primarily covers firms that are privileged importers. For another, data on import allocations to industries have also been based partly on information pertaining to the privileged industries.

To the extent that there are firms in the industry which have the same input structure but do not receive import licenses for their raw materials, the rate of effective protection to those firms would be overstated. This would also imply that the nonprivileged firms, which are generally small, would show smaller

---

[21] The reason the cases are at the extremes is that an entrepreneur becomes a privileged importer at the time his investment is sanctioned by the licensing authorities, and his claim on future foreign exchange resources is established then. If a firm is established without obtaining capital equipment through the industrial licensing procedures, it is highly unlikely that it could ever become a licensed industrial importer, since its investment would not have been sanctioned.

profits than the privileged ones. A study made by Gustav Ranis suggests that the reverse is true: rates of return on capital are substantially higher for smaller firms than for larger ones.[22] The study also suggests that the input structure of firms in the same industry differs among firms of different sizes, chiefly because of the different access they have to imported inputs. Thus, the small firms would appear to be more efficient users of imported raw materials than the larger firms, presumably because, not being privileged importers, the small firms are forced to pay higher prices and therefore economize on the use of raw materials.

These results do not necessarily mean that smaller firms are more efficient; the use of unpaid family help, long working hours, and low wages—all contribute to the observed high rate of return on capital. Incidentally, according to Stephen Guisinger's unpublished results, there is no definite pattern of differences in output per worker between large and small firms.[23] Note further that in a study of Colombian industry, Nelson found large firms to be more efficient than smaller ones.[24]

The calculations in Table 10.10 are thus representative of the levels of protection enjoyed by the large-scale (or modern) manufacturing sector of Pakistan while smaller firms receive less protection. This does not mean, however, that smaller firms are often more efficient. The estimates based on the domestic input-output table do not permit a numerical comparison of levels of protection provided to privileged and nonprivileged firms but such calculations can be made by the use of free trade coefficients. The use of free trade coefficients is convenient for this purpose although ideally one would like to take account of differences in input proportions if substitution in response to differences in relative prices does occur.

Table 10.11 provides estimates of nominal and effective rates of protection based on free trade input-output coefficients for two groups of firms: firms that enjoy import privileges and those that do not receive any such privileges. We have not prepared calculations for industries that do not exist in Pakistan. Nor do we provide estimates of protection to nonfavored firms in industries which had only privileged firms producing at the time the price data were collected; in these industries raw materials were available to privileged firms only.[25]

---

[22] G. Ranis, *Industrial Efficiency and Economic Growth: A Case Study of Karachi* (Karachi: Pakistan Institute of Development Economics, 1961).

[23] The results are, however, affected by the greater capital intensity of large firms and the lack of inclusion of unpaid family help in family enterprises.

[24] R. R. Nelson, "International Productivity Differences," *American Economic Review*, December 1968, pp. 1219–48.

[25] For example, since paper and paperboard firms are all privileged, there is no internal market in pulp, which precludes a calculation of protection granted to industries which purchase pulp on the internal market. The calculation given for the pulp industry is based on the tariff rates on pulp.

TABLE 10.11: Effective Protection Calculated from Free Trade Input-Output Coefficients: A Comparison of Protection to Firms with and without Direct Licensing Privileges in Pakistan, 1963/64

(*Percent*)

Industry	Nominal implicit protection	Effective implicit protection	
		Firms with import privileges	Firms without import privileges
Agriculture (01)	7	**	−19.8
Fishing (02)	30	**	−5.5
Nonferrous metals (06)	60	56.8	27.7
Petroleum and natural gas (07)	30	23.7	*
Preserves (other than meat) (11)	251	591.5	555.1
Sugar (12)	204	504.3	*
Dairy products (14)	56	248.2	−75.7
Beverages (17)	123	182.9	148.4
Fats and oils (18)	102	191.4	120.7 .
Tobacco (19)	207	335.6	157.9
Thread and yarn (21)	23	16.7	−43.5
Cotton yarn	23	36.8	8.2
Cotton cloth	37	42.7	18.6
Textile fabrics (22)	105	198.2	149.3
Hosiery (23)	126	157.3	104.1
Clothing (24)	225	392.4	382.4
Shoes (26)	60	61.6	36.6
Sawn wood (28)	73	111.9	57.1
Wood pulp (31)	12	−38.3	*
Paper and paper products (32)	94	156.3	*
Printed matter (33)	28	1.6	−21.1
Leather (35)	45	97.0	69.1
Leather goods (except shoes) (36)	60	67.3	58.1
Rubber goods (37)	153	297.9	239.0
Plastic articles (38)	236	458.7	386.8
Synthetic materials (39)	224	469.1	*
Other chemical materials (40)	65	83.8	*
Chemical products (41)	65	91.4	32.7
Petroleum products (44)	47	62.9	*
Nonmetallic mineral products (45)	91	118.2	79.7
Glass and glass products (46)	164	212.0	187.1
Ingots and other primary forms of steel (49)	24	60.6	*
Rolling mill products (50)	55	165.1	102.9
Other steel products (51)	69	177.1	81.1
Nonferrous metals (54)	90	273.7	*
Metal manufactures (56)	95	166.8	113.1
Nonelectrical machinery (58)	89	125.2	90.6
Electrical machinery (59)	66	83.4	48.8
Automobiles (62)	249	514.1	*
Bicycles and motorcycles (64)	221	460.1	387.9
Precision instruments (66)	110	145.4	110.0
Other industries (67)	65	67.8	16.1

Sources: Computed from free trade input-output coefficients and price and tariff data for Pakistan described in Appendix E. See also Table 3.4.

* No firms without import privileges.

** No privileged firms.

The estimates shown in Table 10.11 indicate that the differential advantage given to the privileged, large-scale producers is quite high. Exceptions are processed food products, clothing, leather goods other than shoes, and glass and glass products, where differences are rather small. In turn, the differential advantages of privileged over nonprivileged firms are most pronounced in the case of sugar, thread and yarn, tobacco, sawn wood, chemical products, steel products, electrical machinery, and the miscellaneous groups of "other industries." Nonprivileged producers of sugar and thread and yarn actually receive negative protection.

At the same time, the range of effective rates of protection to privileged producers is much narrower if calculated from free trade rather than from domestic input-output coefficients. This is hardly surprising since, as we have seen, the indirect calculation of free trade value added can give rise to very small and even negative figures, while value added is by definition positive in the free trade input-output table.

The use of free trade coefficients also lowers the rate of effective protection to Pakistan's most important manufacturing industry—cotton textiles. Even this is not decisive, however, since the free trade input-output table does not separate cotton from other textiles. Moreover, the effective rates of protection calculated from the free trade input-output table are reduced by the greater importance of intra-sectoral deliveries of semi-finished products which have been deflated by the export bonus rate. Still, privileged firms producing cotton fabrics enjoy a 43 percent effective rate of subsidy according to the results of Table 10.11.

In some of the other industries which grew rapidly in the late fifties and early sixties—particularly metal-working—one finds very high effective rates of protection to firms that had import privileges. Naqvi's work, and some additional analysis of his data by Lewis,[26] suggest that a large part of the growth of output has come in firms that received import privileges, since import licensing to these industries was increasing at a rapid rate.

Effective Rates of Protection for Major Industry Groups

We have considered so far the results obtained by the use of domestic and free trade input-output coefficients for individual industries in Pakistan. Since the industry breakdown of the two sets of coefficients differs greatly, it is of interest to compare nominal and effective rates of protection for major industry groups. This is done in Table 10.12 where the results for privileged firms are shown under both alternatives, while those for nonprivileged firms are given under free trade coefficients only.

---

[26] Naqvi, "The Allocative Biases of Pakistan's Commercial Policy," and Lewis, *Economic Policy and Industrial Growth in Pakistan*, ch. 6.

TABLE 10.12: Nominal and Effective Protection for Major Product Categories in Pakistan, 1963/64

Industry group	Estimates based on domestic coefficients						Estimates based on free trade coefficients		
	Nominal tariff protection	Nominal implicit protection	Effective tariff protection		Effective implicit protection		Nominal implicit protection	Effective implicit protection[a]	
			Balassa	Corden	Balassa	Corden		Privileged firms	Nonprivileged firms
I Agriculture, forestry, and fishing	na	na	na	na	na	na	8	na	-19
II Processed food	42	133	54	26	-164	-307	154	379	196
III Beverages and tobacco	na	na	na	na	na	na	130	195	149
IV Mining and energy	na	na	na	na	na	na	35	29	28
V Construction materials	39	54	39	32	72	51	91	118	80
VI-A Intermediate products I	6	44	-19	-14	139	69	71	147	42
VI-B Intermediate products II	87	55	547	179	846	188	91	173	121
VI Intermediate products I and II	67	53	153	84	427	148	77	155	87
VII Nondurable consumer goods	91	100	38	28	77	65	112	156	123
VIII Consumer durables	78	234	-282	150	-164	-2,100	247	510	388
IX Machinery	24	86	25	20	272	139	80	110	75
X Transport equipment	b	b	b	b	b	b	b	b	b
I-X All industries	na	na	na	na	na	na	63	112	48
I+IV Primary production	na	na	na	na	na	na	18	10	-15
II, III,									
V-X Manufacturing	59	85	120	65	-2,584	271	97	188	109
VI-X Manufacturing less food, beverages, tobacco, and construction materials	66	70	144	78	471	154	88	164	92

Sources: Table 10.10 and text.
[a] Calculated by using the Corden formula.
[b] Included with consumer durables.

Averages of nominal implicit protection (the percentage excess of domestic over world market prices) for manufacturing industries are 85 percent for estimates obtained by the use of domestic coefficients and 97 percent for estimates using the free trade coefficients. The differences are greater for intermediate products at lower, as well as at higher, levels of fabrication, and also for consumer nondurables. In these three groups, the larger weight in world trade than in domestic supply of some items with high nominal implicit protection (synthetics in the first-mentioned group, plastics and wool textiles in the second, and clothing in the third) is responsible for the observed differences.

Effective rates show larger discrepancies since there is more escalation in the results derived by domestic coefficients than in those derived by free trade coefficients. Averages of effective rates for manufacturing are 271 percent (3.2 times the average nominal rate) if domestic coefficients are used, and 188 percent (2.0 of the nominal rate) if free trade coefficients are used. These are estimates for privileged firms; the average of effective rates for nonprivileged firms, calculated by the use of free trade coefficients, is 109 percent (1.1 times the average nominal rate). Thus, there is little escalation in the protective structure for nonprivileged enterprises.

The ranking of major industry groups by effective rates of protection is much the same, irrespective of whether estimates are made by the use of domestic or free trade coefficients. Effective rates are the highest for processed food (largely because of the high protection of sugar and edible oils) and for consumer durables (because of motor vehicles). In both industry groups, value added at world market prices is negative if domestic coefficients are used in the calculations, while rates of protection exceed 300 percent with free trade coefficients. Intermediate products at higher levels of fabrication as well as beverages and tobacco come in the second category, with effective rates of protection approaching 200 percent under both alternatives.

The third group, with effective rates not exceeding 160 percent, includes nondurable consumer goods, machinery, intermediate products at lower levels of fabrication, and construction materials. However, except for machinery, effective protection is considerably higher if it is calculated by free trade rather than by domestic coefficients. For nondurable consumer goods, this discrepancy is explained by the relatively small weight of the highly protected clothing industry in the domestic input-output table; for intermediate products at lower levels of fabrication, this is due to the large share of export products in the domestic table. For construction materials, however, the reasons for the differences could not be pinpointed.

The data obtained by the use of free trade coefficients also indicate that agriculture is at a considerable disadvantage relative to manufacturing activities. This is, of course, a direct result of the policies which turned the terms of trade against agriculture in the postwar period. If calculations were made for the mid-fifties, the extent of discrimination against agriculture and in favor of manufacturing would have been even greater. Calculations based on domestic coefficients, however, do not cover the agricultural sector because of a lack of data on its input-output structure. Still, some general observations can be made.

Intermediate purchases of the Pakistani agricultural sector from the manufacturing sector are very small relative to its gross output and value added, although structural interdependence is increasing with modernization.[27] A second characteristic is the variation in the incentives provided by government policies to the production of individual crops. A particularly vivid example appears in West Pakistan, where cotton (an export crop, subject to export duties) competes for land and water resources with sugar cane (which is supplied to the import-substituting sugar refining industry).[28] It is quite clear that, to utilize resources more efficiently, Pakistan should be substituting cotton for sugar cane. The policies work in the opposite direction, however. Thus, raw sugar prices are above world market prices at the official exchange rate, while cotton prices are below f.o.b. export prices at the same exchange rate. There are similar differences for other crops.

There are variations in input prices as well. Whereas the government provides pesticides at a 100 percent subsidy, the domestic price of fertilizer is above the world market price. And although rebates are available to farmers for excise taxes paid on diesel fuel used in farm machinery, diesel fuel prices exceed import prices by more than the excise tax. Furthermore, the prices of metal products and machinery are especially high because of the scarcity margin received by their producers. By contrast, irrigation water is provided in most cases below its opportunity cost to the economy, and is rationed by traditional arrangements.

On balance, the intermediate inputs and capital goods used in agriculture, weighted by estimated purchases of manufactures by this sector, are almost twice world market prices, since subsidized inputs are small, relative to non-subsidized inputs. One should remember, however, that the principal inputs into the agricultural sector are from other parts of this sector, where the prices are not much above world market prices at the official exchange rate.

Earlier studies[29] suggest that in 1963/64 the prices received by farmers in Pakistan (weighted by sales of agricultural goods) were approximately 5–10

---

[27] Some aspects of interdependence are discussed by Falcon, "Agricultural and Industrial Interrelationships in West Pakistan."

[28] This competition and the uneconomic effects of the pricing policies are discussed by Ghulam Mohammad, "Some Physical and Economic Determinants of Cotton Production in West Pakistan," *Pakistan Development Review*, Winter 1963, pp. 491–526.

[29] See Lewis, "Effects of Trade Policy on Domestic Relative Prices: Pakistan, 1951–64."

percent above world market prices at the official exchange rate. It appears then that the effective rate of protection to the agricultural sector as a whole may be zero as an upper limit, and it is certainly negative for various crops. Moreover, as will be shown below, the agricultural sector shows a substantial negative rate of effective protection if the evaluation is made at a more realistic exchange rate than the present official rate.

The major conclusions derived from the results of our calculations in Pakistan seem to be the following.

1. In the presence of import licensing or quantitative restrictions, tariffs are a poor guide to the relative price structure.

2. The ranking of industry by nominal implicit protection, defined as the percentage difference between domestic and world market prices, differs considerably from ranking by effective rates of protection.

3. The effective rate of protection to export industries in the manufacturing sector is generally quite high in Pakistan.

4. The distortions in domestic relative prices introduced by multiple exchange rate systems and quantitative import restrictions can become so severe as to make processes of production privately profitable in the country when they would not be adopted by a firm facing world market prices.

5. There is a considerable degree of discrimination in favor of manufactured goods and against agriculture.

6. Manufacturing, food processing and consumer durables are the most highly protected, followed by intermediate products at higher levels of fabrication and beverages and tobacco. The ranking among the remaining industry groups is dependent on the choice of the input coefficients.

Overvaluation and Net Effective Protection

The official exchange rate in Pakistan (4.76 rupees per U.S. dollar) is supplemented by import and export duties, import quotas, and the Export Bonus Scheme. The exchange rates implied by comparisons of domestic and world market prices generally range from Rs 4.00 to Rs 20.00 per dollar. Under such conditions, the measurement of the effective rate of protection or subsidy at the official exchange rate badly misstates the *level* of protection received by various industries. If the official price of foreign exchange were raised and the export taxes, export subsidies, and import taxes were changed at the same time in such a way as to leave domestic relative prices unchanged, the measured effective rates of protection would decline even though no real reallocations in the economy occurred. To evaluate the effects of the system of protection in imports and exports, it is necessary, therefore, to adjust the measured rates of effective protection for overvaluation as compared with the free trade situation. The formula for the adjustment is described in Appendix A and it is discussed elsewhere by the present authors.[30]

Estimates of the appropriate change in the price of foreign exchange should be made by taking into account existing tariffs and export subsidies, as well as the relevant elasticities of world and domestic supply and demand for tradable goods. Among Pakistan's major exports, estimates on world demand are available for raw jute; for all primary exports, somewhat arbitrarily we have used elasticities ranging from 1.0 to 4.0. The elasticities are higher for manufactured exports so that their average may reach 5.

The elasticity of supply of exports has been assumed to vary between 0.4 and 1.0 for agricultural commodities and much higher for manufactured goods; we have calculated with average values of 2.0 to 4.0. Finally, a range of 1.0 to 3.0 has been assumed for the elasticity of domestic demand for imports, and in conformity with the other country studies, the elasticity of supply of imports has been taken to be infinite.

Since, in the presence of quantitative restrictions, tariffs do not reflect the extent of nominal protection of imports, we have used the average difference between the domestic and world market prices of imports which has been estimated at 80 percent. Estimates of the extent of the average export subsidy have been made by taking account of export subsidies to manufactured goods and export taxes on agricultural products. We have further included the export of invisibles, the most important item of which is the repatriation of earnings of Pakistanis living abroad. These transfers were placed on the eligible list for the Export Bonus Scheme during the Second Plan Period, and they contributed substantially to the improved earnings of foreign exchange during the Plan. The estimate of total net subsidies divided by total export and invisible earnings for 1963/64 yields an average net subsidy of 26 percent.

Under these assumptions the extent of overvaluation as compared to the free trade situation has been estimated to be in the 40–60 percent range.[31] In Table 10.13 we compare the rate of effective implicit protection calculated at the official exchange rate and at a rate 50 percent higher. In the table we also show the exchange rate at which each industry would be able to compete on the world market (i.e., the exchange rate that would provide the same protection actually applied).

---

[30] S. R. Lewis, Jr., and S. E. Guisinger, "Measuring Protection in a Developing Country: The Case of Pakistan," *Journal of Political Economy*, November/December 1968, pp. 1170–98, especially Appendix on Method.

[31] The extent of overvaluation would be higher if we excluded raw jute where Pakistan has a near-monopoly position. The average net subsidy on exports other than jute comes to 39 percent, thereby raising the extent of overvaluation.

The effect of evaluating protection at a higher price of foreign exchange is
to lower the rate of protection on each industry. The protection to the median
industry (paper, and paints and varnishes) falls from 133 percent when valued
at the official exchange rate to 55 percent when valued at the higher price of

TABLE 10.13: Effective Rate of Implicit Protection Evaluated at Different Exchange
Rates, 1963/64[a]

Industry	Effective protection		Exchange rate at which industry would be fully competitive (Rupees per U.S. dollar)
	At official exchange rate	When foreign exchange is 50% more expensive	
	(Percent)		
Consumer and related goods			
Sugar	−329	−253	*
Edible oils	−189	−159	*
Tea	−6	−37	4.5
Cotton textiles	213	109	14.9
Silk and silk textiles	9,900	6,567	476.0
Footwear	59	6	7.6
Wearing apparel	1,900	1,233	95.2
Printing and publishing	16	−23	5.5
Soaps	223	115	15.4
Matches	9	−27	5.2
Plastic goods	335	190	20.7
Sports goods	75	17	8.3
Pens and pencils	186	91	13.6
Electrical appliances	72	15	8.2
Motor vehicles	−2,100	−1,433	*
Average	883	555	46.8
Intermediate goods			
Jute textiles	183	89	13.5
Thread and threadball	84	21	8.7
Saw milling	92	28	9.1
Tanning	96	31	9.3
Rubber products	525	317	29.8
Fertilizer	186	91	13.6
Paints and varnishes	133	55	11.1
Chemicals	113	42	10.1
Petroleum products	−5	−37	4.5
Paper products	144	63	11.6
Average	88	25	9.0
Investment and related goods			
Nonmetallic mineral products	72	15	8.2
Cement	49	−1	7.1
Basic metals	194	96	14.0
Metal products	270	147	17.6
Nonelectrical machinery	170	80	12.9
Sewing machinery	82	21	8.7
Electrical machinery and equipment	72	15	8.2
Average	155	70	12.1

Sources: Table 10.10 and text.

[a] Calculations have been made by the use of the Corden formula. In cases where an asterisk
appears in the third column, the value of inputs exceeds that of output at world market prices;
no exchange rate would equalize value added at domestic and world market prices.

foreign exchange. There is no change in the ranking of industries, since Corden's treatment of nontraded inputs makes rankings insensitive to the change in the value of the exchange rate. Nor is the dispersion of effective rates affected by the adjustment.

There are now ten industries with rates of protection in excess of 100 percent, including three with negative value added at world market prices. All of these industries have been discussed earlier and need no further consideration. It should be emphasized, however, that the high net effective rates of protection of such important industries as cotton and jute textiles (109 and 89 percent, respectively) indicate serious possibilities of inefficiencies although some of the protection certainly went into excess profits. In turn, five industries are shown to be discriminated against in absolute terms; i.e., they have negative protection, if the price of foreign exchange is 50 percent higher than the official exchange rate.

Table 10.14 shows net effective rates of protection for major industry groups. The data indicate the existence of considerable discrimination against agriculture; it is also apparent that the average net effective protection of manufacturing is about 100 percent, irrespective of whether domestic or free trade coefficients are used in the calculations. Needless to say, the ranking of industry groups by effective protection is not affected by the adjustment.

An alternative way of evaluating the system of protection in Pakistan is to calculate the exchange rate at which the industry would receive no protection or subsidy. If we use Corden's approach—i.e., if nontraded inputs are included in value added—this rate can be derived by adding one to the effective rates of protection and multiplying the results by the official exchange rate (4.76 rupees to the U.S. dollar).[32]

Calculating the exchange rate necessary to make an industry competitive permits us to ask whether it is likely that the price of foreign exchange will be raised to this height. If not, domestic industry will be uneconomical provided the rate of effective protection correctly expresses the excess of domestic over foreign costs. In intuitive terms, this means that the direct domestic cost of saving or earning foreign exchange is too high to be justified at a reasonable rate of exchange.

From Table 10.13, we find that twenty of the thirty-two industries included in our study would not be fully competitive if the price of foreign exchange were twice its official value; twelve industries would not be competitive even if foreign exchange were valued at three times the official rate; and eight industries would still not be competitive even if the value of foreign exchange were

---

[32] If the rate of exchange at which the industry would become competitive on the world market is R_c, the official exchange rate R, and the effective rate of protection Z, the relevant formula is

$$R_c = (1 + Z)R$$

TABLE 10.14: Net Nominal and Effective Protection for Major Product Categories in Pakistan, 1963/64

(Percent)

Industry group	Estimates based on domestic coefficients				Estimates based on free trade coefficients		
						Effective implicit protection	
	Nominal tariff protection	Nominal implicit protection	Effective tariff protection[a]	Effective implicit protection[a]	Nominal implicit protection	Privileged firms[a]	Non-privileged firms[a]
I Agriculture, forestry, and fishing	na	na	na	na	−28	na	−46
II Processed food	−5	55	−16	−238	69	219	97
III Beverages and tobacco	na	na	na	na	53	97	66
IV Mining and energy	na	na	na	na	−10	−14	−15
V Construction materials	−7	3	−12	1	27	45	20
VI-A Intermediate products I	−29	−4	−43	13	14	65	−5
VI-B Intermediate products II	25	3	86	92	27	82	47
VI Intermediate products I and II	11	2	23	65	18	70	25
VII Nondurable consumer goods	27	33	−15	10	41	71	49
VIII Consumer durables	19	123	67	−1,433	131	307	225
IX Machinery	−17	24	−20	59	20	40	17
X Transport equipment	b	b	b	b	b	b	b
I-X All industries	na	na	na	na	9	41	−1
I+IV Primary production	na	na	na	na	−21	−27	−43
II, III, V-X Manufacturing	6	23	10	147	31	92	39
VI-X Manufacturing less food, beverages, tobacco, and construction materials	11	13	19	69	25	76	28

Sources: Table 10.12 and text.

[a] Effective rates of protection have been estimated by using the Corden formula; both nominal and effective rates have been adjusted for over-valuation as compared to the hypothetical free trade situation.

[b] Included with consumer durables.

four times the official price. There are finally three industries—those with negative value added at world market prices—which would not be competitive at any price of foreign exchange.

Earlier in this chapter we urged caution in interpreting the findings. We urge similar caution here, for two reasons. First, since we have used price data, not cost of production, we have necessarily included in domestic value added all windfall profits. To the extent that there is profit in excess of the opportunity cost of capital, measured protection will then overstate excess costs, and the exchange rate at which the industry would be competitive in terms of *costs* is below the rate calculated from price comparisons. Second, if a different, more neutral, set of trade policies were adopted as the economy moved toward a more realistic exchange rate, there could be a series of substitutions at the firm level, and the use of factors and material inputs would change, affecting in turn relative costs.

Evaluation and Policy Recommendations

This study has concentrated primarily on the Pakistani manufacturing sector which is heavily subsidized relative to the agricultural sector. In 1963/64 the agricultural sector paid approximately 8.08 rupees when it purchased one dollar's worth of manufactured goods, while it received about 5.15 rupees for its sales of one dollar's worth of agricultural products. This price differential is equivalent to paying 57 percent more, or receiving 36 percent less in trading domestically than agriculture could have paid or received if it could have traded in free international markets.

On a value added basis, agricultural products had a small negative protection at the official exchange rate, so that the extent of discrimination against agriculture surpasses 50 percent if a more realistic exchange rate is used in the comparisons. This is the counterpoint to the high levels of effective protection found in most manufacturing industries, even after an adjustment has been made for the overvaluation of the rupee. It should be added that since agricultural products are the principal wage goods for industrial labor, the low prices of agricultural goods relative to manufactures also kept pressure off wages, and increased the profitability of domestic manufacturing activity in general. If this factor could be adequately taken care of, the measured degree of "protection" afforded investors in most lines of manufacturing in Pakistan would be even larger than calculated here.

Our major conclusions concerning the protective system in Pakistani manufacturing are based on an appraisal of the licensing system, export bonuses, and other factors which kept tariffs from being the sole, or even the principal, determinant of the difference between domestic and world market prices. Introducing direct price comparisons for inputs and for output increased the average levels of protection in most cases, although in industries where the process of import substitution had been completed and exports had begun under the Export Bonus Scheme, domestic prices fell below the tariff-inclusive c.i.f. import price estimated at the official exchange rate.

Nevertheless, even allowing for the overvaluation of the exchange rate as compared to the free trade situation, the average net effective protection of manufacturing industries was about 100 percent. There are three industries where value added at world market prices is negative, six industries with net effective protection exceeding 100 percent, seventeen industries with net effective protection between zero and 100 percent, and five industries with negative net effective protection.

In the face of the evidence on the inefficiency of Pakistan's manufacturing industry suggested by the data on effective protection, one finds that large-scale manufacturing industry grew at approximately 15 percent per year for almost twenty years. This performance requires explanation since, if the inefficiencies suggested by our analysis were present, one would expect the growth potential in protected industries to have run out after a shorter period of time.

The reasons for the continued growth of the manufacturing sector behind high protective walls are complex, and are developed at some length elsewhere.[33] It is important to recall that Pakistan began its history in 1947 with virtually no modern manufacturing capacity. Analysis of the "sources" of manufacturing growth in Pakistan has shown that in the early 1950s almost all the growth in output or value added was "due to" import subsitution, that in the First Plan (1955–60) the growth of domestic demand and exports began to play an important role, and that during the Second Plan (1960–65) import substitution was a very unimportant source of growth, and the growth of domestic demand absorbed virtually all of increased manufacturing output.[34]

The rate of industrial growth slowed down in the second half of the fifties. The diagnosis of the deceleration was spelled out in an article by John Power who suggested that the bias of the protective system in favor of the finishing stages of fabrication and against earlier stages and exports is responsible for these results.[35] The growth rate of manufacturing accelerated again in the early sixties for three main reasons: first, the domestic market for manufactured goods expanded rapidly, as the rate of investment rose from less than 10 to more than 15 percent of GNP, and as the agricultural growth rate accelerated and rural living standards began to rise. Second, some of the established

---

[33] See Lewis, *Economic Policy and Industrial Growth in Pakistan*, ch. 6.

[34] Import substitution is defined here as increase in the share of domestic production in total supply.

[35] See J. H. Power, "Industrialization in Pakistan: A Case of Frustrated Take-Off?" *Pakistan Development Review*, Summer 1963, pp. 191–207.

industries were given export subsidies, and industries which sold in world markets were not limited in size as were those which catered only to protected domestic markets. Third, inadequate supplies of capital equipment and raw materials did not constitute a problem because of a sharp increase in the inflow of foreign aid and an acceleration in export earnings due in part to the Export Bonus Scheme.

Thus, one might argue that the reasons Pakistan had not run into serious trouble from her protectionist policies by the mid-sixties were (a) the potential for import substitution due to rising incomes,[36] (b) the fact that subsidies were shifted from import substitutes to exports during the sixties, and (c) an accelerated inflow of foreign aid just at the time when the difficulties with import substitution began to appear.

A further consideration is that while inefficiencies have been prevalent in Pakistani manufacturing, the system of protection has also led to high profit rates in protected industries. Nonetheless, it should not be assumed that protection has primarily resulted in transfer payments to owners of capital stock in the form of excess profits, and that little real cost has been involved. Nurul Islam has recently completed an analysis of the Tariff Commission investigations and reports from 1951 to 1966, which supports the conclusion that the high degree of protection has permitted Pakistan's manufacturing industries to operate despite a substantial cost disadvantage.[37] Having compared his results with Pal's data on relative prices utilized in the present investigation, Islam concluded: "In spite of the differences in methods and sources of data as well as in the commodity composition of the two samples, the overall comparability of the two sets of cost ratios adds to the degree of confidence in the general level of cost disability of the different manufacturing industries in Pakistan as evidenced from the present study."[38]

Although he has not calculated effective rates of protection, it is encouraging that Nurul Islam found similar levels of nominal protection for goods included in both Pal's data and the Tariff Commission reports. "It appears . . . that the unweighted simple average cost ratios for the selected items which are comparable as between the two studies, are about the same, i.e. 2.12 and 2.05 (times the c.i.f. price) respectively."[39] Since the principal possibility for error in our study came in the estimation of price differentials for the major indus-

---

[36] Lewis, *Economic Policy and Industrial Growth in Pakistan*, ch. 7, develops this argument more completely.

[37] Islam, "Comparative Costs, Factor Proportions, and Industrial Efficiency in Pakistan." See also his *Tariff Protection, Comparative Costs and Industrialization in Pakistan*, Research Report No. 57 (Karachi: Pakistan Institute of Development Economics, 1967).

[38] "Comparative Costs, Factor Proportions, and Industrial Efficiency in Pakistan," p. 218.

[39] *Ibid.*, p. 243.

trial goods, the reasonable comparability of the results of the two studies bear out our conclusions concerning effective rates of protection.

It should be added that since during the fifties import restrictions made it profitable to produce virtually any manufactured product domestically, the choice among industries has been dictated partly by the fact that the industries in which real cost advantages were greatest (cost disadvantages the smallest) showed the greatest profit opportunities. As production began in many industries, and the system of protection became more differentiated, however, the distortions in the price system have increased, and the potential for errors in investment decisions has also risen.[40] Although the introduction of the Export Bonus Scheme in 1959 represented a change in the right direction, the failure to apply the scheme to all exports creates inefficiencies and/or provides excess profits.

Still, an important advantage Pakistan enjoys is the awareness of the adverse effects the distortion in the price system has had, and can continue to have, on the development process. The Third Plan noted that

> ... high rates of growth in a highly protected market have tended to mask the basic problems of the relative inefficiency of the industrial sector, lack of appropriate technology and technical skills and absence of any definite relationship between industrial programming and market demand. The cost of many industrial products has not come down even after a decade of production experience. . . . Even after fifteen years of high industrial growth rates, the country cannot claim to have built up a sufficient reservoir of technical skills on which it can draw for the next phase of more sophisticated industrial development.[41]

The Third Plan also argued for replacing quantitative restrictions and licensing by tariffs. Despite the steps that have been taken to liberalize the system of protection, however, a considerable task remains before the economy will be freed of distortions in the price system and in resource allocation. These may be extremely harmful to continued growth of real income and to the best use of capital and foreign exchange.

---

[40] *Ibid.* Other things being equal, industries based on domestic raw materials would tend to be profitable relative to industries based on imported raw materials.

[41] Planning Commission, Government of Pakistan, *Third Five-Year Plan, 1965–70*, Karachi, 1965, p. 116.

CHAPTER 11

THE STRUCTURE OF PROTECTION IN THE PHILIPPINES

John H. Power
with the assistance of Cristina Crisostomo and Eloisa Litonjua

Economic Growth and International Trade

Structural Change since the Turn of the Century

The Republic of the Philippines extends over some seven thousand islands in Southeast Asia. Its geographical area is comparable in size to that of Italy and it had a population of 35 million in 1967. Its fertile land permits the cultivation of a variety of tropical products, but much of the country's territory consists of mountains and rain forests which are less amenable to cultivation. Manufacturing activities were largely limited to the simple processing of primary products when U.S.-Philippine free trade arrangements were in force; they have become widely diversified over the last decade and a half.

During the first two-thirds of the century, the gross domestic product of the Philippines appears to have grown at an annual average rate of about 3.5 percent, while per capita incomes rose at a rate of 1 percent a year. Separating agricultural and nonagricultural activities, we find that in per capita terms the former rose scarcely at all, while the latter increased at an average annual rate of 1.6 percent. Among nonagricultural activities, manufacturing output per head grew as much as 2.7 percent a year.

John H. Power is Visiting Professor of Economics at the University of the Philippines.

The estimates shown in Table 11.1 are subject to considerable error, particularly in earlier years, but are nevertheless indicative of general trends. For individual subperiods, the data reveal an uneven time pattern of growth. During the first sixteen years and the last eighteen, both total and per capita incomes grew rapidly; during the intervening years, total output stagnated and per capita output declined.

Agriculture led the economy in the earlier period of rapid growth when exports expanded in response to the trade preferences enjoyed in the U.S. market. By contrast, in the 1950s, the leading sector was manufacturing which exploited the opportunities due to the imposition of import controls. But the growth of manufacturing slowed down during the sixties, since the possibilities for easy import substitution had become by and large exhausted.

Hooley has attempted to produce estimates of the sources of long-term growth for both agriculture and manufacturing. If his results are indicative of actual productivity trends, the picture is a depressing one. In agriculture, labor productivity increased only 17 percent between 1902 and 1961, and the productivity of all inputs combined (land, labor, machinery, and animals) declined 15 percent. In the same period, labor productivity in manufacturing rose by about one-half but this required a more than doubling of the capital-labor ratio, so that total input productivity declined. Part of this unimpressive performance can be explained by the depression of the 1930s and World War II. But even in the two periods of more rapid growth, at the beginning and at the end of the period under consideration, productivity gains were rather small.[1]

TABLE 11.1: Growth Rates in the Philippines, 1902–67

(*Percent*)

Category	1902–18	1918–38	1938–48	1948–61	1961–67	1902–67
Gross domestic product						
Total	4.4	1.9	−0.5	6.9	5.1	3.4
Agriculture	5.0	0.5	0.0	3.8	4.8	2.6
Nonagriculture	3.6	3.4	−1.0	9.1	5.3	4.0
Manufacturing	4.1	4.7	−3.8	12.0	4.7	5.1
Population	1.9	2.2	1.9	3.1	3.4	2.3
Per capita GDP						
Total	2.7	−0.3	−2.4	3.5	1.6	1.0
Agriculture	3.0	−1.7	−1.9	0.7	1.4	0.2
Nonagriculture	1.7	1.2	−2.8	5.8	1.8	1.6
Manufacturing	2.2	2.4	−5.6	8.6	1.3	2.7

Sources: For 1902–61, Richard W. Hooley, "Long-Term Economic Growth in the Philippines, 1902–1961," *Proceedings of the Conference on Growth of Output in the Philippines,* Los Baños, December 9–10, 1966. For 1961–66, *National Economic Council,* revised national income accounts.

---

[1] Richard W. Hooley, "Long-Term Economic Growth in the Philippines, 1902–1961," *Proceedings of the Conference on Growth of Output in the Philippines*, Los Baños, December 9–10, 1966, pp. 4–25.

Focusing our attention on the postwar period, we find that economic growth was especially rapid during the first half of the fifties when manufacturing output grew at an average annual rate of 12.8 percent, agriculture at 7.3 percent, and the gross domestic product at 8.6 percent. Growth slowed down in the following decade, with the rate of increase of GDP averaging 5 percent a year (see Table 2.2). The share of investment in the gross national product increased, however; this implies either a rise in the marginal capital-output ratio or growing excess capacity. The higher share of investment was made possible by a higher saving ratio as well as by an increase in the inflow of foreign capital.

While agriculture's growth was sluggish in the second half of the fifties, after 1960 the slowdown was concentrated in manufacturing. Correspondingly, after a rapid increase during the fifties, the share of manufacturing in national income declined. The contribution of manufacturing to the net national product was 10.2 percent in 1950, 17.9 percent in 1960, and 17.2 percent in 1967. Meanwhile, agriculture's share fell from 39.8 percent in 1950 to 31.0 percent in 1967. Similar trends are shown if we consider the relative contributions of agriculture and manufacturing to commodity production, since the share of service industries changed little during this period (see Table 2.3).

The transformation of the structure of Philippine manufacturing is also of interest. Before World War II much of the gains in manufacturing were made in food processing, particularly sugar, yet in the postwar period growth occurred across a broad front of import substitutes. During this period, a variety of fabricating, assembling, and processing industries gained in importance at the expense of food, beverages, and tobacco. This can be seen in Table 11.2 which shows long-run changes in percentage shares for eighteen manufacturing subsectors.

Composition of Exports and Imports

This transformation of the structure of manufacturing was accompanied by substantial shifts in the composition of Philippine imports of manufactured goods. Imports of consumer goods declined substantially during the period of import controls, and increases in absolute terms after decontrol in the early sixties were not large enough to prevent a continuing decrease in their relative share. By 1965, consumer goods accounted for only 7 percent of imports of manufactures as against 27 percent in 1950. During the same period, the share of capital goods rose from 19 to 45 percent, while that of intermediate goods and inputs into construction hardly changed (Table 11.3). Thus the trend of imports shows the usual pattern in the process of import substitution, with capital goods increasingly replacing consumer goods in the import bill. Imports, in fact, accounted for less than 5 percent of total supply (production plus imports) of manufactured consumer goods in 1965.

TABLE 11.2: Distribution of Value Added in Philippine Manufacturing by Industry Groups, 1902–67

(Percent)

Industry	1902	1918	1938	1948	1956	1967
20 Food manufacturing	25.7	50.9	52.1	30.8	27.0	25.8
21 Beverages	12.7	5.3	4.7	25.1	10.7	8.7
22 Tobacco products	24.2	9.6	7.2	4.7	6.1	4.6
23 Textile products	0.5	0.5	0.8	2.6	3.7	4.5
24 Footwear and wearing apparel	5.9	3.5	7.8	6.6	5.1	7.0
25 Wood and cork products	8.0	5.4	5.3	9.7	5.0	4.6
26 Furniture and fixtures	2.3	1.3	1.9	1.8	1.3	1.6
27 Paper and paper products	0.0	0.0	0.0	0.0	1.7	2.2
28 Printing and printed products	4.9	1.7	3.6	3.7	3.1	3.4
29 Leather products	0.7	0.3	0.1	0.0	0.2	0.3
30 Rubber products	0.0	0.0	0.0	0.6	0.9	3.3
31 Chemicals and chemical products	1.9	10.9	6.9	2.9	9.9	10.1
32 Products of coal and petroleum	a	a	b	b	b	b
33 Nonmetallic mineral products	3.9	0.7	3.3	2.1	4.7	4.3
34 & 35 Basic metal and metallic products	0.9	0.8	0.7	1.9	4.7	6.9
36 & 37 Machinery	3.6	0.8	0.2	0.5	2.1	4.8
38 Transportation equipment	a	1.3	0.4	1.0	2.2	3.0
39 Miscellaneous manufactures	4.2	5.9	3.9	5.7	11.2	4.9
Unallocated	0.6	1.1	1.1	0.4	0.4	0.0
Total manufacturing	100.0	100.0	100.0	100.0	100.0	100.0

Source: Salvador Umana, "Growth of Output in Philippine Manufacturing: 1902–1960," *Proceedings of the Conference on Growth of Output in the Philippines;* Bureau of the Census and Statistics, *Survey of Manufactures, 1966.*
a Negligible.
b Included in miscellaneous manufactures.

With the increase in the domestic production of intermediate goods, their share of the imports of manufactures, however, did not rise. Increases in the domestic production of these commodities were especially large after decontrol, but the growth of output tended to level off in later years as tariff rates on some of the commodities were lowered. By contrast, the share of capital goods in domestic production remained practically unchanged in the period 1956–65, while their share in the imports of manufactured goods increased (Table 11.3).

Data arranged according to the Standard International Trade Classification show similar trends, with the share of machinery and transport equipment in total imports rising from 13 percent in 1950 to 35 percent in 1967. Despite the fall of consumer goods imports, the share of manufactured goods in total imports also rose. The share of food, beverages, and tobacco, however, declined somewhat and that of industrial materials used in domestic manufacturing activities increased (see Table 2.8).

The Philippines continued to depend on a relatively few traditional exports of agricultural and mineral origin that undergo little processing. The ten principal primary exports accounted for over 85 percent of total exports during most of the postwar period but their share fell below 80 percent in 1967. The broad composition of exports remained by and large unchanged, except that

TABLE 11.3: Philippine Manufacturing Production and Imports, 1948–65

	1948		1956		1960		1965	
Product category	Million pesos	Percent	Million pesos	Percent	Million pesos	Percent	Million pesos	Percent
Intermediate goods								
Production	28.3	3	147.3	8	507.6	15	1,318.9	21
Imports	263.8	36	317.5	46	348.4	42	751.2	39
Production/total supply		10		32		59		64
Inputs into construction								
Production	35.9	4	117.4	7	230.7	7	395.8	6
Imports	91.4	13	92.6	13	66.4	8	173.3	9
Production/total supply		28		56		78		70
Capital goods								
Production	10.9	1	61.8	3	89.9	3	218.2	4
Imports	92.8	13	178.3	26	340.1	41	866.7	45
Production/total supply		11		26		21		20
Consumption goods								
Production	612.9	65	953.4	52	1,698.3	52	2,748.7	43
Imports	274.3	38	105.6	15	74.7	9	134.8	7
Production/total supply		69		90		96		95
Export goods								
Production	167.3	18	242.6	13	285.2	9	952.7	15
Rice mill products								
Production	11.1	1	11.1	1	21.5	1	28.1	…
Sugar mill products								
Production	78.4	8	285.1	16	411.1	13	684.1	11
Total								
Production	944.8	100	1,818.7	100	3,244.3	100	6,346.5	100
Imports	722.3	100	694.0	100	829.6	100	1,926.0	100
Production/total supply		57		72		80		77

Sources: Bureau of the Census and Statistics, "Annual Surveys of Manufacturers of Years 1956–1960 and 1962–1963"; *Census of the Philippines: 1948*, Economic Census Report, vol. 4, pp. 618–22; *Economic Census of the Philippines*, vol. 3 (Manufacturing), 1961; Bureau of the Census and Statistics, *Foreign Trade Statistics*.

manufactured goods (chiefly plywood, veneer, and clothing) gained at the expense of primary commodities. In 1967, industrial materials provided approximately 65 percent of Philippine exports; food, beverages, and tobacco, 25 percent; and manufactured goods, 10 percent (see Table 2.7).

Among primary exports, the shares of copra and desiccated coconut fell substantially, and this was only in small part offset by the rise in the shares of coconut oil and copra cake. With the increased use of synthetics in developed countries, the exports of abaca declined in relative, as well as in absolute, terms; there was also a fall in the share of canned pineapple exports. By comparison, the share of tropical logs and copper ores and concentrates in total exports increased to a considerable extent, while fluctuations in sugar prices contributed to the irregular movement of the value of sugar exports (Table 11.4).

Another approach to export performance is to consider changes in Philippine exports in relationship to world demand as in Table 2.6. We then find that the expansion of Philippine exports of tropical logs is explained by the rapid growth of world demand rather than by an increase in its relative share in world exports. The Philippines made gains, however, in world markets for sugar and abaca. In the first case, access to the U.S. market provided advantages to the Philippines; in the second, its share in declining world sales rose from 85 to 95 percent. By contrast, the share of the Philippine copra exports in world trade in oilseeds declined, and this loss was not fully offset by gains made in coconut oil. All in all, the exports of these five commodities, which together accounted for three-fourths of Philippine exports, increased only slightly faster than their world demand.

Table 11.4: Principal Exports of the Philippines, 1950–67

(Percent of total exports)

Commodity	1950	1955	1960	1965	1967
Copra (SITC 221.2)	42.0	29.8	24.8	21.4	15.9
Desiccated coconut (051.7)	7.4	3.2	3.4	2.6	2.1
Coconut oil (422.3)	3.8	4.2	2.8	8.4	6.9
Copra cake and meal (081)	1.2	1.1	0.9	1.5	1.3
Tropical logs (242)	3.3	10.5	16.4	18.5	24.4
Sugar (061)	14.0	26.7	23.9	18.0	15.2
Copper ores and concentrates (283.1)	0.5	1.4	3.3	5.0	6.5
Abaca (265.5)	12.7	7.0	7.5	3.1	1.7
Canned pineapple (053.2)	2.9	1.5	1.3	1.5	1.4
Chromium ores and concentrates (283.9)	0.7	2.6	3.1	1.5	1.1
Plywood and veneer (631.1, 2)	0.0	0.2	1.2	2.3	3.8
Total principal exports					
Including plywood and veneer	88.5	88.2	88.6	83.8	80.3
Excluding plywood and veneer	88.5	88.0	87.4	81.5	76.5
Total exports ($ million)	331	401	560	794	875

Sources: Central Bank, *Statistical Bulletin;* Bureau of the Census and Statistics, *Foreign Trade Statistics.*

In the same period, the commodities included in the minor export category in Table 2.6 increased two-and-a-half times and exceeded the rate of expansion of world trade. The Philippines made considerable gains in several commodities which have come to assume increasing importance in its exports. Among primary products, exports of copper ores and concentrates and of iron ore rose rapidly. Among manufactures, exports of plywood and veneer increased in periods when they received appropriate price incentives, but 1964 levels of exports were not again reached by 1967. Finally, clothing articles accounting for about 4 percent of total exports in 1967 consist principally of embroidery and undergarments produced on a consignment basis.

All in all, the value of exports grew at an average annual rate of 6 percent and that of imports at a rate of 7 percent between 1950 and 1967, while the terms of trade declined on the average of 2 percent a year (see Table 2.5). In the 1950–55 period this decline was due to the fall in export prices after the Korean war; during the sixties it was explained by the rise in import prices.

The System of Protection

Until the 1950s the free entry of U.S. goods greatly limited the protective effects of the tariff which served mainly revenue purposes. The establishment of an independent system of protection began with the import controls imposed in 1949. While the initial impetus was given by a balance-of-payments crisis, import controls soon became a weapon for stimulating industrialization. Protection was accorded to new industries both by restricting foreign exchange allocations for importing the final product and by permitting the importation of the necessary inputs—capital goods, intermediate goods, and raw materials. The result was a rapid burst of manufacturing growth, characterized by emphasis on the finishing stages of processing and assembly. But by the end of the fifties there was little discretion left to exercise in exchange control; the import bill comprised almost exclusively essential investment goods, intermediate products, and raw materials required to sustain the new industries.

Decontrol accompanied by devaluation began early in 1960. By the end of 1960 about half of the foreign exchange transactions had been freed; by March 1961 another 25 percent had been liberalized; and on January 21, 1962 decontrol was virtually completed. Devaluation also proceeded by stages from April 1960 and likewise was virtually completed by January 1962. However, until the end of 1965, exports continued to be penalized by the requirement that 20 percent of foreign exchange proceeds be converted at the old rate.

The various stages in the process of devaluation and the complexity of the rate structure during this process are shown in Table 11.5. For a while a system of multiple exchange rates prevailed, with the export rate gradually increasing and a rising proportion of imports paying the penalty of the higher

TABLE 11.5: Philippine Exchange Rate Structure, 1945–66

(Pesos per U.S. $)ᵃ

Category	1945–50	1951–55	1956–58	1959	Apr. 25–Sept. 11, 1960	Sept. 12–Nov. 27, 1960	Nov. 28, 1960–Mar. 1, 1961	Mar. 2–14, 1961	Mar. 15, 1961–Jan. 19, 1962	Jan. 20, 1962–Nov. 5, 1965	Nov. 6, 1965 to date
Basic rate											
Official rate	2.00	2.00	2.00	2.00	2.00	2.00	2.00	2.00	2.00	2.00	3.90
Free market rate	—	—	—	—	3.20	3.00	3.00	3.00	3.00	3.90	—
Effective buying rate	2.00	2.00	2.00	2.00	—	—	—	—	—	—	3.90
Export receipts					2.30	2.30	2.50	2.75	2.75	3.51	
U.S. government expenditure					2.30	2.30	2.50	2.75	2.75	3.90	
Invisibles, others					2.30	2.30	2.50	2.75	2.75	3.90	
Foreign investments					2.30	3.00	3.00	3.00	3.00	3.90	
Gold proceeds					3.20	3.00	3.00	3.00	3.00	3.90	
Tourist receipts					2.30	3.00	3.00	3.00	3.00	3.90	
Veterans and Filipino citizens					2.30	2.30	3.00	3.00	3.00	3.90	
Personal expenses of diplomatic personnel	2.00		2.00								
Effective selling rate											
Imports and invisibles at official rate exempted from margin		2.00	2.00	2.00	2.00	2.00	2.00	2.00	2.00	—	—
Imports and invisibles at official rate not exempted from margin		2.358ᶜ	2.00	2.519ᵈ	2.50	2.50	2.40	2.40	2.30	—	—
Other imports and invisibles at the free market rateᵇ					4.00	3.75	3.60	3.60	3.45	3.91	—
Foreign travel					3.49	3.27	3.27	3.27	3.27	3.91	—

Source: Central Bank News Digest, July 26, 1966, p. 11.
Note: Dashes indicate no separate rate.
ᵃ No allowance has been made for the normal spread between buying and selling rates.
ᵇ From April 25, 1960 to January 19, 1962, in the case of the special privilege given to 90 percent of dollar earnings of Philippine suppliers to the U.S. Armed Forces, the effective rate would be the free market rate.
ᶜ From March 29, 1951 to December 31, 1955, a 17 percent tax was imposed.
ᵈ On July 16, 1959, a margin fee of 25 percent was imposed on sales of foreign exchange, was reduced to 20 percent on November 28, 1960 and to 15 percent on March 15, 1961; it remained at 15 percent until its suspension on January 20, 1962.

rate. In the end the price of foreign exchange was 95 percent higher than in 1956–58; this implied a devaluation of the peso of about 49 percent.

While Table 11.5 shows changes in the exchange rates applicable to various transactions, in Table 11.6 average export and import rates are shown, with adjustments made for changes in domestic prices. The resulting series of real exchange rates varies only slightly from the nominal rates during the fifties; but following devaluation and decontrol a considerable gap has emerged between the two. Real exchange rates continued to rise until 1962—although more slowly than nominal rates—and declined afterward. During much of the period, import rates exceeded export rates because of special fees on imports and the delay in completing the devaluation for exports. By 1966, however, the two rates were equalized.

The real rates of exchange have been further adjusted for changes in world market prices. The adjusted real rates for exports show a sharper decline in the early part of the period and a more rapid increase afterward. In addition, the discrepancy between the adjusted real import and export rates is more pronounced and it fails to disappear in 1967. Rather, on a 1950 basis, the adjusted real exchange rate for imports exceeds that for exports by nearly 40 percent.

With the elimination of foreign exchange restrictions, the Tariff Law of 1957 has become the main instrument of protection.[2] This law amended substantially the tariff code of 1909, which had some importance as a revenue measure but, because of the free entry of U.S. goods, had little protective effect until the Revised U.S.-Philippines Trade Agreement (Laurel-Langley) became effective January 1, 1956.

The new law had four avowed aims: (1) protection, (2) aid for economic development, (3) the increase of revenues, and (4) preparation for decontrol. The protective effect of the tariffs was rather high so that the transition to exchange convertibility was less of a problem than might have been expected. Still, after 1960 there were pressures for upward adjustments in rates, and some increases did indeed take place. Using total supply (production plus imports) as weights, we estimated average tariffs on manufactured goods to have risen from 46 percent in 1961 to 51 percent in 1965. The structure of protection has not changed much as compared with the period of exchange controls. Consumer goods are subject to the highest rates, averaging 70 percent in 1965, followed by inputs into construction (55 percent); rates are relatively low on intermediate goods (27 percent) and capital goods (16 percent).[3]

----

[2] The discussion which follows, concerning the Tariff Law of 1957, depends heavily on F. H. Golay, *The Philippines: Public Policy and National Economic Development* (Ithaca: Cornell University Press, 1961), ch. 8.

[3] This comparison of average rates understates the change that occurred between 1961 and 1965, however, since the proportion of duties to which U.S. goods were liable increased from 50 percent to 90 percent over the period. At the same time, the U.S. share of total imports declined from 50 percent to 35 percent.

TABLE 11.6: Nominal and Real Exchange Rates in the Philippines, 1950–66ᵃ

(Pesos per U.S. $)

Year	Wholesale price indexᵇ 1	Export unit value 2	Import unit value 3	Export rate			Import rate		
				Nominal 4	Real 5 (4)/(1)	Adjusted real rate 6 (5) × (2)	Nominal 7	Real 8 (7)/(1)	Adjusted real rate 9 (8) × (3)
1950	100.0	100.0	100.0	2.00	2.00	2.00	2.01	2.01	2.01
1951	110.0	106.7	112.8	2.00	1.82	1.94	2.36	2.15	2.43
1952	103.3	84.0	111.0	2.00	1.94	1.63	2.36	2.28	2.53
1953	101.3	102.6	106.0	2.00	1.97	2.02	2.36	2.33	2.47
1954	96.2	91.1	101.4	2.00	2.08	1.90	2.36	2.45	2.48
1955	94.9	83.5	101.4	2.00	2.11	1.76	2.36	2.49	2.53
1956	96.8	84.7	102.8	2.00	2.07	1.75	2.01	2.08	2.14
1957	100.7	85.9	106.1	2.00	1.99	1.71	2.01	2.00	2.12
1958	102.9	89.3	108.5	2.00	1.94	1.73	2.01	1.95	2.12
1959	101.2	96.8	110.8	2.00	1.98	1.92	2.52	2.49	2.76
1960	106.1	95.3	113.1	2.22	2.09	1.99	na	na	na
1961	111.4	87.7	114.8	2.71	2.43	2.13	na	na	na
1962	113.5	88.7	117.0	3.51	3.09	2.74	3.91	3.44	4.03
1963	123.4	93.4	124.7	3.47	2.81	2.63	3.91	3.17	3.95
1964	132.1	92.6	125.9	3.51	2.66	2.46	3.91	2.96	3.73
1965	135.5	94.2	128.0	3.58	2.64	2.49	3.91	2.89	3.70
1966	143.4	95.1	130.0	3.88	2.71	2.58	3.91	2.73	3.55
1967	151.4	97.2	133.8	3.88	2.58	2.49	3.91	2.58	3.45

Source: Central Bank of the Philippines, Statistical Bulletin.
ᵃ The import rates for 1951–55 and 1959 include special taxes and margin fees Some imports were exempted from these charges. Import rates were so numerous and varied in 1960 and 1961 that no attempt has been made to estimate an average.
ᵇ Locally produced goods for domestic consumption.

An additional element of protection arises from the discrimination against imported goods inherent in the sales tax system. Under this system the same percentage tax is applied to a different basis depending on whether the commodity is imported or domestically produced; in the first case, it applies to the c.i.f. price augmented by the tariff and a percentage markup;[4] in the second, to only the portion of manufacturer's price that represents inputs not already taxed (for the most part, value added plus electricity, fuel, and depreciation). The sales tax rate and the markup are 7 percent and 25 percent, respectively, on most goods; 30 percent and 50 percent on "semi-luxuries" (for example, electric appliances, synthetic textiles, and furniture); and 50–100 percent on "luxuries" (for example, automobiles, jewelry, and perfumes).

Thus, imported goods are often taxed much more heavily than similar domestic goods of an equal value. If, for example, the taxable proportion of the price of a domestic "semi-luxury" product is 40 percent and the duty on the comparable import 50 percent, the sales tax rate on the c.i.f. value of the import will be 67.5 percent, and on the domestic product 12 percent. On some commodities, this discrimination can be more important than the tariff.

Nominal and Effective Protection

Potential and Realized Protection

As noted in Chapter 1, ideally we should estimate the effective rate of protection from direct comparisons of world and domestic prices for homogeneous categories of goods. However, in manufacturing, where protection is the most important, we often observe product differentiation that makes price comparisons difficult. It may then be more practical to deduce the degree of protection of value added from the system of protection itself. This method yields a measure of potential protection and, whenever imports are competing in significant volume with domestic products, also a measure of realized protection.

Where there is import competition, this method offers advantages over the direct comparison of world and domestic prices, since it is not easy to distinguish price differentials due to quality differences from those due to protection. In other words, when foreign and domestic goods are competing, it is a reasonable inference that the system of protection is fully effective in equating for the user the prices of domestic and foreign goods of comparable quality. Now, if the actual price differential is less than the tariff, the implication is that domestic products are of lower quality than imports.

---

[4] There is no markup, however, on goods imported for own use.

A qualification needs to be made for the case of a bias against domestic goods based on consumer ignorance—a bias widely believed to exist in the Philippines. If this were the case, a part of the protection accorded to domestic suppliers may be simply offsetting such a bias. The consequences for welfare in this eventuality are the opposite of those usually attributed to protection, inasmuch as the effect is to bring domestic prices more nearly in line with world market prices for goods of comparable quality. It is impossible, however, to estimate the importance of this factor quantitatively.

The potential rate may have significance in itself, even when the rate of realized protection is judged to be less, insofar as it measures the margin of protection from foreign competition accorded to an industrial activity. While domestic competition may keep prices below the sum of c.i.f. import prices and the tariff, the incentives to reduce costs and prices and to improve quality are likely to be less than without protection.

To indicate the extent of realized protection, it is necessary to make price comparisons whenever imports do not compete with domestic commodities. In this study, we have attempted to make such comparisons whenever imports represented less than 10 percent of domestic production. In most cases, an adjustment has also been made for assumed differences in quality. The resulting rates of realized protection are generally below potential rates, in some cases by a substantial margin.

An industry has been considered an export industry if exports were more than 10 percent of production, although beer—with less than 3 percent of output exported—has also been put in the export category because of its world-competitive price and quality. One important export commodity, sugar, is a special case since its exports go entirely to the highly protected U.S. market under a preferential quota arrangement. For sugar we have compared the f.o.b. export unit value (for the portion exported) and the manufacturers' domestic price (for the portion consumed domestically), with a "world market price" represented by an average of c.i.f. import values of Japan, Hong Kong, and Malaysia.

During most of 1965, the year the calculations refer to, exporters were required to surrender 20 percent of their foreign exchange earnings at the old rate of 2 pesos per U.S. dollar. Hence, there was an implicit tax on exports equal to the difference between the net export rate and the new official rate applicable to imports. The tax on exports, weighted by the proportion of the year for which it prevailed, comes to 8 percent. This has been taken, with a negative sign, as the nominal tariff on export industries for the year 1965.

Potential rates of protection have been estimated for ninety manufacturing industries (at the four-digit level of the International Standard Industrial Classification), for eleven product groups in agriculture, as well as for forestry and logging, fisheries, and metallic and nonmetallic mining. The input-output data for manufacturing is from the 1965 Survey of Manufacturing, made available by the Bureau of the Census and Statistics. For nonmanufacturing, the data is from the input-output table of the Office of Statistical Coordination and Standards (National Economic Council), based on the 1961 Census of Manufacturing. Since the various elements affecting protection for the nonmanufacturing sectors showed virtually no change from 1961 to 1965, the 1961 coefficients have been taken to represent the 1965 structure without correction.

We have further estimated, by direct price comparisons, rates of realized protection for thirty-four manufacturing industries in the non-import-competing category where imports account for less than 10 percent of domestic production. In some cases, it has been possible to judge that quality was clearly comparable. In others, calculations have been made by assuming that the Philippine product suffered a modest quality disadvantage.

In estimating effective rates of protection, we have used both the Corden and the Balassa methods in regard to nontraded goods. Differences in the estimates are relatively small, however, largely because the data from the Philippines Survey of Manufacturing do not identify nontraded inputs other than electricity and water. But the construction element in the depreciation coefficient has been estimated in each case, and direct and indirect value added in construction, along with that in electricity and water, have been calculated. Any other nontraded inputs—for example, advertising—are included in value added in processing; this entails a small downward bias in the estimates of the effective rates of protection.

The Pattern of Effective Rates

Owing to the tax on exports and the protection of material inputs, there is negative effective protection on the products of export industries in the manufacturing sector defined in a wider sense (i.e., including food processing, beverages, and tobacco). The range is from −11 percent on coconut oil, copra cake, and meal to −33 percent on veneer and plywood, averaging −20 percent (Table 11.7). Sugar is an exception because exports are sold under the U.S. preferential system at prices far exceeding world market prices, while import restrictions are prohibitive and domestic prices are controlled.

On import-competing products where differences between domestic and foreign prices are determined by tariffs and indirect tax differentials, nominal rates of protection range from 1 to over 100 percent. These rates are 1 percent on dairy products, and 5 percent on canned meat; 10 to 100 percent on machinery, some intermediate products, and consumer goods; 100 to 200 percent on industrial refrigerators and air conditioners, clay tiles, metal furniture, leather, jute mill products, electric lamps, household radios, phonographs, and television sets; and 252 percent on jewelry (Table 11.8).

TABLE 11.7:   Nominal and Effective Protection in Manufacturing Export Industries in
the Philippines, 1965

(*Percent*)

| | | | Effective protection | |
ISIC Code	Industry	Nominal protection	Balassa	Corden
2521	Veneer and plywood	−8	−33	−32
2031	Pineapple canning	−8	−27	−27
2093	Desiccated coconut	−8	−27	−27
2611	Rattan furniture	−8	−25	−25
2315	Ramie products	−8	−25	−24
2511 & 2513	Lumber	−8	−20	−19
2331	Cordage, rope, twine, and net	−8	−18	−17
2131	Beer	−8	−14	−13
3121	Coconut oil, copra cake, and meal	−8	−11	−11
2072	Sugar	35	186	183
	Average	9	12	13

Source: See text.

The averages and the dispersion of effective rates of protection are considerably higher than for nominal rates. If weighted by "derived" free trade value added (i.e., the difference between the domestic value of output and that of material inputs, deflated by the nominal rates of protection), average effective rates on import-competing goods are 62 or 59 percent depending on whether the Balassa or the Corden method is used, nominal rates weighted by total supply average 30 percent (Table 11.10). The results indicate the extent of escalation of the tariff structure which has contributed to disparities in rates. Effective protection is negative on canned meat and dairy products; at the other extreme, value added at world market prices is negative for metal furniture, stationery, refrigerators and air conditioners, leather, jute mill products, household radios, phonographs, and televisions, as well as for jewelry.

The apparent penalty on the canned meat and dairy products industries stems from the activities of the National Marketing Corporation which in 1965 imported duty-free substantial quantities of canned corned beef, sardines, and milk while several of the inputs of these industries were protected. Duty-free importation ceased after 1965; this raised nominal rates in the two industries to 53 and 12 percent, respectively.

Industries with negative value added at world market prices seem to display extreme cases of inefficiency since it would appear cheaper to import the finished product than to import its material inputs. These results indicating absolute waste of resources, however, should be considered with some skepticism. It is possible that the bias against domestic products noted earlier has in some cases contributed to such a result. Or, owing to widespread evasion, the actual level of protection may be lower than the apparent level.

Having made these disclaimers, we should note that there are several reasons why the production techniques employed under extremely high pro-

TABLE 11.8: Nominal and Effective Protection in Manufacturing, Import-Competing Industries in the Philippines, 1965

(Percent)

ISIC Code	Industry	Nominal protection	Effective protection Balassa	Effective protection Corden	Bias against exporting[a]
2014	Canned meat	5	−72	−70	184
2024	Dairy products	1	−29	−26	4
3832	Vehicle engines, parts, bodies	18	5	4	128
3621	Agricultural tractors	14	6	5	85
3622	Farm machinery, except tractors	16	6	5	147
3392	Lime	12	7	7	28
3632	Metal forming machinery	12	9	8	19
3412	Iron and steel foundry products	10	10	7	44
3196	Agricultural chemicals	15	13	13	28
3111	Inorganic acids, alkali, chlorine	18	14	10	81
2056	Flour mill products	15	15	12	243
3651	Industrial pumps and compressors	16	16	14	77
3192	Pharmaceutical preparations	25	22	22	56
3319	Structural clay products	19	23	21	33
3113	Compressed and liquefied gases	24	28	25	64
3092	Processed rubber	27	29	23	31
3646	Woodworking machinery	15	29	27	66
3199	Inks and dyes	30	38	34	186
3211	Petroleum refinery products	13	45	42	133
3511	Packers' cans	25	50	49	273
3021	Tires and inner tubes	51	54	52	342
3591	Metal barrels, drums, etc.	40	64	59	199
3641	Rice milling machinery	41	65	65	134
2712	Paper and paperboard products	31	66	59	167
3831	Trucks and buses	29	77	75	*
3321	Glass containers	45	82	81	115
3322	Flat glass and mirrors	44	83	77	124
3198	Polishing preparations	51	94	91	233
3411	Steel mill products	29	96	88	236
3731	Batteries	50	101	92	533
3734	Electric wires and wiring devices	20	103	103	187
3114	Fertilizers	16	104	72	80
3551	Wire nails, brads and spikes	29	109	107	*
3992	Fabricated plastic products	74	161	156	834
3532	Architectural metal work	60	164	151	1,556
3923	Eyeglasses and spectacles	98	183	165	974
3312	Clay tiles	102	261	243	350
3749	Sewing machines, household	78	363	318	2,010
3531	Structural iron and steel	81	431	335	*
3115	Plastic and resin materials	69	504	485	*
3732	Electric lamps	125	4,155	2,320	*
2641	Metal furniture	104	−9,750	784	*
2721	Stationery	71	−1,250	−2,600	*
3742	Industrial refrigerators and air conditioners	101	−380	−447	*
2911	Leather	105	−390	−461	*
2316	Jute mill products	110	−2,050	−3,154	*
3722	Household radios, phonos, and TV	147	−563	−604	*
3941	Jewelry	252	−307	−323	*
	Average	30	62	59	325

Source: See text.

[a] Calculated by using the Corden formula.

* Denotes negative value added in case of exporting; thus, the extent of discrimination against exporting is infinite.

tection, may in fact entail negative value added at world market prices. First, there are various kinds of sheer inefficiency, ranging from a higher incidence of breakage, theft, and substandard products to a failure to produce the entire range of possible by-products, with a resultant higher proportion of waste and scrap. Second, high prices may be paid for imported inputs owing to the monopoly power of the foreign supplier, especially where the local investment is foreign-owned and the domestic activity is by and large limited to assembly. Finally, nontraded inputs, such as electricity, may cost more at home than abroad. A combination of these could easily produce a situation with negative value added at world market prices.

Several non-import-competing industries, for which direct price comparisons have been made, also show negative value added at world market prices; they include automobiles, bags and canvas products, ham and bacon, vermicelli and noodles, household refrigerators and air conditioners, as well as pianos. These results are shown in Table 11.9, which also permits a comparison of potential and realized protection.

The percentage excess of domestic over import prices differs greatly from the nominal tariff for all non-import-competing goods. Realized rates of nominal protection are less than one-third of the tariff in twenty-one industries, between one-third and two-thirds in eleven, and more than two-thirds in only one. On soft drinks, wood furniture, rubber shoes, knitting mill products, ready-made garments, distilled liquors, paints, cigarettes, sausages, and bags and canvas products, the tariff rate exceeds 100 percent, yet domestic prices exceed import prices by less than one-fifth. On non-import-competing goods, taken together, the average rate of realized nominal protection on this group of products averages 17 percent, lower than the 30 percent average for import-competing goods. However, effective rates of protection on non-import-competing goods average nearly 100 percent, almost one-third higher than on import-competing products (Table 11.10). It appears, then, that the escalation in the structure of protection is greater for the former group of products than for the latter.

We have noted that realized rates of nominal protection have often been adjusted by an arbitrary but modest margin of protection for quality differential. This has been based on the existence of a premium in the Philippine market on imported versions of similar products. It should be added, however, that Philippine manufacturers generally attribute this premium to an irrational prejudice on the part of Philippine buyers.

On the other hand, the large discrepancies between potential and realized rates of protection in non-import-competing industries suggest the possibility that similar downward adjustments might be necessary in some of the import-competing industries. There is a general belief in the Philippines that the evasion of the protection system is widespread so that domestic output must com-

TABLE 11.9: Nominal and Effective Protection in Manufacturing, Non-Import-Competing Industries in the Philippines, 1965

(Percent)

ISIC Code	Industry	Nominal protection Poten-tial	Nominal protection Real-ized	Potential Corden	Realized Balassa	Realized Corden	Bias against exporting[a]
3391	Structural concrete products	67	7	129	14	13	14
3394	Asbestos products	92	9	179	18	18	18
2411	Shoes, except rubber	71	7	71	20	20	20
2412	Slippers, except rubber	70	7	125	23	22	23
2141	Soft drinks	110	11	400	24	23	23
2621	Wood furniture	102	10	1,279	24	23	24
3011	Rubber shoes	104	10	1,992	32	31	32
2096	Feeds for animals	49	5	248	33	32	31
2320	Knitting mill products	111	11	115	43	42	41
3191	Matches	49	25	81	48	46	47
2431 & 2433	Ready-made garments	110	11	821	53	52	50
2111	Distilled liquors	162	16	375	58	55	57
3194	Soap	27	14	69	59	52	20
3341	Cement	56	25	93	59	58	55
3131	Paints, etc.	113	11	−318	71	70	69
2211	Cigarettes	191	19	−268	76	74	75
2094	Vegetable lard and margarine	79	8	−158	87	85	92
2722	Paper bags, boxes	87	9	−525	89	87	87
2034	Vegetable sauces	119	54	−3,800	106	100	1,508
2081	Candy	149	66	−315	300	297	*
2314	Cotton textiles	91	30	−400	330	317	196
2082	Cocoa and chocolate	85	39	381	350	336	325
2012	Sausages (uncanned)	102	10	−180	400	400	275
2541	Wooden boxes	220	22	−160	400	400	283
3193	Perfumes, cosmetics, etc.	228	95	1,171	450	433	319
3851	Bicycles	91	31	1,630	474	466	356
3831	Autos	167	54	−164	533	495	*
2441	Bags and canvas products	109	11	−143	−300	−300	*
2013	Ham, bacon, etc.	114	71	−257	−833	−1,052	*
2091	Vermicelli and noodles	113	91	−345	−640	−800	*
3742	Household refrigerators and air conditioners	163	90	−233	−500	−580	*
3961	Pianos	318	180	−1,600	−1,500	−1,520	*
	Average	114	26	−1,397	85	83	144

Source: See text.

[a] Calculated by using the Corden formula.

* Denotes negative value added in case of exporting; thus, the extent of discrimination against exporting is infinite.

pete with imports at a lower rate of protection. Unfortunately, no quantitative estimate of the importance of evasion has been made. However, the existence of evasion weakens the presumption that when imports and domestic products are competing in significant volume, the protective system is fully effective in permitting higher prices or lower qualities.

All in all, the nominal rate of protection on nonexport industries in the manufacturing sector defined in a wider sense (i.e., including food processing, beverages, and tobacco) averages 29 percent and effective rates 85–89 percent. This result indicates a high degree of discrimination in favor of import substitution and against exports. The discrimination against exporting is also strong in protected industries since, in the absence of export subsidies, domestic pro-

TABLE 11.10:   Average Rates of Protection in Philippine Manufacturing, 1965

(*Percent*)

Industry group	Nominal protection	Effective protection	
		Balassa	Corden
Exports (excluding sugar)	−8	−19	−19
Import-competing	30	62	59
Non-import-competing	26	85[a]	83[a]
Sugar	35	186	183
All manufacturing	24	49	48
Except exports	28	74	71

Source: See text.
[a] Realized protection.

ducers would have to sell in foreign markets at world market prices. The bias against exports in individual industries is shown in Table 11.7 and 11.8.

In Table 11.11 average rates of nominal and effective protection have been calculated for major industry groups. From data on effective protection, it appears that the bias in the system of protection not only penalizes exports, but also discriminates against capital goods and intermediate goods in favor of consumer goods. This bias comes from the escalation of tariffs, with rates tending to rise from earlier to later stages in the production process (capital goods are treated here as inputs). The bias against machinery industries is especially pronounced if we eliminate industrial refrigeration equipment from the group. If we further exclude rice milling machinery, the protection of domestically produced machinery becomes negligible.

Potential rates of effective protection exceed realized rates on nondurable consumer goods by a considerable margin. For consumer durables, however, the effective rate remains high even after the adjustment to realized protection. Furthermore, the protection of intermediate products at higher levels of fabrication exceeds that of intermediate goods at a lower level, irrespective of whether we consider potential or realized protection. Estimates based on free trade input-output coefficients yield the same general conclusions, although the averages for broad categories are usually higher.

Capital goods production includes construction, a nontraded output whose effective rate of protection has been assumed to be zero.[5] But, under the assumption of some positive elasticity of demand for construction, these costs will nevertheless inhibit the growth of the industry. The high protection of inputs into construction points, then, to another bias against the production of capital goods.

Rates of protection have also been estimated for nonmanufacturing sectors, including fisheries, agriculture, mining, and forestry and logging. Despite

---

[5] Cf. Chapter 1, pp. 16–18.

TABLE 11.11: Nominal and Effective Protection for Major Product Categories in the Philippines, 1965

	Industry group	Estimates based on domestic coefficients					Estimates based on free trade coefficients		
		Nominal protection		Effective protection			Nominal protection	Effective protection[a]	
		Potential	Realized	Potential	Realized			Balassa	Corden
				Corden	Balassa	Corden			
I	Agriculture, forestry, and fishing	8	8	0	0	0	31	35	33
II	Processed food	24	15	77	47	46	37	112	89
III	Beverages and tobacco	115	10	183	15	15	1	3	3
IV	Mining and energy	4	3	−25	−25	−25	11	−3	−9
V	Construction materials	59	25	102	50	50	42	67	56
VI-A	Intermediate products I	14	13	15	16	16	18	39	28
VI-B	Intermediate products II	57	33	175	88	85	34	76	63
VI	Intermediate products I and II	39	25	85	55	53	22	50	38
VII	Nondurable consumer goods	107	22	287	55	53	32	52	46
VIII	Consumer durables	150	68	−232	1,355	1,062	52	96	81
IX	Machinery	27	27	103	112	103	26	27	24
X	Transport equipment	29	29	75	77	75	16	−4	−3
I–X	All industries	27	15	15	8	8	25	47	37
I+IV	Primary production	7	7	−1	−1	−1	22	18	14
II, III, V–X	Manufacturing	52	24	128	49	48	29	66	53
VI–X	Manufacturing less food, beverages, tobacco, and construction materials	53	30	145	70	68	25	48	38

Source: See text.
[a] Realized protection.

high potential protection, fisheries is treated as a nontraded goods industry with a zero rate of effective protection; although a world market price for fresh fish is not available, fresh seafood appears to be relatively cheap in the Philippines. Mining and forestry are export sectors that sell at world market prices and cannot pass on the costs arising from the protection of their inputs; therefore, the rates of effective protection are negative. Among agricultural products, tobacco is a similar case, although the situation is complicated by the subsidy accorded to Virginia-type tobacco. Despite the subsidy, however, the price received by growers seems to be no higher than the c.i.f. import price of what is considered to be tobacco of comparable quality.

The degree of aggregation makes price comparisons impractical for fruits and nuts and vegetables which seemingly enjoy high protection. Price comparisons have, however, been made for rice, corn, and sugar cane. For rice and corn this was necessary because exports and imports are government-controlled. On sugar cane, the growers' return is determined in proportion to the value of manufactured sugar; hence they share in the protection accorded to the latter.

Taken together, then, it appears that manufacturing is heavily protected when compared with the other major sectors. The predominantly exporting mining and forestry sectors are discriminated against, while agriculture stands in between. For the eleven agricultural subsectors, however, Table 11.12 shows a wide range of values with negative rates on export commodities and fairly high protection of vegetables, root crops, and fruit and nuts.

TABLE 11.12:   Nominal and Effective Rates of Protection in Nonmanufacturing Industries

(Percent)

Industry	Nominal protection	Effective protection
Agriculture	13	17
Coconut	−8	−16
Fiber crops	−8	−12
Tobacco	−8	−11
Palay	11	6
Livestock and poultry	12	12
Corn	23	24
Sugar cane	38	52
Coffee and cacao	41	55
Fruits and nuts	46	56
Vegetables	55	62
Root crops	75	78
Fisheries	0	0
Forestry and logging	−8	−26
Mining	3	−25
Copper, chromite, iron mining	−8	−30
Nonmetallic mining and quarrying	22	21

Source: See text.

Overvaluation and Net Effective Protection

Effective rates of protection measured at actual exchange rates indicate the extent of discrimination among domestic activities. But, in order to estimate net protection against imports and net discrimination against exports, adjustment has to be made for overvaluation as compared to the free trade situation. This has been done using the formulas shown in Appendix A.

In accordance with the assumptions made in the other country studies, the elasticity of supply of imports to the Philippines has been assumed to be infinite. In turn, elasticities of demand for its major export products have been estimated by utilizing available information on the Philippines' share in world exports and on demand elasticities for these products in the world market. In 1963–66, the Philippines provided 95 percent of the world exports of abaca, 62 percent of copra, 51 percent of coconut oil, 33 percent of tropical logs, and 6 percent of sugar. The Philippines has an even smaller share in the world market for most of its minor exports which provided one-third of its export earnings in 1963–66.

World demand elasticities for individual commodities are not available for a recent time period, and we have had to rely on the results of a study by B. A. de Vries which was based on an investigation carried out by the U.S. Tariff Commission in 1945.[6] An exception has been made for sugar where a zero export demand elasticity has been assumed since exports to the United States, the only Philippine market, are regulated by quotas. Using these estimates for the major export products of the Philippines, and assuming very high elasticities for the remainder, we have derived demand elasticities for Philippine exports in the range of 16 to 20.

Estimates on the long-term elasticities of domestic demand for imports and the domestic supply of exports are not available. We have, therefore, used estimates derived for the industrial countries,[7] and have made adjustments for the relative size of the foreign sector in the Philippines. The domestic import demand elasticity has been taken to be 4, while a range of 3 to 5 has been used for the elasticity of export supply.

The average nominal rate of protection on all industries excluding exports was 28 percent in 1965, while an 8 percent tax was levied on exports. The corresponding estimate of the extent of overvaluation ranges between 8.7 and 12.9 percent, with 10.6 percent as the median estimate. Were we to ignore the export tax which was abolished in November 1965, the relevant estimates

---

[6] Barend A. de Vries, "Price Elasticities for Individual Commodities Imported into the U.S.," *IMF Staff Papers*, April 1951, pp. 397–419.

[7] Bela Balassa, "Tariff Protection in Industrial Nations and Its Effects on the Exports of Processed Goods from Developing Countries," *Canadian Journal of Economics*, August 1968, pp. 583–94.

would be 13 and 16 percent, with a median of 14.5 percent. This assumes, of course, that after 1965 balance-of-payments equilibrium required the absence of the export tax.

Tables 11.13–11.15 show the estimates of net effective protection, adjusted for the overvaluation of 14.5 percent. A detailed discussion of the results is not given here since the changes are rather small. For the same reason, estimates of net effective protection in the detailed tables have not been reproduced.

Evaluation and Policy Recommendations

Although the principal characteristics of the structure of protection in the Philippines have been described above, a brief summary might prove useful before we attempt an evaluation of its implications for trade and growth. The system appears to correspond to the guidelines for tariff policy set forth in an

TABLE 11.13: Net Nominal and Effective Protection in Manufacturing Export Industries in the Philippines, 1965[a]

(*Percent*)

ISIC Code	Industry	Nominal protection	Effective protection
2521	Veneer and plywood	−20	−41
2031	Pineapple canning	−20	−36
2093	Desiccated coconut	−20	−36
2611	Rattan furniture	−20	−34
2315	Ramie products	−20	−34
2511 & 2513	Lumber	−20	−29
2331	Cordage, rope, twine, and net	−20	−28
2131	Beer	−20	−24
3121	Coconut oil, copra cake, and meal	−20	−23
2072	Sugar	18	147
	Average	−5	−1

Sources: Table 11.7 and text.

[a] Effective rates of protection have been estimated by using the Corden formula; both nominal and effective rates have been adjusted for overvaluation as compared to the free trade situation.

TABLE 11.14: Net Average Rates of Protection in Philippine Manufacturing, 1965[a]

(*Percent*)

Industry group	Nominal protection	Effective protection
Exports (excluding sugar)	−20	−29
Import-competing	14	39
Non-import-competing	10	60
Sugar	18	147
All manufacturing	8	29
Except exports	12	49

Sources: Table 11.10 and text.

[a] Effective rates of protection have been estimated by using the Corden formula; both nominal and effective rates have been adjusted for overvaluation as compared to the hypothetical free trade situation.

TABLE 11.15: Net Nominal and Effective Protection for Major Product Categories in the Philippines, 1965[a]

(Percent)

		Estimates based on domestic coefficients				Estimates based on free trade coefficients	
	Industry group	Nominal protection		Effective protection		Nominal protection	Effective protection
		Potential	Realized	Potential	Realized		
I	Agriculture, forestry, and fishing	−6	−6	−13	−13	14	16
II	Processed food	8	0	55	28	20	65
III	Beverages and tobacco	88	−4	147	0	−12	−10
IV	Mining and energy	−10	−10	−34	−34	−3	−21
V	Construction materials	39	9	76	31	24	36
VI-A	Intermediate products I	0	−1	0	1	3	12
VI-B	Intermediate products II	37	16	140	62	17	42
VI	Intermediate products I and II	21	9	62	34	7	21
VII	Nondurable consumer goods	81	7	238	34	15	28
VIII	Consumer durables	118	47	−215	915	33	58
IX	Machinery	11	11	77	77	10	8
X	Transport equipment	13	13	53	53	1	−15
I-X	All industries	11	0	0	−6	9	20
I + IV	Primary production	−7	−7	−14	−14	7	0
II, III, V-X	Manufacturing	33	8	99	29	13	34
VI-X	Manufacturing less food, beverages, tobacco, and construction materials	34	14	214	47	9	21

Sources: Table 11.11 and text.
[a] Effective rates of protection have been estimated by using the Corden formula; both nominal and effective rates have been adjusted for overvaluation as compared to the hypothetical free trade situation.

unofficial statement by an official of the Tariff Commission.[8] In addition to the general criterion of "protection for deserving domestic industries," the statement emphasizes low rates of duty on essentials, high rates on non-essentials, and lower rates on materials than on finished products. These criteria are taken to be "no longer debatable," and to "hardly need justification."

What is "essential" is not spelled out, but we might think of certain consumer goods—like milk products, flour mill products, and medicines—as essential and note their corresponding low rates of protection. Consumer durables, plus jewelry, cosmetics, candy, and tobacco products—which might be thought of as less essential—have, in contrast, very high effective rates.

But the question of essentiality is probably more closely tied to production needs than to consumption needs. So the really essential imports are the machinery and intermediate inputs needed to maintain and expand production and employment in the manufacturing industries that have been established. The general pattern of tariffs, therefore, shows low rates for machinery, moderate rates for intermediate inputs, and generally high rates for finished consumer goods. This tends to augment the protection given to the finishing-stages activities in comparison to what the structure of nominal tariff rates would suggest. The result is a strong bias in favor of investment in finished consumer goods industries that are heavily dependent on imported supplies. Moreover, the pattern of industrial growth and trade over the past decade and a half in the Philippines tends to confirm the existence of this bias.

Exports are, however, the most heavily penalized group, especially when we exclude sugar, which derives its relatively high degree of protection from preferential treatment in the protected U.S. market. The negative rates of effective protection for exports derive, of course, from the fact that they are not protected from world competition, but must pay the penalty of higher prices owing to the protection accorded some of their inputs. Exports are further penalized by the lower price for foreign exchange generated by the system of protection.

This is brought out in a comparison of net effective rates (i.e., after adjustment for overvaluation as compared to the free trade situation). Exports are penalized by an average net rate of about −30 percent, while consumer goods, at the other end of the scale, have an average net effective rate of protection of 80 percent. The result for exports needs to be qualified, however, by two considerations. First, the less favorable exchange rate for exports, implying an 8 percent tax, ended in November 1965. Second, the government is making efforts to implement a drawback on import duties, which has heretofore been ineffective. With these two changes, the net penalty on exports would be

---

[8] *Manila Times*, August 18, 1967.

simply the overvaluation of the peso plus the excess cost of domestically produced inputs.

To the extent that the system of incentives produced by the structure of protection influences resource allocation, we would expect the Philippine system to have given strong encouragement to finishing stages of production of consumer goods, relatively less encouragement to intermediate goods, much less to capital goods, and rather severe penalties on exports. This expectation is generally confirmed by the trade and production figures shown earlier. Imports of consumer goods declined absolutely and relatively to other imports, while imports of capital goods rose more rapidly than any other category and by 1965 were the largest of the four groups of imports in Table 11.3.

Production trends in manufacturing complemented the trade trends with the output of consumer goods increasing most in absolute terms and capital goods least. In relative terms, however, intermediate goods gained most rapidly and reflected the smaller bias against that group. It may be suggested, however, that relative rates of growth are less significant than absolute rates in the assessment of the direction of the allocation of resources, since there is no presumption that proportionality is in any sense neutral. The key question is, rather, where was most of the new investment allocated? And the answer seems clear—to consumer goods output.

Apart from plywood and veneer, no manufacturing exports developed during the 1950s. But, following the increase in the export exchange rate in 1965, several new export commodities have emerged. While their total contribution to export earnings is still relatively small, the results are encouraging enough to suggest that further corrections in the bias against manufactured exports may prove rewarding.

Traditional exports performed quite well during the decade and a half following the reconstruction after World War II; increases in their value averaged about 5 percent a year. As the data of Table 3.6 indicates, this result has been due largely to the rapid growth of world demand for some of the Philippines' export products, since the share of the Philippines in the world exports of these commodities hardly increased during this period.

It should be added that the response of the major primary exports of the Philippines to devaluation has been relatively modest, although there have been no adverse price movements after devaluation. What may be true is that these traditional export industries offer relatively advantageous employment to Philippine resources even after the implicit taxes imposed by the system of protection and the exchange rate it defends. Nonetheless, these taxes probably go beyond what would be optimal in the light of world demand elasticities. In effect, then, the taxes implicit in the system of protection entail a transfer of income away from export industries to the protected manufacturing sector.

Even if this transfer could be defended in terms of forcing saving for development priorities, objections can be raised to the method of transfer. For, apart from possible adverse effects on traditional exports, the system of incentives discourages the development of new exports by penalizing *all* exportation. This bias has a harmful effect on the wide range of potential new exports that might otherwise emerge.

Manufacturing growth in substituting for imports was most rapid in the 1950s. But the process of import substitution slowed sharply after 1956 as Table 11.3 indicates. This is consistent with the hypothesis that the system of protection was effective in encouraging the relatively easy capture by domestic manufactures of the existing market for finished consumer goods; but, as this process approached completion in many lines of activity, the growth of manufacturing began to be constrained by the rate of growth of the domestic market itself, and by the greater difficulties of moving backward to the earlier stages of manufacturing and into the export market.

It is no doubt true that there is considerable evasion of the system of protection in the Philippines, so that the distortions indicated by this assessment may be exaggerated. Moreover, a variety of other forces at work influences resource allocation. Nevertheless, it seems that it will be difficult for manufacturing to again become a leading sector in Philippine growth unless the protection system is revamped to correct the relative bias against production at the earlier stages, and even more against exports. Thus the protection system is seen as inhibiting the future growth of the Philippine economy.

It should be added that the existence of this system in the past may have led to an overstatement of real growth that has occurred; prices of the more rapidly growing manufacturing sector are rendered artificially high by the system, and this increases the weight of that sector in growth calculations. Accordingly, if we attempt to measure growth in terms of world market prices by correcting values in each sector by its effective rate of protection (adjusted for overvaluation), we find that the average annual growth rate of net domestic product from 1950 to 1965 is reduced from 5.4 to 5.1 percent.

The natural growth avenues for industry, following import substitution in finished consumer goods, are backward-linkage import substitution (intermediate and capital goods) and new exports of industrial products. Yet, what emerges clearly from an analysis of the protection system is that distortions in prices discourage investment in these growth areas. Ironically, it is also these activities that could save and earn foreign exchange to ease the balance-of-payments problem. Finally, the poor investment climate that results from these price and profit distortions tends to encourage the repatriation of foreign capital and the expatriation of Philippine capital; this further intensifies the pressure on the balance of payments. In fact, since 1965, the balance of payments of the Philippines has worsened to the point where some controls on foreign exchange transactions have been reintroduced.

Of course the protection system is not all-powerful. There are other influences at work on investment and resource allocation. In particular, the Board of Investments, a new addition to the plethora of planning agencies in the Philippines, seems to be set on the right track. Backward integration and new exports rank high in its investment priorities. But it is not at all clear that the Board's weapons—principally tax credits and exemptions—are sufficient to overcome the biases of the protection system. So in order to accelerate economic growth through the expansion of manufacturing industries, a general reform of this system seems to be needed.

What would be the nature of the reform? Without spelling out details, we would indicate two broad goals that should be met. First, the bias against backward integration should be removed. This means that the tariff system should move toward general uniformity of rates. Second, the bias against exports should disappear. This means providing subsidies to exports to match the uniform tariff. The subsidies could be withheld (or reduced) for those traditional exports whose foreign demand elasticities are thought to be significantly less than infinite. While one would not realistically hope for perfection in the application of these principles, it is difficult to imagine that a resurgence of industrial growth could occur in the Philippines without some progress in their application.

CHAPTER 12

THE STRUCTURE OF PROTECTION
IN NORWAY

Bela Balassa and Preben Munthe

Economic Growth and International Trade

Developments until 1949

In the nineteenth century, Norway's economic development was largely oriented toward the exploitation of its natural resources and location. Forest products and fish played an important role in exports, and Norway exploited its favorable geographical position for ocean shipping. In turn, given the country's relatively unfavorable soil and climatic conditions, agriculture produced almost exclusively for the domestic market and Norway relied on the imports of food and agricultural raw materials to a considerable extent.

Toward the end of the century, a shift occurred toward exporting resource products in processed form. Exports of logs gave place to lumber, and later to wood pulp and paper, while exports of processed fish were substituted for raw fish. Manufacturing industries were also established to serve the shipping and fishing sectors and to provide nondurable consumer goods for home consumption. It is noteworthy, however, that manufacturing developed behind relatively low tariffs; thus we can speak of "natural" import substitution in Norway.

Preben Munthe is Professor of Economics at the University of Oslo. He has been responsible for the section on the protection system in Norway, and has advised on other parts of the study.

The forestry and fishing industries continued to expand in the early part of the twentieth century while the availability of cheap hydroelectricity led to the establishment of electro-chemical industries. Industries based on electric power developed further during the interwar period, with concentration on intermediate goods of relatively simple fabrication, such as aluminum, ferroalloys, fertilizers, and carbide. Moreover, increased protection during the thirties, responding largely to protectionist measures taken elsewhere, provided a stimulus to the growth of nondurable consumer goods industries.

In describing the structure of the Norwegian economy, we shall depart slightly from the industrial classification scheme used elsewhere in this volume and distinguish three major product groups within the commodity-producing sectors: primary producing activities, industries producing intermediate products at lower stages of transformation, and manufacturing industries at higher levels of fabrication. The first group includes agriculture, fishing and whaling, forestry, and mining; the second encompasses processed food, processed fish, pulp and paper, fertilizers and carbide, unwrought nonferrous metals, and ferroalloys; and the third comprises commodity classes 5 to 8 of the U.N. Standard International Trade Classification *less* paper, fertilizers, carbide, unwrought metals, and ferroalloys.

This scheme of classification permits us to separate the production of primary goods and standardized products requiring relatively simple technological processes from manufacturing industries at higher levels of fabrication. Industries producing primary commodities and intermediate products at lower stages of transformation other than the basic electro-chemical industry (fertilizers and carbide) have further been combined into four major sectors, so that we can indicate changes in the relative importance of processing activities within each. The sectors in question are agriculture and processed food; fisheries and fish processing; forestry and forest products; and mining, nonferrous metals, and ferroalloys.

In 1949, primary activities accounted for 41.6 percent, intermediate products at lower stages of transformation for 21.3 percent, and manufactured goods at higher levels of fabrication for 37.1 percent of value added in the commodity-producing sectors (Table 12.1). Among primary activities, agriculture was of greatest importance, followed by forestry, fishing and whaling, and mining. The ranking was the same in regard to the intermediate goods produced in these sectors except that unwrought metals and ferroalloys, which in large part use imported materials, ranked higher than processed fish.

Comparisons with other countries at similar levels of industrialization are of further interest. Among countries that may be classified as semi-industrial,[1]

---

[1] On the definition used, cf. Bela Balassa, "Growth Strategies in Semi-Industrial Countries," *Quarterly Journal of Economics*, February 1970, p. 27.

TABLE 12.1: The Sectoral Distribution of Value Added and Exports in the Commodity-Producing Sectors in Norway, 1949-66[a]

(Percent)

Sector	1949 Value added	1949 Merchandise exports	1953 Value added	1953 Merchandise exports	1958 Value added	1958 Merchandise exports	1961 Value added	1961 Merchandise exports	1966 Value added	1966 Merchandise exports
Primary activities	*41.6*	*13.0*	*37.5*	*14.6*	*33.9*	*12.7*	*29.9*	*10.9*	*24.4*	*7.6*
Crops and livestock	20.3	1.1	18.8	2.2	16.5	2.5	15.3	3.1	11.0	3.1
Fishing and whaling	7.6	7.7	7.5	7.4	6.6	5.8	5.3	3.7	5.8	1.1
Forestry	9.8	1.5	8.2	1.3	7.8	0.5	6.4	0.5	4.2	0.2
Mining	3.9	2.7	3.0	3.7	3.0	3.9	2.9	3.6	3.4	3.2
Intermediate products at lower levels of transformation	*21.3*	*77.8*	*23.9*	*73.4*	*22.7*	*68.4*	*24.0*	*65.6*	*27.2*	*61.3*
Processed food	9.1	2.2	10.0	2.3	7.8	2.2	9.0	2.6	9.1	1.6
Processed fish	1.7	24.8	2.9	21.9	2.7	18.3	2.0	14.2	2.6	13.4
Pulp and paper	5.2	27.0	5.2	24.0	5.4	20.3	5.6	19.8	5.9	15.1
Nonferrous metals	2.5	11.0	2.7	13.1	3.0	16.2	3.2	17.1	4.1	18.9
Ferroalloys	0.5	5.4	0.8	4.7	1.1	4.7	1.1	4.8	1.1	4.5
Fertilizers and carbide	2.3	7.4	2.3	7.4	2.7	6.7	3.1	7.1	4.4	7.8
Manufactured goods at higher levels of fabrication	*37.1*	*9.2*	*38.6*	*12.0*	*43.4*	*18.9*	*46.1*	*23.5*	*48.4*	*31.1*
Commodity producing sectors	*100.0*	*100.0*	*100.0*	*100.0*	*100.0*	*100.0*	*100.0*	*100.0*	*100.0*	*100.0*
Million kroner	8,365	2,758	9,641	3,899	10,794	5,193	12,193	6,441	15,161	9,934

Source: Norwegian input-output tables.
[a] Data are expressed in 1955 prices.

value added in all manufacturing industries—including intermediate as well as final production—accounted for 25–30 percent of the gross domestic product in 1950; the relevant figures were Argentina, 30 percent; Denmark and Norway, 28 percent; and Japan, 25 percent. By comparison, in the major industrial countries of Western Europe (France, Germany, and the United Kingdom), this share was in the 38–40 percent range.[2]

Although intermediate products at lower levels of transformation accounted for a higher proportion of value added in the industrial sector in Norway than elsewhere, Norway was behind other semi-industrial countries as regards the relative importance of manufacturing industries at higher levels of fabrication. Around 1950, the share of these industries in the gross domestic product was 15 percent in Norway, as compared with 17 percent in Denmark and Japan and 21 percent in Argentina; in France, Germany, and the United Kingdom the corresponding figures were 27–29 percent.[3]

It should further be added that the intermediate goods produced in Norway are generally material-intensive and/or utilize large amounts of electrical energy; hence, their share was much larger in terms of production value (39.6 percent) than in terms of value added (21.3 percent). The importance of these products is put in even stronger focus if we consider that they provided nearly four-fifths of Norwegian merchandise exports in 1949. Processed fish and pulp and paper each accounted for one-fourth of the total, with aluminum, ferroalloys, fertilizers, and carbide supplying much of the remainder (Table 12.1).[4]

By contrast, manufacturing activities at higher levels of fabrication were oriented toward the home market. Consumer goods industries supplied domestic needs behind moderate protection; the manufacture of wood products benefited from the availability of cheap raw material; and the engineering industry specialized in shipbuilding and in the production of machinery used for the processing of domestic materials. In 1949, only 3 percent of the combined output of these industries was exported and such exports provided less than one-tenth of total merchandise exports. In the same year, one-fourth of the domestic consumption of these commodities was supplied by imports (Table 12.2).

---

[2] United Nations, *Yearbook of National Accounts Statistics, 1964*, New York, 1965.

[3] *Ibid.* and United Nations Statistical Office, *The Growth of World Industry, 1938–1961* (New York, 1963). Data refer to value added in the case of Argentina, Germany, Norway, and the United Kingdom and to employment in Denmark, France, and Japan. For each country available figures for a year nearest to 1950 have been used.

[4] We do not consider here the contribution of shipping services to foreign exchange earnings. Shipping accounted for 42 percent of the exports of goods and services in 1949, and 32 percent in 1967. International Monetary Fund, *Balance of Payments Statistics*.

TABLE 12.2: Selected Data on Norwegian Manufacturing Industries at Higher Levels of Fabrication, 1949–66

(In 1955 prices)

Industry	Production (mill. kroner)			Exports (mill. kroner)			Imports (mill. kroner)			Exports/production (percent)					Imports/consumption (percent)				
										Average			Marginal		Average			Marginal	
	1949	1958	1966	1949	1958	1966	1949	1958	1966	1949	1958	1966	1949–58	1958–66	1949	1958	1966	1949–58	1958–66
Textiles	848	870	1,235	4	61	160	511	572	1,137	0.5	7.0	13.0	259.1	27.1	37.7	41.4	51.4	225.9	68.1
Clothing	674	928	1,172	...	11	55	32	114	377	0	1.2	4.7	4.3	18.0	4.5	11.1	25.2	25.3	56.7
Footwear	397	316	400	...	1	6	2	15	81	0	0.4	1.5	...	6.0	0.5	4.5	17.1	...	45.5
Leather and leather products	197	126	122	...	4	28	38	31	71	0	3.4	23.0	...	...	16.2	20.4	42.8	...	285.7
Wood and cork products	1,214	1,386	2,154	33	87	146	54	78	253	2.7	6.3	6.8	31.4	7.7	4.4	5.7	11.2	16.8	16.4
Wallboard and paper products	270	422	721	13	47	89	10	31	134	4.8	11.1	12.3	22.4	14.0	3.7	7.6	17.5	15.0	28.7
Printing, publishing	603	777	1,051	1	2	15	4	15	79	0.2	0.2	1.4	0.6	4.7	0.7	1.9	7.1	6.0	19.7
Rubber products	165	167	302	3	19	55	33	60	147	1.8	11.4	18.2	800.0	26.7	16.9	28.8	37.3	207.7	46.8
Other chemicals	448	949	2,445	55	159	639	563	998	2,414	12.3	16.7	26.1	20.8	32.1	58.9	55.8	57.2	52.2	58.2
Nonmetallic mineral products	358	591	921	17	29	109	64	124	222	4.8	4.9	11.8	5.2	24.2	15.8	18.0	21.5	21.3	28.3
Iron and steel	167	462	975	19	136	471	433	456	933	11.4	29.4	48.3	39.7	65.3	74.5	58.3	64.9	11.4	72.8
Engineering products	1,342	2,295	3,859	50	279	671	651	1,191	2,977	3.7	12.2	13.4	24.0	25.1	33.5	37.1	48.3	42.7	60.4
Electrical machinery	405	720	1,537	8	74	260	202	314	727	2.0	4.7	16.9	21.0	22.8	33.7	32.7	36.3	31.0	39.5
Shipbuilding	661	1,095	1,835	49	52	282	52	123	320	7.4	4.7	15.4	0.7	31.1	7.8	10.6	17.1	14.2	27.8
Miscellaneous manufactures	208	335	861	3	19	107	48	183	611	1.4	5.6	12.4	12.6	16.7	19.0	36.7	44.8	54.9	49.4
Manufactured goods at higher levels of fabrication, total	7,957	11,439	19,590	255	980	3,093	2,697	4,305	10,482	3.2	8.6	15.8	20.8	25.9	25.9	29.2	38.9	36.8	50.6

Source: Norwegian input-output tables.

Structural Changes in the Postwar Period

It appears then that in the early postwar period Norway showed the characteristic features of a semi-industrialized country. Although various manufacturing activities had been established, primary activities and the relatively simple transformation of foods and raw materials had a preponderant place in the Norwegian economy. The development of these sectors largely reflected the availability of natural resources and hydroelectricity, and they supplied much of Norway's export earnings.

Given the limitations of fishing, forestry, and mining resources, the continuation of this pattern of specialization would not have permitted, however, the full utilization of all productive factors and a rapid rate of growth of the Norwegian economy. Accordingly, Norway faced the choice between fostering domestic industry through import substitution or through export-based expansion. The decision was made for the latter, with appropriate policy measures taken to stimulate exports and to increase foreign competition in domestic markets.

In the early fifties, successful efforts to maintain price stability contributed to the profitability of sales in foreign markets, and exports were also favored by the government's investment policy.[5] Subsequently, the maintenance of realistic exchange rates and low tariffs on imported inputs have benefited exports. In turn, the elimination of quantitative restrictions, reductions in tariffs, and participation in the European Free Trade Association have diminished the extent of import protection.

The policies followed in the postwar period have provided both the stick and the carrot of foreign competition in Norway. Rather than being sheltered from foreign competition, domestic industries have had to compete with imports. At the same time, cost reductions obtainable in large-scale production have induced firms to search for export markets and these incentives have not been frustrated by the disadvantages of overvalued exchange rates and high input prices observed in countries where industrialization has taken place in the confines of highly protected domestic markets.

The export orientation of manufacturing industries has led to a rapid rise of exports. Between 1949 and 1966, the volume of exports of manufactured goods at higher levels of fabrication grew more than twelve times, and their share in merchandise exports increased from 9 percent in 1949 to 31 percent in 1966. Meanwhile, the average ratio of exports to manufacturing output rose from 3 to 16 percent, and the share of exports in the *increment* of output approached one-fourth.

---

[5] Cf. Alice Bourneuf, *A Planned Revival* (Cambridge, Mass.: Harvard University Press, 1958), p. 11, ch. 6 and 7, and The Ministry of Finance, *The Norwegian Long-Term Program, 1954–1957* (Oslo, 1957).

Exports assumed especial importance for the growth of manufacturing after the establishment of the European Free Trade Association. Incremental export-production ratios rose from 21 to 26 percent between 1949–58 and 1958–66, and the rate of growth of output accelerated. Value added in manufacturing industries at high levels of fabrication grew at an annual rate of 4.7 percent in the first period and 5.8 percent in the second (Tables 12.1 and 12.2).

While exports contributed to the growth of manufacturing in Norway, none of the commonly used measures of import substitution show evidence of import replacement. Thus, the share of imports in the consumption of manufactured goods at higher levels of fabrication rose from 26 percent in 1949 to 29 percent in 1958 and to 39 percent in 1966; this acceleration occurred after the establishment of EFTA.[6] The results are explained by the fact that, apart from providing inducements to exports, an outward-looking strategy of industrial development also stimulates imports through the liberalization of trade.

The expansion of manufacturing industries at higher levels of fabrication brought about an increase in the share of this sector in value added in the total commodity-producing sectors from 37.1 percent in 1949 to 48.4 percent in 1966; three-fifths of the increment of value added in the commodity-producing sectors was in manufacturing during this period. The share of primary producing activities declined from 41.6 to 24.4 percent, while that of intermediate products at lower stages of transformation rose from 21.3 to 27.2 percent. The shift from primary activities to industries at lower stages of transformation reflects the limitations of the domestic material base, and the growing importance of processing activities, as well as the increased reliance on hydro-electricity.

Among the four major nonmanufacturing sectors, the combined share of agriculture and food processing in value added in commodity production declined from 29.4 percent in 1949 to 20.1 percent in 1966. The entire decline took place in the share of crops and livestock, where production remained stationary although productivity increased. The soil and climatic conditions for Norwegian agriculture being unfavorable, the result represents an improvement in the efficiency of resource allocation in the national economy. In food processing, value added nearly doubled, and food exports rose at a somewhat higher rate.

Value added in fishing and whaling also increased at a relatively low rate in the period under consideration. With the continuing establishment of processing plants, increases were more rapid in fish processing, and there was a shift toward the exportation of fish in processed form. Thus, a one-half decline

---

[6] Similar trends are shown in the ratio of imports to the sum of production and imports, a measure of import substitution suggested by H. B. Chenery ("Patterns of Industrial Growth," *American Economic Review*, September 1960, p. 640). This ratio increased from 25 percent in 1949 to 27 percent in 1958, and to 35 percent in 1966.

in the exports of raw fish between 1949 and 1966 was accompanied by a doubling of the exports of processed fish. Still, limitations in the catch led to a decrease in the share of fishery products in merchandise exports from one-third in 1949 to one-seventh in 1966.

Similar developments occurred in forest products; although supply limitations led to a decline in value added in forestry, the share of pulp and paper in commodity production increased during this period. Moreover, Norway virtually ceased to export logs and pulpwood while the combined exports of pulp and paper taken together more than doubled, with paper gaining at the expense of wood pulp. The combined share of forest products in Norwegian exports, however, fell from 28.5 percent to 15.3 percent.

By contrast, the share of nonferrous metals (aluminum and to a lesser extent nickel and copper) and ferroalloys both in commodity production and in exports increased during the 1949–66 period. Supply limitations hardly played a role here since Norwegian aluminum production relies on imported bauxite and alumina; nickel and copper ores, as well as most alloying metals, are also imported. The availability of hydroelectricity further contributed to the expansion of these industries and largely explains the increase in the share of Norwegian aluminum in world markets.

Within the manufacturing sector, too, there has been a shift in production and in exports toward processed goods at higher levels of fabrication. Among wood products, the shift has been from paper and simple wood products to paper products, wallboard, and furniture. In chemicals, increases in the production of fertilizer and carbide were overshadowed by the development of more advanced branches of the chemical industry, including the production of carbide-based synthetic chemicals. Thus, by 1966 the exports of synthetic fibers and resins, petroleum derivatives, and a variety of inorganic chemical products taken together approached the value of fertilizer and carbide exports as against a ratio of about one-fourth in 1949. Finally, among rubber products, the export of tubes and tires assumed importance.

There has further been a shift from industries with a lower to those with a higher skill requirement. Industries relying to a large extent on unskilled and semi-skilled labor grew at a relatively slow rate (textiles, clothing, and footwear) or even experienced a decline in output (leather and leather products) whereas the share of imports in the domestic consumption of these commodities increased substantially. Nevertheless, exports of specialty products, such as knitwear and ski clothes, rose also; between 1949 and 1966, two-fifths of the increase in textile production was destined for export.

The rapid expansion in skill-intensive industries, such as engineering and electrical machinery, has been largely oriented toward exports. While the Norwegian engineering and machinery industries produced almost exclusively for the home market in 1949, foreign sales accounted for nearly one-fourth of the increase of output between 1949 and 1966. Increases came in a variety of products, including mechanical handling equipment (cranes, hoists, and excavators), calculating machines and cash registers, as well as radios and tape recorders. In conjunction with the growing importance of specialization within these industries, the share of imports in domestic uses also increased. Nevertheless, industrial development in Norway led to a rise in the ratio of exports to imports in the engineering and machinery industries from 7 percent in 1949 to 25 percent in 1966.

Nor did Norway follow the example of several developing countries in producing a great variety of shapes and forms of steel. Rather it has concentrated on specialty products, such as quality pig iron containing titanium and vanadium, high-quality alloyed steel, as well as heavy castings for shipbuilding. Apart from heavy castings, much of the output is exported: between 1958 and 1966 two-thirds of the increase in output was sold abroad. At the same time, steel ingots and many finished steel products are imported, accounting for two-thirds of the rise in domestic consumption during this period.

While shipbuilding (including repairs) was already a large industry in Norway in the interwar period, it assumed importance in export markets only after 1958. Tankers continue to dominate shipbuilding activity, but in recent years Norway has also started to export hydrofoils and pleasure boats. Finally, in the group of miscellaneous manufactured products, exports of plastic articles and sporting goods are noteworthy.

It should be emphasized that within individual industries Norwegian firms tend to specialize in narrow ranges of products for domestic, as well as for export, use while other product varieties are imported. This so-called intra-industry specialization is especially characteristic of Norway's trade in steel products, machinery, and equipment. Moreover, a number of firms produce parts and components of automobiles for assembly abroad, especially in Sweden. There are also cooperative arrangements with foreign producers; an example is the agreement between Norwegian and Danish manufacturers for the production of hydraulic deck fittings for ships.

For the sake of comparability, these results are also presented according to the classification scheme used elsewhere in this volume. It appears then that the share of agriculture, forestry, and fishing in commodity production declined from 28.6 percent in 1950 to 16.0 percent in 1967 whereas that of manufacturing increased from 48.8 to 58.9 percent (see Table 2.3). Within this period, the rate of expansion of manufacturing increased and led to an acceleration of the growth of the national economy. Thus, while the annual average rate of growth of GDP in Norway was 3.3 percent in 1950–60, it was 5.0 percent between 1960 and 1967. In per capita terms, increases were 2.3 percent in the first part of the period, and 4.2 percent in the last seven years (see Table 2.2).

The high capital requirement of hydroelectrical installations and the investment needs of the transportation and communication network necessitated by the long distances within the country, partly explain the large proportion of investment in national income in Norway. During the fifties, the average share of gross domestic investment in GNP approached one-third, implying a marginal capital-output ratio of about 9. In 1960–67, however, this ratio declined to 5.8, possibly reflecting the contribution of investments in infrastructure undertaken in earlier periods (see Table 2.4).

The Pattern of International Trade

Norway had a continuing current account deficit during the postwar period, largely financed by the inflow of foreign capital. This deficit declined, however, from nearly 4 percent of GNP in the early fifties to 2 percent during the 1960s. During that time, there was also an increase in the relative importance of foreign trade for the Norwegian economy. The share of merchandise exports in the gross national product rose from 18.6 in 1950 to 19.5 percent in 1960 and again to 20.9 percent in 1965, with imports rising somewhat less.

The increase in export shares is chiefly the result of the rapid growth of merchandise exports. Between 1950 and 1967, these exports increased at an annual rate of 9.2 percent while imports grew at a rate of 8.6 percent. As noted above, export growth was accompanied by changes in the composition of exports from commodities at lower to those at higher levels of fabrication. Using the SITC classification, we find that the share of primary products in total exports declined from 56.9 percent in 1951 to 43.8 percent in 1967, while the share of machinery and transport equipment rose from 11.0 percent to 22.2 percent. Reductions in tariffs and participation in EFTA led to similar changes in the structure of imports although their magnitude was smaller here (see Tables 2.7 and 2.8).

Structural changes in Norwegian exports were associated with increased export diversification. The share of the eight major export commodities (fresh fish, dried fish, preserved fish, wood pulp, paper and paperboard, aluminum, ships and boats, and fertilizers) in total exports declined from 54 percent in 1950 to 45 percent in 1967 (Table 12.3). Among these commodities, Norway experienced a fall in its share in the world exports of fishery products, wood pulp, and fertilizers, and an increase in aluminum. In the case of wood pulp, this change reflects the limited supply of the raw material (timber) as well as the shift to exporting paper and paper products; fertilizers have lost ground to the more advanced branches of the chemical industry. But, as noted earlier, the major development has been the growth in the exports of manufactured goods at higher levels of fabrication that are included among minor exports. The expansion of these exports exceeded the world average so that, on balance,

Norway's competitive position has improved. Norway further benefited from the rapid increase in world demand for its major export commodities and the increase in export prices (see Table 2.6).

The System of Protection

Trade Policies Prior to World War II

When Norway gained its independence in 1814, it inherited a liberal trade policy from the Kingdom of Denmark and Norway. Although economic difficulties following independence and poor market conditions for major Norwegian exports led to increases in some tariffs in the 1830s, these were reduced again. With reductions in protective tariffs, duties were mainly concentrated on commodities, such as coffee, tea, sugar, tobacco, and fuels, which were not —and could not—be produced in the country. These tariffs served revenue purposes, with customs duties accounting for over four-fifths of government revenue throughout the nineteenth century.

The liberal trade policy followed by Norway corresponded to the needs of a country whose natural resources made it possible to attain relatively high living standards by exporting a few staple items and importing a variety of manufactured goods. Public discussions at the time were dominated by the idea that free trade results in low prices to the consumer and that protection would "unjustly" redistribute incomes to those who would benefit from it.

In 1875 a public commission even recommended the abolition of all protective tariffs. Although this recommendation was not followed, tariffs were not raised until the turn of the century when the termination of the free trade agreement with Sweden adversely affected Norwegian exports. This arrangement was established in stages from 1815 until 1875 when full exemption from duties was provided to practically all manufactured goods traded between the two countries.

TABLE 12.3: Principal Exports of Norway, 1950–67

| | | | | | (*Percent of total exports*) |
Commodity	1950	1955	1960	1965	1967
Fish, fresh (SITC 031.1)	3.0	4.0	3.5	3.9	3.0
Fish, dried (031.2)	7.8	7.8	5.8	3.2	3.1
Fish preparations (032.1)	4.7	3.1	2.6	1.8	1.5
Wood pulp (251)	11.1	12.0	9.0	6.0	4.5
Paper and paperboard (641)	12.3	10.4	10.6	8.2	7.5
Aluminum, unwrought (684.1)	3.2	4.3	7.7	8.0	8.9
Ships and boats (735)	4.2	5.0	5.2	9.7	13.7
Fertilizers, manufactured (561)	7.5	5.5	4.7	4.5	2.8
Total principal exports	53.8	52.1	49.8	45.3	45.0
Total exports ($ million)	390	633	880	1,443	1,736

Source: U.N., Yearbook of International Trade Statistics.

The Swedish-Norwegian free trade arrangement came to an end as increased protection in Sweden brought with it demands for abolishing the duty exemption accorded to Norwegian goods. As a first step, in 1887 and 1890, the Swedish government introduced more stringent rules for accepting a commodity originating in Norway as a "domestic product" eligible for duty exemption. In 1897, the free trade arrangement between the two countries was terminated and their commodities were henceforth given equal treatment with those originating elsewhere.

The unfavorable effects of the termination of the arrangement on Norwegian exports, together with Sweden's example of raising tariffs, led to protectionist pressures in Norway. The growing economic importance, and the commensurate political influence, of industrialists were further contributing factors. Nevertheless, increases in protective tariffs were small in absolute terms and the average of these tariffs did not exceed 10 percent.

In the period following World War I, Norwegian agricultural producers demanded protection and called for "trade policy equality" with manufacturing industries. The reasoning of agriculturalists was along effective protection lines. While price increases during the war reduced the average ad valorem equivalent of specific tariffs on manufactured goods to 6.5 percent, it was calculated that, with value added being higher in agriculture than in manufacturing, an average tariff of 9 percent on foodstuffs would be required to give equal protection to the two sectors.

These demands were met by increasing tariffs on foodstuffs and by introducing domestic market regulations. The specific duties imposed on manufactured goods were also raised, but these increases hardly offset the rise in prices after World War I. Increases in specific duties, along with the fall in prices during the depression, however, augmented the ad valorem equivalent of duties on manufactured goods during the thirties. Specific duties on manufactures were raised again in 1940, while agriculture became increasingly separated from the world market through a series of market regulations.

Tariffs and Economic Integration

Norway, along with other European countries, imposed quantitative restrictions on imports in the immediate postwar period and these, rather than tariffs, were binding at that time. In subsequent years, Norway took part in the dismantling of quantitative restrictions in the framework of the Organization for European Economic Cooperation although it lagged somewhat behind other European countries in the pace of quota liberalization. These delays were considered necessary to avoid large balance-of-payment deficits during the reconstruction period when pent-up consumer demand and investment needs, including the rebuilding of the merchant fleet, strained domestic resources.

Norway has also participated in negotiations on tariff reductions undertaken in the framework of GATT. Although reciprocity on the part of small countries was of secondary importance in the negotiations, Norway has chosen to reduce her tariffs to a considerable extent. This decision reflects the understanding of the importance of foreign trade for a small country and the desire to keep domestic producers competitive.

As a result of this policy, Norwegian tariffs are not only substantially lower than levels of protection in other countries included in this investigation but are also below the tariff levels of the major industrial countries. In 1958, the year for which comparable data are available, Norwegian tariffs on manufactured goods averaged 11.7 percent while the corresponding figures were 18.2 percent for the United Kingdom, 14.5 percent for the European Common Market, and 16.8 percent for the United States.[7]

We can thus classify Norway as a low-tariff country even in comparison with the major industrial nations that possess a highly advanced manufacturing sector. Furthermore, the structure of protection contains fewer peaks and valleys in Norway than in the United States and Britain, so that particular industries are not protected at the expense of others.[8] In 1958, Norwegian tariffs exceeded 20 percent in only 11 of the 91 industrial categories, while this occurred in 37 categories in the U.S. and 35 categories in the U.K. Norwegian duties are the highest on synthetic materials and fabrics, or clothing and travel goods, and on passenger automobiles. But, as Norway does not produce automobiles, tariffs on cars have the function of an excise tax.

Changes in Norwegian attitudes toward economic integration are of further interest. Along with Denmark and Sweden, Norway participated in negotiations for the establishment of a Nordic Union in the early postwar period. But the talks then were unsuccessful, largely because of Norway's reluctance to face Swedish competition in a customs union of the Scandinavian countries. Opposition was especially strong on the part of industrialists who feared that they would not be able to stand up to the more advanced Swedish industry.[9]

Attitudes had changed, however, by 1958 when the Norwegian industrial federation joined similar organizations of the other Scandinavian countries, Austria, Switzerland, and the United Kingdom in calling for the establishment of an all-European free trade area. Apparently, the ability of domestic producers to meet foreign competition despite reductions in tariffs, their increasing success in exporting manufactured goods, and the fear of being excluded

---

[7] Average of tariffs for 91 three- and four-digit SITC categories weighted by the combined imports of the OECD countries. Based on data published in Political and Economic Planning, *Atlantic Tariffs and Trade* (London: Allen & Unwin, 1962), pp. 3–62.

[8] This conclusion does not hold for the EEC where the averaging of the tariffs of the member nations reduced the dispersion of duties.

[9] For a detailed account of the negotiations, see Frantz Wendt, *The Nordic Council and Co-operation in Scandinavia* (Copenhagen: Munksgaard, 1959).

from the markets of the participating countries, led many industrialists to favor this scheme. On the part of the Norwegian government the major consideration appeared to be that the disadvantages of the small size of the home market could be overcome through participation in a larger area.

After the breakdown of negotiations for an all-European free trade area, Norway became one of the founding members of the European Free Trade Association, established in 1959. The other member countries of EFTA are Austria, Denmark, Portugal, Sweden, Switzerland, the United Kingdom and, first in an associate status and later as a full-fledged member, Finland. Since its creation, tariffs on intra-EFTA trade in nonagricultural products have been successively reduced and ultimately eliminated.

As of January 1, 1967, all Norwegian imports of manufactures from the other EFTA countries and Finland are duty-free. The only exception in force is that for goods which Norway has declared to be subject to fiscal duty, such as automobiles and hard liquor. On July 1, 1968, the tariff rate on automobiles was reduced from 30 to 10 percent, but the domestic excise duty was increased proportionately; this left the total charge unchanged. Taxes on hard liquor are also maintained by other member countries.

Participation in the European Free Trade Association has also entailed the elimination of drawbacks on exports to EFTA countries. This scheme, under which duties paid on goods used in the production of exported commodities are refunded, has been an integral part of Norwegian tariff policy. It is of importance to several branches of the manufacturing sector, and especially to the shipbuilding industry.

The provisions of the EFTA Convention on the elimination of drawbacks have led to pressures by producers for reductions in duties on intermediate products and have thereby strengthened Norway's free trade orientation. This was given expression in positions taken at the Kennedy round of tariff negotiations. The negotiations were attended by a joint delegation of Danish, Norwegian, and Swedish representatives who bargained as a unit. The three countries, together with Finland, have also started negotiations to establish a Nordic Economic Union.

Nontariff Measures

Protective measures other than tariffs are not generally applied in Norway; the major exception is restrictions on trade in agricultural products. Thus a government monopoly makes it possible to maintain a dual price system on cereals. Domestically produced cereals provide one-third of total consumption and are used chiefly as animal fodder. In 1954, the year for which our calculations were made, the domestic production of barley and oats was the largest, with output levels of 215 and 170 thousand tons, respectively. Wheat output (used exclusively as fodder) was 40 thousand tons, while little rye and no maize was produced.[10] In the same year, a comparison of prices paid to domestic producers and import prices shows a difference of about 30 percent for barley, 25 percent for oats, and 80 percent for wheat.[11]

Imports of fruits and vegetables are also subject to quantitative restrictions during periods when domestically produced varieties are available. Price comparisons are difficult to make for these commodities because of differences in quality. An exception is potatoes which is by far the most important product in the group; domestic prices here do not seem to exceed foreign prices.

Meat, eggs, and dairy products are subject to quantitative restrictions, and imports are admitted only during periods when domestic supplies are not sufficient to provide for home consumption. Our comparisons indicate that in 1954, domestic prices exceeded import prices by 26 percent for beef, 14 percent for pig meat, 36 percent for milk, and 11 percent for eggs.

On the basis of these data we have estimated the implicit nominal protection of agriculture (crops and livestock) in Norway. Weighting by the value of output, we have derived a 25 percent average implicit tariff for this sector in the year 1954. The implicit tariff on the agricultural inputs used in meat processing has been taken to be 20 percent and in the dairy industry 30 percent. Calculations of effective rates of protection have been made by utilizing these figures.

We have provided here a brief description of the development of the system of protection in Norway. The evaluation of the effects of the present system of protection on resource allocation is, however, made difficult by the differential treatment of imports from EFTA and from non-EFTA sources. Were we to assume that prices are determined in non-EFTA markets, the domestic price would equal the world market price plus the tariff, with exporters in EFTA countries receiving a preferential margin that would increase profits or permit operations at higher than world market costs in the EFTA countries. In such an eventuality, the nominal rates of protection in Norway would equal the tariffs levied on goods imported from non-EFTA sources. If, however, EFTA countries compete on the world market and do not engage in price discrimination, they would supply all Norwegian imports of standardized commodities and the nominal rate of protection on these commodities would be nil.

It follows that information on the sources of Norwegian imports would permit us to determine the nominal rate of protection on standardized com-

---

[10] Averages for 1953–54 and 1954–55. Food and Agriculture Organization, *Production Yearbook*.

[11] Price data on various commodities are from OECD, *Prices of Agricultural Products and Fertilizers;* FAO, *Monthly Bulletin of Agricultural Economics and Statistics;* and Norwegian import statistics.

modities. But most manufactured goods imported into Norway are differentiated products, on which price differentials lead to shifts in sources of supply, without entailing the disappearance of higher-priced imports. Since this fact makes it almost impossible to evaluate the present protection of Norwegian industries, we have decided to make calculations for a year prior to the establishment of the European Free Trade Association. The year 1954 has been used for this purpose because of the availability of detailed input-output data. This choice seems appropriate since by showing Norway at an earlier stage of industrial development, it increases comparability with the developing countries included in the study.

Nominal and Effective Protection

Table 12.4 shows estimates of nominal and effective rates of protection for fifty-two Norwegian industries, of which seven belong to the primary and forty-five to the manufacturing category. As noted above, implicit tariffs have been calculated for the major agricultural products while nominal tariffs have been utilized for all other products, since there are no prohibitive tariffs or quantitative restrictions on nonagricultural commodities in Norway. In the absence of information on domestic production in the appropriate breakdown, tariff averages for the individual industries have been derived by using international trade weights. Estimates of effective rates pertain to net value added, while value added has been defined in two alternative ways, depending on whether it includes (Corden method) or excludes (Balassa method) value added in the production of nontraded goods.

We have noted that the tariff average on manufactured goods calculated from PEP data was 11.7 percent in 1958. This result is practically identical to the tariff average of 11 percent obtained for 1954. In the same year, nominal rates of protection averaged 14 percent on primary products, largely because of the high protection accorded to agricultural activities carried out under favorable conditions in Norway (Tables 12.5 and 12.6).

We have further separated export and import-competing industries. In the former group we have put all industries where exports account for over 15 percent of domestic production. They include fishing, whaling, canned fish, other fish preparations, wood pulp, paper and paperboard, wallboard, manufactured fertilizers, fish oil and fish meal, whale oil, ferroalloys, aluminum, and shipbuilding. All other industries have imports exceeding 10 percent of domestic consumption and thus belong to the import-competing category.

While the nominal protection of exports is nil, their effective protection averages about −4 percent, indicating a small degree of discrimination against export industries. Nor is there a substantial bias against exports in import-competing industries. In these industries tariffs average 14 percent, the average

TABLE 12.4: Nominal and Effective Protection in Norway, 1954

(*Percent*)

Industrial category	Classifi- cation[a]	Industry	Nominal protection	Effective protection Balassa	Corden	Bias against exporting[b]
1110	IC	Agriculture	25	40	39	52
1121	IC	Forestry	1	1	1	1
1130	IC	Hunting	7	9	9	12
1140	X	Fishing	0	−3	−3	...
1150	X	Whaling	0	10	−8	...
1170	IC	Coal mining	0	0	0	0
1181	IC	Metal mining	0	−1	−1	−1
1190	IC	Nonmetallic minerals	0	0	0	0
1201	IC	Meat and meat preparations	18	16	16	*
1202	IC	Dairy products	31	20	20	−49
1203	IC	Margarine	14	44	41	163
1204	X	Canned fish	0	−6	−6	...
1205	X	Other fish preparations	0	−4	−4	...
1206	IC	Grain mill products and livestock feed	4	8	6	*
1207	IC	Bakery products	19	39	37	65
1208	IC	Confectionery	5	6	6	11
1209	IC	Other food preparations	4	3	3	15
1211	IC	Liquors	46	61	60	*
1213	IC	Breweries and soft drinks	26	38	36	51
1220	IC	Tobacco	111	243	236	812
1230	IC	Spinning and weaving	12	24	23	50
1232	IC	Knitting mills	17	29	27	98
1233	IC	Cordage, rope, and twine	7	4	3	19
1241	IC	Footwear, fur goods, and gloves	15	22	21	54
1243	IC	Clothing	18	30	29	102
1251	IC	Saw mills, planing mills, and wood preserving	0	−2	−2	0
1259	IC	Other wood and cork products, furniture, wood fixtures	5	6	6	13
1271	X	Wood pulp	0	−4	−4	...
1273	X	Paper and paperboard	0	−4	−3	...
1274	X	Wallboards	0	0	0	...
1275	IC	Paper and paperboard products	10	32	31	40
1281	IC	Publishing	0	−11	−9	0
1282	IC	Printing, bookbinding, etc.	6	11	10	11
1290	IC	Leather and leather products	14	52	48	62
1300	IC	Rubber products	15	31	29	48
1311	X	Calcium carbide, cyanamide, and other fertilizers	0	−5	−4	...
1315	IC	Other industrial chemicals	3	3	2	9
1317	X	Fish oil and fish meat	0	−3	−3	...
1318	IC	Vegetable oil	3	0	0	−1
1319	X	Whale oil	0	−7	−6	...
1330	IC	Nonmetallic mineral products	7	9	8	17
1340	X	Ferroalloys	0	−2	−1	...
1341	IC	Iron and steel works	3	4	3	7
1342	IC	Iron and steel foundries	7	9	8	14
1343	X	Refining of aluminium	0	−3	−2	...
1344	IC	Nonferrous metals	0	−2	−2	0
1356	IC	Wire and wire products	3	8	8	11
1356	IC	Other metal building articles	6	9	8	11
1356	IC	Other metal products	14	27	25	17
1356	IC	Metal packaging and household articles	9	19	18	27
1356	IC	Nonelectrical machinery	12	19	19	27
1356	IC	Railroad equipment	6	8	7	10
1356	IC	Motor vehicles	28	51	50	63
1356	IC	Bicycles, motorcycles	13	20	18	19
1370	IC	Electrical machinery	11	19	18	31
1380	X	Shipbuilding	0	−4	−4	...
1390	IC	Miscellaneous manufacturing	9	15	14	24

Sources: See text.

[a] X = export industries; IC = import-competing industries.

[b] Calculated by using the Corden formula.

* Denotes negative value added in case of exporting; thus, the extent of discrimination against exporting is infinite.

TABLE 12.5: Nominal and Effective Protection in the Major Sectors of the Norwegian Economy, 1954

(Percent)

Sector	Nominal protection	Effective protection Balassa	Effective protection Corden	Bias against exporting[a]
Primary production				
Exports	0	−5	−4	...
Import-competing goods	17	21	20	27
Total	14	15	15	21
Manufacturing				
Exports	0	−4	−4	...
Import-competing goods	13	19	18	35
Import-competing goods less beverages and tobacco	10	14	13	26
Total	11	12	12	24
All exports	0	−4	−4	...
All import-competing goods	14	19	19	32
All import-competing goods less beverages and tobacco	12	16	16	27
All commodites	11	13	13	23

Source: Table 12.4.
[a] Calculated by using the Corden formula.

TABLE 12.6: Nominal and Effective Protection for Major Product Categories in Norway, 1954

(Percent)

	Industry group	Estimates based on domestic coefficients Nominal protection	Estimates based on domestic coefficients Effective protection Balassa	Estimates based on domestic coefficients Effective protection Corden	Estimates based on free trade coefficients Nominal protection	Estimates based on free trade coefficients Effective protection Balassa	Estimates based on free trade coefficients Effective protection Corden
I	Agriculture, forestry, and fishing	15	16	16	24	36	34
II	Processed food	11	7	6	4	1	0
III	Beverages and tobacco	67	107	104	57	128	103
IV	Mining and energy	0	−1	0	0	−8	−7
V	Construction materials	5	6	6	6	9	8
VI-A	Intermediate products I	1	−1	−1	3	4	3
VI-B	Intermediate products II	7	12	11	7	16	14
VI	Intermediate products I and II	4	5	5	4	8	7
VII	Nondurable consumer goods	12	17	16	16	28	25
VIII	Consumer durables	25	39	38	27	68	57
IX	Machinery	12	19	18	12	20	18
X	Transport equipment	1	−2	−2	1	−7	−6
I–X	All industries	11	13	13	10	13	12
I + IV	Primary production	14	15	15	13	16	16
II, III, V–X	Manufacturing	11	12	12	7	11	10
VI–X	Manufacturing less food, beverages, tobacco, and construction materials	7	9	8	7	14	12

Source: Table 12.4.

rate of effective protection is 19 percent, and the bias against exports 32 percent; the latter is reduced by tariff drawbacks on imported inputs. The extent of protection is even lower if we exclude beverages and tobacco where tariffs serve revenue as well as social purposes. Nominal rates now average 12 percent, effective rates 16 percent, and the extent of discrimination against exports 27 percent.

The excess of effective over nominal rates indicates the escalation of the tariff structure in Norway. Effective rates are more than double the nominal rates on margarine, grain mill and bakery products, tobacco, paper and paperboard products, leather and leather products, and metal articles. In all these cases, the major input is imported duty-free or it is an export commodity. By contrast, nominal duties exceed effective tariffs on meat and meat preparations, dairy products, miscellaneous food preparations, cordage, rope, and twine, and miscellaneous chemicals.

The results for meat and dairy products are of especial interest since tariffs on these commodities are high by Norwegian standards: 18 and 31 percent, respectively. While the high cost of inputs due to agricultural protection reduces the effective protection of these products, they and several other processed foods (margarine, and bakery products) still have higher than average effective protection. Effective rates are also higher than the average in agriculture where nominal rates of protection are 25 percent and effective rates 40 percent.

Apart from agriculture and various processed foods, nominal and effective rates of protection are the highest on motor vehicles. But Norway produces only parts and accessories of automobiles for export so that protection serves the function of an excise tax. Among import-competing manufactures, nominal and effective rates of protection also exceed the average for spinning and weaving, knitting mills, shoes, clothing, leather and leather products, and rubber products. Effective, but not nominal, rates are above average for miscellaneous metal products, electrical and nonelectrical machinery, and bicycles and motorcycles whose inputs are subject to relatively low duties.

Among major product groups, the ranking in terms of nominal as well as effective tariffs is (from high to low): nondurable consumer goods, machinery, intermediate products at higher levels of fabrication, construction materials, intermediate products at lower levels of processing, and transport equipment. The same ranking is shown whether we use estimates derived by using domestic or free trade input-output coefficients. However, owing in good part to differences in weighting, the latter are usually higher than the former.

In Table 12.7, the estimates for Norway are compared to those for the major industrial countries. In the table the Norwegian results obtained under the Balassa method are used because these are more comparable to the estimates for the industrial countries than the results derived under the Corden

TABLE 12.7: Manufacturing Protection in Major Industrial Countries and in Norway, 1962

(Percent)

Industry group	United States		United Kingdom		Common Market		Sweden		Japan		Norway[a]	
	Nominal	Effective	Nominal	Effective	Nominal	Effective	Nominal	Effective	Nominal	Effective	Nominal	Effective
Intermediate products I	9.6	21.9	11.8	27.6	6.5	11.1	3.0	6.7	11.2	26.6	4.8	8.6
Intermediate products II	11.5	18.9	14.0	25.5	12.7	24.7	6.9	14.8	15.4	28.0	6.5	15.8
Nondurable consumer goods	21.1	32.9	23.0	38.0	16.1	26.2	10.5	19.0	22.4	36.5	16.1	27.7
Consumer durables	7.4	6.7	23.0	41.2	19.6	37.0	14.9	30.9	35.0	73.3	27.1	67.6
Machinery	10.6	15.0	17.3	24.3	12.0	16.0	9.6	14.1	17.5	23.4	11.7	20.3
Transport equipment	5.7	2.7	4.9	-5.5	1.6	-11.8	1.7	-3.7	13.3	12.8	1.3	-6.6
Manufacturing, total[b]	11.5	20.0	15.2	27.8	11.0	18.6	6.6	12.5	16.1	29.5	7.0	14.0

Source: Bela Balassa, "Tariff Protection in Industrial Countries: An Evaluation," *The Journal of Political Economy*, December 1965, pp. 573-94; and Table 3.1.
[a] Data refer to 1954.
[b] Excludes food processing, tobacco and beverages, as well as construction materials. Some of the averages have been corrected as compared to the original sources.

procedure. The comparisons pertain to manufactured goods defined in a narrower sense, i.e., excluding processed food, beverages and tobacco, as well as construction materials. Free trade coefficients have been used in deriving the estimates for all the countries in question.

The results confirm the PEP estimates according to which nominal protection is lower in Norway than in the United States, the United Kingdom, or the European Common Market. The same result is obtained for effective protection on all manufactured goods as well as for intermediate goods, nondurable consumer goods, and transport equipment. The effective protection on machinery is, however, somewhat greater in Norway than in the United States and the European Common Market. In addition, due largely to the high tariffs on automobiles, average effective rates on durable consumer goods are higher in Norway than in the U.S., U.K., and the EEC. Finally, effective rates of protection in Norway are generally somewhat higher than in Sweden but substantially lower than in Japan.

Overvaluation and Net Effective Protection

As noted in Chapter 1, in order to estimate net protection against imports and net discrimination against exports, we have to adjust for overvaluation as compared to the hypothetical free trade situation. For Norway, the range of possible values of the "free-trade" exchange rate is relatively small since the extent of the overvaluation cannot exceed the 13 percent average tariff on import-competing goods.

In making calculations, we have assumed that the elasticity of supply of Norway's imports is infinite. The elasticity of import demand for the major categories of nonagricultural products has been taken to be the same as for the Continental member countries of EFTA: 2.3 for finished manufactures, 1.1 for intermediate products, and 0.2 for industrial materials;[12] weighting by Norwegian imports, we obtain an average of 1.4. But the elimination of import barriers would have a profound effect on the agricultural sector where Norwegian producers would hardly be able to compete with imports under free trade conditions. Taking account of the possible expansion of agricultural imports, we have assumed a total import demand elasticity of 1.6 in Norway.

Norway's share in the world market of its major export commodities was in the range of 15–18 percent for fresh and dried fish and for aluminum as compared to 5–7 percent for fish preparations, wood pulp, ships, manufactured fertilizers, and paper. With a world demand elasticity of about 0.5 for these commodities, the corresponding average elasticity of demand for Nor-

---

[12] Bela Balassa, *Trade Liberalization among Industrial Countries* (New York: McGraw-Hill Co., 1967), p. 180.

way's major exports is around 5. The export demand elasticity is substantially higher for Norway's minor export commodities which accounted for about one-half of its total exports during the period under consideration. In estimating the extent of overvaluation as compared to the hypothetical free trade situation, we have assumed a demand elasticity of 8 for Norwegian merchandise exports, taken together.

The elasticity of supply of exports is also rather high in Norway. On the one hand, in the presence of intra-industry specialization, the freeing of trade permits a rapid expansion of exports through changes in product variety; on the other, the degree of interindustry mobility of resources is high in Norway. We have assumed here that a 1 percent rise in export prices would lead to a 6 percent increase in Norwegian exports.

These estimates pertain to merchandise exports. Yet, in 1954, two-fifths of export earnings were provided by shipping services for which the elasticities of demand and supply are likely to be smaller than for merchandise exports. We have arbitrarily assumed that for shipping, the relevant elasticities were one-half of those for merchandise exports.

Under these assumptions, we have estimated the extent of overvaluation as compared to free trade to be 4 percent. Since choosing other values for the elasticities would affect the outcome very little, alternative estimates have not been provided. Rates of net protection for the principal economic activities are shown in Tables 12.8 and 12.9; the relatively small adjustment did not warrant reproducing the detailed table containing information on individual industries. Net effective protection of import-competing goods other than

TABLE 12.8:   Net Nominal and Effective Protection in the Major Sectors of the Norwegian Economy, 1954[a]

(Percent)

Sector	Nominal protection	Effective protection
Primary production		
Exports	−4	−8
Import-competing goods	13	15
Total	10	11
Manufacturing		
Exports	−4	−8
Import-competing goods	9	13
Import-competing goods less beverages and tobacco	6	9
Total	7	8
All exports	−4	−8
All import-competing goods	10	14
All import-competing goods less beverages and tobacco	8	12
All commodities	7	9

Sources: Table 12.5 and text.

[a] Effective rates of protection have been estimated by using the Corden formula; both nominal and effective rates have been adjusted for overvaluation as compared to the hypothetical free trade situation.

TABLE 12.9: Net Nominal and Effective Protection for Major Product Categories in Norway, 1954[a]

(*Percent*)

	Industry group	Estimates based on domestic coefficients		Estimates based on free trade coefficients	
		Nominal protection	Effective protection	Nominal protection	Effective protection
I	Agriculture, forestry, and fishing	11	12	19	29
II	Processed food	7	2	0	−4
III	Beverages and tobacco	61	96	51	95
IV	Mining and energy	−4	−4	−4	−11
V	Construction materials	1	2	2	4
VI-A	Intermediate products I	−3	−5	−1	−1
VI-B	Intermediate products II	3	7	3	10
VI	Intermediate products I and II	0	1	0	3
VII	Nondurable consumer goods	8	12	12	20
VIII	Consumer durables	20	33	22	51
IX	Machinery	8	13	8	13
X	Transport equipment	−3	−6	−3	−10
I–X	All industries	7	9	6	8
I + IV	Primary production	10	11	9	12
II, III, V–X	Manufacturing	7	8	3	6
VI–X	Manufacturing less food, beverages, tobacco, and construction materials	3	4	3	8

Sources: Table 12.6 and text.

[a] Effective rates of protection have been estimated by using the Corden formula; both nominal and effective rates have been adjusted for overvaluation as compared to the hypothetical free trade situation.

beverages and tobacco now appears to be 12 percent and net discrimination against exports 8 percent. Similar conclusions apply if we separate primary production and manufacturing activities.

The results for the major industry groups (Table 12.9) are identical to those in Table 12.6 except that they are scaled down slightly. Among these groups, there appears to be a net discrimination against construction materials, intermediate products at lower levels of transformation, and transport equipment. By contrast, net effective rates of protection were in the 10–15 percent range for nondurable consumer goods and machinery, and were even higher for durable consumer goods. In the latter case, however, the results reflect the revenue on automobiles.

Evaluation and Policy Recommendations

The results show little discrimination among economic activities, in favor of import substitution, or against exports. The adoption of a liberal trade policy has in turn had beneficial effects on the development of an efficient manufacturing sector in Norway. For one thing, foreign competition has contributed to improvements in production methods in domestic industries. For another, cost reductions obtainable in large-scale production have not been frustrated by discrimination against export activities in the form of overvalued exchange rates and high duties on imported inputs.

The result has been a rapid growth of manufacturing industries, characterized by an export orientation. Between 1949 and 1966 value added in manufacturing industries at higher levels of fabrication rose at an annual rate of 5.2 percent and the exports of these manufactures at a rate of 15.8 percent. The impact of exports on the expansion of manufacturing output has assumed special importance after the establishment of EFTA. This is shown by increases in incremental export-production ratios in manufacturing—from 1949–58 to 1958–66, this ratio rose from 21 to 26 percent. As a result, the rate of growth of output accelerated; value added in manufacturing industries at higher levels of fabrication grew at an annual rate of 4.7 percent in the first period and 5.8 percent in the second.

The expansion of the manufacturing sector has entailed a shift toward industries with a high skilled-labor requirement, as well as to a higher level of processing. Interindustry specialization which has accompanied specialization within individual industries has led to a narrowing of product variety in individual firms. Norwegian firms also participate in the international division of the production process by manufacturing parts and components for assembly abroad.

The record of the Norwegian economy indicates the possibilities of expanding manufacturing industries behind low trade barriers in semi-industrial countries. The Norwegian example thus has implications for developing countries that have already built a manufacturing base. It has relevance especially for countries such as Argentina and Chile where industries have been oriented toward the domestic market.[13] It further indicates the advantages for a small country of participating in regional integration schemes.

Note should be taken, however, of the special advantages enjoyed by Norway. Exports of manufactured goods have benefited from the availability of nearby markets in countries that have long followed a liberal trade policy and have been eager to participate in regional integration schemes. Nevertheless, Norway has had success in faraway markets too.

The continuation of present policies as regards trade in manufactured goods augurs well for the future growth of the Norwegian economy. Norway would obtain further benefits from joining the Common Market since one-fourth of its exports go to the EEC countries as compared with two-fifths of EFTA. There would be need, however, for lessening agricultural protectionism.

---

[13] For a comparison of the experiences of Norway, Argentina, Chile, and three other semi-industrial countries, see Bela Balassa, "Growth Strategies in Semi-Industrial Countries."

APPENDICES

APPENDICES

THE EFFECTIVE RATE OF PROTECTION: THEORETICAL AND METHODOLOGICAL ISSUES

Bela Balassa

Nominal and Effective Protection in a Partial Equilibrium Context

The concepts of nominal and effective protection will first be defined in the framework of a simple partial equilibrium model. Let us assume that the elasticity of substitution among inputs is zero, production takes place under constant returns to scale, factor prices are unchanged, there is pure competition, transportation costs are nil, and both the foreign demand elasticity for the country's exports and the foreign supply elasticity of its imports are infinite. Now, if a_{ji} and a_{vi} are the amount of material inputs (j) and primary inputs (v) used per unit of output (i), P_j and P_v their world market prices, the world market price of output is taken to be unity, and m denotes the percentage excess of domestic over world market prices, we can express world market values as in (1a) and domestic values as in (1b).[1]

(1a) $$1 = \sum_j a_{ji}P_j + \sum_v a_{vi}P_v$$

(1b) $$1 + m_i = \sum_j a_{ji}P_j(1 + m_j) + \sum_v a_{vi}P_v(1 + m_v)$$

Next, assume that the product and its material inputs are traded while primary inputs are not. Since, under the stated assumptions, differences

---

[1] This formulation is based on a suggestion by Benjamin B. King.

between the domestic and the world market prices of traded goods can be due only to tariffs and other protective measures, we can reinterpret (1b) as in (2).

$$(2) \qquad Z_i = \frac{(1 + m_i) - \sum_j a_{ji}P_j(1 + m_j)}{\sum_v a_{vi}P_i} - 1$$

$$= \frac{(1 + T_i) - \sum_j a_{ji}P_j(1 + T_j)}{\sum_v a_{vi}P_i} - 1$$

The percentage excess of domestic over world market prices for the output and for material inputs is termed the nominal rate of protection (T). In turn, taking the contribution of primary inputs to output (for short, value added) as a unit, we define the effective rate of protection (Z) as the percentage excess of the domestic price of the value added unit over its world market price.[2]

As long as input coefficients are assumed to be constant, this general formulation of effective protection can be reinterpreted as the percentage excess of domestic value added (W) over world market value added (V), which is the expression utilized in Chapter 1. We will return to the general formulation below when we remove the assumption of zero substitution elasticity among inputs.

The Use of Input-Output Coefficients

In practice, effective rates of protection are calculated by the use of input-output coefficients which refer to the value of inputs per unit of output. Under free trade conditions, input-output coefficients (A_{ji}) will equal the corresponding input coefficient defined in natural units (a_{ji}) times the ratio of the world market price of the input to that of output. Taking again the world market price of output to be one, we can rewrite (2) as in (3).

$$(3) \qquad Z_i = \frac{W_i - V_i}{V_i} = \frac{(1 + T_i) - \sum_j A_{ji}(1 + T_j)}{1 - \sum_j A_{ji}} - 1 = \frac{T_i - \sum_j A_{ji}T_j}{1 - \sum_j A_{ji}}$$

---

[2] The relevant world market prices are those a country faces in foreign trade: c.i.f. prices for actual and potential imports and f.o.b. prices for exports. In the following, we will assume for the sake of simplicity that domestic prices equal the sum of the c.i.f. price and the tariff in the first case and the sum of f.o.b. price and export subsidies in the second; i.e., the nominal rate of protection is taken to equal, respectively, the rate of tariff and the rate of export subsidy. However, the formulas can be reinterpreted in terms of the other protective measures described in Chapter 1 (pp. 10–11).

This formula can be used to obtain the results shown in Chapter 1 (pp. 5–6). In the clothing example, T_i is .10, while A_{ji} and V_i are .60 and .40, respectively. The numerator of (3) can now be calculated either as the difference between domestic and world market value added (.54 − .40) or as the difference between the tariff on the product and the tariff on the material input weighted by the latter's share in the product price on the world market (.20 − .06). The numerator will thus be .14 while the denominator is .40, so that we obtain an effective rate of protection of 35 percent.[3]

In the case of an export product (meat), the rate of export subsidy (S) replaces the rate of tariff (T) in the formula. In the absence of subsidies, and with the other variables (T_j, A_{ji}, V_i) assuming the same values as beforehand, the numerator of the expression will be negative (−.06) and so will the effective rate of protection (−15 percent). In turn, with a 6 percent export subsidy, the numerator and hence the effective rate of protection will be zero. More generally, the effective rate of protection will be positive, zero, or negative, depending on whether the "subsidy element" due to the nominal protection of the product—the first term in (3)—is greater than, equal to, or less than the "implicit tax" due to the protection of material inputs—the second term in (3).

If calculations are made by using domestic (post-protection) rather than free trade (pre-protection) input-output coefficients, the effective rate of protection is estimated from (4).

$$(4) \qquad Z_i = \frac{W_i - V_i}{V_i} = \frac{W_i}{V_i} - 1 = \frac{P_i - \sum_j A_{ji'}}{\dfrac{P_i}{1 + T_i} - \sum_j \dfrac{A_{ji'}}{1 + T_j}} - 1$$

In this eventuality, we observe the domestic price of output (P_i) and the domestic value of inputs per unit of output ($A_{ji'}$) and derive world market values by deflating domestic values by the relevant price ratios.

Under the assumption of constant input coefficients, (3) and (4) will give the same result if identical data are used for both. In practice, however, we obtain domestic input-output coefficients for each country from that country's input-output table while, in the absence of direct information on the input-output coefficients that would prevail under free trade conditions, these have to be "borrowed" from elsewhere.

Free trade coefficients, including that for value added, are by definition

---

[3] In (3) the world market price of the product is taken as unity and all variables are expressed in percentage terms. The equation can also be reinterpreted in expressing all magnitudes in absolute terms; this has been done in the example in Chapter 1. World market values will then be multiplied by the exchange rate to make them comparable to domestic values.

positive. However, using domestic coefficients, we may obtain negative "derived" world market value added in the sense that the world market value of material inputs exceeds that of output.[4] If (4) is applied, negative "derived" world market value added will give rise to negative effective rates, as does "genuine" negative protection when the implicit tax on inputs outweighs the subsidy provided by nominal protection.

To avoid problems of interpretation, it has been suggested that an alternative measure (U)—defined as the ratio of the difference between domestic and world market value added to domestic value added—be used instead of Z. This measure assumes negative values only in the event of genuine negative protection; it has a value greater than one if world market value added is negative.[5]

It is apparent, however, that U does not provide additional information since it is obtained as a simple transformation of Z (5a).

$$(5a) \qquad U = \frac{W - V}{W} = \frac{(W - V)V}{WV} = Z\frac{V}{W} = \frac{Z}{Z + 1}$$

$$(5b) \qquad Z = \frac{W - V}{V} = \frac{(W - V)W}{VW} = U\frac{W}{V} = \frac{U}{1 - U}$$

If world market value added (V) is positive and less than domestic value added (W), Z will assume values between 0 and ∞ and U between 0 and 100 percent; if V is positive but exceeds W, Z will be between 0 and -100 percent and U between 0 and $-\infty$; finally, if V is negative, Z will be in the range between -100 percent and $-\infty$ and U between 100 percent and ∞. Thus the magnitude of negative values of Z permits us to make a distinction between genuine negative protection $(0 > Z > -100)$ and negative value added at world market prices $(Z < -100)$.

It should be added that, irrespective of the measures applied, ranking by effective rates of protection is subject to difficulties whenever world market value added is negative. As the following example indicates, both Z and U will rise or fall depending on whether an increase in protection takes the form of a smaller V (case II) or a larger W (case III). This difficulty can be obviated if we reinterpret the effective rate of protection as a measure of the cost of foreign exchange, i.e., the amount of domestic resources (value added) spent to save (or earn) a unit of foreign exchange. Case II will now show a decline and case III an increase in domestic value added per unit of

---

[4] For the circumstances that may give rise to negative "derived" world market value added, see Chapter 4, p. 74.

[5] Cf. R. Soligo and J. J. Stern, "Tariff Protection, Import Substitution, and Investment Efficiency," *Pakistan Development Review*, Summer 1965, pp. 249–70.

	W	V	Z	U
I	600 pesos	−400 pesos	−250%	167%
II	600	−500	−220	183
III	800	−400	−300	150
IV	450	−300	−250	167

foreign exchange lost in the form of negative value added. Thus, in terms of the domestic cost of foreign exchange, an increase in the values of Z and U indicates an improvement, and a decrease, a deterioration.

Note further that the Z-measure provides information on the relative magnitudes of the nominal rates of protection on the product and its material inputs taken together. From (3) it is apparent that Z_i will be greater than, equal to, or less than T_i depending on whether T_i is greater than, equal to, or less than the weighted average of the T_j's. No simple relationship is shown for the U-measure.[6] Considering also the straightforward economic interpretation of the Z-measure as the percentage excess of domestic over world market value added, we have opted for it in measuring effective protection.

Calculations of effective rates of protection have also involved problems of classification and averaging which are discussed in Chapter 1 (pp. 18–21). Averages of effective rates ($\bar{Z}$) have further been calculated for various industry groups. Estimates based on domestic input-output tables have been averaged by using "derived" world market value added as weights.[7] As shown in (6), the averages are unbiased in the sense of being equal to effective rates calculated directly from aggregated data.[8]

$$(6) \quad \bar{Z} = \frac{\Sigma ZV}{\Sigma V} = \frac{\Sigma \frac{W - V}{V} V}{\Sigma V} = \frac{\Sigma W - \Sigma V}{\Sigma V}$$

This weighting scheme could not be applied in calculations based on free trade coefficients since the latter are given in percentage terms. Instead, effective rates have been averaged by using as weights the combined imports of the industrial countries that are taken to represent the relative importance of individual commodities and commodity groups in the world market.[9]

---

[6] If Z_i equals T_i, however, U_i will equal $T_i/T_i + 1$.

[7] I am indebted to Maurice Scott on this point.

[8] It will be observed that, under this method of averaging, the product of the effective rate and world market value added will be positive whenever the latter is negative. Furthermore, high effective rates due to the smallness of "derived" world market value added will not distort the averages since their weight in the averaging will be small.

[9] On the origin of the free trade coefficients and the weighting scheme applied, see Chapter 1, pp. 15–16.

Treatment of Indirect Taxes

In Chapter 1, we have noted that the imposition of indirect taxes on the product does not affect its protection as long as indirect taxes are levied at the same rate on both domestically produced and imported varieties. By contrast, the imposition of indirect taxes on material inputs will reduce the extent of protection of domestic industry by raising the cost of these inputs while leaving net receipts unchanged.

Equations (3a) and (4a) admit the possibility that rates of indirect taxes on the domestically produced variety (T_{di}) and on imports (T_{mi}) of the same commodity are different.

$$(3a) \quad Z_i = \frac{(1 + T_i)(1 + T_{mi} - T_{di}) - \sum_j A_{ji}(1 + T_j)(1 + T_{mj}) - \left(1 - \sum_j A_{ji}\right)}{1 - \sum_j A_{ji}}$$

$$= \frac{T_i + T_{mi} - T_{di} + T_i T_{mi} - T_i T_{di} - \sum_j A_{ji}(T_j + T_{mj} + T_j T_{mj})}{1 - \sum_j A_{ji}}$$

$$(4a) \quad Z_i = \frac{\dfrac{P_i}{1 + T_{di}} - \sum_j A_{ji'}}{\dfrac{P_i}{(1 + T_i)(1 + T_{mi})} - \sum_j \dfrac{A_{ji'}}{(1 + T_j)(1 + T_{mj})}}$$

The formula includes, however, only the rate of indirect taxes applicable to imported inputs (T_{mj}); from the point of view of protection, the tax rate on domestically produced inputs (T_{dj}) is irrelevant unless it exceeds the combined rate of tariffs and indirect taxes on imported inputs.

If rates of indirect taxes on the domestically produced and on the imported variety of the product are identical, (3a) assumes a simpler form (3b).

$$(3b) \quad Z_i = \frac{T_i - \sum_j A_{ji}(T_j + T_{mj} + T_j T_{mj})}{V_i}$$

This is the assumption made in the following example, where the rate of indirect taxes on both the output and the material inputs is taken to be 10 percent, the rate of tariff on the commodity 20 percent and on its material inputs 10 percent. Since indirect taxes are levied on tariff-inclusive values, the rate of tariff *cum* indirect taxes will be 21 percent on inputs and 32 percent on the output, while the effective rate of protection on the latter will be 18.5 percent.

By contrast, in the absence of indirect taxes, the domestic value of material inputs would be 66 pesos and that of output 120 pesos, resulting in a domestic value added of 54 pesos. Accordingly, the imposition of indirect taxes on inputs has reduced the effective rate of protection from 35 to 18.5 percent. This difference indicates the importance of adjusting for indirect taxes in the calculations.

	World market values (*pesos*)	Difference (*percent*)	Domestic values (*pesos*)
Material inputs	60	21.0	72.6
Value added	40	18.5	47.4
Output at factor cost	100	20.0	120.0
Indirect tax	10		12.0
Output at market prices	110	20.0	132.0

Treatment of Nontraded Goods

In Chapter 1 we have noted that the Corden procedure of treating non-traded goods includes value added in the production of nontraded goods with value added in processing so that the extent of protection is calculated with respect to the sum of the two. Conversely, under the Balassa method, it is assumed that nontraded goods are supplied to the processing industry at constant costs and the protection of value added in processing alone is measured.

To derive the Corden measure, the direct and indirect contributions of primary factors are summed up through the various stages of producing a nontraded good; i.e., one goes down the input-output structure until a material input is reached. This entails dividing the value of nontraded inputs into (1) direct and indirect material inputs which are combined with the value of material inputs used in the production process, and (2) direct and indirect value added which are combined with value added in processing. Tariffs on material inputs used in producing nontraded goods are thus assumed to increase the cost of these inputs to the producer. The Balassa method also assumes the forward shifting of such tariffs; i.e., the effective rate of protection of nontraded goods is taken to be zero.[10]

Let us denote the input-output coefficients for nontraded goods by A_{ni}, when A_{ni} is divided into (1) the cumulated value of material inputs and (2) value added in the production of nontraded goods. This division is effected on the basis of information on the elements of the matrix of direct and indirect material and value added input-output coefficients for nontraded goods which are denoted by r_{jn} and r_{wn}, respectively. The effective rates of protection under the Balassa (B) and Corden (C) methods are estimated from free trade input-output coefficients by using (7) to (12).

---

[10] Similar adjustments could be made for labor and capital if we were to assume that the cost-push effects of protection would raise their prices above free trade levels. Cf. D. B. Humphrey, "Measuring the Effective Rates of Protection: Direct and Indirect Effects," *Journal of Political Economy*, September/October 1969, pp. 834–44.

(7) $\qquad \sum_n A_{ni} = \sum_j \sum_n A_{ni} r_{jn} + \sum_w \sum_n A_{ni} r_{wn}$,   when $r_{jn} + r_{wn} = 1$

(8) $\qquad V_i^B = 1 - \sum_j A_{ji} - \sum_n A_{ni}$

(9) $\qquad V_i^C = 1 - \sum_j \sum_n A_{ni} r_{jn} = V_i^B + \sum_w \sum_n A_{ni} r_{wn}$

(10) $\qquad W_i^B = (1 + T_i) - \sum_j A_{ji}(1 + T_j) - \sum_j \sum_n A_{ni} r_{jn}(1 + T_j)$

$$- \sum_w \sum_n A_{ni} r_{wn}$$

(11) $\qquad W_i^C = (1 + T_i) - \sum_j A_{ji}(1 + T_j) - \sum_j \sum_n A_{ni} r_{jn}(1 + T_j)$

$$= W_i^B + \sum_w \sum_n A_{ni} r_{wn}$$

(12a) $\qquad Z_i^B = \dfrac{W_i^B - V_i^B}{V_i^B}$

(12b) $\qquad Z_i^C = \dfrac{W_i^C - V_i^C}{V_i^C}$

$$= \dfrac{(W_i^B + \sum_w \sum_n A_{ni} r_{wn}) - (V_i^B + \sum_w \sum_n A_{ni} r_{wn})}{V_i^B + \sum_w \sum_n A_{ni} r_{wn}}$$

$$= \dfrac{W_i^B - V_i^B}{V_i^B + \sum_w \sum_n A_{ni} r_{wn}}$$

It follows that the difference in the formulas used for estimating the effective rate of protection under the Corden and the Balassa methods is that the former includes, and the latter excludes, in the denominator of the equation, the term

$$\sum_w \sum_n A_{ni} r_{wn}$$

(the cumulated value added elements of nontraded inputs). Since this term is always positive, the Corden formula will give a smaller or greater result depending on whether the effective rate of protection is positive or negative. The same conclusion pertains to the estimation of the effective rate of protection from domestic input-output coefficients; in the latter case, domestic and world market value added under the two definitions can be expressed as follows:

(13) $\qquad W_i^B = P_i - \sum_j A_{ji'} - \sum_n A_{ni'}$

(14) $W_i^C = P_i - \sum_j A_{ji}' - \sum_j \sum_n A_{ni}' r_{jn} = W_i^B + \sum_w \sum_n A_{ni}' r_{wn}$

(15) $V_i^B = \dfrac{P_i}{1 + T_i} - \sum_j \dfrac{A_{ji}'}{1 + T_j} - \sum_j \sum_n \dfrac{A_{ni}' r_{jn}}{1 + T_j} - \sum_w \sum_n A_{ni}' r_{wn}$

(16) $V_i^C = \dfrac{P_i}{1 + T_i} - \sum_j \dfrac{A_{ji}'}{1 + T_j} - \sum_j \sum_n \dfrac{A_{ni}' r_{jn}}{1 + T_j}$

$= V_i^B + \sum_w \sum_n A_{ni}' r_{wn}$

Thus,

(17a) $Z_i^B = \dfrac{W_i^B - V_i^B}{V_i^B}$

(17b) $Z_i^C = \dfrac{W_i^B - V_i^B}{V_i^B + \sum_w \sum_n A_{ni}' r_{wn}}$

In practical instances, it is rarely necessary to go back for more than two stages in calculating the value added and the material content of nontraded goods. Let us assume, for example, that output at free trade prices is 100 pesos, material inputs 50 pesos, value added 35 pesos, and the nontraded input is valued at 15 pesos. In turn, the breakdown of the nontraded input is 4 pesos value added, 7 pesos material inputs, and 4 pesos other nontraded inputs, with the latter divided between 3 pesos material inputs and 1 peso value added. Assuming tariffs of 20 percent on the output and 10 percent on the material inputs, and substituting into equations (7) to (12), we get

$$\sum_n A_{ni} = (7 + 3) + (4 + 1) = 10 + 5 = 15$$

$$V_i^B = 100 - 50 - 15 = 35 \qquad V_i^C = 35 + 5 = 40$$

$$W_i^B = 120 - 55 - 11 - 5 = 49 \quad W_i^C = 49 + 5 = 54$$

$$Z_i^B = \frac{49 - 35}{35} = 40 \text{ percent} \qquad Z_i^C = \frac{54 - 40}{40} = 35 \text{ percent}$$

The Balassa and Corden methods are two possible alternatives for treating nontraded goods. Maurice Scott suggests a third alternative that he calls the "ideal" method. This method, used in the study undertaken by the OECD Development Centre is based on the hypothesis that the proportionate differences between the domestic and the free trade values of nontraded inputs equaled the weighted average of the nominal protection for manufacturing and agriculture (i.e., for practically all industries producing traded goods).[11] Deflating the domestic value of nontraded inputs by the weighted average of

[11] Ian Little, Tibor Scitovsky, and Maurice Scott, *Industry and Trade in Some Developing Countries* (London: Oxford University Press, 1970), Appendix to Chapter 5.

nominal rates can be regarded as a proxy for adjusting for the difference between the actual and the free trade exchange rate, the need for which is indicated on pp. 7–9. But, as seen from (26), the exchange rate adjustment will equal the weighted average of nominal rates only under special assumptions as regards the relevant variables. Correspondingly, we have not made use of the Scott method.

Calculation of "Net" Effective Rates

Net effective rates of protection can be derived by adjusting effective rates estimated at the actual exchange rates for the extent of overvaluation as compared to the hypothetical free trade situation, or by expressing world market values in terms of domestic currency at the exchange rate that would obtain under free trade conditions.

In the application of the first method, use is made of (18a) and (18b) which express domestic prices of a particular commodity under protection and under free trade in terms of world market prices, exchange rates, and tariffs.

(18a) $\quad P_{id} = P_{iw}R(1 + T_i)$

(18b) $\quad P_{id}' = P_{iw}R'$

In the equations, P_d denotes the domestic price expressed in terms of the domestic currency, P_w is the world market price expressed in foreign currency, and R the exchange rate. Unprimed magnitudes refer to the situation under protection and primed magnitudes pertain to free trade values. The world market price of the commodity in question is taken to be unaffected by production in the importing country.

The net nominal rate of protection, (T'), the percentage excess of the domestic price under protection over that under free trade, can now be expressed as in (19).

(19) $\quad T_i' = \dfrac{P_{id}}{P_{id}'} - 1 = (1 + T_i)\dfrac{R}{R'} - 1$

Thus, if the actual exchange rate (R) is 100 pesos to the dollar, and the free trade rate (R') 110 pesos to the dollar, a 20 percent nominal rate of protection (T) will correspond to a net nominal rate (T') of 9.1 percent.

In the absence of nontraded inputs, the same adjustment is made in the effective rate of protection (19a), since output as well as input values are adjusted in the same fashion.

(19a) $\quad Z_i' = \dfrac{R(1 + Z_i)}{R'} - 1$

If we assume a 10 percent overvaluation as compared to the free trade situation (i.e., R'/R equals 1.1), the 35 percent effective rate of protection for clothing calculated at the going exchange rate (pp.5–6) will correspond to a net effective rate of 22.7 percent. Furthermore, the -15 percent effective rate of protection on meat will become a net effective rate of -22.7 percent, and the zero effective rate a net effective rate of -9.1 percent.

Under the alternative procedure we recalculate the effective rate of protection by expressing world market values in domestic currency at the free trade exchange rate. Estimates of net rates of protection—nominal and effective—can then be derived by taking the percentage difference between domestic values under protection and world market values converted at the free trade exchange rate. This is shown in the following example.

| | World market values | | | | World market values in | Net |
	in foreign prices (*dollar*)	in domestic prices at actual exchange rate (*pesos*)	Nominal and effective rates of protection (*percent*)	Domestic values (*pesos*)	domestic prices at free trade exchange rate (*pesos*)	nominal and effective rates of protection (*percent*)
Clothing						
Material inputs	0.60	60	10	66	66	0
Value added	0.40	40	35	54	44	22.7
Product value	1.00	100	20	120	110	9.1
Meat						
Material inputs	0.60	60	10	66	66	0
Value added	0.40	40	0	40	44	−9.1
Product value	1.00	100	6	106	110	−3.6

It is easy to see that the described adjustment for overvaluation does not affect the ranking of industries by effective rates. Nor does the introduction of nontraded inputs modify either the method of adjustment or the ranking of industries by effective rates as long as the Corden method is applied; for this method combines value added in producing nontraded inputs with value added in processing. On the other hand, the adjustment is made by the use of a more complicated formula, and the ranking of industries by effective rates may change under the Balassa method, which regards the value added component of nontraded goods as an input whose value does not vary with the exchange rate. The differences between the results are, however, small and we report only those obtained with the Corden formula.

It will be recalled that effective rates of protection are estimated under the assumption of infinite foreign demand elasticities, i.e., constant world market prices. Although it can be assumed that the imports of developing countries are supplied at constant costs, their exports rarely face infinitely elastic world demand. To the extent that this is not the case, the degree of discrimination against export industries will be overstated; the lower is the elasticity of foreign demand for a country's exports, the less will the overvaluation of the exchange rate associated with protection reduce the domestic prices of these exports.

Less than infinite elasticities of export demand thus call for an additional adjustment in the estimates of effective protection for export industries. Because of the error possibilities associated with the assumed values of the relevant elasticities for particular products, such adjustments have not been made for individual industries. However, the estimates of nominal and effective protection on primary exports, the exports of manufactured goods, and the total exports of the individual countries have been adjusted on the basis of the elasticities of export demand assumed in the country studies.

Estimation of the Extent of Overvaluation

In this volume, we have applied the first method of estimating net effective rates of protection that involves adjusting effective rates calculated at existing exchange rates for the extent of overvaluation as compared to the hypothetical free trade situation. Logically, the estimation of the extent of overvaluation proceeds in two stages. First, we estimate the decrease in exports and the increase in imports that would result from the elimination of protective measures; second, we calculate the extent of the devaluation which would be necessary to remedy the ensuing deficit in the balance of payments.[12]

Under the assumption of infinite foreign supply elasticities, changes in imports due to the elimination of tariffs can be calculated alternatively by the use of a direct and an indirect method. Under the first method (20), changes in imports due to the elimination of tariffs (ΔM_1) are estimated on the basis of information on actual imports (M), the elasticity of import demand defined as a positive number (η_m), and changes in the average prices of imported goods that result from the removal of tariffs ($T/1 + T$).[13]

$$(20) \qquad \Delta M_1 = \eta_m \frac{T}{1 + T} M$$

Under the second method, (21), the import demand elasticity is replaced by the elasticities of domestic demand (η) and supply (ϵ), and changes in imports are separated into changes in domestic demand (ΔC) and supply (ΔP).

$$(21) \qquad \Delta M_1 = \Delta C - \Delta P = \eta \frac{T}{1 + T} C - \epsilon \frac{T}{1 + T} P$$

The mathematical identity of the two formulations is shown by (22); thus the two methods give identical results if the relevant elasticities are estimated without error.

---

[12] On the conditions of an outcome when free trade is accompanied by an appreciation rather than a depreciation of the currency, see H. G. Johnson, "A Model of Protection and the Exchange Rate," *Review of Economic Studies*, vol. 33, no. 2, pp. 159–67.

[13] For simplicity's sake, formulas (20) to (26) relate to estimations for total imports and exports. On disaggregated estimation, see pp. 330–31 below.

$$(22) \qquad \eta_m = \eta \frac{C}{M} + \epsilon \frac{P}{M}$$

One should further take account of the elimination of tariffs on the material inputs used in the production of protected goods. Accordingly, (21) is replaced by (21a) where the elasticity of supply of output (ϵ) is replaced by the elasticity of supply of value added (ϵ').[14]

$$(21a) \qquad \Delta M_1 = \eta \frac{T}{1+T} C - \epsilon' \frac{Z}{1+Z} P$$

This formula would permit separating the consumption and the production effects of the elimination of protective measures and making use of estimates of effective protection. In the absence of information on domestic demand and supply elasticities, however, it has not been possible to employ this procedure and we have used the direct method instead. The latter has also been employed in estimating changes in exports.

Changes in exports due to the elimination of export subsidies will depend on the original amount of exports, the rate of export subsidies, and the elasticity of supply of foreign exchange (ϵ_f); the latter is, in turn, determined by the elasticities of demand for (η_x) and supply of (ϵ_x) exports. The resulting changes in exports (ΔX_1) can be estimated by (23) where S refers to the rate of export subsidy; an export tax is taken to be a negative subsidy.

$$(23) \qquad \Delta X_1 = - \frac{\epsilon_x(\eta_x - 1)}{\epsilon_x + \eta_x} \frac{S}{1+S} X = - \epsilon_f \frac{S}{1+S} X$$

Next, we need to estimate the percentage devaluation ($R'/R - 1$) necessary to remedy the deficit that would result from the elimination of protective measures in the case of initial balance-of-payments equilibrium. The relevant formula (24) is composed of the same elements as (20) and (23) except that the price change due to the elimination of protective measures is now replaced by that due to devaluation with corresponding changes in the signs of the terms representing changes in exports and imports.

$$(24) \qquad \Delta M_1 - \Delta X_1 = \Delta X_2 - \Delta M_2$$
$$= \left(\frac{R'}{R} - 1 \right) \left[\frac{\epsilon_x(\eta_x - 1)}{\epsilon_x + \eta_x} X + \eta_m M \right]$$
$$= \left(\frac{R'}{R} - 1 \right) (\epsilon_f X + \eta_m M)$$

---

[14] For a derivation of this result, see H. G. Johnson, "The Theory of Effective Protection and Preferences," *Economica*, May 1969, pp. 119–38.

In actual estimation we combine (20), (23), and (24), with account taken of the simultaneity of changes in tariffs, export subsidies, and exchange rate. The condition for balance-of-payments equilibrium after the elimination of tariffs and subsidies and the compensating devaluation is indicated by (25). In turn, from (25), we can express the ratio R'/R (26) which is substituted into (19) to calculate net effective rates of protection.

(25) $\quad \epsilon_f \left[\dfrac{R'}{R(1 + S)} - 1 \right] X - \eta_m \left[\dfrac{R'}{R(1 + T)} \right] M = 0$

(26) $\quad \dfrac{R'}{R} = \dfrac{\epsilon_f X + \eta_m M}{\dfrac{\epsilon_f X}{1 + S} + \dfrac{\eta_m M}{1 + T}}$

It is easy to see that in the usual case when the rate of tariff exceeds the rate of export subsidy, the extent of overvaluation will be smaller than the former rate and greater than the latter. Correspondingly, in (25) the term in the first brackets will be positive and the term in the second brackets negative, i.e., both exports and imports would rise after the elimination of tariffs and subsidies *cum* devaluation. It is further apparent that if the rate of tariff exceeds the rate of export subsidy, the extent of overvaluation will be positively correlated with the elasticity of import demand and negatively with the elasticity of supply of foreign exchange. The latter, in turn, is positively related to the elasticities of demand for, and supply of, exports. The extent of overvaluation is independent of the values taken by the elasticities only if average rates of tariffs and export subsidies are identical, and it will then be equal to these rates.

Thus far we have assumed that the country's balance of payments is initially in equilibrium, in the sense that, given the protective measures actually applied, there is no unplanned reserve loss or temporary short-term capital movements. Under this definition the balance of payments was in equilibrium during the period under consideration in the countries in question, except for Chile. In Chile's case, equations (25) and (26) have been replaced by equations (25a) and (26a) which express the need to eliminate the unplanned deficit in the balance of payments (D).

(25a) $\quad \epsilon_f \left(\dfrac{R'}{R(1 + S)} - 1 \right) X + \eta_m \left(\dfrac{R'}{R(1 + T)} - 1 \right) M = D$

(26a) $\quad \dfrac{R'}{R} = \dfrac{\epsilon_f X + \eta_m M + D}{\dfrac{\epsilon_f X}{1 + S} + \dfrac{\eta_m M}{1 + T}}$

Adjustment for Overvaluation

The sensitivity of the results to the assumptions made in regard to the elasticities is shown in Table A.1. Assume, for example, that exports and imports are initially equal, the rate of export subsidy is 5 percent, the rate of tariff 30 percent, the import demand elasticity (η_m) 4, while the elasticities of demand (η_x) and supply (ϵ_x) of the country's exports are 12 and 6. The elasticity of supply of foreign exchange (ϵ_f) will then be 3.67 and the extent of overvaluation as compared to a free trade situation 16.6 percent. Adjusting for overvaluation by substituting this value into equation (12) will reduce the tariff from 30 percent to 11.5 percent; in turn, the 5 percent average export subsidy becomes a 9 percent export tax. Similar adjustments would need to be made in regard to the effective rate of protection.

These results are obtained under the medium assumptions made in Table A.1 in regard to the relevant elasticities. The two extremes are an overvaluation of 10.5 and 23.5 percent. These assume variations in all three elasticities—and all in the same direction from the point of view of the extent of overvaluation—by a factor of three. If we consider twofold variations in each, the range will be nine percentage points.

But we can hardly assume that errors in all three elasticity values would affect the extent of overvaluation in the same direction. With compensating errors, the variation in the estimated extent of overvaluation will be relatively small. If instead we vary one of the elasticities but keep the others unchanged, a twofold variation will give a range of only four percentage points.

TABLE A.1:   Estimation of Overvaluation under Alternative Assumptions

			Extent of overvaluation as compared with free trade $(R'/R - 1)$		
η_x	ϵ_x	ϵ_f	$\eta_m = 2$	$\eta_m = 4$	$\eta_m = 6$
	3	1.67	17.3	21.4	23.5
6	6	2.67	14.5	18.7	21.1
	9	3.00	13.6	17.8	20.3
	3	2.20	15.4	19.7	22.0
12	6	3.67	12.5	16.6	19.1
	9	4.71	11.3	15.1	17.6
	3	2.43	15.1	19.3	21.6
18	6	4.25	11.8	15.7	18.2
	9	5.67	10.5	14.0	16.5

Source: See text.

Note: The table indicates the extent of overvaluation as compared to a free trade situation $(R'/R - 1)$ under alternative assumptions as regards the elasticity of import demand (η_m), the elasticity of supply (ϵ_x) and demand (η_x) of exports. It is assumed throughout that exports equal imports under protection while average tariffs of 30 percent and export subsidies of 5 percent apply.

It appears, then, that the results are only moderately sensitive to the assumptions made. At the same time, for what may be considered as reasonable assumptions concerning the relevant elasticities, adjustment for overvaluation will substantially affect the estimates of the effective rate of protection. The adjustment for overvaluation would be small only if the elasticities of demand for, and supply of, exports were very large or the elasticity of demand for imports very small. No adjustment is required if the elasticities of demand and supply of exports are infinite *or* the elasticity of demand for imports is zero and exports receive no subsidy. In the first eventuality, the elimination of protection would entail reallocating resources from import-competing to export industries without a loss in the terms of trade, and effective rates of protection calculated at existing exchange rates would correctly measure the cost of protection. There would be no reallocation of resources in the second case but this would require that both domestic demand and domestic supply of importables were completely unresponsive to price changes.

The estimation of the extent of overvaluation requires information on tariffs and export subsidies, exports and imports, as well as on export demand and supply and import demand elasticities. While (20) to (26) relate to total imports and exports, estimation should ideally take place from data for individual commodities or industries. Averages of tariffs and subsidies and the values of exports and imports are shown in the breakdown of the input-output tables. However, in most instances, the elasticities of import demand were available only for total imports. Also, while export demand elasticities could be derived for the main export products of the individual countries, there are but few estimates of export supply elasticities.

The elasticity of demand for a country's exports of a given commodity depends on the elasticity of world demand for the commodity in question and on the elasticity of supply on the part of competing suppliers. The relevant formula is shown in (27) where η_{xw} refers to the world demand elasticity, ϵ_{xw} is the supply elasticity of competing suppliers, and k is the country's share in the world market.[15]

$$(27) \qquad \eta_x = \frac{\eta_{xw} + (1 - k)\epsilon_{xw}}{k}$$

It follows that the elasticity of demand for a country's exports will equal the world demand elasticity divided by the country's share in the world market, if competing suppliers do not reduce their exports in response to a fall in prices. While this assumption may not always be realistic, we have adopted

---

[15] For the derivation of this formula, see Staffan Burenstam Linder, *Trade and Trade Policy for Development* (New York: Praeger, 1967), p. 158.

it in the present investigation in order to give expression to market conditions in most primary commodities and to possible reactions in other developing countries. On the one hand, reductions in prices by one supplier often lead to price-cutting by others; on the other, we would overestimate the export prospects of individual countries if we considered these in isolation without taking account of policy changes in other nations.

For the seven countries under study, estimates on the average shares of their major export commodities in the world market in 1963–66 are shown in Table A.2. In making calculations, we have further utilized available information on the price elasticity of world demand for individual commodities.

Bias against Exports

Thus far we have considered the formulas applied in estimating the extent of protection for individual industries; we can further indicate the relative incentives the system of protection provides to production for domestic markets and for exports within each industry. Equation (28) shows the bias

TABLE A.2: Share of Country Exports in World Exports, 1950–53 and 1963–66

(*Percent*)

	1950–53	1963–66		1950–53	1963–66
Brazil			**Malaya**		
Coffee	48.4	32.9	Rubber	33.7	31.6
Cotton	4.4	5.7	Tin	63.5	73.7
Iron ore	2.6	3.2	**Pakistan**		
Sugar	0.6	3.5			
Lumber	3.9	2.4	Jute	98.6	88.3
Cocoa beans	13.7	7.7	Cotton	9.5	3.4
Chile			Jute textiles	0.3	22.2
			Cotton textiles	0.0	4.3
Copper	28.9	20.5	**Philippines**		
Iron ore	4.6	8.5			
Saltpeter	100.0	100.0	Copra	45.2	61.9
Mexico			Sugar	4.9	5.7
			Tropical logs	34.9	33.5
Cotton	8.0	10.0	Coconut oil	21.1	50.9
Coffee	2.9	2.9	Abaca	84.0	94.5
Sugar	0.2	2.6	**Norway**		
Shellfish	11.9	16.6			
Maize	0.0	2.6	Aluminum, unwrought	8.7	18.2
Lead, unwrought	28.6	15.7	Paper and paperboard	3.9	4.1
Copper, unwrought	3.8	0.6	Ships and boats	5.7	5.8
Fish, fresh	11.7	0.3	Wood pulp	12.1	6.8
			Fertilizers, manuf.	8.0	5.6
			Fish, fresh	17.9	17.4
			Fish, dried	24.1	14.7
			Fish preparations	10.0	6.8

Sources: FAO, *Trade Yearbook;* FAO, *Yearbook of Forest Products;* FAO, *Yearbook of Fishery Statistics;* U.N., *Commodity Trade Statistics;* U.N., *Yearbook of International Trade Statistics;* Great Britain, Institute of Geological Sciences, *Statistical Summary of the Mineral Industry;* Metallgesellschaft, *Metal Statistics.*

against exporting in a particular industry (X_i) for the case when free trade input-output coefficients are used in the calculations.[16]

$$(28) \quad X_i = \frac{W_i - Y_i}{Y_i}$$

$$= \frac{[(1 + T_i) - \sum_j A_{ji}(1 + T_j)] - [(1 + S_i) - \sum_j A_{ji}(1 + T_{jx})]}{(1 + S_i) - \sum_j A_{ji}(1 + T_{jx})}$$

This bias is defined as the percentage excess of domestic value added obtainable as a result of protection in producing for domestic markets over that obtainable in exporting.

It is apparent that the numerator of the equation will equal the difference between the rate of tariff and the rate of export subsidy provided that tariffs on material inputs are the same irrespective of whether these are used in producing for domestic markets or for exports. Thus, in the previous clothing example with a 20 percent tariff on the product and a zero export subsidy, the bias against exports will be 58.8 percent. As the formula includes only domestic values, no adjustment is made for overvaluation as compared with the free trade situation.

Input Substitution in Partial Equilibrium

We have noted that, in a partial equilibrium framework, effective rates of protection are measured under the assumption of zero substitution elasticity among inputs, constant returns to scale, unchanged factor prices, pure competition, no transportation costs, and infinite foreign demand and supply elasticities. In Chapter 1 (pp. 17, 22–23), we have considered the implications of removing the constant returns to scale, pure competition, and no transportation cost assumptions. Furthermore, in this appendix (pp. 325–26), we have indicated the adjustments made necessary by less than infinite foreign demand elasticities. We will next consider the question of input substitution under the assumption of unchanged factor prices. In response to changes in relative product prices following the imposition of protective measures, substitution may take place (1) between primary factors, taken as a unit, and material inputs; (2) among material inputs; (3) between individual primary factors and material inputs; and (4) among primary factors.

It will be recalled that, in the presence of substitution, the effective rate of protection should be interpreted as the proportionate change in returns to primary factors due to protection. This is the case because the change in

---

[16] In the equation, Y_i refers to value added obtainable in exporting, and T_{jx} is the rate of tariff on material inputs used in producing for exports.

value added from the preprotection to the post-protection situation will now consist of (1) a change in the quantity of primary factors per unit of output, and (2) a change in the price of the bundle of primary inputs (the value added unit). An appropriate concept of the effective tariff should take into account solely the second of these elements. Only thus will it be comparable to the nominal tariff which represents a price change and not a quantity change.[17]

Using this definition of the effective rate of protection, we can easily show that substitution between primary factors, taken as a unit, and material inputs will give rise to a bias in the estimates. The direction of this bias can be indicated if we consider the measurement of the effective rate of protection as an index-number problem. The employment of free trade (presubstitution) input-output coefficients entails an underestimation of the effective rate of protection since we take no account of the gains obtainable through substitution in response to changes in the relative prices of the product and its material inputs. Conversely, the use of post-protection (post-substitution) coefficients will overestimate the effective rate.[18]

Substitution among material inputs will also give rise to a bias in estimating the effective rate of protection. Irrespective of the elasticity of substitution between material inputs, the results will be subject to a downward bias if free trade coefficients are used in the calculations, and to an upward bias if domestic coefficients are used. This is because producers will tend to replace materials whose prices have risen as a result of protection, thereby moderating increases in the cost of inputs.

The magnitude of the bias due to substitution between value added, taken as a unit, and material inputs and among the material inputs themselves will depend on the extent of differences in tariffs on the product and its inputs (there will be no bias if all of these are equal) and on the substitution elasticities among the inputs. This raises the possibility that the size of the error in estimates of effective rates due to substitution will differ among industries and that these differences will affect the ranking of industries by effective rates. For example, if effective rates of protection estimated by using free-trade coefficients are higher for industry A than for industry B because the material inputs used in the latter are subject to high tariffs, resources might still move from A to B if industry B can escape the effects of the rise in the cost of material inputs by substituting primary factors for such inputs.

The direction of the bias due to substitution between primary factors

---

[17] On the definitional issue, see W. M. Corden, *The Theory of Protection* (Oxford: Clarendon Press, 1971), ch. 6.

[18] For proof, see J. C. Leith, "Substitution and Supply Elasticities in Calculating the Effective Protective Rate," *Quarterly Journal of Economics*, November 1968, pp. 588–60; and J. M. Finger, "Substitution and the Effective Rate of Protection," *Journal of Political Economy*, November/December 1969, pp. 972–75.

and material inputs is indeterminate if substitution elasticities differ between individual primary factors on the one hand, and material inputs, on the other. In this eventuality, the interindustry movement of resources will also depend on differences in substitution elasticities among pairs of primary factors and material inputs and in relative factor intensities among industries. Thus, if substitution effects tend to raise capital-labor ratios, the ensuing rise in the price of capital may more than offset the impact of high-measured effective protection on capital-intensive industries.[19]

Finally, substitution among primary factors in response to changes in relative prices due to the application of protective measures will not give rise to bias. This is because value added is derived as a residual—the difference between the value of output and that of material inputs—and hence cannot be affected by substitution among primary factors.

In Chapter 3, we have attempted to test the importance of the bias in the measurement of effective rates due to substitution between primary factors, taken as a unit, and material inputs and among the material inputs themselves, as well as the errors in estimation due to substitution between pairs and primary factors and material inputs and among primary factors. Some comments will now be offered on the use of the free trade input-output coefficients which is intimately related to the substitution issue.

We have noted in Chapter 1 (pp. 15–16) that free trade input-output coefficients have been derived largely from the input-output tables of Belgium and the Netherlands that have nil or low tariffs and thus approach a free trade situation.[20] However, the question arises: would the same coefficients apply under free trade conditions to developing countries with different resource endowments?

This will happen if (1) production functions are identical among countries or differ by a multiplicative constant that may vary from industry to industry, and (2) there is no substitution between primary factors and material inputs. Regarding the first point, the originators of the CES production function have assumed that differences in efficiency are neutral among countries and have obtained reasonable results under this assumption in a comparison of individual industries in the United States and Japan.[21]

---

[19] On this point, see V. K. Ramaswami and T. N. Srinivasan, "Tariff Structure and Resource Allocation in the Presence of Substitution," in *Trade, Balance of Payments and Growth: Papers in International Economics in Honor of Charles P. Kindleberger*, ed. J. Bhagwati, R. Jones, R. A. Mundell, and J. Vanek (Cambridge, Mass.: M.I.T. Press, 1971).

[20] These coefficients were first utilized in my "Tariff Protection in Industrial Countries: An Evaluation," *Journal of Political Economy*, December 1965, p. 578.

[21] Cf. Kenneth Arrow, H. B. Chenery, B. Minhas, and R. M. Solow, "Capital-Labor Substitution and Economic Efficiency," *Review of Economics and Statistics*, August 1961, pp. 225–50.

U.S.–Peruvian comparisons tend to support this conclusion.[22] At any rate, there is no definite bias in measurement due to differences in production functions.

The direction of the error is also uncertain in the presence of substitution between primary factors and material inputs. While lower labor costs in developing countries would entail the substitution of labor for intermediate inputs, high capital costs would tend to increase the use of intermediate inputs. But the magnitude of the error is likely to be small: empirical studies give evidence of little substitution between primary factors and material inputs in response to price changes,[23] and a calculation based on French data showed a substitution elasticity of 0.09 between value added and raw materials.[24] In addition, with the prices of material inputs being identical everywhere under free trade, they will be used in identical proportions. Nor does substitution among primary factors give rise to error since, with the prices of traded goods equalized under free trade, value added should be the same irrespective of factor substitution.[25]

Substitution among material inputs will, however, bias the calculations made for a particular country by the use of free trade and domestic input-output coefficients in the manner indicated above, and thus measurement by the two sets of coefficients serves a useful purpose even if substitution elasticities between primary factors and intermediate inputs were low. Moreover, such estimates provide an indirect test of the practical importance of the substitution issue.

These considerations indicate the usefulness of estimating effective rates of protection by using both domestic and free trade input-output coefficients. It should be noted, however, that the results are affected by errors of observation of the nominal rates of protection[26] and input-output coefficients, as

---

[22] Christopher Clague, "An International Comparison of Industrial Efficiency: Peru and the United States," *Review of Economics and Statistics*, November 1967, pp. 487–94.

[23] For a survey of the pertinent literature, see H. Theil and C. B. Tilanus, "The Demand for Production Factors and the Price Sensitivity of Input-Output Coefficients," *International Economic Review*, September 1966, pp. 258–73.

[24] Cf. B. Balassa, S. E. Guisinger, and D. M. Schydlowsky, "The Effective Rate of Protection and the Question of Labor Protection in the United States: A Comment," *Journal of Political Economy*, September/October 1970, pp. 1150–62.

[25] It is assumed that value added in nontraded inputs is included with value added in processing à la Corden.

[26] If quotas or prohibitive tariffs are applied, nominal rates of protection refer to the percentage excess of domestic over world market prices (c.i.f. prices for imports and f.o.b. prices for exports). However, as Bhagwati has repeatedly shown, quotas are equivalent to tariffs only if we assume universal competitiveness—in foreign supply, in quota-holding, and in domestic production (Jagdish Bhagwati, *Trade, Tariffs, and Growth* [Cambridge, Mass.: M.I.T. Press, 1969]). Should this not be the case or should quota allocation be combined with investment licensing, the amount imported will not be the same under the

well as by differences in product composition, and in the weights used in averaging nominal and effective protection.[27] Again, whatever these errors, they do not introduce a definite bias in the results.

Effective Protection in a General Equilibrium Framework

In general equilibrium, protection will affect particular activities not only through changes in product prices but also through changes in factor prices. Even in the absence of substitution among primary factors and material inputs, these factor-price effects may reverse the product-price effects of protection. Thus, commodity A, having a lower effective rate than commodity B, may still enjoy greater protection if it is complementary in factor use with unprotected commodity C, and hence benefits from a protection-induced decline in the price of the primary factor it uses intensively.

The error possibilities due to the neglect of protection-induced changes in factor prices in estimating effective rates will depend on the magnitude of these changes relative to changes in the prices of final products and their intermediate inputs. In the framework of a Heckscher-Ohlin model, the relative importance of the product-price and the factor-price effects will in turn depend on intercommodity differences in factor intensities and in nominal rates of protection. Under *ceteris paribus* assumptions regarding factor-price effects, the greater is the variability of tariffs and other protective measures, the greater will be the relative importance of the product-price effects of protection.

In the developing countries under study, intercommodity differences in nominal rates of protection are large, and it can be surmised that the effects of protection on output and input prices tend to outweigh its effects on factor prices. Thus, for example, if effective rates of protection, estimated in a partial equilibrium framework, are 10 percent on commodity A and 30 percent on commodity B, factor-price effects are unlikely to reverse the ranking by effective rates.

This conclusion is strengthened if we admit international differences in efficiency to vary among industries as shown in the comparative studies referred to in footnotes 21 and 22 above. This will mean that protection is designed to compensate for high costs due to the application of inferior technology and organization rather than for the high prices of factors of

---

quota as it would be if a tariff equal to the observed price difference was applied (cf. Jagdish Bhagwati and Padma Desai, *India—Planning for Industrialization* [London: Oxford University Press, 1970], ch. 17).

[27] In averaging nominal rates of protection for individual industries, we have used supply weights (domestic production plus imports) in applying domestic coefficients and world trade weights in applying free trade coefficients. The results are thus influenced by the economic structure of the individual countries as compared to the pattern of world trade.

production used intensively in protected industries. Finally, note that input substitution in a general equilibrium framework will create much difficulty in the interpretation of the results if we can assume that substitution elasticities between primary factors and material inputs are low.[28]

Effective Rates of Protection and the Cost of Foreign Exchange

In Chapter 1, we have noted that the effective rate of protection can be reinterpreted as representing the domestic cost of earning or saving foreign exchange. While effective rates of protection indicate the excess of domestic over foreign costs in a particular activity (direct costs), some writers have suggested the inclusion of the costs of processing domestically produced inputs (indirect costs) in a measure of the domestic cost of foreign exchange.[29] For a given commodity, this would equal the sum of direct and indirect domestic resource costs incurred in domestic production divided by the difference between the foreign price of the product and the foreign exchange cost of direct and indirect imported inputs.[30] Denoting elements of the matrix of direct and indirect domestic (W) and imported (N) input requirements by r_{ji}, the direct plus indirect cost of a dollar earned or saved by the domestic production of commodity i (for short, the B-measure) can be expressed as

$$(29) \qquad B_i = \frac{\sum_j W_j r_{ji}}{P_i - \sum_j N_j r_{ji}}$$

For the sake of comparability with the effective rate of protection, let us reinterpret this measure by expressing foreign values in terms of domestic currency (i.e., multiplying the denominator by the exchange rate). It can then be shown that the B-measure equals unity plus a weighted average of the effective rate of protection at different levels of fabrication—the weights being the contribution of direct and indirect value added to output produced under free trade conditions.[31]

---

[28] For a detailed discussion, see Bela Balassa, "Effective Protection: A Summary Appraisal," to be published in the *Proceedings of the Conference on Effective Protection* (the conference was held December 17–20, 1970, in Geneva).

[29] Under both definitions, adjustment should be made for above-normal profits and wages.

[30] Michael Bruno, *Interdependence, Resource Use and Structural Change in Trade* (Jerusalem: Bank of Israel, 1963); "The Optimal Selection of Export-Promoting and Import-Substituting Projects," in *Planning the External Sector: Techniques, Problems and Policies*, Report on the First Inter-regional Seminar on Development Planning (New York: United Nations, 1967); Anne O. Krueger, "Some Economic Costs of Exchange Control: The Turkish Case," *Journal of Political Economy*, October 1966, pp. 466–80.

[31] Bela Balassa and Daniel M. Schydlowsky, "Effective Tariffs, Domestic Cost of Foreign Exchange, and the Equilibrium Exchange Rate," *Journal of Political Economy*, May/June 1968, pp. 348–60.

(30) $B_i = 1 + \sum_j Z_j \dfrac{V_j r_{ji}}{V_{jr} r_{ji}}$

The relationship of the B-measure and the effective rate of protection can also be indicated by an example. Let us consider two import-competing industries: clothing manufacturing and precision equipment. Assume that, in the country in question, the manufacturing of precision equipment involves the use of steel produced under protection while the fabrics used by the clothing industry are not protected. Assume further that the production of precision equipment is efficient in the sense that domestic value added equals value added under free trade conditions, while this is not the case for clothing manufacturing. Input coefficients are taken to be constant in the production of both commodities, and costs are expressed in terms of direct and indirect inputs (processing costs and foreign exchange).

The figures of Table A.3 permit us to estimate the effective rate of protection and the B-measure by the use of equations (3) and (29). We find then that the rate of effective protection is 50 percent on clothing and nil on precision equipment. However, in terms of the direct plus indirect domestic cost of foreign exchange, the clothing industry ranks ahead of precision equipment manufacturing: the cost of foreign exchange is 1.2 in the first case and 1.4 in the second.

The explanation is easy to find: the cost of foreign exchange is lower in clothing manufacturing—a relatively inefficient industry—than in the production of precision equipment because the material input of the former (textile fabrics) is produced at world market prices while the latter is penalized by the protection of the domestic steel industry. Accordingly, while the effective rate of protection indicates the relative costs of processing activities, the B-measure is affected not only by the costs of manufacturing the product itself but also by the cost of production of its inputs.

TABLE A.3:   Evaluation of Clothing and Precision Equipment Projects

(Pesos)

	Domestic production			Foreign production		
	Processing costs	Foreign exchange	Total	Processing costs	Foreign exchange	Total
Clothing						
Fabrics	6	10	16	6	10	16
Processing costs	6	—	6	4	—	4
Price	12	10	22	10	10	20
Precision instruments						
Steel	10	10	20	6	10	16
Processing costs	4	—	4	4	—	4
Price	14	10	24	10	10	20

Source: See text.

It follows that the ranking of activities according to the B-measure reflects the implicit assumptions that (1) all existing industries will be maintained, and (2) the expansion of the output of any one industry will bring forth increased output of all domestic industries providing direct and indirect inputs into it (that is, the direct and indirect marginal input coefficient of domestic resources and of imports is equal to the corresponding average coefficient). Thus, it is assumed that policy changes would not lead to the substitution of foreign for domestic inputs either in existing output or in future output.

One may question the usefulness of this proposition since policy recommendations should properly cover the inefficient input-producing industry also. In the present example, it would hardly be appropriate that the past establishment of a high-cost steel industry should jeopardize the chances for setting up a precision equipment industry if, for example, its labor intensiveness gives a developing country comparative advantage.

Alternatively, we may accept inefficiencies for the sake of noneconomic objectives and envisage the maintenance of protection in input-producing industries for an indefinite period. This circumstance does not require a modification in the conclusions as long as the additional inputs necessary for the expansion of the user industries are imported since these should be valued at the cost of acquisition. However, to avoid discriminating against industries using domestically produced inputs, the production of the latter would need to be subsidized.

If we were to assume instead that political pressures would entail the expansion of some inefficient input-producing industries *pari passu* with the user industries, the products of these industries would be treated as if they were nontraded goods. But instead of equating all domestically purchased inputs with nontraded goods as is done by using the B-measure, we should judge such cases on their individual merits, with appropriate adjustments made in the effective protection measure. This conclusion also holds when the market prices of some primary factors are not equal to their opportunity costs; primary factors should then be valued at opportunity costs and we should calculate the "social" as against the "private" effective rate of protection. For lack of information, however, such an adjustment has not been made in the present study.

DERIVATION OF FORMULAS FOR ESTIMATING THE COST OF PROTECTION

Bela Balassa

Let us adopt the following notation (all values expressed in domestic prices at the free trade exchange rate): Y = gross domestic product, X = value of exports, Q_x = quantity of exports, M = value of imports, Q_m = quantity of imports, C = consumption, W = domestic value added, V = world market value added, π = world market price, p = domestic price, ϵ_x = elasticity of supply of exports, η_x = elasticity of demand for exports, η_m = elasticity of demand for imports, T = nominal rate of protection of import substitution, S = nominal rate of export subsidy, $\dot{R}$ = percentage devaluation associated with the elimination of tariffs and subsidies, and T' and Z' the net rates of nominal and effective protection (i.e., after adjustment for overvaluation as compared with the free trade situation).

It is assumed that each country engages in three types of productive activities: exports (W_1), import-competing goods (W_2), and non-import-competing goods (W_3). The move to free trade would represent an increase in the imports of import-competing goods, in part because their consumption rises and in part because domestic production disappears under the assumption of constant costs. In the case of agricultural products, however, increasing costs have been assumed; the same assumption has been made for exports, many of which originate in the primary sector. Finally, we have assumed that foreign competition will lead to cost reductions to world levels in the production of non-import-competing goods that is taken to occur under constant costs.

The separation of commodities into import-competing and non-import-competing necessarily involves a considerable degree of arbitrariness. We have derived value added in the production of non-import-competing goods indirectly, by taking the difference between the increases in imports estimated by using the formulas shown in Appendix A and the increases in the consumption of non-import-competing goods following the decline in their prices due to the elimination of tariffs. In so doing, we have applied the ratio of consumption to world market value added (α) which is observed in the case of goods where imports account for less than one-tenth of domestic consumption. The following equations pertain to the case of initial balance-of-payments equilibrium where the elimination of tariffs and subsidies *cum* devaluation must lead to an identical increase in the value of exports and imports.

Derivation of V_1

(1) $\qquad dX = dM = dM_c + dM_p$

(2) $\qquad dM_c = \eta_m \dfrac{T'}{1+T'} C_1 = \eta_m \dfrac{T'}{1+T'} \alpha V_1$

(3) $\qquad dM_p = V_1 = dX - dM_c = dX - \eta_m \dfrac{T'}{1+T'} \alpha V_1$

(4) $\qquad dX = V_1 \left(1 + \eta_m \dfrac{T'}{1+T'} \alpha \right)$

(5) $\qquad V_1 = \dfrac{dX}{1 + \eta_m \dfrac{T'}{1+T'} \alpha}$

Derivation of changes in prices (products of differentials neglected)

(6) $\qquad \dfrac{dX}{X} = \dfrac{dQ_x}{Q_x} - \dfrac{d\pi_x}{\pi_x}$

(7) $\qquad \dfrac{dQ_x}{Q_x} = \eta_x \dfrac{d\pi_x}{\pi_x} = \epsilon_x \left(\dfrac{\dot{R}+1}{1+S} - 1 - \dfrac{d\pi_x}{\pi_x}\right)$

$\qquad\qquad = \epsilon_x \left(\dfrac{\dot{R}+1}{1+S} - 1\right) - \epsilon_x \dfrac{d\pi_x}{\pi_x}$

(8) $\qquad \dfrac{d\pi_x}{\pi_x} = \dfrac{\epsilon_x \left(\dfrac{\dot{R}+1}{\dot{R}+S}\right) - 1}{\eta_x + \epsilon_x}$

(9) $\qquad \dfrac{dp_x}{p_x} = (1 - \pi_x)\left(\dfrac{\dot{R}+1}{1+S} - 1\right)$

Derivation of changes in the value of exports and imports

(10) $\qquad \dfrac{dX}{X} = \epsilon_f\left(\dfrac{\dot{R}+1}{1+S} - 1\right)$

(11) $\qquad \dfrac{dM}{M} = \eta_m\left(\dfrac{\dot{R}+1}{1+T} - 1\right)$

Estimation of welfare cost

Static or allocative cost: $\qquad Z_1'V_1 = Z_1'\ \dfrac{dX}{1 + \eta_m \dfrac{T'}{1+T'}\alpha}$

Dynamic cost of protection: $\qquad Z_2'V_2 = Z_2'\left[\dfrac{\Sigma W_1 - V_1(1 + Z_1')}{1 + Z_2'}\right]$

Terms of trade effect: $\qquad \dfrac{d\pi_x}{\pi_x}X$

Consumer surplus: $\qquad \dfrac{1}{2}\dfrac{T'}{1+T'}dC_1 = \dfrac{1}{2}\dfrac{T'}{1+T'}\eta\dfrac{T'}{1+T'}C_1$

Excess cost of increased exports: $\qquad \dfrac{1}{2}\dfrac{dp_x}{p_x}dX$

DERIVATION OF THE FREE TRADE EXCHANGE RATE IN BRAZIL

Bela Balassa and Joel Bergsman

In this Appendix the assumptions made for deriving the free trade exchange rate for Brazil by the authors of the Brazilian study and by the director of the project are described. The calculations based on these assumptions are shown in Tables C.1 and C.2.

In conformity with the other country studies, the elasticity of supply of imports to Brazil was taken to be infinite. In turn, time series estimates for the postwar period show import demand elasticities of 0.4 and 0.6 for Brazil.[1] Bergsman and Malan use 0.5 in their calculations and note that higher values would imply greater overvaluation and therefore less net protection. Balassa maintains that these estimates tend to understate the true value of the elasticity, partly because of the effects of quantitative restrictions on imports and partly because of the excess protection in the tariff structure during the period in question. Rapid increases in consumer goods imports following the tariff reductions undertaken in 1966 and 1967, and results obtained by the application of the indirect method of estimation also point to higher elasticities. In the latter case, import demand elasticities are derived from the

---

[1] Paul Clark and Richard Weisskoff, "Import Demands and Import Policies in Brazil," mimeographed, February 1967; Paul Clark, "Brazilian Import Liberalization," mimeographed, September 1967; and Samuel A. Morley, "Import Demand and Import Substitution in Brazil," in *The Economy of Brazil*, ed. Howard S. Ellis (Berkeley and Los Angeles: University of California Press, 1969), pp. 283–313.

domestic elasticities of demand and supply of importables and the share of imports in domestic consumption and production. Balassa suggests the use of 0.5 as the minimum value of the import demand elasticity, 2.5 as the maximum, and 1.5 as the most likely estimate.

Apart from coffee, Brazil's share in the market for its exports is relatively small. In 1963–66, Brazil provided the following proportions of world exports: coffee, 32.9 percent; cocoa beans, 7.7 percent; cotton, 5.7 percent; sugar, 3.5 percent; iron ore, 3.2 percent; and lumber, 2.4 percent. Coffee is not relevant for the present discussion; for Brazil's minor exports the proportion supplied does not exceed 1 or 2 percent. Taking an average of 3 percent for noncoffee exports and assuming that the price elasticity of world demand for these commodities is about 0.3, the demand elasticity for Brazil's noncoffee exports would appear to be about 10. This is the value suggested by Balassa with a lower limit of 7 and an upper limit of 13. Bergsman and Malan also use a lower limit of 7 but adopt an upper limit of infinity.

Time series estimates of the elasticity of domestic supply of a few Brazilian primary exports are between 0.8 and 1.3;[2] the elasticity of domestic supply of all of these, taken together, would probably be less. The elasticity of supply of exports is also affected by the share of exports in output. Taking these considerations into account, Bergsman and Malan maintain that a reasonable estimate of the supply elasticity for all noncoffee exports would be around 1 or 2. They further submit that time series data on the volume and prices of noncoffee exports are consistent with the assumptions of unitary supply and infinite demand elasticities. The former assumption could be contradicted by a regression of the export quantity on the real domestic price. Such a regression gives an estimated elasticity of 0.98. The latter assumption could be contradicted by a regression of the quantity on the foreign price. Such a regression does not show a statistically significant relationship; this is consistent with an unshifting, infinitely elastic demand curve. The absence of a relation between the export quantity and the world price can also be seen in a regression of the quantity on the real exchange rate. This regression gives the same elasticity (1.03) with respect to the exchange rate as the first equation's estimate with respect to the exchange rate times the foreign price.[3]

These results have led Bergsman and Malan to conclude that infinite demand and unitary supply elasticities for Brazilian exports make an appro-

---

[2] Antonio Delfim Netto *et al.*, *Agricultura e Desenvolvimento no Brasil*, Estudos ANPES No. 5, São Paulo, 1967.

[3] The results are as follows:

$$\log Q = .44 + .98 \log rp \qquad R^2 = .39$$
$$(1.30 \quad (.28)$$
$$\log Q = .14 + 1.03 \log r \qquad R^2 = .67$$
$$(.78) \quad (.17)$$

priate combination for calculating Brazil's free trade exchange rate. They note that the former is probably on the high side and that the latter may be on the low side, but maintain that any errors in the assumed elasticities tend to compensate.

According to Balassa, however, these estimates have little usefulness in indicating possible changes in the event of the adoption of free trade policies. In his view, it would be unrealistic to assume that the elasticity of demand for the exports of a country as large as Brazil would be infinite. Also, information on the share of exports in domestic production suggests that the elasticity of supply of Brazil's exports far exceeds one. The share of exports is one-half to two-thirds for iron ore and cocoa beans, one-sixth to one-fifth for sugar and lumber, and it may not exceed one-tenth for most other export commodities. Calculating with an average ratio of one-fifth would correspond to a supply elasticity of exports of about 4. But the supply elasticity of the exports of manufactured goods is considerably higher and the removal of discrimination against exports might lead to a substantial expansion of the foreign sales of manufactures from a rather small base. Correspondingly, Balassa suggests 4 to 6 as the range for the elasticity of supply of Brazilian exports, with 5 as the median figure.

The extent of overvaluation in 1967 estimated under the assumptions made by Bergsman and Malan is shown in Table C.1; the corresponding estimates obtained under Balassa's assumptions are given in Table C.2. Bergsman and Malan consider the third alternative to be the most appropriate; in turn, Balassa suggests the use of the estimate derived on the basis of the median elasticities. The Bergsman-Malan estimates, compared to those of Balassa, imply a smaller expansion of both exports and imports in response to a given price change. These differences compensate for each other in the determination of the free trade equilibrium exchange rate; in fact, the estimates of overvaluation suggested under the two alternatives happen to be the same.

---

where Q = quantum of noncoffee exports (*Conjuntura Econômica*, index No. 70)

   r = average export exchange rate for products other than coffee, deflated by the domestic wholesale price index. (See Table 6.10.)

   p = average dollar price of noncoffee exports (*Conjuntura Econômica*, index No. 84.

Data cover 1946–66. Both elasticities are significantly different from zero at the one percent level. The regression of Q on p gives an R^2 of .11, which implies that the relationship is not significant at the 5 percent level.

TABLE C.1:   Estimation of Overvaluation under Alternative Assumptions: Brazil, 1967[a]

		Assumed elasticities		Extent of overvaluation as compared to free trade
	η_x	ϵ_x	η_m	$(R'/R - 1)$
1.	7	2	0.5	14%
2.	7	1	0.5	19
3.	∞	1	0.5	14
4.	7	2	2	27
5.	∞	1	2	29

Source: See Appendix C.
[a] Assumptions suggested by Bergsman and Malan. Notations: η_x = export demand elasticity, ϵ_x = export supply elasticity, η_m = import demand elasticity.

TABLE C.2:   Estimation of Overvaluation under Alternative Assumptions: Brazil, 1967[a]

Assumed values as regards foreign demand and supply elasticities			Extent of overvaluation as compared with free trade $(R'/R - 1)$					
			$\eta_m = 0.5$		$\eta_m = 1.5$		$\eta_m = 3.5$	
η_x	ϵ_x	ϵ_f	$t = 85$	$t = 37$	$t = 85$	$t = 37$	$t = 85$	$t = 37$
	4	2.18	14.8	8.2	32.9	17.1	43.5	21.8
7	5	2.50	13.2	7.4	30.2	15.8	40.6	20.5
	6	2.77	12.1	6.8	28.2	14.9	38.5	19.6
	4	2.57	12.9	7.2	29.6	15.6	40.0	20.3
10	5	3.00	11.3	6.4	26.7	14.2	36.8	18.9
	6	3.38	10.2	5.8	24.6	13.2	34.3	17.7
	4	2.82	11.9	6.7	27.9	14.7	38.1	19.4
13	5	3.33	10.3	5.8	24.8	13.3	34.6	17.9
	6	3.79	9.2	5.2	22.6	12.2	32.0	16.7

Source: See Appendix C.
[a] Assumptions suggested by Bela Balassa. Notations: ϵ_f = elasticity of supply of foreign exchange, t = nominal rate of protection. See also Table C.1.

SPECIAL REGIMES IN CHILE

Teresa Jeanneret

Chilean law provides preferential treatment—chiefly in the form of tax, tariff, and credit privileges—to particular industries, regions, and institutions. In estimating the extent of protection of the industries that benefit from these special regimes, one should therefore take account of the concessions accorded to them. But even if such adjustments are not made either because of the lack of appropriately detailed data or because they affect only a few firms or a particular industry, information on the special regimes applied adds to our knowledge of the system of protection in Chile.

A rough idea of the relative importance of the special regimes is afforded by the fact that in 1961 about 40 percent of total imports were exempt from specific duties. In Table D.1 we show the incidence of these exemptions by aggregating the data furnished by the Superintendency of Customs on duty-free imports under each law that provides exemptions. Note, however, that while we have taken account of exemptions accorded to particular industries, regions, and institutions, there is some degree of double-counting and over-lapping in the figures. Moreover, the data relate only to exemptions from specific duties and exclude other types of concessions.

The determination of how the special regimes modify the estimates of effective protection has involved three well-defined stages. First, it was neces-sary to obtain information on the nature and content of each special regime in 1961. Second, we had to determine whether these regimes affected the

TABLE D.1:   Value of Total Imports Made Free of Specific Customs Duty under Certain
             Special Regimes in 1961

(*Millions of U.S. $*)

Department of Arica	35
Provinces of Chiloé, Aysén, and Magallanes	22
Provinces of Tarapaca and Antofagasta and Department of Chañaral	6
Departments of Iquique, Pisagua, Taltal, and Chañaral	8
Nitrate mining	14
Coal mining	2
Iron and copper mining and export promotion	10
Iron and steel ingots (also includes iron mining)	35
Agricultural machinery	13
Sugar industry	4
Fishing	3
1960 earthquake	1
Total	152
Others	87
Total imports made free of specific duty	239
Total Chilean imports, 1961	590

protection of any industry and, if so, in what way. Finally, we had to ascertain whether and to what extent their effects were implicitly allowed for in the input-output table.

While we have endeavored to take account of all important special regimes, it has not been possible to cover each of them because of the lack of information at one or other of the above three stages. Moreover, in conformity with the purpose and the general outline of this study, our attention centers on preferential treatment through lower customs duties and indirect taxes, although mention will also be made of other types of concessions, such as reductions in profit taxes or low interest credits. In the following we will consider individually the various special regimes.

Department of Arica

The Department of Arica contains about 50,000 people, i.e., 0.6 percent of the total population of Chile. It borders on the Peruvian frontier and is separated from Santiago by a distance of about 1,500 kilometers and the vast Atacama desert. In 1953, a special regime was instituted,[1] with the objective of preventing the progressive de-Chileanization of this Department and promoting its industrial development. The broad outlines of this scheme as of 1961 may be summarized as follows:

1. A 90 percent reduction in profit and real estate tax rates for all industrial enterprises established in Arica during the years 1959–69

---

[1] Decree-Law No. 303 of July 1953, as amended by Law No. 13039 of October 1958, Law No. 14555 of April 1961, and Decree No. 316 of January 1959.

2. A special credit system, not subject to the general margins established by the Central Bank, for all industrial enterprises that used exclusively raw materials produced in the area
3. Exemption from indirect taxes for industrial enterprises located in Arica
4. Exemption from customs duties on the imports of certain products (chiefly raw materials and capital goods) into the Department and a single customs duty of 10 percent on other products; an additional duty of 15 percent for some articles classified as luxury goods
5. The movement of goods from Arica to the rest of the country subjected to the importation rules applicable in the country generally, except in the following cases: (a) tourists are allowed to take with them, not more than once every six months, goods free of customs duty up to a specified amount as well as goods against payment of only the specific and ad valorem duties up to another specified limit;[2] (b) goods produced in Arica and not produced in the rest of the country are subject only to one-half of the specific and ad valorem duties on the import content and are exempt from the additional tax and the prior deposit; (c) goods produced in Arica and also produced in the rest of the country but, in the judgment of the Ministry of Economic Affairs, only in "inadequate quantity," are subject to 75 percent of the specific and ad valorem duties on the imported components and are exempt from the additional tax and the prior deposit requirement
6. A system of drawbacks on the exportation of products assembled or produced in Arica

Estimation of the effective protection afforded to industrial enterprises in Arica would be of interest as a means of checking to what extent the special regime has accomplished its purpose of promoting the development of the area. However, the objective of this study is to consider the effective protection of Chilean industries and not of particular firms so that the excess protection of firms located in Arica has been taken to provide compensation for the additional costs involved in manufacturing in the area or to afford extra profits. The declining importance of the special regime in Arica since 1961 supports this decision.

Table D.2 provides data on the most important of the industries located in Arica and their relative shares in the Chilean total. They include fish meal, textiles and clothing, sewing machines, television and radio receivers, automobiles, motorcycles and bicycles. The exports of fish meal receive benefits under a special scheme applicable throughout the country;

---

[2] These amounts were not fixed in terms of the c.i.f. value of the goods, but related to the specific and ad valorem duties applicable (approximately $40 and $110 of duty, respectively).

TABLE D.2:   Main Industries in Arica, 1962

Industry	Number of plants[a]		Percent of total value of production in Arica	Value of imports (1961) (In thousands of U.S. $)		Arica as a percent of total
	Country	Arica		Country	Arica[b]	
Fish meal	12	3	36	export good		
Textiles and clothing	102	2	33	na		
Sewing machines	3	1	63	3,310	317	10
T.V. sets	3	3	100	145	23	16
Radios	9	2	17	2,828	1,015	36
Automobiles	19	18	84	10,969	132	1.2
Motorcycles	4	2	77	30	15	50
Bicycles	5	1	51	128	30	23
Auto chassis	0	0	...	30,545	2,042	7

[a] *Source: Rol Industrial*, 1962. These figures may be underestimated in varying unknown degrees, but in general there is a bias tending to inflate the proportion of plants located in Arica.

[b] In some cases, the Arica import statistics aggregate the imports of the final product and its parts. This again tends to inflate Arica's proportion.

this is discussed separately. For textiles and clothing, implicit rates of protection have been estimated, as indicated in the text of Chapter 7.

Although the Department of Arica accounted for 63 percent of all sewing machine assembly, the domestic price of sewing machines is likely to have been determined by the c.i.f. price plus the equivalent tariff, since the import statistics include under this heading both machine heads and other components together with complete machines, and imports to Arica account for only 10 percent of total imports into Chile.

Similar considerations apply to other commodities produced in Arica. Among these, the manufacture or assembly of television receivers was experimental in 1961, since transmissions did not begin until 1962. Furthermore, the proportion of radio receivers assembled in Arica was relatively small while imports were large. Imports also predominate in transportation equipment, particularly if we consider that the trade statistics frequently include automobiles under the heading "Chassis." Although 18 of Chile's 19 motor vehicle assembly plants were located in Arica in 1961, the total number of motor vehicles assembled in the country was small in comparison with the number of vehicles imported so that domestic prices could be taken to have been determined by the price of imports and the equivalent tariff.

Although under these assumptions the Arica regime does not modify the effective rates of protection for the industries in question, the calculations made from the domestic input-output table would need to be adjusted because the table shows inputs into Arica at lower duties. Such adjustments have been made for transport equipment manufacturing. As noted elsewhere, textiles and clothing have been handled in a different fashion; in other industries Arica accounts for less than 10 percent of output and thus adjustments have not been deemed to be necessary. Finally, because of their relative unimportance, no account has been taken of exemptions from indirect taxes.

Provinces of Chiloé, Aysén, and Magallanes

These provinces, located in the extreme south, account for about one-third of the country's total area but only 3 percent of its population. There are practically no roads leading to them, and access to the rest of the country is by sea or air. Climatic conditions are very difficult because of excessive rainfall and strong winds. Magallanes, the most developed of the three provinces, contains the country's petroleum deposits and is an important producer of sheep and their products. In 1956 the area was exempted from import duties on all nonluxury products, while the reshipment of imported products to the northern region of the country was made subject to the same rules that apply to the Department of Arica.[3]

Petroleum is governed by a special regime which is examined separately in this appendix, while products derived from sheep-raising involve a minimum of imported components so that this special regime does not modify the estimation of effective protection for the agricultural sector. Finally, in 1961 there was not a single important industrial enterprise that qualified for the concession of customs duties.

Provinces of Tarapaca and Antofagasta and the Department of Chañaral

With the objective of compensating, at least in part, for the impossibility of producing agricultural goods in this region, located in the northern part of the country and including the entire Atacama desert, in 1958 it was authorized to import duty-free a number of food products, the domestic production of which is insufficient to supply the national demand.[4]

This special regime modifies the protection provided to the industries of this region that use any of those goods as inputs. It does not, however, affect that of the entire Chilean food processing industry, since in 1961 the region produced at most 6 percent of the gross value of domestic output and its privileges can be regarded as compensation for excess costs.

---

[3] Law No. 12008 of February 1956, Article 10 of the Transitory Provisions of Law No. 12084 of August 1956, Decree No. 7880 of October 1960, Decree No. 8413 of July 1959, Law No. 13039 of October 1958, and Law No. 14555 of April 1961.

[4] Law No. 12858 of February 1958.

*Departments of Iquique, Pisagua, Taltal, and Chañaral and the
Province of Antofagasta*

Certain exemptions[5] have been applied since 1958 to all productive activities in the Departments of Iquique, Pisagua, Taltal, and Chañaral and to small- and medium-scale copper mining in the Province of Antofagasta, with the exception of the El Salvador copper deposits[6] located in the Department of Chañaral. These were (a) the exemption from import duties on capital goods, fuels, and raw materials to be used by agricultural, fishing, mining, transportation, and industrial enterprises located in the area, with the transfer of these goods to other areas of the country being subject to payment of normal customs duties; (b) a special credit scheme for industrial enterprises that use exclusively raw materials produced in the area; and (c) a system of export drawbacks for products assembled or produced in the area.

These departments, located in the provinces of Tarapaca, Antofagasta, and Atacama, account for 12 percent of the total area of the country and 1.5 percent of its total population. Their main products are fish and its derivatives, copper, iron ore, and lead ore. In 1962 about three-fourths of the country's fish meal, oil, and processed fish was produced in this area. Small- and medium-scale copper mining in the Province of Antofagasta accounts for less than 4 percent of the country's total copper production while the area had 13 percent of the production of iron ore and 6 percent of that of lead ore.

The effects of the system of export drawbacks on the estimation of effective protection are discussed below, together with other export promotion laws, while the effects of the credit scheme are outside the scope of this study. With regard to exemptions from customs duties, the only industries of any importance (fish derivatives, iron ore, and copper) benefited from the more general laws which are discussed separately.

Nitrates (Saltpeter)

The Agreement between the Chilean Government and the major nitrate enterprises provides, among other things for the following exemptions: (a) exemption from indirect taxes on their inputs and from profit taxes; (b)

---

[5] Law No. 12937 of August 1958, Articles 12 and 40 of Law No. 13039 of October 1958, Decree No. 337 of January 1959, Meeting No. 34 of the Central Bank of October 1960, and Article 256 of Law No. 13305 of April 1959.

[6] This deposit, which is worked by the Anaconda Copper Co., is assigned to the category of large-scale mining, since it produces more than 25,000 tons a year.

exemption from customs duties on imports of equipment and machinery; and (c) exemption from duties on imports of gasoline, crude and diesel oil, electrical detonators, chemical inputs, and containers.[7]

Moreover, duty-free importation of other inputs was permitted with the authorization of the Board of CONVENSA.[8] But, although by law the industry was exempt from indirect taxes on its inputs, in practice no use was made of this concession so that input values include indirect taxes.

In calculating the rate of effective protection of the nitrate industry from the domestic input-output table, we have made adjustments for the duty privileges accorded to this industry. No such adjustment has been made in estimates based on free trade coefficients since the latter do not separate nitrates from the group of other minerals and their share in the total is small.

Coal

With the declared purpose of reducing coal-mining costs, a policy of promoting mine mechanization and modernization was introduced in 1960. The following are the principal measures adopted:[9] (a) exemption from tax on profits reinvested in accordance with plans approved by CORFO;[10] (b) accelerated depreciation; (c) exemption from the turnover tax on the transportation of inputs and the production of the coal-mining enterprises; (d) exemption from all customs duties on the importation of machinery and equipment under investment programs approved by CORFO; and (e) exemption from customs duties on industrial or domestic coal-using equipment.

The described duty exemptions have been allowed for in calculating the equivalent tariffs for the major input items of the coal industry. For depreciation, a tariff rate of zero percent has been assumed. However, no account has been taken of the exemption from the freight tax since, the domestic matrix being computed at user prices, any method that seeks to allow for the effects of this exemption on effective protection is subject to substantial error.

---

[7] Law No. 5350 of January 1934, as amended by Laws 12018 of September 1956, 12033 of August 1956, and 13305 of April 1959, and Decree-Law No. 229 of March 1960. The Agreement lapsed in 1968 and a new regime for nitrates was introduced.

[8] Under the Agreement, CONVENSA (Corporacion de Venta de Salitre y Yodo ["Saltpeter and Iodine Marketing Corporation"]) has a monopoly of the sales of the products of the industry. Its Board of Directors consists of representatives of the enterprises and of the government; the governmental representatives have the power to veto resolutions.

[9] Decree-Law No. 255 of April 1960.

[10] Corporación de Fomento de la Producción ("Production Development Corporation").

Export Promotion Schemes

On export products other than nitrates, iron ore, and copper from large-scale mines, there was in 1961 a complex system of exemptions from all taxes affecting their cost and selling price. The existing laws provided for three different mechanisms for accomplishing this objective, depending on the characteristics of the exporting firm and on the type of tax concerned.[11] These mechanisms were (a) indirect taxes and customs duties on material inputs that were not payable by the firm if they applied to operations directly concerned with exporting or to enterprises that exported 100 percent of their production; (b) taxes that were not paid, or were paid but could be recovered, provided that the exporter could demonstrate that they affected the cost of his exports; and (c) taxes that had been paid but were refunded automatically when exportation took place.

To examine in detail all the modifications that these mechanisms entail in the estimation of effective protection is practically impossible. Taking account of mechanism (a) for enterprises exporting less than 100 percent of their production, one would require information that would take much time and effort to obtain. Furthermore, many exporters may not have taken advantage of concessions under mechanism (b) because of the difficulties they face in proving that they were entitled to them. The cost of proving entitlement to such concessions often turned out to be as high or higher than the benefit obtained. Correspondingly, we have not taken account of these entitlements in the following discussions.

By contrast, the taxes refunded to exporting firms under mechanism (c) are easily ascertainable; the refund was fixed for a list of export products as a percentage of the f.o.b. export value. This percentage varied from 0.015 percent for copper or brass flats or sheet to 26.8 percent for bulk wine shipments; for the majority of products it was around 3–6 percent. Finally, the fixed percentage of tax refunds applicable to enterprises that exported only a part of their production appears as a subsidy in the domestic input-output table; this reduces the amount of indirect taxes collected and thus raises the reported value of production at producer prices.

Firms that exported all their production benefited from mechanisms (a) to (c), since they were exempt from all indirect taxes and customs duties on their inputs. In 1961 these were chiefly the small- and medium-scale copper and mining enterprises, some firms producing other metallic and nonmetallic minerals, a producer of explosives, and a few sawmills. Among these, the most important were small- and medium-scale producers of iron ore and

---

[11] Article 93 of Law No. 12861 of February 1958 and Decree-Laws No. 256 and No. 257 of April 1960.

copper; in 1965, these accounted for 80 percent of iron ore output and 12 percent of copper output. They will now be discussed in some detail.

Iron Ore and Copper. Small- and medium-scale producers of iron ore are exempt from all indirect taxes and customs duties on their material inputs while large-scale firms are exempt from the advance deposit requirement and additional taxes[12] so that they pay only the specific duty and the ad valorem tax. In calculating the effective rate of protection of iron mining from both the domestic and the free trade input-output table, we have made appropriate adjustments for these exemptions.

It has not been possible, however, to obtain a breakdown of the inputs that corresponded to small- and medium-scale mining within the total, and we have assumed that the input structure of these firms is similar to that of large-scale iron mining. This assumption appears fairly reasonable since the distinction between medium-scale and large-scale iron mining is a legal one[13] and it does not relate to production capacity. Cases exist of enterprises classified as "medium-scale" that are in fact larger than those included in the "large-scale mining" category and that use similar technologies.

Small- and medium-scale producers of copper received the same exemptions as their counterparts in iron ore production. Large-scale copper mining, too, enjoyed lower tariffs in the same way, as did large firms in iron mining (Table D.3). Correspondingly, estimates derived from the domestic input-output table have been adjusted in a similar fashion in the two cases.

There is, however, a substantial technological difference between large-scale and small- and medium-scale copper mining. The legislation defines an enterprise in the large-scale copper mining category as one that produces more than 25,000 tons of refined copper a year. In point of fact, the smallest of the three large copper enterprises produced in 1961 about 60,000 tons. As ODEPLAN data were available on the inputs of the two types of enterprises, we have made separate calculations for each of them and aggregated the results. However, in the absence of a breakdown of the nonferrous minerals and nonferrous metals sector, calculations based on free trade coefficients could not be so adjusted.

---

[12] They were exempt because, historically, the advance deposit requirement was established primarily as a precondition of the right to buy foreign exchange to pay for imports. Since these enterprises possess foreign exchange of their own, the deposit requirement was not considered relevant in their case. Subsequently, the additional tax was introduced to replace the prior deposit. Since the large-scale mining enterprises had already obtained exemption from the prior deposit requirement, they were exempted also from the additional tax. As the advance deposit was not abolished, the enterprises remained exempt from both obligations.

[13] "Large-scale" enterprises are those that enjoy free disposition over the foreign exchange earned by their exports. This means that they sell on the Chilean exchange market only the amounts of exchange necessary to meet their domestic costs and to pay their taxes.

TABLE D.3:   Equivalent Tariffs for Inputs Used in the Large-Scale Iron and Copper
Mining Industry and in Other Sectors, 1961

Input	Large-scale mining (1)	Other sectors (2)	(1)/(2)
Coal	0.370	0.370	1.00
Wood and cork	0.248	0.352	0.70
Chemical products	0.539	0.900	0.60
Petroleum and coal products	0.445	0.495	0.90
Nonmetallic manufactures	0.887	1.371	0.65
Basic metallic industries	0.373	0.624	0.65
Metallic manufactures	0.387	0.591	0.65
Machinery (except electrical machinery)	0.376	0.794	0.47

Source: See text.

Although, as already stated, no attempt has been made in this study to allow for the effects of profit taxes on effective protection, it is noteworthy that in 1961 special profit taxes were applied to large-scale copper mining.[14] The profits of these firms were taxed at rates that varied, depending on the rate of expansion of the enterprises, from 50 percent to more than 80 percent, instead of the 45 percent that was applied to the majority of enterprises in Chile. The extra profit tax may be regarded as a rent paid for the exploitation of Chile's copper deposits.

Other Export Development Schemes. Outside the general system of promotion of exports just examined, there existed in 1961 in the Departments of Arica, Pisagua, Iquique, Taltal, and Chañaral special systems of export drawbacks for products originating in those departments.[15] No information is available concerning the way in which this system of drawbacks operated, their magnitude, and the type of enterprises that benefited from it. However, the only enterprises for which the amount of these drawbacks may have been of any significance are those manufacturing fish preserves, meal, and oil, which account for only a small proportion of the relevant sectors of the Chilean input-output table.

Iron and Steel

The only enterprise producing iron and steel ingots in Chile was established in 1946 and is exempt from all taxes, including customs duties and profit taxes.[16] In 1961 this enterprise accounted for one-half of the value of production of the basic metal industry. To calculate the effect of the special

---

[14] Law No. 11828 of May 1955, Supreme Decree No. 150 of October 1956, Decree Law No. 258 of April 1960, and Laws 14603 and 14688 of September 1961.

[15] Laws 13039 of October 1958 and 12937 of August 1958. Cf. our earlier discussion.

[16] Law No. 7896 of October 1944, and Decree No. 1896 of April 1946.

regime for iron and steel on the effective protection of the basic metal industry, we have estimated the value of the inputs used by this enterprise by utilizing information from ODEPLAN.

In the free trade input-output table, two industries—pig iron and ferromanganese and steel ingots—benefit from this regime, and we have accordingly assumed tariffs and indirect taxes on their inputs to be zero. About 50 percent of rolled steel products, too, comes into this category; hence we have calculated with duty-free and tax-free entry for one-half of inputs into this industry.

Sugar Industry

In 1956 Chile introduced a policy of promoting the refining of beet sugar to replace imports of sugar cane which cannot be grown in Chile. For this purpose total exemption was granted from import duties on beet-refining machinery.[17] A corresponding adjustment has been made in calculations based on the free trade input-output table that includes sugar as a separate industry. In the domestic input-output table, however, sugar is part of food processing and accounts for at most 6 percent of the output of the latter.

Fishing and Fish Products

In 1960 the government adopted a policy of promoting fishing, fish processing (canned and frozen fish, fish meal, and fish oil), and ancillary industries (shipbuilding and repair). The principal measures adopted[18] are summarized as follows:

1. A 90 percent reduction in the profit tax and real estate tax rates for fishing enterprises that reinvest their profits in the industry for a period of 10 years; a 90 percent reduction in the income tax rate for profits distributed to shareholders; a 90 percent reduction in the profit tax rates for profits derived from other activities but invested for a period of at least 5 years in the fishing or related industries[19]

---

[17] Article 60 of Group 2, Transitory Provisions, Law No. 12084 of August 1956.

[18] Decree-Law No. 266 of April 1960, Decree No. 133 of May 1961, and Article 140 of Law No. 14117 of October 1960. They affect Sector 2 and (partially) Sectors 9 and 27 of the domestic matrix, and Sector 2 and (partially) Sectors 11, 16, 18, and 51 of the standard matrix.

[19] This is a notable case of the effect that income and profit tax discriminations can have on the allocation of investment resources. When these regulations were enacted, no one anticipated that the response of the investors would be so favorable, and no thought was given to the problem of optimum capacity, having regard to the characteristics of Chile's marine fauna. Since 1966, a number of fish meal plants have had to close down for lack of raw material.

2. Exemption from all indirect taxes on both inputs and products of the fishing industry (with the exception of lobsters, sea urchins, oysters, and centolla crabs)
3. Exemption from duties on machinery and equipment, fuel, and petroleum derivatives used by the fishing industry; exemption from duties for all other inputs, the domestic production of which is considered to be inadequate and the domestic price of which exceeds the c.i.f. price plus 20 percent.

In estimating rates of effective protection for the fishing industry from both the domestic and the free trade input-output table, we have calculated with 20 percent tariffs and nil indirect taxes on inputs. A similar adjustment could not be made for fish processing and for shipbuilding that are, respectively, part of the food processing and transport equipment industries. But the error committed thereby is likely to be small since the products in question have a very small share in the above industries. Nor have adjustments been made on the account of these products in estimating effective protection from the free trade input-output table.

Machinery for the Earthquake Area

In May 1960 southern Chile was struck by a violent earthquake which destroyed the installations of numerous industrial enterprises. One of the principal measures adopted to facilitate reconstruction was to permit the importation of machinery and equipment by the industrial enterprises of the region against a sole customs duty of 15 percent of c.i.f. value.[20] This provision was applicable until 1965.

The only industry where this area accounts for a substantial part of Chilean production is basic metals. About 50 percent of its production comes from Huachipato (an enterprise located in Concepción which possesses the country's only blast furnace). However, the iron and steel enterprises enjoyed even greater concessions under the special regime applicable to them. As these have been incorporated in the estimation of the protection of the sector, a further adjustment is not called for.

Petroleum Extraction and Derivatives

Since its establishment in 1950, the National Petroleum Enterprise (Empresa Nacional de Petroleo—ENAP) has enjoyed total exemption from

---

[20] Article 133 of Law No. 14117 of October 1960. The area covers the provinces from Nuble to Aysen (inclusive) and includes Concepción, the country's second largest industrial center after Santiago.

all taxes, including indirect taxes on its inputs, customs duties, and profit taxes.[21] This firm produces all of Chile's crude petroleum and practically all of its petroleum derivatives. Between 1959 and 1968—the period relevant for our study—the method of application of customs duty exemptions was as follows: ENAP had to pay the duties at the time of importation but then had them refunded by the Treasury; this refund appears in the domestic input-output table as a subsidy. Indirect taxes, however, were not paid at all.

ENAP accounts for part of the production of "other mining" and for almost the whole of the production of petroleum and coal derivatives in the domestic input-output table and that of petroleum and natural gas and petroleum derivatives of the free trade table. In the absence of available information on the relative share of petroleum, it has not been possible to adjust the estimates for the "other mining" industry in the domestic matrix, and hence the effective protection of this sector is somewhat understated. In the other cases referred to above, however, appropriate adjustments have been made and inputs have been valued net of tariffs and indirect taxes.

Agricultural Machinery and other Capital Goods

Since 1950, the imports of machinery destined for agriculture, small- and medium-scale mining and fishing, as well as machinery for equipping new industries (i.e., industries that do not yet exist in Chile) at least 80 percent of whose raw materials are of domestic origin, have been exempt from customs duties.[22] In regard to small- and medium-scale mining and fishing, this exemption has already been taken into account in the preceding discussion of these sectors.[23]

In the absence of information on new industries that might have enjoyed this exemption in 1961 on the grounds that the raw materials they used were more than 80 percent of domestic origin, no adjustment has been made in such cases, but it is believed that they were of little importance.[24] Duty-free imports of agricultural machinery, however, were large—over $13 million in 1961 and over $21 million in 1966. Therefore, in the estimation of the effective rate of protection of the agricultural sector, a zero tariff has been used on depreciation.

---

[21] Law No. 9618 of June 1950, Article 165 of Law No. 13305 of April 1959, and Law No. 16768 of March 1968.

[22] Law No. 9839 of November 1950.

[23] See pp. 357 and 359. Under laws subsequent to 1950 much wider concessions were granted to these sectors than under Law No. 9839.

[24] The value of machinery imported duty-free for this reason was less than $1.5 million in 1966 and even lower in 1961.

Deferred-Payment Imports

As an incentive to the importation of capital goods, exemption from the advance import deposit requirement has been given since 1959 on imports of machinery purchased on deferred payment terms (i.e., using foreign suppliers' credits or loans granted to the government by international agencies) in excess of one year. In addition, the deferred payment of the specific customs duty and the ad valorem and additional tax is permitted in such cases.[25]

The exemption from the advance deposit requirement, together with the deferred payment of the duties, amounts to a reduction in equivalent duties. Unfortunately, sufficient information is not available to determine the extent to which these concessions have been used and we have not taken account of them in making calculations.

Imports on Consignment

In 1961, regulations were enacted permitting the importation of a number of products on consignment; this means that importers were authorized to pay their foreign suppliers and the corresponding customs duties at the time of sale of the product to the Chilean user (but not later than 60 days after loading in the foreign port) instead of at the time of importation. The principal advantage of this scheme was the lower financial cost resulting from the delayed payment of customs duties. However, it is practically impossible to quantify the resulting benefit to individual industries and it has not been taken into account in this study.

---

[25] Article 164 of Law No. 13305 of April 1959, Decree No. 18673 of December 1959, and Meeting No. 530 of August 1959 of the Central Bank. It is noteworthy that this mechanism discriminates in favor of investors who need loans and, therefore, against those able to finance their investments out of their own resources.

SOURCES OF DATA AND INPUT-OUTPUT COEFFICIENTS FOR PAKISTAN STUDY

Stephen R. Lewis, Jr., and Stephen E. Guisinger

The input-output structure for 1963/64 has been taken from the Tims-Stern table which appeared in a mimeographed publication of Pakistan's Planning Commission.[1] The table separates all flows by domestic and imported origin. It is expressed in terms of user prices, including both trade and transportation margins and indirect taxes in the value of the flows. This made necessary an adjustment in the table since, in order to compare the value of domestic output with c.i.f. (for actual or potential imports) or f.o.b. values (for exports), indirect taxes had to be deducted from the value of output, and the domestic trade and transport margins had to be deducted from both the input and the output side.[2]

---

[1] Planning Commission, International Economics Section, "Methodology of Estimating Import Requirements," mimeographed (Karachi, March 1967). The table was constructed by Wouter Tims and Joseph J. Stern.

[2] It is also likely that the Pakistan table and the Census of Manufacturing Industries use the "all other services" inputs as a residual category, or balancing them. The Census of Manufacturing Industries, on which the table was based, has numerous defects, which undoubtedly affect the accuracy of the input-output table. Some discussion of the problems of the Censuses is given by S. R. Lewis, Jr., and R. Soligo, "Growth and Structural Change in Pakistan's Manufacturing Industry, 1954–1964," *Pakistan Development Review*, Spring 1965, pp. 94–139; by G. F. Papanek, "Industrial Production and Investment in Pakistan," *Pakistan Development Review*, Autumn 1964, pp. 462–90; and by J. J. Stern, "On the Present State of Inter-Industry Studies in Pakistan," mimeographed (Karachi: Pakistan Institute of Development Economics, 1965).

Indirect taxes can be easily accounted for but trade and transport margins cause difficulties, since these are combined with "all other services." Several different methods were explored to adjust for this group of inputs.[3] In the method used for the text calculations we deducted two-thirds of the value of the input "all other services" from both the input row and from the value of the output of the industry, and computed all rates of effective protection with the adjusted industry structure. The two-thirds proportion was adopted on the basis of the importance of wholesale and retail trade and transportation in the entire service sector of Pakistan's National Accounts. Estimates prepared under other alternatives (not reported here) show that while measured levels of protection are sensitive to the treatment of unallocated and non-traded inputs, the ranking of industries by effective rates of protection is hardly affected.

When the value of "all other services" inputs is reduced by two-thirds, the average and the median levels of protection calculated by the use of the Balassa method fall substantially, as does the average level of protection in each subgroup of industries. The decline is particularly large in industries with large deliveries from "all other services" in the original table. Notable decreases occur in edible oils, dyeing and finishing, thread- and threadball-making, saw milling, tanning, paper products, metal furniture, metal products, and sewing machines.[4]

Tariff and indirect tax data have been taken from Radhu, as updated in Lewis and Radhu.[5] Price comparisons, or implicit exchange rates, have been obtained from several sources and by the use of several methods. For many manufacturing industries, particularly in the intermediate and capital goods producing industries where total domestic supply is dominated by imports, price comparisons for imported goods were made for a large number of

---

[3] Some alternatives were explored empirically and theoretically in S. R. Lewis, Jr., and S. E. Guisinger, "Measuring Protection in a Developing Country: The Case of Pakistan," *Journal of Political Economy*, November/December 1968, pp. 1170–98, especially Appendix on Method.

[4] R. Soligo and J. J. Stern ("Tariff Protection, Import Substitution, and Investment Efficiency," *Pakistan Development Review*, Summer 1965, pp. 249–70) and S. R. Lewis, Jr., and G. M. Radhu (Chapter 4 in Lewis, *Economic Policy and Industrial Growth in Pakistan* [London: George Allen & Unwin, Ltd., 1968]) both used the unadjusted "all other services" coefficients. In their calculations, the unweighted average effective rate of tariff protection fell from 809 to 138 percent and the median fell from 400 to 139 percent when the adjusted "services" coefficients were substituted for the unadjusted figures. Other adjustments resulted in similar declines in the average rates. However, the rankings were not significantly affected by the adjustments in the coefficients. Rank correlation coefficients among the several adjusted measures were .90 to .96, while the rank correlation coefficients between the measure using unadjusted coefficients and those using adjusted coefficients were between .84 and .88.

[5] Lewis and Radhu in Lewis, *Economic Policy and Industrial Growth in Pakistan*, ch. 3.

products by Pal[6] in two separate surveys. Domestic price data were gathered from wholesalers, from market reports, and from purchasers of goods, in order to double-check the results. The price for each item was an average of several reported prices. The c.i.f. prices of identical commodities were obtained from customs records, and a markup above c.i.f. price plus duties and fees was computed. At this stage, several specific grades or sizes of an item were averaged to get a markup for a broader type of good (for example, steel bars and rods). Since Pal reported the duty and markup for each good, it was easy to convert to a price differential for those goods.

This procedure is based on the assumption that the price of domestically produced goods is determined by the price of imports, and that, therefore, the price differentials for imported goods represent the nominal rate of protection the domestic industry is receiving. This assumption seems appropriate for those industries in which imports are the dominant part of total supply. It has the advantage of avoiding the comparison of the prices of domestically produced and imported goods which may not be of identical quality.

A second method has been used to obtain price differentials in cases where an industry exported in sufficient volume. We have assumed that the exchange rate at which the industry exported was a good representation of the ratio of the domestic prices to the f.o.b. price of exports. The underlying rationale is that producers equilibrate marginal revenue in the domestic and the foreign market, and that marginal revenue is equal to price. Fortunately, most of the exporting industries have fairly large numbers of firms domestically to make this a reasonable assumption.

The third method employed to estimate price differentials was that of direct price comparisons of domestic and some form of world or international price. Such comparisons had been made elsewhere for agricultural goods, and we have made some price comparisons for a few manufactured goods not included in the first two groups, such as hydrogenated vegetable oils, and paper products.

For most industries we had only a few representative goods, and price differentials for these goods have been averaged to arrive at an average for the industry. Price observations were available for larger numbers of individual goods in the case of chemicals, basic metals, and metal products, but for fewer goods for electrical and nonelectrical machinery, paper products, and refined petroleum products. Nevertheless, we believe the price differentials are fairly representative for the industries. The problems for a few specific industries (sugar, jute textiles, edible oils, motor vehicles, cotton textiles) are discussed in Chapter 10, since these are important industries which gave unexpected results.

---

[6] M. L. Pal, "The Determinants of the Domestic Prices of Imports," *Pakistan Development Review*, Winter 1964, pp. 597–622, and "Domestic Prices of Imports: Extension of Empirical Findings," *ibid.*, Winter 1965, pp. 547–88.

INDEX